Blood Road

Shen Dingyi standing behind Sun Yat-sen
Guangzhou, August 1924

Shen Dingyi xiansheng shilue
[A brief biography of Mr. Shen Dingyi]. N.p., n.d.

Blood Road

The Mystery of Shen Dingyi in Revolutionary China

R. Keith Schoppa

With best wishes,

Keith Schoppa

UNIVERSITY OF CALIFORNIA PRESS

Berkeley / Los Angeles / London

University of California Press
Berkeley and Los Angeles, California

University of California Press, Ltd.
London, England

First Paperback Printing 1998

Library of Congress Cataloging-in-Publication Data
Schoppa, R. Keith, 1943–
    Blood road : the mystery of Shen Dingyi in revolutionary China /
R. Keith Schoppa.
        p.   cm.
    Includes bibliographical references and index.
    ISBN 0-520-21386-6 (pbk : alk. paper)
    1. Shen, Dingyi, dd. 1928.   2. Revolutionaries—China—
Biography.   3. China—History—1912–1928.   I. Title.
DS777.15.S53S36   1995
951.04′1′092—dc20   94-22072
[B]

Printed in the United States of America

9   8   7   6   5   4   3   2   1

The paper used in this publication meets the minimum requirements
of American National Standard for Information Sciences—Permanence
of Paper for Printed Library Materials, ANSI Z39.48-1984. ∞

With love and gratitude
for my parents
Robert George Schoppa
Dorothy Karcher Schoppa

and for my mother-in-law
Ruth Smith Braaten

Within the mirror there I am.
Outside the mirror there I am.
When I break the mirror, I don't see me.
The broken fragments of the mirror become pieces of me.
When I break the mirror, I am nowhere in the mirror.
When I break the mirror, I have even broken me.
When I have broken me, I don't know how many of me
    there are.

Shen Dingyi
"On Reading Liu Dabai's
'Facing the Mirror'"
1920

Contents

Maps

Acknowledgments

In the years that I have taken on the identity of detective into the mysteries of the Nationalist Revolution and of the life and death of Shen Dingyi, I have built up debts of gratitude to those who have helped at various stages. Foremost are Professors Chen Qiaoyi, Lu Yichun, and Que Weimin in the Department of Geography at Hangzhou University. They gave of their time more generously than one could reasonably expect during my extended stay in Hangzhou at the beginning stage of this book, and they provided important information and assistance in the summer of 1993. On the latter stay, I am especially indebted to Professor Que for his arrangement of the visits to Xiaoshan and Yaqian. For his considerable assistance, I also want to thank Chen Xianxin, head of the Xiaoshan County Local History Bureau. Thanks also should go to Wang Renxin of the Xiaoshan City Planning Commission and to Xu Maiyong, vice-mayor of Xiaoshan City, for serving as kind host.

A special word of thanks goes to Shen Jianyun and Shen Zhongliang, son and grandson respectively of Shen Dingyi, who welcomed me into their home to speak of their father and grandfather. The deep familial pride that they feel in him, despite the trouble and grief that he and his memory have brought the family, was apparent in their warm words about his contribution to modern China, in the informal shrine that they keep in his memory on the wall facing the entry way to their home, and in their insistence that our picture be taken in front of the tree that grew from the seedling brought back from the Soviet Union by Shen Dingyi in 1923. I hope that in their estimation I have represented the actions and roles of their father and grandfather fairly. I also owe a special debt to Professor Liu Qing of the Department of Communications at Hangzhou University who assisted in my conversations with the Shens.

The following colleagues provided comments, assistance, and support at various stages of the project: Parks Coble, Bradley Geisert, John Hazewinkel, Lin Zhimin, Herman Mast, Mary Rankin, Frederic Wakeman, Jr., Wen-hsin Yeh, Zhang Xin, and Zhang Yongwei. For additional comments, I am grateful to the participants in the conference on Oppositional Politics in Republican China held in 1990 at Washington and Lee University and to faculty in the Departments of History at the Massachusetts Institute of Technology, the University of California, Santa Cruz, and the University of Oregon. Special thanks should go as well to the university and college faculty who gave support and understanding during the 1993 LECNA summer seminar. I thank the American Council of Learned Societies for financial support in a Chiang Ching-kuo Foundation grant. For continuing general support, I owe many debts to Valparaiso University, with special thanks to Philip Gilbertson, Roy Austensen, and Richard Baepler.

Finally, deep thanks to my family who must watch with amazement (and perhaps chagrin) as husband and father continues to immerse himself in projects that burrow deeply into Chinese localities. For her patience, understanding, and myriad ways of assistance, Beth, as always, deserves my deep gratitude. For their concerns and questions that pull me (if only temporarily) out of Chinese localities into the joys and rigors of family life, I thank Kara, Derek, and Heather.

Berkeley
May 1994

Introduction

Forty years after two white-garbed assassins cut Shen Ding-yi down at the Yaqian bus station, farmers in the madness known as the Great Proletarian Cultural Revolution blew up his grave with a bomb. It had been an imposing grave site on Phoenix Mountain a half mile northwest of his home in Yaqian—fitting for a man who had lived an extraordinary life. A revolutionary, landlord, politician, journalist, educator, and an early member of both the Communist and Nationalist parties, Shen had been called by Sun Yat-sen after their first meeting "the most talented man in Zhejiang [province]."[1]

Though the mountain was dotted with many graves, Shen's had often been linked with that of Li Chenghu, a farmer with whom Shen worked in organizing a 1921 rent resistance movement, the first in China to be shaped by and infused with Marxist thought. Li had been jailed and had died of illness in prison. In 1935 a Shanghai journalist, Lin Weibao, traveled to Yaqian and described both grave sites. The inscription on Li's tombstone was written by Shen: "Li Chenghu's grave. The first deputy of the Yaqian Farmers Association. 1/24/1922 in the Xiaoshan county jail. His son Zhangbao entreated for his body to be buried."

Thinking of this enthusiastic old farm friend (sixty-seven when he died), we stood silently several minutes by the grave with an unspoken sorrow in our hearts over the tragedy of [his] dying in prison. The small friend who was leading us ran on up the winding path, turning left and then right more than halfway up the mountain. And then we saw a splendid and beautiful grave, imposing and majestic. The grave was built of cement in a very beautiful style. Leading up to the grave were completely even stone steps. Before the grave was a small raised flower bed. Many small white stones taken from streams were used around the grave site. Shen's coffin was surrounded by cement railings. The grave was shaped as a semicircle with dense pine trees all around and behind it was a great lofty majestic cliff.[2]

On the way down the mountain after paying his respects at the grave, Lin noticed a middle-aged farmer going along the road; his young guide told him that it was Li Chenghu's son Zhangbao, who had pleaded with the authorities for the peaceful burial of his father. It was a chance opportunity to get Zhangbao's perspective on the events of 1921 and after, and Zhangbao, on his way to the regional government office, was willing to oblige.

On a hot June day in 1993, I traveled to Yaqian with one goal being a visit to Shen's tomb on Phoenix Mountain. I made known my request to the local Yaqian Communist official, and we left for the mountain. But his intent was to show me only the tomb of Li Chenghu, the farmer who today gets official credit and the titles of hero and martyr for the rent resistance movement that Shen began in 1921. Though I protested and the Chinese man who was accompanying me to deal with the rigors of the local dialect insisted, the official first demurred because "we don't yet know whether Shen was a good or bad man"—this, sixty-five years after his death. Part of this uncertainty, of course, grows out of the history of changing party lines in the People's Republic; but part also comes from Shen's own controversial history.

The next line of the official was "we'd like to show you but we don't know where his grave is." More protesting finally led to a concession: "there might be someone in the town who does." While they attempted to find that someone, I began climbing the steps to view Li Chenghu's tomb, not very far up the mountain. Renovated in 1984, it is an imposing sight. Backed by a semicircular white stone wall about twelve feet tall with decorative geometric designs and topped by a tiled gable, the elevated grave lies on an expansive stone platform. In front is a stone planter with short green bushes and a stone cenotaph reading "the grave of martyr Li Chenghu." Gone is Shen's handwritten inscription. Behind the grave site is the imposingly rugged crest of Phoenix Mountain. I had little time to take in the scene before I heard shouts that they had found a person who knew the way to Shen's grave. That person was a smiling, ruddy-faced man, Li Yuexiao, who (in one of those historical ironies that is almost too perfect to believe) is the grandson of Li Chenghu. He seemed happy, even eager to lead me and six Chinese men from Hangzhou University and the Xiaoshan county and Yaqian town governments to the site.

We walked first on a footpath, cut through thick growths of vines and weeds amid a sparse forest of mostly spindly pines. Then the path ended and we walked on through the knee-high, sometimes waist-high vegetation up the mountain. "This is the pathway to the tomb," Li pointed out, but there were none of the stone steps that Lin had noted in 1935; there was simply the same lush overgrowth that somehow seemed at odds with this place of death. We walked a few more steps; then Li parted some plants to reveal a gaping hole in the ground, in the grave itself, ripped open by the bomb in 1968.

I had known earlier about the destruction but had assumed that the tomb would have been rebuilt with the passage of a quarter century and especially in light of the changes in attitudes brought by the reform efforts of the 1980s and 1990s. But there had been no repair, and the totality of the destruction and the subsequent treatment of the body were horrifyingly vicious. All that is left of the tomb itself is a large chunk of what had been an imposing concrete headstone lying amid the rubble from the bomb. The bones had been thrown down the mountain; they were later reburied by the family with the site known, I was told, only by Shen's seventy-six-year-old son. And those who destroyed the tomb: "Were they student Red Guards?" I asked. "No," came the shocking reply, "they were farmers." Shocking, for as will become clear, much of Shen's later life was spent helping the families of these same area farmers.

What was there about Shen that inspired such bitter emotion? It has been well over a decade since those who were vilified during the Cultural Revolution itself have been rehabilitated. What was there about Shen that sixty-five years after his bloody death leaves such consternation among officials about how to offer some historical judgment, how to deal with his life and legacy? What is the mystery of Shen Dingyi? This book is in part a probing of that mystery through a reconstruction of the last dozen years of Shen's life. Part of that mystery is bound up with his death, for if Shen today still inspires bitter and confused reactions, during his lifetime, for someone or some group, his actions prompted an animosity that turned murderous. His assassination at the Yaqian bus station, a vicious and significant crime (for it took in his forty-fifth year the life of one of China's potential revolutionary leaders), has never been solved.

This study is in part an attempt to solve Shen's murder.

It is primarily, however, a study of the Chinese revolution of the 1920s through an examination of the social, political, and cultural seams and textures of the late 1910s and the 1920s, as they are revealed in the relationships, career, and death of Shen Dingyi. Unlike the Communist phase of the revolution of the 1930s and 1940s, and despite its significance for understanding modern China, the social dynamics of the so-called Nationalist Revolution have not been probed much beyond the dominant political paradigms and approaches of structures, institutions, and ideology: the overriding political polarization between Right and Left; the centrality of ideology in political commitments and motives; the centrality of structures (parties and factions) for revolutionary action; the role of the Comintern in the affairs of both the Communist Party and the Guomindang; and a generally monochromatic depiction of environmental and social contexts.

Several interrelated issues emerge as crucial in the story of Shen and the revolution: the nature of social identity, the roles of social networks, the import of place, and, in historical explanation, the centrality of process. Coupled with academic trends in cultural studies, the recent rapid economic development in China has given rise to considerable interest in and new perspectives on national, ethnic, and locational identities.[3] Indeed, throughout the almost cataclysmic challenges of the twentieth century and the tortuous search for a new political and cultural orthodoxy, the question of Chinese identity has been central. That has not been the case only for the Chinese en masse or for the Chinese as a nation, however. In the context of vast and even dizzying social and political changes, individuals have had to grapple with the question of their own identities in relation to others in society, to the state, and to the nation. Periods of concentrated revolutionary change that posed considerable political and personal insecurity have presented individuals with the greatest necessity to confront the problem of identity and in some cases to construct and reconstruct their own identities. Shen Dingyi is not Everyman or Every Revolutionary, yet the question of identity with which he had to deal was one that all Chinese elites had to confront to greater or lesser degree, even if only in establishing their relationship to the revolution. It is probably the case that identity for many elites was shaded in muted and changeable hues, marked by considerable ambiguity and adaptability in relation to new contexts. Part of the tragedy of life in twentieth-century China, as we will see, grew from efforts to apply starkly specific and unchanging identities to others in the midst of a revolution with an indeterminate outcome. The mystery of Shen coils around this question of identity; what emerges in the details of his life and death in the revolutionary 1920s is a view of "identity as process, as performance, and as provisional."[4]

In a 1975 essay comparing social metaphors that historians use in studying Chinese and Islamic cultures, Ira Lapidus challenged historians of China to think about the possibilities of the network rather than the hierarchy as a way to conceive social dynamics. He asks, "Would it be possible to integrate studies of Chinese local history, which seem to parallel local politics in the Islamic world, into networks rather than hierarchical models? Would China look different if it were studied as the outcome of individual choices and actions rather than from the perspective of the total system?"[5] It is not, of course, as though the network metaphor has been missing from Chinese studies of recent years; in social analyses historians and social scientists have repeatedly pointed to the important roles of networks.[6] And yet the dominant models have generally remained hierarchical: the patriarchy of the family, the political models of centralization and the mass line, the authority-dependence syndrome as a mark of political culture, and, most dominant in recent years, the urban hierarchy of central places.

A Chinese poet in the 1980s characterized Chinese life as "a net": one is linked with others in a net of relationships, tied directly to some and indirectly through intermediaries to others.[7] There is not, however, simply one net of which one is a part but many overlapping nets that hold people in social place and help shape their identity. While networks are important in most societies, the relational emphasis in Chinese society is its central feature: the individual's primary reality is his relationship to others. Chie Nakane has pointed out that, in contrast to Japan where family ethics are based "on the collective group," in China they "are always based on relationships between particular individuals."[8] The Chinese define themselves and are defined, that is, given identity, in large part by their roles in those relationships and by the networks of which they are a part and which are based upon a variety of factors—familial, communal, occupational, political, economic, social, intellectual.[9]

This study envisions society as a linking and coalescence of individuals through a wide range of personal connections; these linkages, which may be both horizontal and vertical, in turn compose the social skeins and networks that are the basic components of social organizations and groupings, including structures like political parties and factions. Elizabeth Perry's study of Shanghai labor organizations in the 1930s noted, for example, that "organizational developments reflected pre-existing informal networks among the workers."[10] In the revolution, such networks became both a significant context and a resource, and their stability and strength (or lack thereof) became an important dynamic; thus they are crucial for an understanding of the direction and contours of the revolution and for the life and death of Shen.

A third significant reality in the story of Shen and the revolution is the importance of place as context and as player. In recent years theorists have set forth the centrality of space as a crucial component of social analysis.[11] In the field of Chinese studies, William Skinner's marketing and regional systems models have provided a significant spatial approach for some studies,[12] but there has seemed to be no general commitment to explore the relations between spatial and situational environments and human outlooks and behavior. In the revolution of the 1920s, for example, key actors have often seemed to move in an undifferentiated, placeless world. A firm notion of context is essential not only for understanding particular social and political networks, structures, and dynamics, but also in appreciating divergent outlooks and mentalities. Robert Darnton's argument that "world views cannot be chronicled in the manner of political events, but they are no less 'real'" points to the significance of attempting to reconstruct such views, especially, I would argue, in analyzing revolutionary situations.[13]

Shen's revolutionary activities occurred primarily in three different arenas: the metropolis of Shanghai, the provincial capital of Hangzhou, and the village of Yaqian. On its face, the general framework for this analysis comprises these three spatial arenas, but in essence, given the gaps among them in social ecology and in economic and political development, it is really (to play on the title of Graham Peck's classic report from western China) an examination of three kinds of time.[14] From Shanghai, which, in Leo Lee's phrase, "constituted a 'spatialization' of 'modernity,'" to the rapidly modernizing Hangzhou, to the dark and dreary thatched huts of Yaqian, Shen's involvement in the three arenas presents a measure not only of the relativity of structures and values in each, but also of the interaction of historical actors, networks, and mentalities among the three.[15]

As I have argued elsewhere, the revolution is not a process to be explained primarily by impersonal social and economic forces or by ideological struggles.[16] (Indeed, the history of this period has often seemed to be a struggle among ideas largely divorced from the people who thought them, among revolutionaries who function primarily as mouthpieces for various isms.) Rather, the revolution is the story of men and women linked in various social relationships and thrust, often without choice, into revolutionary situations and turmoil that they cannot control or direct, where hope and despair seem to follow each other in depressingly endless cycles and where lives are shaped, twisted, and destroyed by treacherously shifting revolutionary currents. Day-to-day decisions and actions in the process of revolution tend to follow or spring from proximate events, developments, and relationships rather than from general ideological and political commitments and developments. To understand the revolution, we must give substantial attention to the daily human experience and social processes from which ideas developed and actions were taken, to flesh-and-blood human beings whose commitments could stem from a wide variety of motives.

Each chapter analyzes a dramatic crisis or development in Shen's revolutionary career as it emerges in one or more arenas. The narrative details the nature and dynamics of the revolution while it offers the clues to possibly explain Shen's death. In many ways this is a story of historical possibilities and contingencies. As we will see, there are at least five possible and even likely suspects and therefore as many different explanations for Shen's murder. In the revolution, too, there were many possibilities for currents in the river of revolutionary change to shift and flow in different directions and in different channels, and thus to produce strikingly different historical outcomes. Whatever the possibilities at the time, in the end the outcome of the Chinese revolution of the 1920s set the political paths that China would follow to the present.

In setting forth the context to probe the mysteries of Shen's life and death and to explore the dynamics of the 1920s revolution, I liberally use passages from Shen's essays, stories, poetry, and speeches. These passages help reveal the nature of the man and the age in which he lived and died.

CHAPTER ONE

Death in Yaqian

August 28, 1928

If one lives as though he were neither alive nor dead or as though he were half alive and half dead—being an idler in years of nonaction, his whole life is not equal to that of a man engaged in action for a single year who finds death on the road.

"Death" (Si), 1922

August had been oppressively hot and humid. Some people thought it likely, in fact, that the great heat had precipitated the explosion of the Zhejiang provincial defense corps' ammunition depot in the capital city of Hangzhou shortly before midnight on August 22. Though the late hour prevented casualties, the tremendous noise of the initial fireball near West Lake and the aftershock of countless exploding shells that kept firemen at bay increased the jitters that many in the city had recently felt.[1] For the past seventeen months, since April 1927, the city in almost yin-yang fashion had been pulled, like much of the province, between Red Scare and White Terror. The successful military campaigns of Chiang Kai-shek in 1926 and 1927 to reunite China after years of warlord depredations had unleashed violent party and factional struggles that continued unabated through the summer of 1928. In the early weeks of August, the provincial defense corps had arrested more than a dozen Communists in Hangzhou hotels. Rumors of sabotage and attacks spread like unchecked flames through the city, fed by newspaper accounts of Communist efforts in counties around the capital and throughout the province.[2]

The heat in itself would have been sufficient reason for forty-four-year-old Shen Dingyi to travel to the mountain resort of Moganshan thirty miles north of Hangzhou, for years the summer destination of Western missionaries and businessmen from Shanghai (ten hours away by rail and motor boat), Hangzhou, and other cities of the Yangzi River region. A two-thousand-foot mountain shaded by a bamboo forest, Moganshan had acquired a reputation as a pleasant vacation retreat from the heat, complete with tennis courts and swimming facilities.[3] But by the 1920s, as Chinese national fervor and resentment against foreign privileges increased, Moganshan came to be seen by Chinese political elites as a healthful retreat that should not be merely a foreign preserve. The construction of a sanitarium in the mid-twenties only enhanced its attractiveness. Shen did not, however, go to Moganshan to escape the heat, but rather to meet some national and provincial leaders in the government and the Nationalist Party who were vacationing or recuperating there. A year before, he had been counted among those leaders, and this was his first informal attempt to reestablish contact.

In the summer of 1928, Shen was directing a bold experiment in economic, political, and educational development in an effort to transform the area around his home village of Yaqian into a model of "self-government." His trip to Moganshan was also in part a chance to describe this program and get reactions from key men in party circles.[4] Whether he was invited to go to the retreat or whether, as one source says, he simply saw in the newspaper that Dai Jitao was resting there and thus decided to initiate the journey himself, we are not certain. For Shen in the early 1920s, Dai Jitao had been something of a lodestar. Personal secretary to Sun Yat-sen, Dai had worked with Shen as a joint editor of a politically progressive Shanghai journal, and they had been involved in the early stages of the formation of the Communist Party. In 1925, amid difficult times for Shen, Dai had provided crucial guidance and support. Yet despite what seemed at one time a significant friendship, it had been almost three years since their last meeting. Perhaps part of Shen's desire to go to Moganshan was to renew an old relationship under new contexts in the Chinese revolution. It would certainly not be a meeting of political equals, for Dai had been elected in February to the standing committee of the party's Central Executive Committee.

Shen did not have many miles to travel as he left on Sunday morning, August 26. Yaqian was no more than fifteen miles east of Hangzhou across the Qiantang River. Yet the bus, ferry, and boat rides to Moganshan could be expected to take much of the day with the inevitable poorly

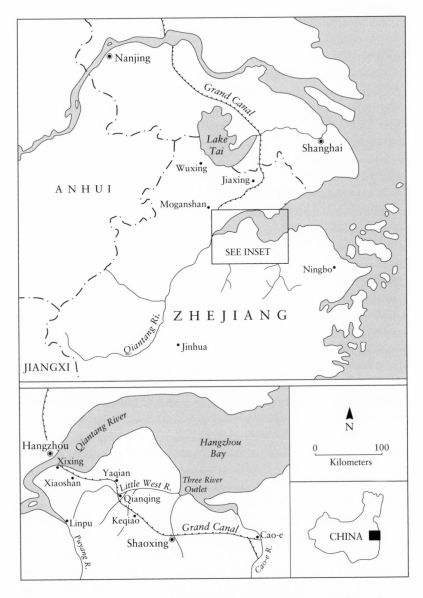

Map 1. The Arena of Shen's Main Activity, including Shanghai, Hangzhou, and Yaqian

coordinated schedules and unpredictable delays. Accompanying him was Wang Nayin, a younger political disciple and coworker who had developed in 1927 into a significant provincial party leader and in 1928 into an important assistant in the self-government experiment.

They arrived at Moganshan in mid-afternoon, taking a brief rest at their hotel, the China Inn, before proceeding to the sanitarium to meet with the political leaders. If Dai and the others had not invited Shen, it is likely that Shen had telegraphed Dai about his planned visit. According to Shen's memorial biography, at the sanitarium with Dai were three other important political figures, two of whom were reportedly involved in the conversations with Shen. Zhang Ji, whose wife was a patient at the sanitarium, was a longtime leader in revolutionary efforts linked to Sun Yat-sen, from the days of the anti-Manchu campaign of the Revolutionary Alliance in Tokyo to the reconstructed Nationalist Party in the early 1920s. With Shen he had been involved in the formation of the Western Hills group, alleged to have been the extreme right wing of the party. Earlier in August he was made chair of the Central Political Council in Beijing. Zhou Bonian was the former official private secretary to the Central Political Council; from a very wealthy family, he was reportedly an old friend of Shen. The third figure was Zhu Jiahua, the commissioner of civil affairs in Zhejiang province. Until 1927 an academic in the fields of geology and German, Zhu would be elected to the Central Executive Committee of the Nationalist Party in 1929. Dai, Zhou, and Zhu all hailed from Wuxing, bound together by the peculiarly strong Chinese cultural tie of native place.

Before dinner on that Sunday evening Shen described to Dai and Zhou details of his self-government program. (How much Zhang and Zhu participated in the conversations we are not told.) During the course of the conversations, Zhou asked Shen to write a couplet for him on a fan. Shen's renown as a calligrapher and author of couplets, which he often composed for various significant national and personal events, was widespread. On the wall of the Wangshunxing Restaurant near the main train station in Hangzhou, for example, hung one of Shen's couplets, which he had written in characters of gigantic size, "beautiful and full of spirit."[5] Complying with Zhou's request that afternoon at the sanitarium, Shen wrote out a poem of Ming dynasty scholar Yu Zhongxiao in a style known literally as "wild draft" (*kuangcao*):

> Steeled by a thousand hammers, by ten thousand chisels
>   before I come out of the mountain,
> I am not afraid of the fierce, raging fire.

I am not afraid if my bones are powdered or my body crushed.
I only want to leave clarity and honor among the people.

Zhou, who had a reputation for a fine sense of humor, joked, "When I write, I like to write about fine bright weather, but you're always writing stuff about powdered bones and crushed bodies. What's going on here?" They both laughed; there is no record that Shen even attempted to respond.[6] After the evening meal, Shen and Wang returned to the hotel for the night.

The next morning Shen, apparently wanting to talk to Dai alone, walked to the country villa where Dai was staying. It was likely at that time that he confided in Dai his deep despair over the recent course of events. "The revolution that originally rose in people's hearts has not been satisfied. Because the situation was [originally] unsatisfactory, we had to have a revolution. But the present unsatisfied nature of people's hearts means that there must be another revolution."[7] Perhaps Dai did not like what he heard, for he used the excuse that Zhang Ji had invited him to visit his ill wife to cut short his conversation with Shen. We can imagine that, in the context of the previous afternoon's description of Shen's own self-government movement, Dai, as a key member of the party leadership, was suspicious about how that effort might relate to "another revolution."

Dai's decision left Shen free to take in the scenery, but in this too he seemed to be thwarted. When he and Wang reached the summit of Pagoda Mountain, the fog was so dense that they had no view. In the afternoon a boat excursion to see the waterfall at Sword Pond was apparently more satisfying: Shen was moved to write a poem with historical allusions to tragic tales of the site's ancient past. On his return to the hotel, he took a nap. It was not until dusk that Shen and Wang made their way back to the sanitarium where they spent the evening with Dai, Zhou, and others reminiscing about the past. Zhou's humorous asides led to frequent outbursts of laughter. Parting came fairly early, with Shen announcing that he and Wang would leave Moganshan at dawn the next morning. Zhou, who seemed to be the only one who was enjoying Shen's presence, pressed him to stay another day. But for Shen, there was little reason to prolong what seems to have been an unsatisfying, even disappointing visit, and he declined Zhou's invitation.

The next morning, August 28, Shen and Wang walked down the mountain and took a steam launch to the Imperial Arch Bridge outside the city wall on the north side of Hangzhou. The headquarters of

transport companies whose steam-powered boats linked Hangzhou to
Jiaxing, Suzhou, Shanghai, and other points, Imperial Arch Bridge was
the center of what would later be considered a suburban community.
When Hangzhou became a treaty port in 1896, the environs of the
bridge became a Japanese market and the location of the English con-
sulate. By 1928 it was a bustling town, a port of entry into the metropolitan area for a large number of travelers and known also for its large
population of prostitutes. It is not likely that Shen and Wang dawdled
in the area once their boat docked. The crowded walkways were always
made more so by worshipers coming and going from a large temple
beside the bridge; a chronicler of Hangzhou noted that the air around
the temple and bridge was often thick with the smoke of incense.[8]

Shen and Wang continued their journey by bus toward the Qiantang
River ferry. On the way, Shen insisted that Wang stop and visit his ill
mother, who lived in the heart of the city. Wang complied, getting off
the bus at the New Market stop, a flourishing government and commercial sector of the city alongside West Lake. Shen continued alone,
arriving in mid-afternoon at the Qiantang River wharves that were the
embarkation point for the ferries crossing the half-mile-wide river to the
east and for the boats going upstream into the center of the province.
It was a busier commercial district than Imperial Arch Bridge, serving
as the entrepot for silk, jute, cotton, and vegetables coming from eastern
Zhejiang and for wood, paper, ink, ink slabs, and tea brought in on the
Fuchun River from southern Anhui province.[9] As in the Bridge district,
the large numbers of people coming and going, the transport and
warehouse workers involved in trade, and attendants providing service
in restaurants, inns, taverns, and brothels created a population in flux,
one not tied to that locality and with little sense of obligation to it. At
times like those in the hot summer of 1928, with fears of a Communist
threat continually aroused, these districts were immediately suspected by
the authorities of harboring Red agents and provocateurs. Evidence
suggests that a temporary imposition of martial law in the area forced
Shen and other travelers to pass through a police search before being
allowed to proceed across the river.[10] Since the middle of August,
authorities had been concerned about an alleged expanding Communist
power in Xiaoshan county (Shen's home), between Hangzhou and the
city of Shaoxing some thirty miles to the east.[11]

Shen crossed the river on the free ferry, established first in the late
Qing by a Hangzhou philanthropist but now funded by a group of
wealthy merchants and other elites.[12] Once on the other side and aware

of the bus schedule, he hurried to the River Bank bus station to buy his ticket for the ride to Yaqian. He then boarded the no. 25 bus for the forty-five-minute ride across flat lands luxuriant in various shades of green—the deep green of cotton, the gray-green of jute, and the chartreuse of rice. It was 4:30 P.M.; ominous rain clouds had appeared in the north and west, turning the sky a deep gray-blue and helping to subdue the intense afternoon heat. Waiting at the River Bank station were two men dressed in white cotton shirts and short trousers. After Shen purchased his ticket, they purchased theirs. Witnesses later said the men pressed to sit near Shen on the bus. Reports later even suggested that he knew the men; some, in fact, claimed that he bought them food.[13]

In any case, there is nothing to indicate that they conversed on the bus. Was Shen aware of their presence? Of what could he have been thinking, in these last forty-five minutes of his life? Perhaps, tired from the travel and the heat, he was dozing. Or perhaps he was thinking of nothing but arriving at Yaqian, walking home, and eating supper with his pregnant wife and two small sons. Perhaps with the glowering rain clouds, he worried, in light of disastrous late June floods, what more serious flooding would do to the coastline of the river and bay. Yaqian was part of a region of alluvial plains that had been formed by the action of shifting Qiantang River currents. Beginning in the mid-twenties, however, currents had shifted once again, and the constructive force of new land formation had been overtaken by an erosive destruction of that same life-supporting land. In June, heavy rains had caused the Qiantang to rise twenty feet, flooding several thousand acres of crop land and collapsing hundreds more into the river and bay.[14] Did the oncoming storms mean more destruction in the offing?

Perhaps his thoughts went to his East Township self-government program and the financial problems that threatened it. Little more than a decade before, he would have had the money to support the effort on his own, but that was now all gone and much of his land parceled out to his second wife and eldest son. If he had hoped for assistance from the party through his contacts at Moganshan, the visit had been a failure. Perhaps most likely, Shen was replaying in his mind the Moganshan conversations and the events in the turbulent year leading up to them. Just one year ago he had been at the height of his political power, the key figure in the provincial party and in governmental and public affairs. But as the star of Chiang Kai-shek rose, Shen's sank. Just five years before at this time, they had been together in Moscow on a mission for Sun Yat-sen. Though Chiang had been the chief negotiator on matters of military aid, Shen reportedly had extensive conversations with Lenin.[15] In the last three years their political careers had gone in strikingly different directions, with Shen's fall from power directly linked to Chiang's rise. Could Shen rehabilitate his career in higher political arenas? Did he even want to do so?

The bus continued its route after a brief stop at the county seat. Especially in light of the continuing Red Scare and the rumors of Communist expansion in Xiaoshan county, perhaps Shen's thoughts turned to his provincial role in the last year as the key leader of the purge of the Communists from the Nationalist Party. It was distasteful, to be sure, to have had to oversee the arrest and punishment of some who had been his disciples, but Shen clearly saw them as betrayers of the revolution and certainly of the special relationships that he had enjoyed with them. Whether he considered the hatred that many of their survivors felt for him we do not know.

Or perhaps, as the eastbound bus neared Yaqian, Shen's thoughts turned to more local matters: the agitation among East Township silk farmers over his new reform policies; the sick, elderly man languishing in the Hangzhou prison largely because of Shen's determination; the Buddhist monk from Yaqian, crazy (or so at least some said), who reportedly was trying to let out a contract for Shen's murder; the rumors that powerful landlords near the county seat were openly talking about trying to hire someone to kill Shen. Could a line from an earlier poem have been coming into his thoughts: *What I pass are nothing but resentful sounds, hateful sounds, despairing sounds—the sounds of killing.*[16]

As the bus pulled in to the station at 5:15 P.M., it was raining heavily. His walk home would fortunately not take long, over the bridge on the Grand Canal and several hundred feet east. From the bus window Shen saw Song Weiqi, a leader of the East Township Education Association, who happened to be returning from the Xiangjia Commoners' School. Shen waved to hail him. When the bus stopped, Shen got off, walking around the back of the bus to talk to Song; he reportedly seemed happy and animated. At the same time, the white-clad men followed Shen around the back of the bus, standing apart from each other. When Shen and Song reached the station master, Shen could not find his ticket, at first mistakenly handing him a name card and then fumbling through his clothes for the piece of paper. While Shen was still searching, the station master turned to Song, whom he thought had also been on the bus. Song was explaining when there was a sudden loud crash—a hail of bullets hitting the window of the station master, who instantly fell to the earth to escape them.

Clasping his hands together, Shen turned around to see where the guns were firing from. Witnesses' descriptions put the killers from twelve to twenty feet from Shen. Then came the second burst of gunfire, followed by a third. Shen was hit first in the chest, then in the head, falling to the ground. Song was not hit but was immobilized by fright, while all others on the station platform fled in panic. The assassins came quickly up to Shen, who was trying to protect his head with his hands, and fired more than ten shots at his body. By the time the shots stopped, Shen had already stopped breathing. A doctor's examination of Shen's body the next day found four wounds from bullets that had exited the body and two, in the head and chest, from bullets that remained lodged in the corpse.

When the killers saw that Shen was dead, they ran west along the highway toward the county seat. Song, steadying himself after what had been only a violent few seconds, yelled at several farmers to pursue the killers. At a small bridge, the assassins wheeled around and fired at the farmers, scaring them into retreat. Three men continued the chase, but again the killers opened fire, further intimidating the pursuers. After this last display of determination, they made their final escape, vanishing without a trace. Shen had met death on the road.

Who did it? And why? To answer those questions, we must understand the person of Shen Dingyi, his social and personal networks, his actions and ideas, and the arenas of the 1920s revolution.

CHAPTER TWO

One's Native Place

Hangzhou, 1916–1917

Lanterns on the shore move like stars in the heavens;
The sound of chickens on the shore; the bellows of the horns
*   urge the boats forward.*
Passengers get up,
Taking with them their native place's broken dreams,
*   half flickering,*
Reluctantly searching for people who can understand them.
Today I arrived in his native place.

"Reaching the Guangzhou Shore"
(Suiyang chuan Guangzhou boan), 1921

Shen Dingyi returned home to China the day that Yuan Shikai died. President Yuan's elevation of his own authority over that of the fledgling National Assembly and his obvious drive to crush the Guomindang had given rise to the summer rebellion of 1913 that, in turn, led to Shen's exile. Called the "second revolution," this rebellion saw pro-Guomindang military governors declaring independence from the Beijing regime and trying to fend off Yuan's formidable army. Shen, a leading member of the provincial assembly with considerable revolutionary credentials from his work in Shanghai during the "first revolution" of 1911–12, worked feverishly in Hangzhou to solicit and gather funds for munitions and supplies. His personal financial commitment, as in 1911, was large; when he personally took the funds to Nanjing, the center of the "revolution," the total was some two hundred thousand *yuan*. But within two weeks, Nanjing was surrounded by Yuan's armies and the effort was crushed, with many of Yuan's opponents, including Shen and Sun Yat-sen himself, forced to flee.

Though the second revolution was only one episode in Yuan's ultimately ill-fated drive to reestablish the imperial system, for Shen and others it produced long-lasting effects and bitter memories. Before he left for Japan, he wrote a poem, ruing the waste of his effort and money:

> Hands scatter two hundred thousand of yellow gold,
> For a time to buy brave actions.
> But down to today
> All that's left is my naked body.[1]

Although he was not yet naked to the point of impoverishment, Shen's financial contributions in 1911 and 1913 had begun to strip him of substantial amounts of the family fortune.

More important for Shen in the short term, the failure of the revolution began three years of exile from family, native place, and position. "Floating in a foreign land, weeping," was a friend's description of how Shen handled the exile.[2] Shen himself described it as a tragedy: "For three years I fled for my life, for ten thousand *li* going into the wilderness. . . . It was an even worse tragedy than being a vagrant on account of poverty."[3] "Going into the wilderness": a graphic metaphor for separation from his culture, social networks, and native place. Years later, in the poem cited above about his arrival in Guangzhou, he expressed the sense of bewilderment of a solitary sojourner.

China's was a culture that so valued a sense of place as a component of identity, as a vital connection to others, as a pivot of consciousness, and as a point of social and cultural orientation that it developed wide networks of special support associations for sojourners in cities and towns all over the country.[4] Ruan Xingcun, Hōsei University graduate, founder of a private Hangzhou law school, practicing lawyer and entrepreneur, and later Shen associate, headed the Yuyao county native place society in Hangzhou from 1911 to his death in 1928. The society rented a house that served as dormitory, cafeteria, and meeting place for Yuyao students and others from the county who were in Hangzhou looking for or coming to work. Twice each year, in the spring and fall, there were special ceremonies at the house, featuring sacrifices to the memories of Yuyao county's virtuous men of the past.[5] Men like Ruan played a large role in shaping and enhancing a sense of local consciousness, loyalty, and memory. Such organizations, in a society where separation from one's group in a faraway place might be equivalent to exile, were very important.

In Tokyo Shen reportedly studied and tried to control his anger at the turn of events in China. When the Japanese presented the Chinese government with the Twenty-One Demands in January 1915, Shen emerged as a leader in bringing together Chinese to discuss opposition to the Japanese government. Out of the discussions came the General Office for Chinese Students in Japan, with Shen elected as general secretary. This organization discussed, among other strategies, the possibility of Chinese students returning to China en masse to press the government to break off diplomatic relations. By the end of February, Shen's actions had raised the suspicions of Japanese government officials, who assigned high-level police authorities to investigate Shen and the organization. Because he had little freedom of action and the situation promised to become worse, Shen and nine comrades fled Japan.[6] One of the nine, Liu Dabai (1880–1931), a Shaoxing-born imperial degree holder and journalist, had also been forced to flee China because of his anti-Yuan involvement. He would become one of Shen's closest friends.[7]

They traveled first to Singapore, where Shen stayed for six months, living in poverty for the first time in his life; he later said that he barely had the resources to light a cooking fire. The opportunity to edit the *Sumatra News* for overseas Chinese gave him his first taste of journalism and lifted him out of dire poverty. Yet, when he received word on New Year's Day 1916 that southwestern provinces had begun an anti-Yuan uprising, he still could not come up with sufficient cash for a ticket back to China until May.[8] His experiences of exile in an alien world were likely the foundation for the road and travel imagery and dream allegories in many of his later surrealistic poems and short stories.

The problem with financial resources seems ironic. The Shen lineage of Yaqian was one of the wealthiest in the county. Their extensive landholdings in the rich alluvial land produced cotton, rice, and jute; rents from many tenant farmers poured into the family coffers. The imposing Shen residence, surrounded by a solidly constructed stone wall, fronted the eastern extension of the Grand Canal as it flowed past the south side of the village. Above the impressively grand gate were carved the characters that named the ancestral residence: *Guanglu di*, House of Brightness and Prosperity.[9] In front of the gate was an elaborately constructed stone flagpole flying the pennant of the highest civil service degree, the *jinshi*, which Shen's father, Shouqian, had attained in 1886—a continual reminder that the family in this compound was part of the awe-inspiring state apparatus.[10] It is almost certain that during his years of exile in Japan and Southeast Asia, Shen returned in thought many times to that compound and his life there.

Father and Son

Shen's return to the House of Brightness and Prosperity in Xiaoshan county was filled with the hope of helping to create a new China, but the first few months after his return were filled with personal tragedy compounding that of his exile. His oldest daughter drowned. Then his young son died of an unnamed disease. And his father, Shouqian, suddenly became ill and died within little more than a month.[11] It was his father's death to which Shen reacted most openly with deep and sincere grief. He reportedly shuddered when he realized that if his departure from Sumatra had been delayed much longer or if his father had become ill earlier, he might not have seen him alive again.[12] In 1919 he wrote, "My father died more than three years ago. I often think of him and I remember his words."[13]

Their relationship had not been an easy one. Shen was the third son of the family and was known in the community as Third Gentleman. He did not have his two older brothers' caution and reserve, however, but instead was bright, quick, and brash, not bound by hard and fast rules.[14] In almost any traditional Chinese family, such a personality would have created tension with a Confucian patriarch-official. Despite Dingyi's sometimes difficult personality, Shouqian recognized his son's intellectual ability and groomed him to take the examination. At age eighteen, he passed the first-level examination, receiving the *xiucai* degree. That degree in itself was not enough to obtain any sort of official position, but Shouqian purchased for his son a magistracy in distant Yunnan province, to which Dingyi journeyed in 1904. He likely saw his more-than-two-year stay in that impoverished hinterland quite as much of an exile as his later period in Japan and Southeast Asia. His actions at the end of his tenure of office clearly did not redound to the honor of his family.[15]

Compromising himself by becoming involved in revolutionary activity in 1907 on the border between Yunnan and Vietnam, Shen simply left his official post, took a train to Hanoi and, from Haiphong, a ship to Japan. Forsaking one's post without permission was a serious matter. The Yunnan civil governor impeached Shen, and on the basis of his report, the Board of Personnel in Beijing ordered as a punishment that Shen be stigmatized as "forever unemployable." Word of Dingyi's actions shocked and outraged Shouqian even as the government penalty saddened him. Suspecting that Dingyi was continuing to participate in revolutionary activities in Japan, Shouqian wrote him that he should never return. To officials and the public in Xiaoshan, he openly denounced Dingyi as an "unfilial and rebellious son." We do not know if, as some commentators later said, such a display of public displeasure merely concealed a concerned father who continued to send money to Dingyi in Japan for his support.[16] Nor is there information on the relations between father and son in the period of the 1911 revolution.

After Dingyi's flight to Japan in the wake of the second revolution, Zhejiang's military governor sent investigators to the House of Brightness and Prosperity. According to a letter Dingyi received in Singapore from Shouqian, the government deputies in veiled threats against the Shen household ordered father to call his son home for arrest. Shouqian answered, "Jianhou [Dingyi's name taken at adulthood] is a man; he has his principles. I am old. If you want to arrest him, then do it. Don't drag me into this." While such a response might be seen as further washing his hands of his son's affairs, Dingyi wrote that when "I received my father's letter, I was very happy. Early on, I had supposed that only I was aware that I had made myself a man; but my father in his seventies had already recognized the man I had become."[17] It is certainly in this context that Shen's grief for his father should be understood: the two had come to an apparent mutual respect.

Subcultures and Identity by Association

The China to which Shen returned in the summer of 1916 was much like that of late Qing China. The difference was that with the passing of the imperial system and the array of ideas, forms, and structures that had given it life, there was no moral center to provide social and political direction and, even more serious, stability. For centuries the core of Chinese culture had been that represented by the flag on the flagpole at the entrance to the Shen compound, the literate, humanistic culture of the scholar. Trained in the thoughts of Confucius and his interpreters, young men and old were inculcated with the values of patriarchy, submission to higher authority in family and state, paternalism toward subordinates, and harmony in society. The civil service examination was the centerpiece of classical culture, for it was the passage through which all would-be scholar-officials had to travel. The educational system exalted the scholar as master of the worlds of society and politics, while the examination, beyond the reach of 90 percent of China's people, provided a demarcation between those scholars and the masses.[18] But it also helped to provide the parameters of cultural consensus that guided scholar and non-scholar alike. Elite cultural concepts shaped the core values of all Chinese, permeating a myriad of subcultures with the essence of what was a basic Chinese identity and in doing so playing the crucial role in integrating those subcultures.[19]

With the abolition of the examination system in 1905, the special status associated with the social term "gentry" began to decline. In a world where elites now came from many sources, new ways of expressing social identity and reality emerged. One Chinese character appears repeatedly in newspaper and other narrative accounts of events in the last years of the Qing and the early years of the Republic: *jie*, often translated as circle or circles, as in government circles, commercial circles, and so on. This word, in Chinese perhaps even more than in English, links social and occupational groupings to the spatial concept of a domain with boundaries. When used with the wide array of early Republican social groups, it suggests a multifocal world of subcultures (*jie*), readily designatable and on the surface quite discrete. But for all their denotation as bounded interest groups, the subcultures were coalescences of many networks and groups based on a variety of personal connections and usually linked to other subcultures by individuals. Perusal of newspapers from the last years of the Qing dynasty reveals that the "circles" that participated in public meetings and demonstrations were gentry (*shen*), merchants (*shang*), gentry-merchants (*shenshang*), and scholars, i.e., students and teachers (*xue*).[20] As the Republic began, the number of subcultures and therefore of perceived social identities in the public realm increased, making the problem of social and political consensus potentially more difficult: by 1916, newspaper reports of public gatherings had dropped gentry, but added police (*jing*), journalists (*bao*), and educators (*jiaoyu*). One other subculture did not appear until after 1911: the military (*jun*). The pivotal legitimating event bringing the military into the world of public circles was their role in the revolution that overthrew the Manchus. In their handling of the Manchu garrison forces in Hangzhou and in their convincing victory at Nanjing, the Zhejiang military leadership had experienced the exultation of military success with its consequent social-occupational bonding and its heightened sense of self-conscious power.[21]

In the rapidly developing world of Republican Hangzhou some subcultures became more significant, with others changing according to the evolving political context: merchant circles, for instance, became increasingly important, underwriting the expansion of business as well as government and revolution. In many ways this subculture was the least bounded domain, its members linking themselves to the wielders of the brush (gentry), the pen (government), and the gun (military) through financial support. Without the traditional social and ethical orthodoxy there were no social structures to articulate the public interest amid these increasingly self-conscious and largely occupational groups, and because there was little agreement on the source of political legitimacy, the ultimate arbiter in clashes between the subcultures was power, held most openly by the military.

The traditional core values had positively excluded martial values: "good men are not used for soldiers," says a Chinese proverb. Though dynasty after dynasty had come to power with bow, sword, and gun, the valued man, the man of learning, wielded the brush. Civilian elites assumed that the culture of brain was clearly superior to that of brawn. The old dynastic military examinations had incorporated physical tests of strength while the civil service examinees wrote their poems and essays with brushes held in long-nailed fingers, a pointed indicator that physical labor and exertion were beneath their dignity. While modern soldiers continued to rely directly upon the strength and agility of their bodies as they wielded artillery and bayonets, new civilian leaders in the flush of Republican hopes used pens to draft constitutions and verbally debated and maneuvered inside elected assemblies.

In the revolutionary efforts of 1911, there had been no outward antagonism between the military and civilian leadership. Networks among the civilian (gentry, merchant, and scholar) subcultures and the military subculture together planned and carried out revolutionary activities. These groups in the early twentieth century shared certain values, foremost among them the assertion of Chinese nationhood predicated on the elimination of the Manchus. They also shared the core cultural values of duty and loyalty and stressed graded social relationships and submission to authority. The process of revolution itself forged new networks that further blurred subculture boundaries. An example of this blurring can be seen in the career of civilian leader Xu Zuqian, journalist, reformer, and provincial assemblyman. Xu lived with Gu Naibin, commander of the Third Battalion of the New Army's Eighty-Second Regiment. The bulk of the planning for the Hangzhou revolution took place at their home, with the main military commanders and the powerful Qing assemblyman Chu Fucheng present. Both Gu and Xu were also said to have ties with the underworld organization, the Green Gang.[22] Many revolutionaries in this period had ties to secret societies, but the possible connections of Gu and Xu with the notorious Green Gang suggest that the subcultures of legitimate civilian and military elites during this revolutionary period were not far removed from a subculture that fed on smuggling, prostitution, and the opium trade.[23] They converged in the direct and sometimes violent action chosen to achieve their ends. Revolutionary networks freely used tactics of terror and assassination and often approached situations as heroic, knight-errant, devil-may-care adventurers.[24] Hallmark approaches were Dare-to-Die Corps and the launching of plots and conspiracies against overwhelming odds.

Although social and political consciousness varied among individual revolutionaries, military officers, or students returning from overseas, even within the same group, they obviously shared many attitudes and ideas and linked themselves in networks and groups of like-minded people. Ties to revolutionaries like Qiu Jin and Xu Xilin, both involved in the 1907 assassination of a Manchu governor in Anhui province, provided exciting prospects of heroic adventure in the saving of the nation. Connections with civilian reformers, many of them members of prestigious and well-to-do elites whose achievements were widely known, offered the potential for government position. Links to the military circles provided a sense of connection to an increasingly powerful force in Chinese society. As each group acted politically using particular assumptions and tactics, its members built up an array of common experiences and memories of challenges, enemies, allies, successes, and failures. Such memories could provide potent motivation and dedication to attaining further group goals.

Once political and social connections were made, moreover, others formed perceptions of a particular individual in the social spectrum, and these perceptions began to have their effect on social interactions. Anyone perceived to be linked to a particular revolutionary or military or civilian elite cause assumed what might be called, in a culture where identity always came in large part from one's relationships, identity by association. That identity allowed others "to organize [their] action with reference to that person."[25] What made this phenomenon particularly misleading and dangerous was the rumor-mongering which seemed so much a part of early Republican culture. A particular example comes from the career of revolutionary Wang Jinfa, a Restoration Society member and one of the Dare-to-Die squad in Hangzhou in November 1911, who became commander of the local military government in Shaoxing. Though his revolutionary credentials were unassailable, once in power he became known, whether fairly or unfairly, as an autocrat whose main goal was to wax fat on what he could take from the local populace.[26] He remained, however, in the network and good graces of major revolutionary leaders like Chen Qimei and Huang Xing. Even in an egregious personal assault case in September 1912, Huang Xing himself provided the bail money for Wang's release. But rumors began to be spread that Lu Gongwang, commander of Zhejiang's Sixth Division, had played a role in Wang's release, thereby identifying and linking Lu with Wang. Lu was so desperate to disassociate himself from such a tie that he maneuvered to have key provincial elites send an open telegram attesting to his lack of involvement in the affair and to the maintenance of his good name.[27]

Shen himself mused more generically about the implications of identity by association with regard to the military. "Soldier. Soldier. Gun. Dagger. Boots. Cartridge cases at the waist. Backpacks. How awe-inspiring! What bearing! But your brain's nerve cells register 'robber' and 'bandit.' A soldier, but he's also a man. What bitterness compels people to be afraid of him? One morning strip him nude from head to toe, and he's just like an intimate brother."[28]

Military Culture and Provincial Politics

For Shen and others the unhappy memory of 1913 did not stem simply from their forced exiles, but from the cause of these exiles. The president, the founder of the New Army, had crushed constitutional government and had used military force to extinguish the second revolution. For Shen and his constitutionalist allies, 1913 became in effect the crucial memory, overshadowing in its bitterly negative implications the increasingly unclear meaning of 1911, legitimating and making imperative civilian leadership over the military. Shen and his fellow assemblymen faced the difficulty of coming to grips with the changed context, where military power was now a key determinant in Chinese political life. It was a hard reality to swallow—that the political power equation had shifted so dramatically in only a decade after the end of the civil service examination and that educated civilian elites were being displaced. The provincial drama from June 1916 to June 1917 that embroiled Zhejiang politics and made Shen a man both admired and hated stemmed from the fundamental clash of subcultures, of the collective mentalities of the civilian and the military elites.

The key structures and approaches of Zhejiang's military culture emerge from an overview of developments among its networks and factions in the period from the 1911 revolution until 1916; they provide insights into the social boundaries and mentalities of this subculture. From the military perspective, the 1911 revolution had been the joint undertaking of officers from four military academies.[29] Those who had attended Japan's Army Officers' Academy, like key figure Jiang Zungui, were the elite, having studied overseas after obtaining government scholarships or using their family's resources; they were known as the most politically progressive of the graduates. Next in order of prestige were the Nanjing and Baoding academies. Jiang's early choice to serve as commander of Zhejiang's New Army regiment was Nanjing graduate Zhu Rui, a major planner of the revolution in Hangzhou and hero of Zhejiang forces at the battle of Nanjing.

Even though men from all schools were involved in plotting and carrying out the revolution, graduates of the Chinese academies from early on markedly resented the Japanese-trained officers. Graduates of the least prestigious Zhejiang Academy, which provided 70 to 80 percent of the lower army officers and the majority of the middle-level officers, grumbled about the "imported goods" who became the key staff officers under the first military governor.[30] Even some of the Nanjing and Baoding graduates joined in their complaints: Zhu Rui (Nanjing) and Lu Gongwang (Baoding), who had been Zhu's Chief of Staff at Nanjing, were quite frustrated.[31] It seems clear that the relationships born of common revolutionary activity when life and career had been on the line had produced potent new connections and social linkages among officers who had been graduated from the Chinese academies (Nanjing, Baoding, and Zhejiang). Yet amid changing political contexts, these connections were not long lasting. The military history and therefore much of the political history of Zhejiang in the years from 1911 to 1917 is the story of the unraveling of the 1911 factional coalition formed by networks of graduates from the four academies. One by one each network eventually provided a military governor: Japan's Army Officers' Academy, Jiang Zungui (1912); Nanjing, Zhu Rui (1912–16); Baoding, Lu Gongwang (1916–17); and Zhejiang, Xia Chao (1924–26).

In the rough-and-tumble factional struggles during these years, the frequently brutal military world was marked by intrigue and direct action, by betrayal and sometimes murder. The most important social bonds in the competing networks and factions were the alma maters of the officers, the bonds forged in common revolutionary experiences, and the personal friendships and connections growing out of native place ties. While the strength and cohesion of networks varied according to situation and to the nature and mix of network composition, study of the military competition in the early Republic reveals certain patterns.[32] The order of highest intensity of commitment to lowest seems to have been personal friendships, school ties, native place ties, joint action in past revolutionary activities, and revolutionary organizational commitment.[33] In periods of stress and crisis, personal friendship retained its tensile strength while other associations (including the usually strong native place tie and the common school affiliation or graduation) were more easily eroded or even sundered. If friendship was a powerful instrument for gaining one's ends, personal enmity was an equally potent force. The strength of particular bonds was often tested by the existential process of political interplay when anger and embittered feelings could spring from hastily made decisions in crisis situations.[34] Whether such emotions had lasting effects on relationships depended on the existence of other more positive connections.

Many civilian elites worked in the bureaucracy of the military governments. An account by Ma Xulun, who would remain an important provincial political figure into the 1930s, frankly reveals the modus operandi for attaining positions in the military regimes.[35] Ma had worked closely with one Lou Shouguang, a member of the Qing Provincial Assembly (ziyiju), in efforts of provincial elites to win back control over the British-controlled Shanghai-Hangzhou-Ningbo Railroad in the last years of the dynasty. Lou and his older brother were good friends with Jiang Zungui's father. Because of these connections and their native place tie (they hailed from Jiang's home of Zhuji county), they used considerable clout in backing Jiang over a strong opponent. Once Jiang became military governor, Ma, on the basis of his support and his friendship with Lou, became Jiang's secretary. Lou also received appointment as head of the Bureau of Printing and Engraving, a position which Ma subsequently took when Lou chose a magistracy. The point is not that Ma and Lou were unqualified, but that their jobs came openly on the basis of personal friendship, doled out by military leaders in return for support. It was the traditional power of connections, which tended to become even more significant at a time when old political structures and patterns had been destroyed and new ones were as yet indeterminate.

Shen was dismayed that civilian politicians like Ma and Lou would work closely and thereby identify themselves with military leaders. Such alliances only enhanced the prestige of the military rulers, whose strengthened position might lead to adventurism and thus the greater likelihood of instability. Shen believed that in such linkages the civilian politicians and bureaucrats were always bested. He put it graphically in speaking to one such civilian politician. "Now you've become Yuan Shikai's concubine. Adult men, when they've slept half the night, develop an erection. They pull the concubine who's sleeping on the floor in front of the bed in beside them like a coverlet into which they can ejaculate. Once they've ejaculated, they kick the concubine out of the bed. Be careful! In not long a day will come when you will be kicked out of bed."[36] In perhaps an even stronger image, after World War I Shen described the military man as a corpse and the politician allied with him as "a maggot on the corpse."[37]

Shen and the Origins of His Provincial Assembly Network

The military leadership and its civilian bureaucrats were only part of the governing scene in Hangzhou. Revived in 1916 after almost three years' abeyance was the provincial assembly, in which Shen had served from 1912 until the collapse of the second revolution. We can best understand Shen's identity at various points in his career by acquainting ourselves with those who were his comrades, who made up various networks of which he was a part, who were his friends and his enemies. This approach is based on the premise that more enduring political and social relationships developed from processes of political action and crisis than from membership in social and political organizations in itself, that "identity is a social reality that is continually produced within and by the experience and interaction of individuals."[38]

A number of those assemblymen who joined Shen in forcefully opposing Yuan Shikai in 1913 remained significant figures in Shen's Hangzhou political networks into the mid-1920s. Composed of ten men, they were a youthful cohort, with at least seven born in the 1880s, thus putting them in their late twenties or early thirties in 1913. While the eldest, vice-president of the assembly Liu Kun (b. 1869), held a *jinshi* degree, and Xu Bingkun (b. 1881) had received a *juren* degree, none of the rest had upper level degrees.[39] At least three had studied in Japan, and at least three had been graduated from modern schools in China, two from the forerunner of Beijing University. They were men who, by and large, were starting their public careers in the provincial assembly. Five of them would be attracted to journalism, by the mid-1910s one of the new public circles.[40] Three would become bureaucrats, serving the military governors whom Shen would later excoriate. At least two would become influential entrepreneurs in what has been called the "golden age" of the Chinese bourgeoisie.[41] In short, they represented the rising wave of Chinese public interests. It is also significant that there is little indication of native place connecting the men: the ten came from seven of the nine provincial prefectures. The practical political goal of unseating Yuan gave rise to a network based on political action.

Some are important to note by name for the roles they would play in Shen's career and in Zhejiang politics. Xu Zuqian of Haining county, a graduate of a normal school, began his career in Hangzhou in the first decade of the century as editor of several newspapers.[42] After his deep involvement in the 1911 revolution, he emerged as an assembly spokesman for civilian legislative power.[43] In the summer of 1913, he was one of the most outspoken anti-Yuan assemblymen, called "irrepressible" by a commentator of the times.[44] He was joined in this open opposition by Ren Fenggang, a close friend from Haiyan county, who was also known as "outspoken and contentious."[45] Ren, a *shengyuan* degree holder at the age of seventeen, had been graduated as a lawyer from the special law school of Beijing University in the fall of 1911. The Xu-Ren tandem was a force in the assembly, one that many assemblymen found intimidating. Both were jailed as a result of their urgings for independence in the second revolution.

Assembly Chairman Mo Yongzhen (b. 1876), a graduate of Waseda University, was, perhaps because of his position, the most noted proponent of independence, and like Xu and Ren was jailed for his role. He had been active in the railroad recovery movement from 1908 to 1911 and was closely allied with other important provincial elites. He was vice-chair of the Zhejiang Guomindang; the chair was Qing assemblyman and revolutionary Chu Fucheng. Those with inclinations to Sun's Revolutionary Alliance and later Guomindang (such as Mo, Xu, Ren, and Chu) tended to emphasize liberal parliamentary government and reliance on law, connected at base as these concepts were to constitutionalism. They also more likely tended to be from northern Zhejiang (the prefectures of Hangzhou, Huzhou, and Jiaxing). In contrast, the other main revolutionary organization, the Restoration Society, was based in eastern Zhejiang and focused on nationalism without the liberal political and socioeconomic aspects of Sun's Three Principles of the People.[46]

Where in the range of political commitments and allegiances does Shen Dingyi fit? His record, as it did throughout his life, resists being pigeonholed. A native of eastern Zhejiang, he was not, however, linked to the Restoration Society. In the years of its formation and of its trauma—the conspiracy and execution of some of its key leaders—he was in Yunnan and in Japan. He was associated with the Revolutionary Alliance before eventually joining the Restoration Society. Whereas the identity of association with the society was generally strong among eastern Zhejiang civilian, military, and revolutionary elites, Shen did not seem to share that identity. When organizations were formed to commemorate two of the heroes of the society, Tao Chengzhang and Xu Xilin, in 1915 and 1917 respectively, Shen did not affiliate himself with either, despite the fact that in the latter organization there were a number of key provincial assemblymen and his close associates.[47]

Part of the explanation likely lies in Shen's personality, which exhibited elements of what I have described as a revolutionary mentality. Independent and with a tendency to be impetuous, Shen appears almost the knight-errant in his ultimately self-impoverishing generosity in funding revolutionary causes and in his often unpredictable actions (for example, leaving his post in Yunnan). Along with his intellectual accomplishments, he had always been fond of the martial arts; from boyhood, he had surpassed others in contests of strength; he rode horses; he boxed. He liked to take up cudgels against what he considered injustices.[48] In a culture that valued group relationships and responsibilities, Shen was an individualist who could play that role convincingly so long as he had the resources, both financial and personal, to do it. His was a style that seemed much more conducive to patron-client relationships than to horizontal networks of peers.

Sun Yat-sen in Hangzhou, August 1916

The visit of Sun Yat-sen to Zhejiang inaugurated the fall assembly session. Because of his long-time leadership of the anti-Manchu movement and his championing of the cause of nationalism, Sun seemed the political patriarch to many Chinese. His willingness in early 1912 to turn the presidency of the Republic to Yuan Shikai had been a bitter pill for some of his supporters to swallow. He had briefly served in Yuan's government, but like many others he fled to Japan for asylum in November 1913. After his return to China in April 1916, he spent much of the next year in Shanghai writing about nationalism and people's political rights.

On August 16 he took the five-to-six-hour train ride to Hangzhou, 120 miles west-southwest of Shanghai. The proximity of the two cities was a crucial spatial fact that played important roles in the history of both. Accompanied by an entourage of about a dozen men, including Dai Jitao, his personal secretary, Sun arrived at the main train station within the city wall on the city's east side. Met by a delegation of important people from military, government, gentry, and commercial circles, Sun was taken little over a mile west to a hotel in the New Market area of Hangzhou.[49]

In many ways, the New Market symbolized Republican Hangzhou. The area, lying alongside West Lake, had been a walled Manchu garrison since the 1650s.[50] During that more than two and a half centuries much of Hangzhou had in a real sense been separated from the lake with which it shared such an important historical identity. Under the leadership of Civil Commissioner Chu Fucheng, the decision was made to raze the former military garrison and to construct a carefully designed area marked by broad avenues, gardens, parks, and open spaces. The vistas of the lake would be brought more integrally into the city than ever before, as the symbol of the old was swept away. From the site of the former Yongjin Gate to that of the Qiantang Gate, about three-quarters of a mile, were built public athletic fields, a public education facility, and six public gardens, each designed differently with teahouses, pavilions, and benches and distinguished by different plantings. Docks were built between the gardens for the small skiffs sailing on the lake.[51]

In the New Market area, schools, government buildings, hotels, wine and tea shops, and theaters were also constructed.[52] In addition, units were marked off to be sold for private residences and for shops and other businesses.[53] Hangzhou thus had a clear spatial expression of the newness of the Republic; the area opened the city to the beauties of the natural world and served as space for business and educational enterprises and physical activity (a major emphasis of the public school system begun in the late Qing). For Shen, it was the site of much of his Hangzhou activity. The provincial Lawyers' Association, where Shen often spoke and where in the 1920s the Guomindang would meet, was only a block from the lake; several blocks south and three blocks east of the lake was the

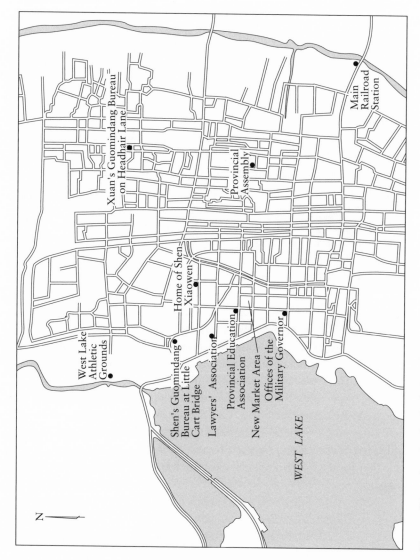

Map 2. Hangzhou in the Early Republic

Zhejiang Education Association, another Shen base. The spatial newness and openness of the New Market area created an appropriately symbolic arena for the political initiatives of the late 1910s and early 1920s.[54] It became the western pole of the east-west axis that symbolized the new Hangzhou; the eastern pole was the train station, the direct link to Shanghai, constructed a decade earlier. It was, however, no accident and can obviously be taken as symbolic that the offices of the military governor, prominently located near the lake shore, were a part of the New Market area while the Provincial Assembly building was not; it met in a large multistory structure north of the east-west axis of Republican Hangzhou.

On August 18, Military Governor Lu Gongwang hosted Sun Yat-sen at a banquet, his first official appearance: protocol revealed the priority of the military as the key political institution.[55] Sun spoke about national reconstruction with a focus on the rather unglamorous topic of road construction. In the afternoon, he was welcomed at the Provincial Assembly Building by the soon-to-be-reconvening assembly. We do not know whether Sun's assembly appearance was Shen's first meeting with the man synonymous with the Republic of China and a man Shen would come to idolize. Sun had visited Hangzhou for a triumphal series of banquets and receptions in December 1912, though there is no record that Shen met him then.[56] There is also no indication that Shen had been involved in Sun's Chinese Revolutionary Party, established in Tokyo in 1914, though many with whom he would later become politically active did participate. Sun's assembly speech focused on what emerged for many in Shen's networks and associations in the next dozen years as an important hope and what would for Shen eventually become a personal mission: local self-government. Like the relativity of native place, "local" self-government depended on one's perspective and could range from village to township to county to province. Sun declared that late summer day that local self-government was "the foundation of the nation's reconstruction."[57]

The Provincial Assembly and Civilian Constitutional Culture

While the values of the military and revolutionary subcultures stressed gaining one's end by direct action, using whatever means necessary, a hallmark of the early Republican civilian elite culture was an emphasis on law and legal processes. This reality is apparent in the agenda and actions of the provincial assembly. From the very beginning of the fall session, the stress lines, if not the battle lines, for the future were clearly evident: tensions between the legislative assembly and the provincial government on one hand and between the provincial and the central regimes on the other. The opening ceremonies of the first meeting on September 4 clearly showed the higher status of the government officials vis-à-vis the assembly. The assemblymen were seated first, then the assembly chair, and last the civil governor and heads of bureaus. After all bowed to the national flag three times, the assemblymen and their chairman bowed to the civil governor and the bureau heads. Military Governor Lu Gongwang's speech offered the hope that provincial government would progress with "the assembly assisting the official executive bureaus." After several speakers had followed with polite responses, assemblyman Zhang Tinglin of Hangzhou countered directly : "In the future we must be able to withstand the power of the official executive bureaus." A newspaper reporter related that these words were greeted by applause "like thunder."[58]

Debate on the first order of business on September 5 illustrates the crux of civilian parliamentary culture at this time. The seemingly minor issue: how to handle Chairman Mo's resignation from the assembly. After his anti-Yuan prison sentence in 1913, Mo had left the assembly for the provincial bureaucracy, becoming an adviser to the civil governor and later head of the Zhejiang Finance Ministry.[59] The problem for the assembly was whether simply to accept his resignation as proposed by what might be called the nonlegalistic assemblymen or whether to follow detailed assembly regulations and submit the case to a special investigative committee as proposed by others. The debate was over procedure, and as inconsequential as it first appears, it went to the heart of the clash between the military-revolutionary cultures and the civilian elite culture.

For the latter, in the new republic "how" was as important as "what," the process as important as the goal, the means as important as the ends. For in the end, of course, the "how" would affect the "what." The legalists were saying that if this is a legal body legislating for the people, then it must follow its own rules. That position was accepted, and the acting chairman appointed an investigative committee which deliberated thirty minutes on Mo's resignation and three others. The committee report recommended acceptance of all resignations, and the assembly accepted the report. In the new political landscape after Yuan's death, the assembly was gingerly making its way in untrod territory; procedural issues and caution about political relationships were crucial concerns. For the outsider perceiving the assembly as a goal-directed body, it seemed a study in endless wrangling, delay, and even incompetence, a case of the "how" having become the "what."

With Mo no longer a member, the assembly's next issue was electing a new chair. Another procedural debate: since there was no precedent for electing a new chair after the resignation of the preceding chair, what should be done? The legalistic assemblymen argued that the National Assembly must give instructions in such a case and that a telegram should be sent immediately. Onto the assembly floor thus came the issue of the relationship between the national and provincial legislative bodies, between the center and the province, an issue that would remain at the heart of political life throughout the twentieth century. In this case the assembly rejected such action and approved a motion calling for an immediate election.[60]

Shen Dingyi was elected chairman of the assembly on four ballots on September 6. His acceptance speech mixed properly polite self-deprecation with his sense of the significance of the reestablished assembly.

The heavy commission from our elders and brothers is to manage our country's preservation, to end the continuing autumn in our country and ourselves. In considering the weight of the responsibility, there is no one else to whom we can delegate it.

You have conferred on me the chairmanship. How great the difficult responsibility of filling that post! In my life I have had miraculous escapes. Many times I have been ill. If I would be thinking of protecting myself, it would be fitting to retire and hide. But if I did not follow and seek out people's ideas, it would be an early rejection of the promise of our country. If the mosquito has other sources of support, it can survive the creek's drying up. . . . If I don't have the will, I'll use this assembly's will as mine; if I don't have the ability, I'll use the assembly's ability. We will work together, following the law. We will build a new provincial assembly.[61]

As chair, Shen played a pivotal role in the appointment of assembly committees. In these selections it is possible to see the sort of assemblymen that Shen (and his close advisers) favored and to get a clearer picture of the political networks in which he operated. In September and October, Shen appointed four committees: a special budget committee (thirteen men), a committee on water conservation (twenty-seven men), a committee to investigate the activities of a particular assemblyman (eleven men), and a committee on a memorial for revolutionary Xia

Zhilin (thirteen men).[62] There were 118 men in the assembly at this time. For the 64 committee posts, Shen assigned 39 different assemblymen; 17 were appointed to serve more than once. One of these served on all four committees, six served on three, and ten served on two. In native place backgrounds, five of the seven (71 percent) who served three or more times were from northern Zhejiang; altogether, ten of seventeen (59 percent) came from that area, made up of only three of Zhejiang's nine prefectures. What is striking is that none of these men came from any county in Shen's native prefecture of Shaoxing. If Shen was building a network for provincial level politics, it would not, at least in this phase of his life, be based on native place; instead it would be a grander coalition. There are two other noteworthy features of these men: at least seven were closely linked to the Revolutionary Alliance or to the electoral Guomindang party in 1912 and 1913 and at least ten had had much experience in local arenas, operating from and frequently returning to a local community base rather than establishing themselves primarily in the provincial arena. In these ways they seem to reflect Shen's own predilections: drawn more to the supporters of Sun Yat-sen than other revolutionary nationalists and maintaining strong, constant connections to native place constituents.

Two of the five with three or more committee assignments were Xu Zuqian and Ren Fenggang, Shen's anti-Yuan colleagues in 1913. The one four-time appointee was Lin Zhuo of Yongjia county (Wenzhou prefecture), who was closely linked to the Guomindang. An anecdote related to Lin reveals much about the political culture of the time.[63] His uncle, Lin Yulin, and two other Guomindang candidates were accused of buying votes in the National Assembly elections. Called to task by an opposing local elite faction, Lin's Guomindang group with several hundred supporters angrily beat up their opponents' leaders, who then were encouraged to take the case to court. At that point, Guomindang provincial head Chu Fucheng intervened by sending a secret telegram to the court's judge, a protégé of the head of a minor party affiliated with the Guomindang. The case was immediately dismissed. Electoral morality was not exhibited by any party, even the one with the largest claim to the best revolutionary bloodline.[64] Local factions and personal connections made their way up and down the political hierarchy; local feuds and connections rose to the provincial level and beyond and national alignments were brought down to the provincial level and below. Thus, while there were immense gaps in terms of modern change among national, provincial, and local arenas, there were important linkages as well.

The transposition of local issues to higher level arenas was facilitated by native place organizations (*tongxiang hui*) in the higher levels. A major difference between the military and civilian subcultures was that the structure and ethos of the military was based on control from the center and thus focused primarily on a top-down process of transmission and control. In many localities there were no official military units; officers and soldiers, often not from elite society, did not necessarily represent local structures and situations. In contrast, the various spatial arenas for civilian elites and nonelites were much more closely integrated, with ideas and personnel transmitted more easily along the spatial spectrum.

In an analysis of the provincial assembly committee assignees, Chu Fucheng, who was serving in the National Assembly at this time, emerges as a node in many personal networks.[65] Guomindang connections linked him to Wenzhou natives Lin Zhuo and Li Se; business interests tied him to Wang Lian, an important Dinghai county merchant assemblyman; native place ties were a basic connection to the seven committee assignees from Jiaxing and Jiashan counties. Chu became an integrating figure in the skein of connections with his multiple ties to the national, provincial, and local levels; such elites made the ties between these arenas of the polity closer than they might first appear. Shen, having developed special links to Jiaxing, thus pulled closer to Chu through his work in the assembly with Chu's varied political associates and in Chu's networks. Alternatively, it might be seen that Shen appointed so many Jiaxing assemblymen as one method to further the development of his ties to the influential Chu.

Personal and social linkages such as those apparent in Shen's committee assignments and his 1913 political network were crucial in the formation, in late fall 1916, of the Zhejiang Political Discussion Society (*Zhejiang zhengfu shangque hui*). In this voluntary association expressive of the ethos of liberal constitutionalism, membership was limited to men actively involved in political affairs on the provincial and local levels.[66] Slated to meet twice a week at the Lawyers' Association office, the society was conceived as one that would offer even more frequent contact for those civilian elites charting a path for the new China.[67] In elections to the society's council Shen (with ninety-one) and Chu (with eighty-eight) were the top vote-getters.

Although the social, educational, and career backgrounds of the membership corresponded with those in Shen's assembly networks, the native place backgrounds based on level of economic development are worth noting.[68] Of the forty-three members on whom such information is available, the inner core zones of Zhejiang's Lower Yangzi and Southeast Coast regions, that is those areas most economically developed, produced 74.4 percent of the total. The Lower Yangzi region clearly predominated, with the three prefectures of northern Zhejiang accounting for sixteen members (37.2 percent) and the prefectures of Ningbo and Shaoxing for thirteen (30.2 percent). The political cohesion produced by dense networks of elites from the core zones, meeting both formally in the business of government and informally in this society, affected provincial politics at least over the next decade. For, to counteract this growing consciousness of commonalities among elites from core zones, coalitions of elites from the provincial interior, which contributed very few elites to this society, would begin to transpose native place ties to regional ties based on political expediency.[69]

The Provincial Crisis,
December 1916–January 1917

Though there were other issues in the fall assembly session, one of the greatest problems was the uncertain relationship between the provincial assembly and the national assembly and government. Throughout the fall the assembly waited for definitive word from Beijing on the assembly's role in the governmental budgeting process and on the reinstitution of local assemblies and other self-government organs. There was still no budgeting answer when the regular fall session ended, thereby necessitating an additional session.[70] On the matter of local self-government, requests had come from county bodies almost from the beginning of the session on the procedures to be followed.[71] Governor Lu and Shen met frequently on this matter; while they allowed certain counties to proceed on their own, they forwarded to the National Assembly the assembly's request to restore the local self-government bodies.[72]

In mid-December Lu and Shen fired off telegrams to Beijing institutions. Shen's (sent to the National Assembly and Senate, the President, and the Cabinet) read:

Local self-government is the foundation of the Republic. To build rule by law in order to nurture government, we must concentrate on local self-government. Therefore, in our proposals we seek to build our country quickly, working with officials who have specified these things in telegrams. But we have not been able to act because there is no law. The President on June 29 already repealed Yuan's 1914 decree by which the Republic was destroyed. But setting forth no [subsequent] law blocks local self-government. How can we talk of the nation and its relationship to the people? We must know now so that this assembly does not go against the law and against the administrative system.[73]

At the scheduled end of the extraordinary session, word on the budget and local self-government had still not been received.[74] The level of frustration for Shen and leading assemblymen must have been great. For a group who had a high consciousness and great expectations of their role in the new China and of the goals that they believed they should achieve, the delay was infuriating. It raised questions about the center at the very time that the center as a source of authority was being elevated in the midst of new governing patterns. And it undercut hopes that with Yuan gone things would be better.

But all this paled in comparison to the crisis that loomed at year's end, one over which they had even less control than over the central government's budget or self-government orders and one which underscored the difficulty of the emphasis on law and procedure in the early Republic. After the overthrow of Military Governor Zhu Rui in April, bitter competition for provincial military leadership had developed between officers from the Baoding and Zhejiang military academies. As with any such struggle, the battle lines shift according to one's perspective. Though there are numerous sub-plots and personal grievances at work in this drama, the main protagonists were Governor Lu, the Baoding graduate, and Xia Chao, the Zhejiang graduate and chief of the provincial and metropolitan police.[75]

The Zhejiang Case against Lu. After coming to power, Lu set out immediately to decrease the power of Zhejiang officers, especially that of Xia. He abolished the provincial police troops that had been under Xia's control. When Lu asked on the occasion of Double Ten to bestow honors on leading military figures, he did not include Xia's name. Lu's arrogance was shown by his appointment of Wang Wenjing as civil commissioner even though Wang was opposed by most leaders and had already been rejected as civil governor. The proximate cause of the confrontation in late December focused on Fu Qiyong, Baoding graduate, close friend of Lu, and father of Lu's god child. Lu was determined to replace Xia with Fu to increase the Baoding grip on the Zhejiang government; it would have been accomplished if the central government had not delayed its response to Lu's request and if Xia's alert spies had not uncovered Lu's devious plot.

The Baoding Case against Xia. In the fall Xia had begun to plot with fellow Zhejiang officer Zhou Fengqi to seize power. Their plan was to overthrow Lu and install a fellow Zhejiang graduate in power as a caretaker for three months. Then Zhou would take the military governorship and Xia the civil governorship. Lu discovered the plot. He felt that Xia, known increasingly as a "man on the take," was behind much plotting and backstabbing in the government hierarchy and that unless Xia were ousted there would not be the stability Zhejiang needed to progress. He wanted to replace him with his friend Fu Qiyong; that appointment was approved by President Li Yuanhong.

On December 26, the day of the transfer of power, Xia struck. Shortly after noon, as the staff of the provincial police force was giving Fu a welcoming banquet, several men dressed in military uniforms and carrying guns burst into the hall. Amid much clamor they dragged Fu from the room, beating and abusing him. With the exception of a few at the dinner who pretended to encourage the attackers to cease and leave, the majority of police officers just stood and watched. Besides the physical injuries suffered in the attack, Fu was humiliated, suffering great loss of face: there was no way he could return to lead the people who had allowed this to happen to him.

At the same time, the police in Hangzhou and its suburbs went on strike in opposition to Fu; most military leaders in the province submitted their resignations in order to coerce Lu to step down. Using his factional support and its extended networks, Xia had prepared well.[76] But the situation threatened to get out of hand. Each side had division force strength and began sending troops into the city. The wooden gates of the main streets were shut and hastily constructed placements for cannon and machine guns set up at key intersections. The military culture's direct, violent action and rapid escalation of the tensions could not provide a starker contrast with the assembly's procedural legalisms and caution. In this crisis for the city of Hangzhou, Shen acted heroically, going to areas of the city where the possibility of fighting was greatest and pleading with military units not to bring devastation to the capital and its people. His actions were all the more remarkable because he was ill and the weather was bitterly cold, with high winds and snow.[77] Later commentators contended that Shen played a major role in preventing open warfare in the streets of Hangzhou.[78]

With internecine war in the balance, Lu sent his resignation to Beijing on December 27, anticipating that it would be rejected.[79] The next day came the bombshell announcement from Beijing: no Zhejiangese would be appointed to either the military or civil governorship. Premier Duan was taking advantage of the threatened turmoil in Hangzhou to bring Zhejiang into the Beiyang camp by appointing as military governor a Beiyang officer, Yang Shande, and as civil governor Qi Yaoshan, a former Qing official from Manchuria.[80] It was the political equivalent of an earthquake. The Hangzhou political world, both military and civil, was stunned, reacting with shock and great fear. Whatever might have been true about the nature and quality of military and civil rule in the province, since 1911 Zhejiangese had been able to say that it was in the hands of natives who supposedly had the best interests of their province at heart. Now that sense of security was threatened.

On the evening of New Year's Day, a gathering of all senior military commanders, the chief of police, Shen Dingyi, and the chair of the Hangzhou General Chamber of Commerce met to work out a provincial compromise and forestall entrance of Beiyang forces. They agreed that they would support Lu's continuation as military governor. Lu quickly telegraphed to Beijing that he would stay in his position.[81] Military leaders who had opposed Lu now supported him out of considerable panic.[82] For the provincial assembly, Shen sent telegrams to the Beijing government requesting Yang's recall and to Chu Fucheng in the National Assembly with a dire prophecy: "With the coming of Yang and Qi to the province, each circle has put aside its ill will and returned to amicable feelings. Uniformly we resist insult. If the outside officials (*keguan*) approach the two Zhes in the morning, there will be rebellion in the evening. We hope that this will be publicly discussed and that the order will be countermanded in order to avoid a tragedy."[83]

It was not, however, a completely united front against the outsiders. Shanghai comprador and Zhejiang native Yu Xiaqing placed his support behind Yang, inciting extraordinarily angry feelings among all Hangzhou circles. Leaders of the Hangzhou General Chamber of Commerce tried to send telegrams welcoming Yang, but the telegraph agent refused to send them.[84] The pragmatic commercial circles clearly preferred peace and stability over fighting to preserve perceived native place rights. And yet the native place "line" held sway. The words of the announcement of a Zhejiang citizens' rally echo this position: "Our accomplishments with regard to center and locality since 1912 came because the province has been controlled by fellow-provincials. . . . The people, wanting to protect their native place, have decided to hold a rally to discuss alternatives."[85]

The assertion that prosperity and good rule in Zhejiang since 1912 stemmed from rule by native sons, heard repeatedly at the rally held on January 5, flies in the face of a report in a Shanghai newspaper two years earlier. A *Shibao* analysis argued that Zhejiang was a hundred times worse off under Zhejiangese rule than in the Qing. Uprisings were allegedly more numerous; the price of rice was rising so quickly that people were forced to live on grass and tree bark and sell cemetery benches for money; taxes were soaking everyone so that officials could attain rank and riches; law-abiding people were for the first time being driven to thievery; and the new, rapidly expanding law profession was tyrannical.[86] Another report from late 1916 purported to show that the level of commerce in the province had not yet been restored to its pre-1911 level.[87] We can dismiss some of this as hyperbole, but any study of developments in the province in the early Republic reveals that these years were not very good ones for many Zhejiangese.

The obsessive championing of rule by native sons seems clearly an example of cultural values of the locality shaping perceptions and consciousness. Family, locality, connections, the "known" were defined as good; strangers, the outside world, the "unknown" were suspect because they could not be defined. They became in that lack of definition unpredictable and dangerous. The emphasis on native place gave rise to seeing the world as divided between those to whom one is connected and those to whom one is not. The "we" against "them" mentality— whether we are from this family and they are strangers; we from this native place and they from that; we from civilian circles and they from military; we from Baoding Military Academy and they from Zhejiang— permeated Republican society and politics. This native place mentality impinged on political thought and action even when issues were national in orientation and scope.

The initiators of the January 5 rally were thirty-two leaders of gentry, government, commercial, scholarly, and journalistic circles and included Shen and ten other Political Discussion Society members. Held at 1:00 P.M. in the First Theater near the train station, the rally reportedly drew almost four thousand people. The main floor and the balconies were full, with people standing shoulder to shoulder and surrounding the stage.

There were eight speakers representing the public circles and several excited the crowd, whose applause vibrated the tiles on the roof. Shen was the fifth speaker. He had come to the rally ill, a condition exacerbated by his peace missions in the snow-blown Hangzhou streets. His speech touched on many of the cultural and political values of the early Republic's civilian elite: native place, local self-government, the symbiotic relationship of the locality and the nation, the importance of law and procedure, and distaste for the military.

Generally it's been said that this time the military and the police had only a small difference of opinion. For the people, even though it was small, it was a cause for fear . . . though we still did not come to suffer hardship because of it. Why not? Because high officials all come from this province. People must be able to care about the common people's suffering. If we have to have outsiders, we have little time to wait [before we will be oppressed].

Zhejiang is the Zhejiang of the people of Zhejiang. If Zhejiangese cannot protect Zhejiang, then the people of the nation cannot protect the nation. What crowning beauty there is in Zhejiang's politics. The whole country's, not only Zhejiang's, affairs are the responsibility of the people of Zhejiang. Likewise the whole of China should bear some responsibility to the people of Zhejiang. If Zhejiangese are not self-governing, then one by one they will appoint outsiders, and will those outsiders not rule by pulling in more outsiders?

Today's effort is not to rebel; we have few slogans of battle. But this great crowd is united and willing to advance. We do not presume to be polite; we are not concerned about treating people with contempt or boastfulness. We will uphold the right and conform to procedures and requirements as our methods of dealing [with this crisis]. . . . Our hearts are determined to achieve our goal in the end. That's it—or else!

But when the Northern soldiers arrive, law-abiding people will no longer be law-abiding people. We must fight fire with fire! We must walk erect in danger! . . . At the most, it can be painful and bitter for our aspirations.

The reporter noted that everyone listened closely to Shen. He spoke in a grieving tone of voice. His illness had weakened him, and although the weather was cold, he was dripping wet with sweat. The thousands of listeners were reportedly deeply moved: Shen's fame as an orator was widely known and much deserved. Punctuated by shouts of "Long live Zhejiang" (*Zhejiang wansui*), the applause was "grand and awe-filling like thunder."[88]

Four delegates were selected to take a petition to the capital requesting the government to countermand the original order. They were Shen Dingyi, long-time revolutionary intellectual Zhang Binglin, First

Normal principal Jing Hengyi, and Chamber of Commerce leader Wang Xirong. The petition read in part: "Since the 1911 revolution, our locality has been peaceful. With our present military and civilian government, we can experience self-government and we can strongly respect and cherish the idea of the native place—for the Zhejiang military is really composed of our sons and brothers. We ask the remanding of the order to benefit the locality and protect the country."[89] The petitions and speeches clearly indicate that on its face there was no contradiction between the locality and the nation.[90] Their relationship was viewed as symbiotic, yet there remained even in this symbiosis an antagonism of the "other." The petition was signed by fourteen of the rally initiators and endorsed by the thirty-seven hundred who attended. Copies of the petition were telegraphed to the Zhejiang native place association in Beijing asking for support (members would have included national assemblymen and officials from Zhejiang) and copies were sent to organizations (chambers of commerce and education associations, for example) in each of the province's seventy-five counties. Zhejiangese at the national, provincial, and local levels were thus informed about the crucial political issues of the day; political action and the political process itself increased the integration of levels of the polity.[91]

A last-ditch effort on the part of the Zhejiangese came early in the morning (12:30 A.M.) of January 8 when three civilian elites were sent to speak with Yang, who had already dispatched a brigade of soldiers into the province. The men were Shen, Ren Fenggang, and Sun Zhiyu, educator, bureaucrat, and provincial assembly secretary. There is no transcript of the meeting, but we may imagine that Shen, Ren, and Sun tried to impress on Yang the sense of fear and embitterment among many people in Hangzhou. From the perspective of the three, the meeting was a disappointment, for they mainly listened to Yang give his opinion on the situation.[92] Yang's troops entered Hangzhou without incident on January 12.[93]

It seems clear that for all the cataclysmic rhetoric of civilian elites, they could not compete effectively with the military force (or threat of it); in the end there was the recognition that an uprising would only end in deaths and destruction. While civilian elites had waited all fall for the National Assembly and civil government in Beijing to take action that would more fully integrate center and province, the military acted quickly and without consultation to integrate province and center in a way that most of the civilians found objectionable. National factional struggle would begin to remake provincial politics through this direct military intervention.

Beiyang Control and the Beginning of Shen's Shanghai Exile

In the subsequent months, there was greater and greater impingement of central control in provincial affairs. However one saw the years of Zhejiang control, at the least they had kept Beijing at arm's length. Now old patterns gave way to new realities, relationships, and connections. Yang cultivated the Zhejiangese, throwing banquets for military officers and powerful bureaucrats like Mo Yongzhen. Xia Chao, fearful of losing his position when Yang entered Hangzhou (he did lose one official title), set out to curry favor with him. One ploy was to have his wife visit Yang's wife daily at the military governor's residence to gain favor through her continual attention; another was to have his subordinates establish connections with the subordinates of Yang and Qi, the new civil governor. One upshot of these efforts was that Qi was so impressed by Xia that he took him as a protégé and restored his lost title.[94] Ousted Lu Gongwang made his way to Beijing and in 1918 went to Guangdong to link up with Sun Yat-sen in the Constitution Protecting Army.[95]

How did Shen Dingyi fare under the new regime? Shen was now perhaps the key civilian leader in the province—chairman of the assembly, de facto head of the Political Discussion Society, and with the added experience and prestige of negotiating and keeping the peace during the winter crisis—and like Zhejiang military leaders he was sought after by the new leadership. Civil Governor Qi, who arrived in the province in late January, at one point sent a special emissary to him to arrange a time when they might finally meet.[96] The military and civilian governmental leadership recognized Shen's significance but, given Shen's role in the January crisis, were quite wary and suspicious of his actions.

Shen battled illness through the winter months, his ill-health often interfering with his work. In early October 1916, Shen had had to take a leave from chairing the assembly because of an illness of the brain (*naobing*). What exactly this was, we are not told. Though he did not have to miss many days, reports suggested that this was a chronic problem.[97] He was well enough by March to begin his own newspaper, the *People's Intelligence Daily* (*Minzhi ribao*).[98] Though there is no extant information about the paper's management or its length of run, its title suggests that its political position likely championed the liberal, parliamentary, deliberative approach for which both the assembly and the Discussion Society stood.

Just as quickly as winter turned into spring, new governor Qi emerged as the bête noire of the assembly and of Shen's networks. By early April, in fact, assemblymen who were also members of the Discussion Society brought an impeachment case against Qi for autocratic use of executive power.[99] The Discussion Society itself telegraphed the central government, decrying the lawlessness of the civil governor, and in its weekly meetings discussed Qi and deficiencies in the central and provincial governments.[100] The assembly itself seemed increasingly ineffective, as it began consistently to break into factions based on native place, especially northern and eastern Zhejiang.[101] On April 13 Shen asked for a leave from the chairmanship and, though he retained the de jure chairmanship, he never returned to lead it actively. Shen later pointed to increasing frustration and pessimism about the political relationship between the assembly and executive and the increasing assembly infighting.[102]

His view of the military was increasingly jaundiced. Even though Shen himself had organized, trained, and completely financed a Student Army in Shanghai in 1911 and 1912,[103] he now saw soldiers as ominous representatives of the old system, of the emperor who "took the land and people as his own private property . . . and used officials as his teeth and claws. . . . What are soldiers? . . . They are truly the emperor's cells, the emperor's shrunken shadows. . . . The cells and shadows remain in great number. Not only do some cherish an imperial China [*Zhonghua diguo*] but even a kind of military state of China [*Zhonghua junguo*]."[104] He had had enough of the quixotic and destructive, increasingly intrusive warlord system. In an essay called "The Future Light," he discussed China's hope in relation to the military:

Why should we make an effort to reform this country? It is because . . . we want to realize a bright world in which all of us can find happiness. . . . Each person must depend on himself in looking for the right road. Each person must walk forward by himself. He can't lie on other people's backs with his eyes closed, ears plugged, and be carried forward.

When we completely realize that gaining individual survival skills is the very basis of reform, we will be able to consolidate this basis and our reform will not need the help of military power. Military power can only destroy.

It never builds anything. It can only kill people, never protect them. We have witnessed so many precedents in this world. The military men when they succeeded in reform were instantly turned into men needing to be reformed. And we don't need the tactics of politicians! The revolution of politicians is always opportunistic. Their greedy eyes always stare at future power and benefits. . . . Since these politicians are swayed by considerations of gain or loss, they stand between reformers and those to be reformed. Now that we exclude both military men and politicians from our reform cause, the success of our reform depends on the power of the common people.[105]

Along with the military he castigated the "politicians" who connected themselves to military lords and milked the system for everything they could, whether they were bureaucrats like Qi or grasping assemblymen; they were "sponging self-interested politicians experienced in the bravery of strengthening themselves."[106] In a caustic essay entitled "Why?" he contrasted the secret why and the public why of the question "Why study?"

The public why: To direct and manage one's ability, to do advantageous things for society, etc.

The secret why: To be an official and make money. To be an official and make money; is or is that not something that's done? For the time being don't ask. To make money? Is that something that should be done? For the time being don't ask. Be an official to make money; to make money be an official: they go together, so it doesn't matter how it's said. It's really an evil thing, a rotten thing, an ugly thing that shouldn't be done. And whenever something is evil, rotten, or ugly, we must protect the secret. Therefore the secret why cannot be the public why—it is only really the criminal why.[107]

Shen believed that the intrusion of the military and the drive toward "making money" in Chinese life were beginning to influence competent young men, enticing them with the likelihood of career success and tempting them, like Lu Xun's misanthrope Wei Lianshu, to compromise their values and work within the military subculture.[108] In early 1920 (five years before Lu wrote about Wei), Shen wrote a dialogue between unnamed brothers about the military and its increasing grasp on people's lives and consciousnesses, capturing the dilemma in very specific terms. The older brother speaks for Shen.

Younger brother: Brother, their high qualifications depend on abuse, on hitting inside, on night watches. *We're* in the middle eating bitterness.
Older brother: Brother, I don't agree. [It's not simply we.] You see everyone in this region—the dead lie there; refugees flee; male, female, young,

old, middle-aged, broken families—not one escapes the fear, deprivation, pain, and bitterness.

Younger brother: . . . Military men in the end are always talking about "obedience": no matter what bitterness they give to other people to eat, the people must obey and keep eating. One day we too, after watching through the night, will be able to give bitterness to others. The military governor obeys higher officials; lower officials obey the military governor. The military governor is willing to eat the High Inspecting Commissioner's shit; those below the military governor then must eat the military governor's shit. We today eat everyone's shit. In the future we can give shit to other people to eat.

Older brother: Brother, I'm not willing to eat shit. I'm also not willing to give people shit to eat. I can't carry out these plans to eat shit.

Younger brother: Brother, you don't understand: there's no other way. . . . That's our meal ticket too. . . .[109]

The central drama of the spring of 1917 involving military and civilian politicians occurred in Beijing; it had a great impact on Shen. Ongoing tensions between President Li Yuanhong and Premier Duan Qirui had reached a crisis point. In March the National Assembly, increasingly seen and treated by Duan as an enemy, had approved the breaking of diplomatic ties with Germany, but it had set as the price for its declaration of war the removal of Duan as premier. In late May Li dismissed Duan from office, an act which led all military governors but one from around the nation to declare their independence from the Beijing government; in Zhejiang Yang Shande did so on May 31. The only one not declaring independence was Zhang Xun, a conservative military leader who was following another part of the conspiracy. The military governors had plotted for Zhang to go to the capital in the guise of mediating the Li-Duan dispute and then to take advantage of his special position to drive Li and the National Assembly out of office. When Zhang reached Beijing, he had sufficient power to demand that Li dissolve the National Assembly as the prerequisite for his settling the dispute. Li did as he was told.[110] The National Assembly, which the Zhejiang Provincial Assembly had looked to and waited for throughout the fall of 1916 as the leader of self-government, was now abolished. Where did that act leave the provincial assemblies? In mid-June representatives from the Zhejiang, Anhui, Shandong, and Fujian assemblies met in Shanghai to discuss strategy. The assemblies' careful reliance on legal methods and orderly procedure was being made a mockery of.[111]

Shen, still titular chair of the assembly, went to the offices of both Yang and Qi to upbraid them for declaring their independence and, in effect, destroying the Republic. Shen was unafraid to confront those whom he believed in error; he did not, however, seem to try to ascertain ahead of time what the reactions of those he accused might be. From the reactions of Yang and Qi, we can be sure that Shen did not mince any words over what he saw as greedy warlords, ready to use violence to further their own private interests. They were furious but dared not arrest him amid the uproar among the elites over the destruction of the National Assembly. Instead they put him under constant surveillance, surrounding his home with military police, in effect placing him under house arrest, in fact if not in name.[112] This lasted more than a month. Then one day, likely in late July, under cover of a great rainstorm, Shen slipped from his home, made it to the train station, and fled for safety to Shanghai.[113] There in the French Concession he would be beyond the reach of the military as he began to explore and write about the future of social relationships and life in the new China.

CHAPTER THREE

Awakening: A Needle of Light
Shanghai, 1919–1920

---

*On that day I walked from Xiafei Road (Avenue Joffre) to
Minguo Road (Boulevard des Deux Républiques). In front of
the Zhong School on Nanyang Road was an iron pillar with
an electric sign: "Meat. (Fine shredded meat). Stored in an
earthenware jar. Take out—in the twinkling of an eye." These
few rows of characters looked like a photograph someone had
taken to save time and had been hung along the road for
people to see. Perhaps it was specially written for me or perhaps
even I wrote it.*

*I passed the "Cow-killing Company," saw herd after herd of
oxen and water buffalo, fat and thin, big and little, being
penned up. I slowly walked down to Bai'er Road where I saw a
small cart to which were tied several piles of new hides. The
hair color was an extraordinarily rich red. Tied on the top
were two skinned cow heads on which two martial horns
extended. As the cart was pushed along, the cowhides shook, the
cows' blood dripped, and the cows' eyes opened wide. It was as if
the two very large eyes were telling me "I. Went in. Was
skinned. In the twinkling of an eye."*

*I met coming toward me a herd of cattle being led—one oxen,
small, fat; the other oxen, big, thin. [To the side] there were
several snow-white, big, fat oxen. Those oxen's eyes grew large
looking at the herd of oxen—as if they were saying [to them]
"in the twinkling of an eye." But the herd of oxen did not take
heed; swaggering, they walked past.*

From "Life and Death" (Sheng he si) 1920

Written after his return to Hangzhou and Yaqian in the early fall of 1920, the short story-essay "Life and Death," called by Marxist intellectual Chen Wangdao "Shen's best work to date," reveals Shen's views of the Shanghai youth culture less than a year and a half after the May Fourth period strike that had paralyzed the city.[1] The locale for Shen's surrealistic sightings of slain and soon-to-be slain cattle was in the middle of residential sections of the French Concession, half a kilometer west of the native Chinese city and only a little more than that northwest of the Public Recreation Ground from which many of the large May Fourth period demonstrations had begun. It was also the arena of Shen's work and life in the period from June 1919 to late summer 1920.

During these fifteen months Shen temporarily shed his role as provincial political leader and turned instead to journalism, writing, and political discussion in new networks of progressive intellectuals in cosmopolitan Shanghai. His interests in parliamentary government and his detestation of the role of warlords were not supplanted in his intellectual development so much as they were expanded and enhanced. As editor, chief bankroller, essayist, and poet for *Weekly Review* (*Xingqi pinglun*) and as essayist and poet for *Awakening* (*Juewu*), the literary supplement of the *Republican Daily News* (*Minguo ribao*), Shen had venues for exploring and advocating views on national developments, feminism and family life, the New Culture movement, and life in general. An analysis of his writings and his actions in what should be seen as a period of self-definition reveals substantial evolution in his thought and especially in his conception of his role in the surge to revolution.

Life in the French Concession

Concerns, agenda, outlooks, and sensibilities are shaped in part by the contexts in which historical actors find themselves.[2] These may be political contexts: the direction of Shen's concerns in Hangzhou was forged by his role as leader of the assembly and by the historical developments of the seizure of the province by Beiyang warlords. They may be social and cultural contexts: the native place, journalistic, and political society networks in which Shen played important roles in Hangzhou. They may also be spatial contexts: the presence of the New Market area along West Lake in Hangzhou with its parks and public activity grounds, visibly symbolizing the abolition of the old, reopening the city to the vistas of lake and mountains, and providing public space for political demonstrations.

For several years and especially in the period 1919–20, Shen lived and worked in roughly two square kilometers of the French Concession. What he encountered in this environment informed and helped shape his writings and his thought. The Concession, located south of the International Settlement, narrowly fronted the Huangpu River at the Bund and flared to wider proportions after it arced around the Chinese City. In 1919 its three main thoroughfares were the Avenue Edward VII (Aiduoya Lu), which served as the northern boundary; the Rue du Consulat (Gongguan malu), which bisected the Concession near the Bund; and the Avenue Joffre (Xiafei Lu), which bisected the Concession from just south of the British Race Course to its western boundary. Each street had its own ambience, evidencing particular aspects of Western influence in a population overwhelmingly Chinese.[3]

Lined with Chinese and foreign businesses, the Avenue Edward VII was described by a Western observer in 1919 as "in a transitional state" where "new foreign buildings" exist "side by side with old 'junk shops,' coolie lodging houses and such like."[4] One imposing foreign-style building was one of two amusement palaces constructed in Shanghai during World War I, the Great World at the intersection of Avenue Edward VII and Tibet Road, described as "a kind of Crystal Palace and Coney Island" rolled into one, a huge, six-storied building with scores of theaters, halls, and restaurants, and attractions ranging from an aviary to roof gardens to a phantasmagoria of entertainments. For example,

the third floor had jugglers, herb medicines, ice cream parlours, photographers, a new bevy of girls their high-collared gowns slit to reveal their hips . . . and under the heading of novelty, several rows of exposed toilets, their impresarios instructing the amused patrons not to squat but to assume a position more in keeping with the imported plumbing. The fourth floor was crowded with shooting galleries, *fan-tan* tables, revolving wheels, massage benches, acupuncture and moxa cabinets, hot-towel counters, dried fish and intestines, and dance platforms. . . . On the top floor and roof . . . a jumble of tightrope walkers slithered back and forth, and there were seesaws, Chinese checkers, mah-jongg, strings of firecrackers going off, lottery tickets and marriage brokers.[5]

From its inaugural issue in June 1919 until February 1920, Shen edited the *Weekly Review* from an office on Xinmin Street that ran into Avenue Edward VII.[6] In his comings and goings, Shen must have walked

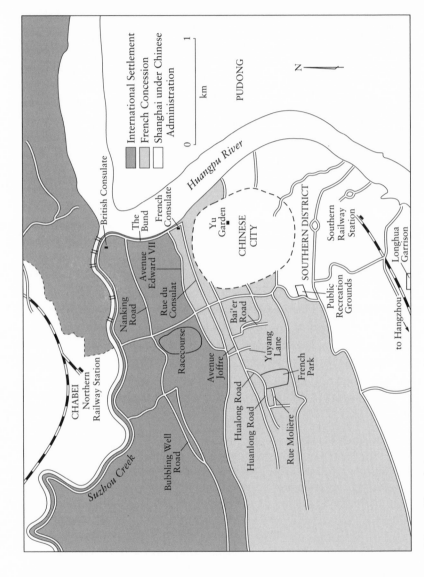

Map 3. Shanghai, 1920

along the avenue many times, noting the mix of things Chinese and foreign. Whether he entered the Great World we do not know, but in an August 1919 essay on the adaptation of human beings to their environment, he noted that the other "pleasure palace," the New World on Bubbling Well Road, had featured the year before "a man with no hands" whose "toes could arrange dominoes and thread a needle."[7]

In contrast to the Chinese-foreign mélange of Avenue Edward VII, the Rue du Consulat (the French Consulate-General was at its intersection with the Bund) was dominated mostly by Chinese shops for about a kilometer running west from the Bund. Despite the presence of a streetcar line, one Western writer in 1919 suggested that "it [had] changed less in twenty years than any main road in Shanghai." The street's shops and those on side streets (depicted as "rather squalid [and] poverty-stricken") sold goods of almost every description: "brasses, pewter figures, snuff bottles, chafing-dishes, bronze josses, and other odds and ends of bric-a-brac." Secondhand stores sold "immense quantities of old Chinese tools, books, clothes, etc."[8] Farther west along the street were municipal buildings, the French Municipal School for Chinese, and just off the thoroughfare, the Ningbo Guild, the native place organization for the Zhejiang men who essentially dominated the Shanghai economy.

Several blocks south of the Rue du Consulat and running straight out to the western boundary of the Concession was its main thoroughfare, the Avenue Joffre, the equivalent of Nanking Road in the International Settlement. In the memory of one Chinese writer, one "could shop for Parisian fashions there, or while away a lazy afternoon sipping coffee and eyeing the girls."[9] After 1918 a tide of White Russian refugees began to flow into Shanghai, making the Avenue Joffre their settlement center; eventually the area became known as "Little Russia." The Russians scandalized the other Westerners, "the way they let the side down and fraternized with the natives, selling their services to all buyers, Chinese and European alike—the men as riding instructors and bodyguards, the women as hairdressers, dance hostesses and whores."[10]

Though there were retail business districts scattered throughout the French Concession, the French authorities were more concerned with municipal zoning than those in the International Settlement. Thus, the neighborhoods along Avenue Joffre were kept largely residential. Sycamore trees, planted by the French, lined many of the major streets and roads, shading the walkways and boulevards. As one traveled farther west the residences became more impressive; especially beyond the Avenue du

Roi Albert wealthy Chinese and foreigners had built mansions surrounded by magnificent gardens and grounds.

South of Avenue Joffre via Route Voyron (Hualong Lu)—but before one reached Avenue du Roi Albert—were the contiguous French Park and Cercle Sportif Français, "one of the most popular resorts" in the city. Comprising about thirty acres, the park that had served as the camp for French troops during the Boxer expedition was an unfenced "vast lawn" with beds of flowers, a lily pond, artificial mounds, and rock works.[11] The veranda of the Cercle Sportif Français offered an excellent view of the park and the Cercle's many tennis courts while the building itself had facilities for dining, drinking, and dancing. A Chinese writer later remembered it as a place "where music once played in the cocktail hour and dinner dances swung to the latest rhythms deep into the night."[12]

The center of most of Shen's activity was the vicinity of the park. Issues of the *Weekly Review* during its last five months were edited and published little more than half a kilometer east of the park in a street off Admiral Bayle Road (Bai'er Lu). Several blocks northeast of the park and the sports club on Yuyang Lane (which ran into Avenue Joffre), he participated in discussions that would lead to the founding of the Chinese Communist Party in the spring and summer of 1920.[13] Shen knew the area well and made it the setting and prologue to one of his most important short stories, "Ripples," highlighting the contrasts between the poverty and drudgery of life of Chinese working women who passed through the area on their way to work and the wealth and privileges of foreign and Chinese elites in the French Concession.[14] Living and working in this arena seem to have deepened his growing sense of the destructiveness of class and other social separations.

In the vicinity of Shanghai's French Park, every day at morning and in the evening there were many female workers carrying small bamboo-plaited meal baskets. Crowd after crowd, coming and going in irregular fashion. Adjacent to the park was the famous Cercle Sportif Français, which only added to the bustle.

  Under the jade-green, trimmed shade trees along Hualong Road, people often walk slowly in the red glow of the late afternoon sun with their shadows, their fresh-smelling clothing, and the carriages of small children. Young boys throw and catch small balls and run along the street chasing butterflies. Large and small, men and women, group after group, coming and going in irregular fashion. Sometimes speedy cars go past. That doesn't even feel annoying because since this is a street in the vicinity of the park it is maintained well. Every evening on both sides of the street a fine spray of water is applied so that no dust will rise. At that time, if it is your first time to walk along Hualong Road, you will almost mistake the spray under the slanting rays as the beginning sprinkles of a rain. Sometimes one has to walk very hurriedly and not amble along to avoid being soaked in this enchanting spot.

Only in the morning and evening, going to and coming from work, women workers—thinking of depending on their twelve-hour wages of twenty to thirty cents. People carrying empty baskets pass quickly. Also passing are perhaps eight people sitting in a small cart with their things going home to prepare dinner.

As Hualong Road goes farther to the west, it curves around and becomes Huanlong Road. The lines of trees on both sides of this road do not have the height and foliage of those on Hualong Road. Both sides of the road are filled with handsome cars, quietly waiting for their masters' bidding after playing tennis or when leaving supper clubs or dance clubs to return home to rest. On this road there are very few hurried people. . . .

The electric lights come on. The tennis games stop; wearing lightweight cotton uniforms, those attendants whose job it is to pick up tennis balls leave. Evening meals begin. In the kitchens, the sounds of basins, pots, bowls, bells; dining rooms with the sound of music, wine glasses being clinked; on the floor the light and urgent footsteps of the "boy." Now and again the happy laughter on the veranda, the sounds of the lute in the music room, the sounds of singing, the bubbling sound of water being poured into glasses—rising and falling in cadence—extravagant joy and rejoicing.

At this time women workers on duty have already worked three or four hours; those off duty have returned home to do women's work at home after the meal has been eaten.

The similarity of Shen's description of female workers "coming and going in irregular fashion" and the herds of cows going to slaughter in "Life and Death" is striking.

Shen and May Fourth in Shanghai

Shen's activities from his arrival in Shanghai in the late summer of 1917 until the summer of 1919 remain a mystery. Shen knew Shanghai well. He had organized and trained the Student Army and established a Citizens' Radical Party there in 1912. It was almost certainly his embarkation point on his flight to Japan in 1913 and his port of entry in 1916. He had also almost been assassinated there.

In 1912 Shen had verbally sparred with Restoration Society leader Wang Jinfa, who had become military head of the Shaoxing military government after the 1911 revolution. Wang had reportedly engorged himself on the local populace and refused to dismantle his regime in order to bring it within the national administrative system. Shen saw Wang's actions as narrow, self-interested, and small-minded, with their emphasis on locality and separateness destructive of the nationalism that infused the founding of the Republic. He upbraided Wang in several open telegrams and went to Shaoxing to draw attention among Shaoxing elites to Wang's misdeeds. In so doing, he enraged Wang.

Shortly thereafter, Wang sent an assassin to kill Shen in a Shanghai hospital where he was being treated. Gaining admittance by claiming to be Shen's friend, the killer approached Shen's bed. Shen was awake and saw the strange man, taking a gun from a large cloth bag, coming near. As an indication of the violent unpredictability of the times, Shen as a matter of course had kept a handgun under his pillow, but when he hurriedly grabbed for it, it was not there: the gun had slid behind the bed and Shen could not reach it. Thinking quickly, he rolled off the bed onto the floor, but he felt that without a weapon, he would in any case meet certain death. Then the man, still with the gun in his hand, reportedly said, "You don't have to do that. I've been assigned to kill you, but I'm not willing to do it. I have heard you speak and feel that your words are correct [*bu cuo*]—I think that you're a good man. So today came; and I want to give you some news. Even though I'm not going to kill you, in the end someone will come to kill you. You must defend yourself." He then put his gun away and left the hospital.[15] Whether the narrow escape altered Shen's outlook on his political actions, we do not know. If anything, such an escape could have led Shen to be even more assertive and daring, certain that he led a charmed life. Whether Shen took the man's warning as an omen, we also do not know. His friends, looking back, recorded the episode in his memorial biography immediately after his assassination; the inclusion of the pointed warning—"in the end someone will come to kill you"—implies that the compilers at least saw the words as a sign.

We do know that Shen not only maintained but strengthened his connections to students in Hangzhou. Yang Zhihua, a female student for whom Shen served for a time as mentor and patron, noted that during the period before the May Fourth Incident Shen regularly sent her progressive books and magazines from Shanghai.[16] In addition, his actions reflect his own intellectual proclivities and role in maintaining an active knowledge of the publications in the vanguard of the intellectual-cultural revolution that had begun to sweep campuses. By this time Chen

Duxiu's *New Youth* magazine was in the fifth year of publication and Cai Yuanpei's educational reforms at Beijing University had burgeoned into their fourth year. As they had since the opening years of the century, students continued to go abroad to universities in Japan, Europe, and the United States. A fertile ground had been prepared among students and intellectuals for the awakening and growth of a consciousness that national change was imperative.

The festering wounds of the damage wrought on the country by Yuan Shikai and his train of warlords were once again ripped open with the news of the apparent acquiescence of Chinese diplomats at Versailles to Japanese demands for maintaining control over Shandong province, an act resulting from the connivance of Chinese officials with the Japanese in 1918. The response in Shanghai to news of the Beijing demonstrations on May 4 was large and tumultuous, with educators and journalists serving as initial leaders. It was among such men as Dai Jitao, Shao Lizi, and Ye Chucang that Shen found a network of like-minded figures.

Deeply involved in Shanghai journalistic circles was Dai Jitao (b. 1891), who would team with Shen as *Weekly Review* coeditor and become a key figure in Shen's political life. Though his family home until the late eighteenth century was Wuxing county in Zhejiang province, he grew up in Sichuan province, obtaining a traditional education but failing in his one attempt to pass the civil service examination. He studied in Japan from 1906 to 1909, becoming a student leader and leaving only after his funds ran out. In 1910 he edited the *Bell* (*Tianduo bao*) in Shanghai; his editorials were strongly anti-Manchu and marked by worry over the moral depravity in Chinese society.[17] To escape imminent arrest, he fled to Penang, where he joined the Revolutionary Alliance.

After his return to China following the Wuchang Rebellion, he met Sun Yat-sen through an interview he was doing for a newspaper. It was the beginning of a special relationship between the twenty-year-old Dai and the forty-four-year-old Sun. In late 1913, Dai became Sun's personal secretary, remaining in that position for the rest of Sun's life. The psychological source of what has been called an essentially "filial relationship" has been speculated upon.[18] Whether Dai found in Sun a strong paternal image that he sought or linked himself to Sun as part of some adolescent identity crisis, we will never know. Perhaps most suggestive for our understanding of the relationship of Shen Dingyi to both Sun and Dai are Herman Mast's and William Saywell's conclusions, based upon an undisclosed number of interviews they conducted with Dai's acquaintances in the early 1970s. "Sun had a boundless ego, which led him to nurture intense individual relationships and dominate them, whenever possible, in high-Confucian patriarchal style. The dependency of others was for him an important symbolic confirmation of his own integrity and leadership. By contrast, Dai sought to anchor himself in personalities more decisive than his own."[19]

Dai often felt unhappy and frustrated by his simultaneous desire to remain at the center of political activity and his reluctance to become involved in the messy business of actual revolutionary work. "Dai attached himself to Sun—a spiritual preceptor from whom he absorbed an irreplaceable, if fragile, self-confidence and sense of purpose. Sun's essential optimism tempered Dai's discouragement."[20] Dai reportedly was "an almost constant companion" of Sun during the 1913–17 period, when both were in exile in Japan following the failure of the second revolution.[21]

Dai and Sun returned to Shanghai in May 1918 following the collapse of an anti-Beijing rival southern government in Guangzhou. Sun established himself in a house in the French Concession on Rue Molière, a street that led west from the greenery of French Park; there he spent the next two and a half years writing a number of his most important works of political philosophy.[22] Dai, despondent over the Guangzhou failure and intensely detesting the city of Shanghai, withdrew to Wuxing, where he reportedly studied Buddhist sutras, with old friends Zhang Jingjiang (wealthy Shanghai businessman, a resident in the French Concession) and Hu Hanmin, a close revolutionary associate of Sun Yat-sen.[23]

We do not know when Shen Dingyi first met Dai, but the mutual compatibility of their thinking about the future of China and the importance of journalism in awakening the consciousness of the Chinese people likely drew them together quickly.[24] Their joint editorship of the *Weekly Review* began only a month after May Fourth activities were initiated in Shanghai. Dai may have been drawn to Shen because of the latter's self-assurance, impulsive optimism, and knight-errant urge to action; in addition, as Dai was drawn to older colleagues, Shen's being almost eight years older may have enhanced the attraction. For Shen, Dai offered connections to Sun Yat-sen and his associates. Shen's encomium to Sun in the *Weekly Review* suggests that Dai's worship of Sun began to shape Shen's view as well. "It is fitting to call it his revolution. He is the revolution . . . he is the protection of the constitution. The government should receive direction from the National Assembly and direction from him as the generalissimo. He is the generalissimo. Call him to abolish a post; he can abolish it. Call him to direct the dismantling of the military government; he can take responsibility. . . . China has this kind of man."[25]

Two other Shanghai journalists linked to Shen were Shao Lizi and Ye Chucang, editors of the *Republican Daily News*. Originally an anti-Yuan paper, it had developed into a vehicle for the views of Sun Yat-sen and his Guomindang. Shao, like Shen a native of Shaoxing prefecture, had received the *juren* degree in 1903, studied at Fudan University in Shanghai, and then studied journalism in Japan in 1907 and 1908, when he joined the Revolutionary Alliance. A reporter for two Shanghai newspapers before teaming with Ye, Shao was also head of the Chinese department at Fudan.[26] Ye, who would later appear in one of Shen's most infamous networks, was a native of Jiangsu province; he had served briefly in official positions before devoting his career to teaching (at Fudan University), journalism (as editor of several newspapers), and writing.[27]

Shao played an important role in Shanghai's initial response to the May Fourth Incident in trying to arouse the public and shape its response, leading educators in the sending of protest telegrams, and initiating a meeting of general community leaders.[28] The period saw large demonstrations (on May 7, ten thousand people unsuccessfully attempted a march through the French Concession), the organization of the Shanghai Student Union, the beginning of a boycott on Japanese goods, and a reception for a student delegation from Beijing by the National Press Union. Ye Chucang presided at the latter, where Shanghainese heard firsthand accounts of the Beijing situation; the press noted Dai Jitao's attendance at this reception, though we do not know if Shen attended.[29] The last days of May saw the intensification of the student movement, the spread of the anti-Japanese boycott, and the increasing involvement of the merchants in the anti-Beijing effort.

Although the initial impetus for the demonstrations and rallies was the events in Beijing and Versailles, as happens in any mass social action local dynamics began to shape the direction of local developments. Student demonstrators on May 31 had marched to the Shanghai County Chamber of Commerce in the Chinese City and to the Shanghai Municipal General Chamber of Commerce to gauge the depth of merchant support. Student meetings with both groups on June 3 turned disorderly, temporarily costing students that support. But when directors of the County Chamber were forbidden by Chinese police from holding a meeting to discuss the issues on June 4, merchant feelings began to turn against the Chinese authorities, seeing them as the antagonist. By sundown students fanned out through the city business districts delivering broadsides and speeches. The general strike began on June 5 in the Chinese City; by noon white banners of strike supporters hung from buildings throughout the French Concession and the International Settlement.

On June 6 industrial workers slowly joined the strike. Leading the way were printers from the Commercial Press, some silk textile workers, and streetcar workers, whose participation paralyzed the city. The Shanghai Student Union deputized students and Boy Scouts to maintain order and to ameliorate the fears of Westerners about the possibility of violence.[30] The first issue of the *Weekly Review* was published on June 8, the day martial law was declared in the Chinese City. Although word came on June 10 that the three Chinese ministers conniving with the Japanese had been dismissed, the strike and protests continued until June 12, when the ousters were confirmed. But from June 21 until July 2 another flurry of demonstrations burst out when word reached Shanghai that the Beijing government planned to sign the Versailles treaty. On June 29 there was a near violent confrontation when demonstrators (who had been forbidden to hold a rally at the Public Recreation Ground) were met by troops with fixed bayonets at the Longhua Garrison. That kind of reception only precipitated a larger demonstration on July 1. The situation, building to what looked to be a bloody climax, was defused by news on July 2 of the Versailles delegation's refusal to sign the treaty.

Shen reacted to the strike and the Shanghai situation in the *Weekly Review*. He saw the goal of the strike as clear: "defending against foreign depredations and eliminating the country's thieves."[31] But more than any additional realization about imperialism and Chinese nationalism was the impact that the protests and demonstrations seemingly had on Shen's conceptions of the capitalist oppression of the proletariat and the unity and power of the underclasses for ends beyond their own self-interest. In an essay in December 1919, Shen wrote that "after the May Fourth and June Fifth [the Shanghai general strike] movements, the whole country has borne much loss. But we have gotten rid of three thieves. If we had only had May Fourth in Beijing, then I'm not sure we would have gotten rid of them. And if June Fifth had only involved students, we also probably would not have gotten rid of them."[32] Shen rhapsodized that the strike was evidence of the "spirit of democracy and constitutional government," of the "growing determination of the people": "the strike is more important [to them] than going to work, than going to their businesses, than going to school. One could say that the people's actions bring national sovereignty."[33]

We do not know whether Shen himself participated in any of the overt protest marches and demonstrations, but his description of events on

June 9 at the New Beijing Wharf on the Huangpu River indicates that he was active in monitoring and reporting the strike. He recounts an affair where some boatmen were at the point of lifting anchors to embark for Ningbo and Yangzi ports in obvious disregard of the strike, but there was disagreement about the action, with some boatmen arguing that there should be unanimity among Ningboese in their patriotism and citizenship.

Before they finished speaking, there were people pointing and saying, "The yellow flags are coming! The yellow flags are coming!" The yellow flags are the flags of workers who keep order. They are also the flags whose meaning is marked clearly. There were about sixty to seventy people wearing dark blue short coats with rows of buttons gradually approaching from the Daji Wharf. They were waving flags on which were written "Maintain order" and "All of one heart" and "Return our Qingdao" and "The conscience of heaven and earth." Arriving at the boats, the people were being directed by one person. The sailors and men on board the boats came ashore.

Shen went on to report that even the Green and Red gangs had issued to their members extremely stringent prohibitions against causing any disturbances during the strike period. The sense of unity against the outside threat among the Chinese and especially among the proletariat and lumpenproletariat impressed Shen, as he enjoined workers to maintain their sense of "resoluteness, forbearance, and peace" and vagrants and members of the gangs to strive for a change of livelihood.[34] Although the subject in Shen's writings in the summer of 1919 remained predominantly national political issues, the strike seems to have awakened in Shen an awareness of the particular morality and potential role of the working classes.

Shen's Themes and Their Evolution, June 1919 to September 1920

In the summer of 1919, Shen arranged a summer job on the staff of the *Weekly Review* for Yang Zhihua. Yang later pointed out that the journal was at this time the center of revolutionary thought and its offices were a magnet drawing many students in the aftermath of the general strike to Shanghai to meet Shen and Dai.[35] One such was Qian Gengxin, a student at Zhejiang's First Normal School, who traveled to meet the two editors during the New Year's holidays in 1920; the personal attention and serious consideration that Shen gave him made Qian very excited.[36] Yang Zhihua stressed that until the journal ceased publishing in June 1920, young Chinese made it a focal point for discussions of change, both at the office itself and in the journal's pages.[37] Therefore, when we discuss Shen's themes and the evolution of his thought, it is not simply an effort to probe Shen's intellectual biography, but it is a gauge of sorts of the general course of intellectual debate and revolutionary thinking during the year after the May Fourth Incident.

Shen's positions and ideas evolved in dialectical form not only with the large political peaks of May Fourth but also with less grand events and in reaction to his colleagues in journalistic circles. He wrote essays and poems in response to the closing of journals in other cities, in answer to letters that he received at the *Weekly Review*, and in reply to queries about his views from his colleagues and students. That his views developed in a process of reaction and response to his environment and did not spring full-blown in some particular ideological identity or proclivity—socialist, anarchist, conservative—points to the contingent nature of participation in the revolutionary flow of the time.

If one analyzes the themes of the essays and poems Shen wrote during the seventeen-month period, there is a considerable shift of focus and emphasis. In the summer of 1919, five of the eighteen works took nationalism and antiwarlordism as their theme, a logical result of the immediacy of the political turmoil after the May Fourth incident, the June strike, and Japan's continued holding of Shandong. In this period of national humiliation and threat, only two focused on the class divergence between rich and poor. In the first three months of 1920, in contrast, twelve of the twenty dealt with themes of class and only one with nationalism.[38] This was a period when the reality of a society separated by class and gender especially seemed to strike Shen. In early 1920 the *Weekly Review* staff assisted in a textile dyers' strike, using cars to distribute more than seven thousand handbills throughout the city.[39] When discussions began later in the spring with colleagues and Soviet agent Voitinsky, Shen was acutely interested in pursuing solutions to bridging the gaps in Chinese society.

NATION AND CLASS

Shen's writings reveal his own awareness of the international arena and China's place in it. His journalistic connections brought him knowledge of world developments that drew his comments and reflections, from the plight of Korean nationalists to the French government's policy on speculation on commodity prices to the role of women in the European and United States governments to an upcoming International Labor Conference to be held in Washington, D.C.[40] His central concern, however, was national danger, especially the plight of China at the hands of Japan. Shen's purpose as a writer and journalist was to activate people: his prose and poetry are, in effect, a call to arms. In an August 24, 1919, piece he wrote that "I have even given up my daily concerns of the last decade of my life *in order to thoroughly awaken the Chinese*" [emphasis added].[41]

He was most explicit about the problem in an essay, "Sacrifice and Fish and Pork," published in the *Weekly Review* on September 7, 1919.

Under the present circumstances, part of the Chinese people and their land has become fish and pork on the cutting board. Three powers in Japan (military, financial, and political) hold their knives and want to push their Chinese counterparts onto the cutting board. The people and land in Shandong have already tasted this cutting. The people and land of the rest of the country, like chickens in a cage, fish in a net, or cows and sheep in a pen, are destined to be pulled out and skinned.

The beans are burning in a pot. We are crying miserably. Flames are reaching our eyebrows; death is coming with haste. But what good will crying and worrying bring us? The day of sacrifice comes. Fellow country-men, get prepared!

The language in this passage foreshadows Shen's trenchant picture in "Life and Death" of skinned cows and of cows going to their deaths unaware—in the middle of the French Concession, i.e., in the midst of the imperialists. Shen's solution? "We should take over the knife, kick away the cutting board, and refuse to be fish and pork."

In Shen's vision, the key to China's success in fending off national calamity comes, like the success of the Shanghai strike, from unity and the interdependence of the Chinese people.

"Breaking one arrow is easy; breaking ten is hard." A country, however large its territory and population, when separated, cannot unite itself automati-cally. A country, however small its territory and population, can conquer and eliminate problems. Considering all the relationships, we can say that the problem of the Qingdao-Jiaozhou-Gaoxu Railroad is the problem of Shan-dong province; the problem of Shandong is the problem of China; the problem of China is our problem, yours and mine. The railroad is lost, which means our way of living is lost. Now that our way of living is lost, we have to rise up and protect [what we have left]. Because of their acts of protection, businessmen have been killed, students have been arrested, publishing houses have been shut down—which means that the lives of you and me were taken, the bodies of you and me were arrested, the mouths of you and me were sealed up, and we were deprived of the right to survive.

Now you and I still have our lives, our bodies, our mouths. If you and I cannot break through this besiegement, we will be cut to pieces. At that fatal time we may cry desperately for help, but it will be too late. Not a single pig, though howling near its death, has ever escaped the butcher's knife.

The specific solutions Shen proposed in this essay were to refuse to recognize the current Chinese government as legitimate (a government that shut down publications championing the New Culture movement), to undertake a general plan for the country's construction (Shen recognized that at this time there was no generally accepted model), and to develop each individual's potential for helping to solve the problems: like a traditional Confucian and a modern liberal, Shen saw education as a, if not *the*, key.

Shen's continual theme, whether discussing nationalism, class, or the family, was the relationship between the individual and the group. Not only did he see natural social and gender divisions splintering groups and fostering isolation, but he was also aware of the centrifugal forces developing from the dynamics of existential movements that threatened to derail or at least hamper those very movements. He analogized the losses suffered by merchants selling Japanese goods during the boycott to losses that watermelon growers suffered when the public stopped buying them during a severe cholera epidemic in Shanghai in the late summer.[42] Although the cries of affected merchants had given rise to schemes "to divide up the losses," Shen argued that any relief supplied by the government would not come close to making up the amount. "What the farmer who plants watermelons loses is little compared to the losses of Japanese stores, though relatively much greater. Why then doesn't anyone show concern for him? Alas! It is melon sacrificed for the sake of health and sanitation and it has already been sacrificed. What about sacrificing [Japanese] goods for the health of the country?" The self-interest of the merchants, he asserted, paled before the interests of the nation.

If the key to saving China was a united, interdependent Chinese society, were the Chinese united and interdependent? Life in Shanghai had clearly awakened Shen to the gulf between the urban rich and the underclasses and to the problem of effecting social and political unity amid such disparity. For his readers, he etched in sharp relief the social demarcations: as in many of his Shanghai descriptions the automobile became a potent symbol of wealth and the capitalist class. "The sounds of motor cars, one after the other. [The poor man] watches with amazed eyes. They outstrip the wind; electrically equipped, they drive past, at their rear a red light. The light reflects on the surprised blackened face, near the corner of the wall. I do not know whether the people in the car were so affected."[43] In "What You See Walking at Night in Shanghai," Shen encapsulates capitalist culture in the fat man and in the drunk's vomiting up expensive soups, while the culture of poverty is depicted in the beggars and prostitutes.[44]

> A fat person says,
>   "Three times a day I put out great energy—
>   in eating three meals."
> A thin person says,
>   "There's no money to buy food;
>   because I feel the strain, I'll take a rest."
> "I beg you to give liberally; I beg you to give liberally!"
> Before the restaurant at the intersection,
>   cars and carriages come and go.
>   Both coming and going, they are innumerable.
> "Eyes full, bellies empty, mouth sweet, heart bitter."
> One sees only a drunk man leaning out of a car window,
>   vomiting uncontrollably.
>   Aiya! "Bird's nest, shark fin."
> There is poetry, poetry; there is need, need—
>   three copper coins for a meal.
> Cold, biting wind; pitch black temple.
> For warmth they sit back to back in their wadded jackets,
>   dozing exhaustedly, yet fitfully.
> I hear that there have been many robberies lately.
> Probably they haven't seen robbers in their dreams.
> Suddenly they are blown awake by gusts of wind.
> They slide further down, looking more exhausted.
> Over there is a woman soliciting men.
> "Come here! Come here!" Her call echoes through the streets.
> The soughing wind.
> The sound gradually lower, stirring things only a little.
> An old woman stands in the middle of the street—
>   angry: moving to the east,
>   lowering her head and heaving sighs;
>   then looking again to the west and strolling that direction.
> The nighttime glow of the electric lights—
>   Why does it not illuminate the thoughts of her heart?

At this hour there are no more cars and carriages.
Only the cries of the two beggars in the corner of the red temple.
   The cry! As of old.

Shen elsewhere instills in laborers a higher morality than that found in capitalists; the urban workers have a more natural and productive life than the wealthy. In "The Song of the Worker," appearing in the January 11, 1920, issue of *Weekly Review*, Shen idealized the virtues of the workers in the midst of their deprivation and brutalization.

> I say, "Our wadded jacket and lined trousers have passed the winter.
> Their red fox and undyed sable still must be dried at the fire.
> Our walk of eight or ten li is light and relaxed.
> Their li or half li must be made by car. . . .
>
> If we did not exist, where would you go to find traces of culture?
> There are clothes that everyone wears, food that the public eats.
> Clothes and food do not come free.
> These are our accomplishments—
>   the results of our hands and brains. . . ."

Shen predicted that such inequity would give rise to "many unfortunate results" in the future.

From his writings and subsequent actions it seems clear that Shen had developed a high degree of personal guilt over his natal identity as a member of a socially and financially privileged elite. It was not at all hidden in a confessional piece called "A Thought" that he wrote in mid-June 1919.[45]

Xuanlu [Shen] has bathed and changed his clothes, rested more than half an hour, eaten, walked to a well-arranged room, rested himself in a rocking chair directly opposite a big mirror, and now suddenly sees Xuanlu sitting.

How can the mirror reveal Xuanlu? Because on the earth there is Xuanlu. Why is Xuanlu on earth? He was born of his mother and father. When he was born, he was small. How did he get to be the big person sitting in the chair? Because he had food to eat and was not hungry. Because he had clothes to wear and was not cold. He had a house to live in and did not receive the bad effects of the wind, frost, rain, snow, sun, thunder and lightning. This man who seeks after life, from the time he burst out with sound straight to the present, has not been sustained and nurtured simply by his mother and father. This support ultimately came from whom?

I have it! Father and mother had property to give me; I then depended on property to live. I infer that my grandfather and grandmother also gave property to my mother and father upon which they depended for life. If everyone had property, how couldn't everyone live? Is it not that propertied people depend on the nonpropertied people to work and make gain? According to this way of speaking, propertied people are not the people who produce and nonpropertied people are the working people, the productive people. . . .

I am also a person. Why must I depend upon other people to support me? Xuanlu thought about this, raised an eye to look and did not ask that kind of thing. Completely full in his mouth was the blood and sweat of the workers. He laughs. I laugh at my life completely dependent on them.

Suddenly I see something more, [though] I didn't perceive that in my anxiety I was breaking out into a sweat all over my body: these are the Japanese goods which I have taken in exchange for the workers' blood and sweat. Forever they make mementos of "my complete loss of conscience."

In addition to revealing considerable guilt over his position, the last paragraph of this piece links national and social concerns. The image of the mirror and of Shen's watching as if detached from himself is one that Shen used more than once to probe the reality of human isolation and separation and the relativity of all relationships.

THE FAMILY SYSTEM AND FEMINISM

As significant as class and political divisions in Chinese society were the gulfs between generation and gender. The thrust of the May Fourth cultural revolution was an attack on the old family system with its ideas of patriarchy, family-arranged marriages, childhood betrothals, and female chastity and subordination. The system had aimed at social harmony but brought instead the destruction of untold numbers of lives and individual dreams. The suicide rate among Chinese women in the early twentieth century was highest among those in their late teens and twenties, the ages when women had most likely been recently betrothed and married, and at roughly the same year (1905) was more than double that in Japan, was over ten times that in Sweden, and more than twenty-five times that in Spain.[46]

Shen's evolving ideas on women and the family seemed to come from his relationships to the youth of the May Fourth period rather than from his first two marriages. His closest relationships seemed to be with younger women and men with whom he initially formed mentor-pupil or patron-client relationships. Yang Zhihua is an obvious example. Seventeen years Shen's junior, Yang came from a small landlord-merchant family in Xiaoshan county with whom the Shens had long-standing ties.[47] Yang married Shen's eldest son, Jianlong. Though a daughter was born to this union, the marriage ended in a divorce—Jianlong having a reputation as a profligate and ne'er-do-well. Yang left Xiaoshan for Shanghai where she continued her studies and married Communist leader Qu Qiubai. As an indication of Shen Dingyi's commitment to the new morality, he had this notification published in a Shanghai news-paper: "Yang Zhihua and Shen Jianlong on this date were divorced in Shanghai. Yang Zhihua and Qu Qiubai on this date were married in Shanghai. Shen Jianlong and Qu Qiubai on this date mutually agree to be good friends."[48]

Shen had come by 1923 to be a strong feminist.[49] But his first journalistic foray into the topic of feminism four years earlier—"Where to Start for Women's Liberation?"—seems to reflect a tentativeness and wariness that his works on nation and class do not show.[50] He wrote, "This essay has been drafted three times. I will appreciate the criticism of all Chinese, including that of Chinese men. Those women who are content with their prosperous family conditions and those men who are hungry for power do not pay enough attention to this problem. The people of the working class, male or female, do not have the opportunity to learn about this problem. Those who are able to criticize are only a few from the intellectual class." Shen then argued two points: "men and women should fully know and firmly believe that women are human beings" with the same qualities as men, and men and women have the right to an equal education. "The tragedy in China is that men have nothing to do with women except the relationship of marriage, con-cubinage, and prostitution. I don't want to mention the sad aspects of trafficking in women, female infanticide, and wife abuse." Shen pointed out that even those women who had studied in Europe or the United States often chose to sit quietly alone in a corner or at the end of a table on social occasions because "people have inherited the habit of regarding women as objects. Because men regard women as objects, women nat-urally think of themselves as objects. . . . All the narrow-mindedness and inequalities between the sexes stem directly from this mistake." Breaking out of this traditional consciousness, Shen argued, was the basis for women's liberation.

Education was thus crucial. Shen charged that the traditional edu-cational system taught women to be objects by teaching such duties as "protecting chastity" and "ordering servants." Now, "since women have equal qualities with men, they should have the right to training in various skills from elementary school through middle school to college. The schools of male students should be the schools of female students. Schools cannot give us knowledge, but they can help us explore our potentiality and obtain knowledge by ourselves. Knowledge is a practical tool. . . . Without knowledge liberation would become an empty word." For Shen, then, women's liberation had to start with an awakening to the reality of sexual equality and the necessity of educational equality.

In December Shen elaborated on the meaning of female equality inside the family.[51] The month before a cause célèbre had erupted at the First Normal School in Hangzhou after a student, Shi Cuntong, had written an essay, "Against Filial Piety," in the newly established journal *New Tides of Zhejiang* (*Zhejiang xinchao*). The essay condemned the family as the source of individual suffering and promoted its destruction as a step in the reconstruction of society.[52] The ensuing brouhaha led to the closing of the journal and the dismissal of four professors involved in its publication: Chen Wangdao, Liu Dabai, Xia Yanjun, and Li Cijiu, the first two of whom were linked in various ways with Shen. Shen, who had been a strong supporter of the school during his provincial assembly chairmanship, maintained close contact with the situation at First Normal.[53] He began to correspond with students there during this period; a mutual respect and admiration grew up, with the students hungrily seeking Shen's advice on revolutionary undertakings and Shen respecting those who wanted to make a new China.[54] A First Normal student, Cao Juren, noted that Shen was one of the student movement's "spiritual directors."[55]

In the December essay, discussing the meaning of fatherhood at a time when patriarchy was in disrepute, Shen argued that a true father treated his sons and daughters as human beings. He exhibited two qualities in his dealings with them, love and equality. Shen described love as unconscious and uncreated, an inheritance from father and ancestors, facing back to the beginnings of time and stretching on without end. Shen's description of love in terms of the traditional longitudinal family raises the question of how his concept diverges from traditional views. In further arguments he differentiated love from filiality and compassion in that the latter are taught. The innate, intuitive nature of Shen's concept of love makes it difficult to analyze in relation to specific existential situations.

His description of equality among daughters and sons in the family is more concrete. Since one can see the equality of sons and daughters at birth, later preference for sons was "false love," stemming from the male-dominated system. Daughters as well as sons, married or unmarried, should inherit family property. In addition, Shen argued that a central reason given for wanting sons—as a defense in old age—should be obviated by the establishment of collective enterprises run by relatives or of public homes for the elderly, new institutions that would alleviate the heavy burdens that fell on children.[56]

Shen thus generally wrote with understanding and compassion about the plight of women, as in a poem about a Shanghai working mother, "One Night."[57]

> During the day she does piecework.
> At night she returns to nurse her son.
> The mother uses her hands to wash the rice, cook the rice,
>   wash the clothes, and mend the trousers.
> The father worked hard all day and now naps—that's all:
>   he doesn't work at night, but gets refreshed.
>
> "Bao Bao, Cheng Cheng." In a low voice there are a series of cries.
> Nursing, she walks; walking, she nurses.
> Small feet alone, a sweating body.
> A pair of small lacquer-like eye-pearls:
> Slowly at Bao Bao's sound, mother and baby come closer together.
> Into the dilapidated room streams moonlight,
> The small palm of the hand glowing like the vapors of a red powder.
> Her dimples and red lips move slightly when she breathes.
> With the two people in the dark shadows, there is already repayment
>   [for added] work: a beaming face.
>
> A yawn penetrates the mosquito netting.
> One head goes down, entering the world of dreams.
> The little one in the mosquito netting, sleeping on the edge
> Allows a still unwarmed place for the mother to sleep.
> She comes to make Bao Bao comfortable.
> There is the hum of the mosquitoes,
>   surrounding the bed's vapor holder
>   as if they thought it were a cup of broth.
>
> Suddenly there is a cry.
> The child with a start in a dream: one hand touches her,
>   the other gives a breast to suckle.
> Bao Bao doesn't cry [after that].
>
> The father awakes—his energy has been restored.
> Outside roosters are crowing: 5 A.M.
> There is the disturbing sound of the car horn.
> There is no alternative. He gets up, puts on his clothes,
>   and goes out.

The tenderness that Shen depicts between mother and baby is notable; the drudgery of her life in work both outside and within the home was relieved only by the relationship she enjoyed with her child. Equally significant in this depiction of domestic life was the separation of both mother and baby from the father. In none of his writings did Shen ever describe the relationship of husband and wife as close or empathetic. The sound of the car (Shen's symbol of capitalism) intrudes and makes the father's leaving for likely factory work the only alternative.

In his extant writings, Shen never commented on his own three marriages. In an interview, his son Jianyun spoke of them.[58] We do not know when or whom Shen first married; it had most certainly been an arranged union. Jianlong, the elder son, would have likely been born from this union about 1902, when Shen was about twenty. We do not know what happened to the marriage. His second marriage produced three children. His elder daughter, Jianbo, drowned at a young age in 1916; his second daughter, Jianhua, was born about that time, and his second son, Jianyun, was born in 1918.[59] Since Shen does not speak of his family in his writings, one wonders about the nature of his family life; Shen was involved in so much public activity that not too much time could have been devoted to those living at the House of Brightness and Prosperity.

In early 1923, Shen in effect dispensed with his second marriage, sending his wife away. His memorial biography attributes the action to Shen's strong feelings about the necessity of women's liberation and the destructiveness of traditional marriage. His wife reportedly left freely and was willing to live elsewhere. He then took a "revolutionary helper" as his wife.[60] Wang Huafen, presumably about twenty years younger than Shen, was from Yuyao county, east of Xiaoshan and Shaoxing. One biographer has suggested that over the years Shen had a weakness for women, and Wang was attractive and youthful; Gao Yuetian, who worked for the Guomindang provincial bureau in 1924, remembered her as "graceful and elegant."[61] Accounts of her educational background vary, but it is likely that she first attended the Shaoxing Women's Normal School and then Hangzhou Women's Normal School.[62] In any case, her decision to gain an education and to leave Yuyao, known for its conservative culture, marked her as a woman of determination and ambition. It is likely those qualities among others appealed to Shen.

Wang became Shen's almost constant companion, taking on the job of transcribing his lectures and speeches. After the transcription, they would rework the draft together to produce a finished essay. Gao noted that Shen and Wang were often in high spirits and that there was much laughter between them.[63] There is some indication that Wang was a sexually liberated woman. Described by one of Shen's biographers as flirtatious, she apparently had built herself something of a reputation in this regard before her marriage to Shen. The story goes that on the day Shen first brought Wang to Xiaoshan, a crowd of young people were there to welcome them. But among the welcoming signs was one that stated: "Welcome to the revolutionary leader Shen Xuanlu; down with the shameless whore Wang Huafen." This biographer alleges that when Shen was traveling away from Yaqian, Wang had an affair with Xu Meikun, a Xiaoshan native and an important early Zhejiang Communist figure.[64] In my 1993 interview in Shen's home with Shen Jianyun, I asked about Wang Huafen, and the response seemed to corroborate reports of Wang's free nature. From family members and associates standing around, there were chuckles and the words "a lot of trouble" (*hen mafan*).[65]

The Problem of Chinese Society: Shen's View

Whether speaking of nation, class, generation, or gender, Shen pointed to a common problem in Chinese culture and society beyond the particulars relating to any of these issues of the New Culture era. For him the isolation and separation of individuals loomed as the critical issue, the solving of which was necessary for China to advance. Two of his important writings focused on this theme, one a surrealistic poem, the other a narrative short story. They are significant enough in their contribution to revealing Shen's vision that I include the poem and portions of the story.

The poem "Friend? Robbed?" appeared in the *Weekly Review* on Double Ten, 1919. Shen prefaces it: "This poem's images are based on several actual events put together—it is not pure fiction." As the surrealism of the description and action quickly reveals, it is difficult to judge Shen's reason for the preface unless it is to play upon the old Chinese preference for history (and the real) over fiction. The bleakness and other-worldliness of the setting, depicting China, give evidence of Shen's view of the situation as China entered the 1920s.

Ten thousand mountains dried up; the light in the sky is like blood.
There are only a few black clouds—they're scaring us to death.
Alas! Friend! We can't move! What can we do?

One asks. One listens. The asker is used to asking.
The listener is used to listening and thus doesn't answer.
There are only these two people facing each other as fated
    without hope under the heavens.

You look at me. I look at you.
If I don't have you, whom am I going to talk to?
If you don't have me, whom are you going to talk to?

On the earth there is no green grass;
    in the sky there are no flying birds.
Our tongues are rotted; our lips are burned; we creep and fall.
Our four red-pupiled eyes moving,
    looking out to the east, out to the west.

There it is! Before me a strip of land destroyed by fire.
There I find just-seared cats and dogs with which I can fill my belly.
Only, there is not a drop of water—what to do?
Huh! Ah! . . . The urine jar.

We come to a place of broken pottery and tiling;
we creep aimlessly, searching. . . .

From before me I heard the distant sound of cannon.
Now hear the laughing sound of thunder.
Suppose it was the sound of cannon: there must be people hit!

"Good, good!" Rain!
These drops of timely rain after the long drought
Fall on the hairy pores of my body.
I grind my teeth and wait for dawn
To bite the new life of the green grass.

The torrents of rain carried a howling wind.
As the lightning passed, it thundered suddenly.
Then I was pulled from the good dream to the eye-opening dream.

The water was several feet deep.
Rolling currents carried several dead carcasses I know not where.
I couldn't move. Crawl! When I was halfway up a mountain,
    I saw bright reflections from a dagger.
Then saw another four red-pupiled eyes.
Four red-pupiled eyes fixed.
"Crash." Inside one fell; inside one spoke, "Go,"
    and gave him something to eat.

I didn't care whether it was sour, sweet, bitter, or hot.
Going along the road. . . . (However my stomach wasn't hungry.)
My friend had gone there. I turned to look.
I could only see a great threatening cliff that was blocking
    with a deep darkness the way to the middle of the mountain.

I pressed on rapidly, hurriedly. Before me was a village. . . .
Walking on, I saw nothing,
    only an empty house with the door half open.
As I entered the door, a great sound for help was heard.

I stopped, but heard only my own sound waves in the empty space—
    nothing else!
The house was so big! Why was there not a single person there?

There were signs—teapots and jars of medicine—
    of efforts to escape the epidemic.
On the bed, under the bed, to the east, to the west, crisscrossed
    and laid out: stiff corpses.
The east of the house and the west of the house were like this.
Why is it like this? . . .

The cooking pot is empty. All others are also completely empty.
There are now only the two red-pupiled eyes looking at them.

Where is the smell of gruel? It blows in on the wind.
    Is it close by on the left?
    It's not certain.
In haste, I let my nose lead me in the direction:
    one li, two li, three li.
I cannot see the people in the mountain.
I can only see the three gigantic characters on the red paper:
    "Soup Kitchen."

"Soup." There's no way to think about it, whether one cares for it.
I snatch it from the outstretched hand. A mouthful.
"Bah! Bah!! Friend. . . . "

This striking context of death, desolation, and destruction with military images (cannons and daggers) and humans brutalized by deprivation and hunger provides a stark arena for the isolation and disconnectedness of individuals. The two people do not communicate or have any affective ties; the narrator, nevertheless, calls the other "friend." They are like animals with red-pupiled eyes, creeping and falling. The absence of subjects in the poem's sentences makes it difficult to tell when the "friend" left, when "we" becomes "I." The complete lack of communication initially makes the parting seem not very noteworthy except for the fact that the only human with whom the narrator can potentially form a connection is now gone. Deliverance from the seared-dry nightmare seemed to come from the "good dream" of rainwater, which seemed to promise life, but the narrator was instead "pulled . . . to the eye-opening dream" of floodwaters and the village of corpses. The search for sustenance marked by the narrator's own echoing cosmic scream ends at the surrealistic soup kitchen, where he is driven to snatch the soup from some hand unconnected to any human. In the end, the narrator despairs of any connections to humanity.

Shen describes the contemporary social equivalent of the good dream that promised more than it could deliver in "Ripples."[66] The themes of class and gender dominate this story, though it is the latter that reveals the good dream as an empty dream. The scene is the living room of a beautiful, foreign-style house near the French Park. Three young Chinese women castigate an editorial that supposedly appeared in the *Weekly Review* calling women prostitutes, thereby, the group decides, ridiculing and polluting women. While these upper-class Chinese women are eating dumplings brought in by the maid, a Mr. Yang, having recently spent time as a student in the United States, makes a call. They draw him into the conversation on feminism, assuming that he had seen much and now knows much from his travels and education abroad. What data, they ask, can be used to deal with the writer of the editorial? This is the "good dream," the youthful May Fourth generation awakening to an awareness of the problems and outlooks of the old family system as it related to women.

Yang's initial response begins the "eye-opening dream." It is avoidance of the problem: "Have you heard the songs and music at the Cercle Sportif Français? What need is there to find these vexing matters to talk about? It's not a crime to carry a little tune and [see] the moonlight outside the window, is it?" The women agree but first demand a story from Yang about his experiences with women. The story reveals Yang as a fop, having no understanding of the meaning of feminism, and it mocks these privileged women listening to him with "bated breath." Yang's attitude toward women: "All through life I've had the greatest respect for women. Even though I'm a religious believer, I've felt that the ancient and modern are at cross purposes. I see women as deities. The words that come out of women's mouths are heaven-sent commands."

He then recounts a winter visit to the countryside with friends that turns into a drunken evening of "guess fingers" and mah-jongg. Hearing of the winter party, the Chinese female host in the mansion near French Park calls her maid to bring in some champagne for them to drink while Yang continues his story. The description stands in marked and ironic contrast to that of "Friend? Robbed?" For here we have civilized sophistication and, at least for a moment, connections between humans brought by the wine. "Yang in a happy spirit lifted his glass and clinked it with the other three. The clear and crisp sounds of the glasses, the transparent color of the wine, the sweet fragrance. For a moment all fused as if the four people were one set of eyes, ears, nose, and mouth communicating."

Yang's story of the winter party ends in a sexual encounter, which he shrouds in mystery for his listeners. Although the initial response of the women was disappointment that so much of the evening had been spent listening to Yang's not-very-satisfying story, they eventually bog themselves down in trying to unravel the identity of Yang's mysterious liaison. Lost in the trivia of Yang's mindless story and their reaction to it was the issue of feminism that they had seemed intent on discussing in the beginning. The "good dream" was only a dream, with Shen's showing that for many of the elite youth, serious concern with this issue and that of class was either nonexistent or ineffectual. None of the four evidence any understanding and, as in Shen's surrealistic poem about friends, there are no real connections among the four. The story ends sarcastically.

Oh! There are sounds of factories changing shifts. Daylight. Four people sit in the car to go to the park for fresh air. Crossing on the road are women going to work. Crowd after crowd, going hither and yon.

Four people getting fresh air in their fast car, in their eyes seeing crowd upon crowd of female workers. Along the road fresh air blowing in causes the words of the people in the car to be indistinct. It seems like they were saying "Pollution . . . prostitutes . . . liberation."

The Solution for the Problem of Chinese Society: Shen's View

Shen's principle image for the solution for China's problems is light. In "Life and Death," he describes his birth as a passage to light.[67] "I remember the days before my birth as a period of dreamless sleep where I did not feel the passage of days. Naturally I grew larger inside a very comfortable world. I didn't know comfort; also I didn't know where I grew larger; I didn't know what world or what me. Suddenly there was a needle seeming many feet long like a light in the gold and black world suspended in front of me. My body was pushed toward this light." For Shen light represents knowledge and a mature awareness, the birth into which can facilitate change. Shen's admonition to live in the light is nowhere clearer than in his poem "Swimming at the Beach."[68]

Naked heavens.
Naked earth.
Naked man.

You begin to walk along the shore, treading along as the waves go—
Everything feels so peaceful.

Sunlight shining on the sea, threads of sand extending into water.
If you open your eyes a bit, you can see light all around.
The heavens and the sea are blue-green jade.

Where can you hide yourself?
You must not hide yourself!
If you must hide yourself, the place—I don't know
    whether it's in the heavens or the sea—is in the light.

"Eyes that are ill," he wrote, "fear seeing the light. But this is the fault of the body and its illness. It is not the fault of the light."[69] Shen's prescription for achieving light is not easy and requires struggle: "After the May Fourth movement, China's future is like cutting one's way bloodily out of darkness. A beam of light—always ahead. We must only go quickly to welcome it."[70]

What, then, is the light according to Shen during this year in Shanghai? What breaks through the eerie blood-light of Shen's nightmarish vision of drought, flood, and plague and through the wan, artificial light of the Western-style house near French Park? While Shen's depiction of China's problem is apocalyptic, his solutions are evolutionary even if their significance is ultimately revolutionary. It is clearly not modern technology and science. In the poem about Shanghai evening sights, the glow of the electric lights are ineffective in illuminating human hearts; the lights at the end of fast automobiles only startle with their seeming inappropriateness.

Shen's answer was a metamorphosis of social outlook and way of life. In an essay in late September 1919, Shen argued that it depended on the individual.[71] "It most depends on me. It's not that I toss away all else and pay attention only to myself. . . . If I care for myself, then can I forever not care for others and depend on them? No! I care for and depend on others. There's mutual dependence and caring."

If each individual in the world would do this, then saying, "From each according to his ability, to each according to his need" would mean "I exhaust my ability, I seek my need." No matter what changes there are in the world, "using my ability" and "seeking my need" are the road of living.

Build an environment so that [each one] progresses. I and he are your environment; I and you are his; he and you are mine.

If you want to change your environment, then you must change my me, your me, and his me. I change my me; you change your me; and he changes his me. Each seeks to be his own teacher and fight his enemy.

The Communist ideal that Shen calls "the road of living" had obviously begun to seem an important element in his views. But Shen's vision in the fall of 1919 for fighting one's enemy was based not in changing structures or revolutionizing gender relationships or restructuring the Chinese nation, but in remaking individuals, in changing their identities as part of a scheme to change the human environment.

Shen's most important essay regarding human relationships appeared in late November 1919. In it human beings become not simply the environment for others but coterminous with each other, their identities merging to create the context for a new society. For Shen, the distinctions between people must be broken down in a context where social identity is fluid. In the piece, entitled "He Really Is You; You Really Are I," opening examples highlight social relativity as evidenced in Chinese cultural, class, and gender separations.[72]

At one point I saw a Northerner take remnants of food wrapped in a dirty, greasy blue shirt sleeve and mix it with dirt and mucus from his nose to eat it. I felt this was extremely outrageous. A Southerner took a bowl of salty boiled vegetables and beans and buried it in front of the door or in an alley way until it became stinky; then he ate it. I also felt that this was outrageous. I once ran into a worker stinking with sweat. His stink came from greasy dirty clothes. His chest smelled as vile as vomit. But when he put on fresh-smelling clothes, the odor was cast off. . . .

I remember after I married that I loved my wife deeply—almost as if we were one. Afterwards we received the influence of old society; I took a concubine. Between the two of us it was as if there were a separation. However, later there was something of a coalescence of emotion—as if one tree was maturing.

Shen then recalls an experience during his days as a magistrate in Yunnan province where light (his symbol for the solution to China's problems) reveals the relativity of reality.

I remember one time in Yunnan when I was hunting and went into deep mountain recesses. The sky was dark and I couldn't find the road. There was only one old temple; and it was quite frightening. I lay down beside the temple guardians. The moonlight was penetrating the foliage, shining on the four frightful statues as if only to frighten me. I was so scared, I jumped up to flee the temple, but the sounds of the wind in the leaves and branches conjured up images of poisonous snakes and wild animals outside. So I didn't dare go out of the temple.

Later in thinking about the statues—even though they were scary—they basically still had a little of the human form. I used some matches to light the shapes a little. And they reminded me of my brother; one had a beard much like my uncle; the female form was my sister. I stared intently and didn't feel afraid. Moreover, the fierce form of a wolf became friendly and lovable. I fell asleep until dawn. When I left the temple, they had no evil attributes in my mind.

I want to make these points from the anecdotes: (1) there are no poor people; there are no rich people; (2) there is no you, I, or he; and (3) whoever under heaven is you, I, or he can all be considered as one person joined together by "love" [*ai*].

By late 1919, Shen had begun to see a new form of human being and new forms of social organization as the solution to the problems of the Chinese polity. As in Chinese tradition, the organizational focal point was the group, but here it was a collective that followed—not preceded—the individual. Responsible individuals who recognized their interconnectedness to others and the relativity of identities and roles amid varying social realities could remake Chinese culture.

Herein is the foundation of the self-government experiment that Shen would try to put into effect nine years later. He details the importance of life in a self-governing collective for breaking down the human barriers built by individual identity, delineating aspects he considered significant for achieving those ends. "My plan emphasizes collective action to establish collective living and focuses on developing economic strength. This is unlike other models. Collective action breaks down the barriers between you, him, and me." An important aspect of Shen's vision is that it is the existential experience—the work of collective action made possible by each sharing identity with the others—that breaks the barriers, not simply being part of the collective. Late in the fall and in the winter of 1920, Shen explored the values of work-study mutual aid teams among the youth as a way of beginning to build the new social environment.[73]

Shen and the Shanghai Communist Group, Spring and Summer, 1920

In the spring and summer of 1920 Shen was involved in initial organizational activities that led to the founding of the Chinese Communist Party, a process that, among other things, highlights the significance of networks. Our understanding of the essentially fluid organizational process is made more difficult to grasp for it emerges mainly from the dreamlike world of memory: most sources are personal accounts retold in the 1950s after years of struggle and war before the eventual Communist victory. There is substantial variation in the description of the nature and timing of groups that were established. Some argue that a Shanghai Communist cell was set up early in 1920, while other sources put its establishment in late summer or near the end of the year; some point to the existence of a Marxist Study Society, while others do not even mention such a group.[74] One writer, Yang Zhihua, Shen's female protégé, suggested that the cell was, in fact, known as the Marxist Study Society, but she does not mark its beginning until the fall or winter of 1920, long after some of its known participants had already left Shanghai.[75] It is not only the haziness of memory that is the difficulty here but the intervening polarization of political views that occurred during the late 1920s and later, well after these events themselves. Judgments about Shen (and others) in 1920 are therefore refracted through the bloodiness of revolution in the memories of men and women.

The earliest account of the beginnings of the Chinese Communist Party came from Samuil Naumov, Soviet adviser at the Whampoa Military Academy in late 1926; it thus predates the Nationalist Revolution of 1926–27 and escapes the revolutionary polarization of accounts in the 1950s.[76] Naumov, using Chinese sources, notes the seven men involved in the Shanghai cell, the first, loosely structured discussion group that met with Soviet agent Gregory Voitinsky: Shen Dingyi, Dai Jitao, Chen Wangdao, Shi Cuntong, Yu Xiusong, Li Hanjun, and Chen Duxiu. It is likely that the group may have been called the Marxist Study Society, as least in its early stage.

Six of the seven were editors and writers for the *Weekly Review*; its offices were thus the obvious center of the movement.[77] One Chen Gongpei remembered that on his arrival in Shanghai he met Voitinsky at the journal's office, where discussions involving Shen, Dai, and a few others covered the situation in the Soviet Union and the potential for a relationship.[78] Yang Zhihua described the revolutionary aura of commitment in the journal's offices, where everyone worked and everyone was equal.[79] Shen's own fascination with work-study and alternative collectives may have been derived from the actual work of the students and intellectuals at the journal's headquarters. Tasks were shared by all, and all communication was on a first-name basis. Most women shaved their heads, "like nuns," Yang noted. She claimed that a good deal of the coherence of the revolutionary effort was lost when the journal ceased publishing, for at that time people scattered.[80]

In addition to the broad roots of the incipient Communist Party organ in the *Weekly Review*, five of the seven—Shen, Dai, Shi, Yu, and

Chen Wangdao—were natives of Zhejiang province, which once again points to the cohesive attraction of native place.[81] Chen (b. 1890, Yiwu county) had been one of the four professors dismissed from the First Normal School in Hangzhou in the trouble over the progressive journal, *New Tides of Zhejiang.* Shi (b. 1899, Jinhua county) and Yu (b. 1899, Yuyao county) had both been Chen's students at the First Normal. Shi had written the conservative-offending essay against filial piety for the journal. Thus, within the Zhejiang cluster in the *Weekly Review* organization and the discussion cell network there were social linkages beyond native place. The close relationships that had existed between teacher (Chen) and pupils (Shi and Yu) added a strength of intimacy to them. Shen's close ties to the First Normal through his support as provincial assembly chairman and as intellectual revolutionary patron have been noted.

All the Zhejiang cluster had come to Shanghai as exiles. Shen had fled the warlord threats and intimidation in Hangzhou. Dai had come with Sun Yat-sen after the collapse of the Guangzhou government. After Chen's dismissal from the First Normal, he had remained in Hangzhou translating the *Communist Manifesto* before making his way to the more hospitable environment of the French Settlement, where he lived at the offices of the *Weekly Review.* In the early winter of 1920, Shi and Yu had left Hangzhou to participate in the Beijing Work-Study Mutual Aid group, lured by the possibility of free tuition at Beijing University. Although they wrote letters to friends about such personages at the university as Li Dazhao and Hu Shi, they did not find the "experiment for new living" to be satisfying. Even before the whole effort collapsed in the spring of 1920, they had decided to leave. Yu wrote, "I did not think any longer of being a scholar, only a revolutionary."[82] Leaving Beijing in mid-March, they made their way to the *Weekly Review* office for work in the journal of revolutionary thought. There they almost certainly discussed the failed project with Shen, who had been so taken the previous autumn with the idea of the Work-Study Mutual Aid group; whether this may have caused Shen to alter his views on the potentials of such collectives we do not know.

The two non-Zhejiang men in the original group were Chen Duxiu and Li Hanjun. Chen (b. 1879), famous as the founder of *New Youth* and as dean of letters at Beijing University, had come to Shanghai in the autumn of 1919 after his three-month imprisonment in the wake of the May Fourth disturbances. While Chen had introduced the ideas of Marxism into the Chinese intellectual debate with articles in *New Youth,* it is said that he was not converted to those ideas until his Shanghai discussions in 1919 and 1920.[83] Li (b. 1890), from Hubei province, had studied many years in Japan. The sixth of the seven in this group to work at *Weekly Review*, he was fluent in Japanese, English, German, and French.[84] Yang Zhihua claimed that Li was the *Weekly Review* group's chief intellectual and that he had numerous connections to the Japanese and Korean Communist parties. She noted Li's help in introducing her into the homes of progressive Koreans and Japanese in Shanghai and to one of his Russian friends for Russian language training.[85]

The seven involved in the initial group were not a discrete unit. The revolutionary circles in Shanghai expanded and contracted continually with the comings and goings of many young adults. Shi Cuntong, for example, had left for Japan by July for study and for treatment of tuberculosis at a sanitarium, a trip for which he was provided letters of introduction by longtime Japan residents Dai and Li.[86] What is noteworthy is the fluidity of the situation, with some participating in political discussions on a single trip to the city, for a short period of time, or—like Shen—consistently over a long period.[87] In addition to the initial seven, four others were reportedly more short-term participants. Three were authors and editors who hailed from Zhejiang: Mao Dun (Shen Yanbing) (b. 1896), based at the Commercial Press, participated irregularly; Shao Lizi, editor of the *Republican Daily News*, was constrained by other duties; and Zhang Dongsun (b. 1886), chief editor of the *China Times* (*Shishi xinbao*), an organ of Liang Qichao's Research Clique, was uncertain about the ideological trends of the group.[88] The other was Li Da (b. 1890) from Hunan province, a returned student from Japan who would emerge as a key spokesman on Marxist ideological issues.[89]

All eleven men in this "expanded" group shared an involvement in journalism and a sense that journalism was the educational tool for awakening the Chinese people. They were young, ranging in age from their early twenties to their late thirties (Chen Duxiu, the only one not in this range, was forty-one). Of the eleven, eight were Zhejiangese. Chen Duxiu and Li Hanjun, from Anhui and Hubei provinces, respectively, worked together very closely in the organizing effort of the party; Li Da clearly seemed the odd man out. His accounts and those of his wife, Wang Huiyu, written in the 1950s, reveal an embittered pair ready to judge harshly their Shanghai colleagues.[90]

If the group was marked by its fluid composition, the arena of its activity was more delimited. Chen Wangdao wrote that all participants lived quite close together in the French Concession, that such proximity led to frequent talks and debates.[91] After the preliminary discussions occurred in the offices of the *Weekly Review*, the meetings moved to Yuyang Lane, where the group had two residences, Numbers 2 and 6, that were used for discussion and a variety of revolutionary purposes. The former was the residence of Li Da, his wife Wang Huiyu, and Chen Duxiu; it was also the office of the journal *New Youth*. When the party would be officially established in 1921, this residence became a frequent meeting place.[92] But for this period, Number 6 was the more significant for group activity. It had been rented in 1919 by Dai Jitao, who stayed in the upper level when he was in Shanghai; it was later rented by Chen Duxiu. The sign on the residence announced a Sino-Russian News Agency, and the presence of the large number of White Russians in the area of Avenue Joffre made such an effort less suspicious. But the downstairs side room and eventually the parlor were actually classrooms for teaching Russian to prepare revolutionary Chinese to travel to the Soviet Union to learn about the revolution and study its applicability to the Chinese situation.[93] In August 1920 the residence also became the center for the Socialist Youth Corps (*shehui zhuyi qingnian tuan*), established by Yu Xiusong.[94]

With people, including Shen, living in the offices of the *Weekly Review* and working in the houses on Yuyang Lane, there was no dichotomy between workplace and living space. The continual presence of idealistic students discussing and arguing about the future of China in the spatial context of the language school, the Socialist Youth Corps office, and publication centers tended to promote the identity of work and life. That reality only enhanced the sense of the immediacy of politics, coupled as it was with such experiences as inspection raids of the premises by Vietnamese and French police.[95] It also threw men and women into a close environment that tested their ability to work together for common ends. We have no records of the group's meetings, but the ideas discussed were undoubtedly those about which Shen and others had written the preceding year. Mao Dun indicated that the contents of the meetings included exchanging news with other Communist groups (in Beijing and Guangzhou), studying the development of a more long-lasting organization, receiving new members, and preparing for the expansion of propaganda work.[96]

For a group composed largely of self-assured intellectuals, some undoubtedly prima donnas but all jealously guarding their own interests, the intimacy and intensity of work and daily life produced clashes that may have at times joined ideological proclivities with personal animus to produce fractured social linkages. Wang Huiyu commented on contentious meetings where opposing views clashed so vehemently that the meetings had to break up.[97] Zhang Dongsun, who had participated only briefly, left the group for ideological reasons.[98] Sharp personality differences even among friends had the potential for increasing and extending such clashes. Qian Gengxin, a visiting student from Hangzhou, noted how different Shen and Dai were. "After we were introduced, Shen came to talk about his opinions, straightforwardly and with clarity; it was like he was speaking to an old friend—earnestly and with genuine sincerity. At lunch I met Dai Jitao whose aura was completely that of the scholar. He didn't speak much, but whatever he said it was very serious."[99]

Yang Zhihua reported an incident that underscores the tensions brought by such idiosyncrasies of personality. One evening Shen, Yu, and about ten others returned from an excursion. Yang heard Dai Jitao crying in his room. On investigating, she found that the men had just formally established a Communist cell. Dai refused to join, fearful of the reaction of Sun Yat-sen. He cried because his own views had not prevailed and because the criticism of the group was unbearable to his psyche.[100] There were other personality clashes as well. Through various anecdotes, Li Da's hatred of Chen Duxiu and Li Hanjun became clear, as did his scorn for Zhang Dongsun and Shen Dingyi.[101] Young Yu Xiusong made known his strong feelings of inferiority and personal intimidation in the face of the arguments and positions of his older colleagues.[102]

The predominance of strong-willed figures in the group militated against the establishment of a stable network. Such stability is enhanced when the strands of connection are of varying strengths and directions of orientation and contain both equal and unequal relationships, so that individuals in a superior position can provide others with needed or desired items or satisfactions. In the Shanghai cell, the strongest linkage was the Zhejiang cluster. In the absence of other strong social bonds, there was little buffer against personal animus and the strains of daily life and ideological differences.

Relativity and Identity:
Shen in the Shanghai Cell

What identities did Shen reveal in Shanghai in 1919 and 1920, a period of self-definition during a significant, extended move into circles beyond his Zhejiang networks? There are three sources for plumbing Shen's identity; the factual historical record, his own writings, and the reports of others. In the first are found firm indications about certain identities. He was a journalist reacting to Shanghai, the effects of imperialism, and the gulf between social classes and gender. He was a reporter about and perhaps a participant in the events of the May Fourth period. He had a close relationship with Dai Jitao through their joint editorship of the *Weekly Review*, and through Dai an increasing admiration for Sun Yat-sen. He was a mentor and patron to young Hangzhou students caught up in the ideological currents of the time.

Shen's own writings convey a sense of his self-identity.[103] Though Shen would surely have seen himself as educator, patron, feminist, supporter of the masses, and proponent of remaking Chinese society through mutual understanding and love, in this period his words and some actions reveal considerable ambivalence. In the "struggle" (a word Shen used) for the new China, he advocated "taking over the knife" as the key to achieving "light," yet the means he prescribed in this struggle were education and mutual love. He championed the lower classes, scorning and satirizing the wealthy, powerful, and prestigious; as one of the elite, he seemed saddled with guilt. He championed feminist rights, serving as patron for younger women, yet he wrote of family emotional relationships that seem similar to those of the past. Who was the real Shen? Proponent of violent change or of peaceful evolution? A man retaining elite outlooks and assumptions or, perhaps driven by guilt, a dedicated supporter of the masses? A fervent supporter of feminism or primarily a man with a weakness for younger women? These unanswered questions may hint at only some of the ambiguities in Shen's identity.

But identity is also "totally social," shaped substantially by the perceiver's outlook, interests, and personality.[104] That created identity in turn provides the touchstone for any social contact with the perceived. Li Da's negative perceptions of many of the participants of the Shanghai cell in the summer of 1920 provide examples of the destructive power of identity-perception on the working of social networks. His 1959 assessment of Chen Duxiu seethes with jealousy and resentment, plays the Chinese cultural trump card of alleged sexual impropriety, and curries favor with Maoists.

Chen was a left-wing capitalist. He didn't understand Marxism-Leninism. He was only a good writer of fluent essays, and he understood much old literature. Therefore, many old scholars feared him. Hu Shi respected him; many youths worshipped him. . . . His leadership style was very high-handed and tyrannical. [After the formal establishment of the party] I was in propaganda work and had written materials coming to my place. . . . He did not originally permit me to go to his place; he had a woman [not his wife] living there. One time he came to my place and saw letters from comrades talking of work difficulties. When he saw them, he gave a curse, picked up a teacup, threw it, and broke it.

Chen didn't understand socialism clearly. He opposed me. . . . In 1922, I went to Hunan to join Mao.[105]

Though other comments revealed Chen's "patriarchal" leadership, especially after his being removed as party chairman in 1927,[106] the personal aggrievement of Li colors his perception and description of Chen. The question raised here is the extent to which individual evaluations of strong-willed and frequently opinionated Shanghai cell members or even statements of fact concerning their activity attain any sort of verity, especially thirty years after the fact.

Apart from specific memories ("Shen came to every meeting in the summer of 1920"—Mao Dun; "Shen was not frequently in Shanghai in the winter of 1921"—Bao Huiceng), three people in and connected to the Shanghai cell constructed a particular identity for Shen from their experiences in Shanghai. For Yang Zhihua, Shen was a New Culture leader who at the *Weekly Review* offices was, with Dai, the major attraction for many students coming to Shanghai—in short, an intellectual and revolutionary leader.[107] Yang's own background, assumptions, and perceptions and her relationship to Shen shaped this identity. For Li Da, jaundiced by his own bitterness, Shen's identity was encapsulated by the social category of "large landlord." For the thoroughgoing Marxist, this social identity made Shen "a very evil man" who "paraded falsely as a good man."[108]

The journalist and fellow Shaoxing native Shao Lizi saw Shen as an ally of sorts. Yet in his 1961 memoirs Shen emerges primarily with a political identity, as a member of the Guomindang. Shao argues that the Shanghai cell was composed from three sources: returned students from Japan, students from the Zhejiang First Normal School, and members of the Guomindang—the last of which he lists as Shen's identity.[109] In actuality, though Shen had ties to several soon-to-be Guomindang provincial assemblymen in Hangzhou, he did not join the Guomindang until more than two years later. Shao's attribution of such membership is anachronistic and, given the subsequent polarization of the political scene, limits the possibilities of seeing Shen in any other way than as a Guomindang member.

More in line with what we know of Shen from his actions and his writings, Shao suggests that there were two opinions about the nature of the political organizing underway in the summer of 1920. Some felt that an essential part of the secret organization was a strict organizational life for its members; others felt that they could approve of a secret organization but that they themselves could not participate in it. Shao claims that the strong-willed Shen, for whom the ideal of individual heroism was relatively strong, could not easily accept the leadership of others in such an organization.[110] The rocky road of Shen's participation in political parties over the next eight years would seem to bear out Shao's evaluation. Revolutionary leader, large evil landlord, Guomindang adherent, knight-errant: did any—or did all—of these perceptions approximate the salient features of Shen's identity?

"I don't know how many of me there are," Shen had exclaimed in a September 1920 poem. "He Really Is You; You Really Are I" had been the title of a November 1919 essay. The relativity both of individual identity and of individual relationships in groups and networks in a culture where values and standards were based on social relationships points to a social fluidity that necessitated continual efforts to define and redefine identity. Such uncertainty and ambiguity were at the heart of Chinese social relationships and also at the center of misunderstandings, misjudgments, and aggrieved feelings. In such a culture, especially at a time of turmoil and flux, political and social categorizations which stamped an identity on an individual or group could become an important weapon, for they in effect defined reality. As seen through this comparison of Shen's identities as gleaned from his writings and actions with those of the perceptions of others, these could range from realistic to fantastic. Shen would be dogged by the discrepancies of identity in his life and after his death. They would be the source of love for and hatred against him. They would be the cause of his death.

CHAPTER FOUR

Rushing to Calamity
Yaqian, 1921–1922

> *Do you like to raise your spirits idealistically? Don't you [rather] like to see harsh tragedy in a penetrating way? I often imagine a scene—and often go to this scene to amuse myself. What kind of scene? It's a deep, black cesspool into which I have fallen. There is no use being frightened or of crying for rescue for there is no one to hear. At that time I even realize that the filth and ugly stench of the excrement cannot dye my blood. I put to use my thoughts and bring my body fully into play to leap out of this deep, black cesspool—I simply must leap out of this deep, black cesspool, because outside the cesspool it must be relatively clean. That moreover is the utility of tragedy. Whatever is tragic must be considered as the reverse of utopia; it cannot be considered to be under the standard of disheartened pessimism.*
>
> "Answering Jiming" (Da Jiming), 1920

Apart from surprise, perhaps, that Shen would "often" choose to return to this nightmarish scene in his thoughts, the thematic similarity of this passage to that of other poems and short stories is striking: personal isolation in the midst of frightening and claustrophobic predicaments where there is no hope of making contact with others and where one must struggle independently. New here is Shen's almost yin-yang vision of tragedy as the reverse side of utopia—the calamitous joined with the ideal—rather than as a complement to some pessimistic weltschmerz. For Shen and his native place of Yaqian in 1921 and 1922, this vision linking the utopian with the tragic seems compellingly real.

The events of these years raise questions about Shen's identity, role, moral judgment, and programs, as he returned to his home community to effectuate the new social and political vision that had evolved during his years in Shanghai.

Natural Tragedy in the Southern Sands

Yaqian, Shen's native village, was located on the natural boundary of two microregions called Within the Dike and the Southern Sands. The former had been inside the original North Sea Dike, constructed centuries earlier to protect the county land from the waters of Hangzhou Bay and the shifting and unpredictable currents of the Qiantang River. The Sands had originally been situated north of the bay, but had become a part of Xiaoshan county when river currents shifted sharply northward in the mid-Qing dynasty. The North Sea Dike had ended just to the north of Yaqian as it abutted several small mountains which had originally been on the coastline, Phoenix Mountain (124 meters) and Hangwu Mountain (299 meters).

The two regions were sharply different.[1] Topographically, Within the Dike was generally flat, but there were isolated small hills and, beginning about two miles southwest of Yaqian, a range of mountains fanning out both east and west, varying from one hundred to four hundred meters in height. The land in the plains area was crisscrossed by a maze of rivers and canals running in every direction; the major mode of transportation (and in many cases, housing) was the boat. The two main waterways were the eastern extension of the Grand Canal, on which Yaqian was situated, and the Little West River, which drained the plains area. The major crops, as they were in the Southern Sands, were rice, jute, cotton, and mulberry. The topography of the Southern Sands was almost completely flat, formed as it was by alluvial deposits. Though there were still canals running in every direction, the region was marked by larger, almost parallel waterways on a northeast-southwest axis, which points to the crucial links in this region to the markets and urban places of Within the Dike.

During the early twentieth century the Southern Sands was the site of an ongoing natural tragedy. Frequently during the nineteenth century sections of the Sands, unprotected by major dikes, had been inundated during storms and washed into the sea. Beginning about 1905,

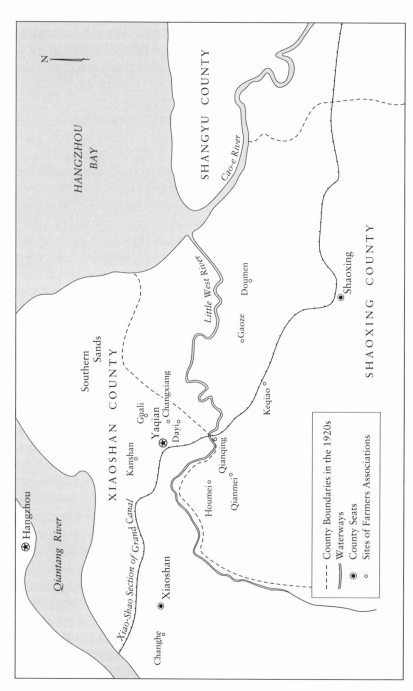

Map 4. The Yaqian Area, with Significant Sites in the 1921 Rent Resistance Movement

however, the main river currents began to shift again, depositing vast quantities of alluvium along the coast. Land-hungry farmers from counties in Shaoxing and Ningbo prefectures quickly began squatting on the new land, which provided excellent soil for the crops: by 1910 scattered thatched-roof farmhouses dotted the area. A 1914 military map of the coastline shows cultivated alluvial deposits over three miles wide, with villages densely studding the area. Nature had seemingly provided, if not a utopia, then at least a much-needed gift to a population historically caught in the squeeze of overpopulation and insufficient land. Greater and greater numbers of settlers poured into the Sands region.

But just as the currents gave life, they also took them back. The process of new land formation was tragically coupled with the erosion of land in other longer-established coastal areas. By the last years of the 1910s, even the newly cultivated land came under potent attack by the treacherous currents. In a continuing environmental and human tragedy, land collapsed into the surging river and was carried into the sea. Shen in a 1923 May Day essay described the horrors, pointing out that in the early 1920s all of one township and parts of three others had collapsed into the Qiantang.[2]

The tide and the wind pass by: with one wave, half the bamboo garden is gone. Another wave—several hills and mulberry gardens disappear. Amid the sound of the tide, the sound of the wind, and sometimes the sound of the rain, there is the sound of [earth] collapsing into the river, the sounds of the shouting and confusion of the house being broken in two and life being snatched away. . . . On moonless nights when there are solitary stars, the great river is very silent. The small glow of the fire in thatched roof houses. The utterly exhausted farmers deep in sleep. The sounds of the crying son, the dry sobbing of the wife, the long sighs of the elderly. Time passes. Suddenly comes the crash of falling rocks. . . . It is enough to turn the blood of the heroes of heaven and earth cold.

This time several people from western Xicang township where land had collapsed into the river came and said, "This time was on the whole a small collapse—only one family." Ah Di was there digging earth. Ah Ge, placing his hands behind his back, walked down to the river to see the force of the collapse. He saw it and knew it couldn't hold up. He limped back, shaking his head. . . . "We can't protect it." Ah Di waited a minute and threw down his hoe. He sat down on the ground, glancing at Ah Ge's sad expression and didn't say a word. From inside the thatched hut several women emerged, throwing down their sericulture implements. Rubbing their hands together, they said to their brothers, "This thing! What should we do?" The man who reported this to me concluded with one sentence: "This time it was only a small collapse."

Shen's image of struggling in the cesspool seems an appropriate metaphor for the human impotence of the victims of this natural disaster ("This thing! What should we do?"). Making the situation in the Southern Sands even more desperate were the exacting social and economic structures with which the farmers had to contend. This region had the highest concentration of landlords in the three ecological regions of the county, and the various kinds of rents they extracted produced almost continual hardships for tenants. The harshest method of assessing rent was requiring the payment of a fixed rate before the planting, most often in the preceding year.[3] If the farmer failed to pay, the landlord could quickly find another renter or send word to the county yamen for county officials to handle the issue. Farmers were in most cases powerless. In years of lean harvests, many farmers became refugees. An economic investigation of a village in the 1930s showed that even in good crop years more than 20 out of 170 households had to resort to begging. Many households were threatened annually with loss of fuel for cooking, and many survived only by traveling to Shaoxing for short-term work making tinfoil for funeral rituals.[4] While the early years of the Republic saw some flourishing industry in several market towns in the area— textile manufacturing, iron-smelting, soy-sauce brewing, rapeseed-oil production, and lace making—the area's economic development was retarded by its location to the north of critical transportation and communication routes, by considerable social unrest spawned by the unpredictable but frequent ravages of nature, and by the threat of destruction by the Qiantang currents.

In addition to social disturbances in the Sands itself, often initiated by settlers fighting over land, social stability in the vicinity of the towns of Yaqian, Qianqing, and Keqiao along the Grand Canal in the Xiaoshan-Shaoxing plains (directly south of the Sands) was also problematic. There the Grand Canal crossed the Little West River, running from the important rice transshipment entrepot of Linpu past a number of thriving market towns to the Three-River Sluicegate on Hangzhou Bay. Yaqian, Qianqing, and Keqiao were thus on and very near to important routes for travelers and merchants; for this reason, the area was a frequent target of thieves, brigands, and kidnappers.[5] Given its potential for both natural disasters and social difficulties and the presence of a population in flux (squatters and settlers, settled and displaced tenants, boatmen and traveling merchants, and criminal types), the region was potentially a combustible mix.

Shen and the Farmers

In the fall of 1920, armed with May Fourth optimism and revolutionary ideas about the importance of a new, group-directed individualism and new social forms, Shen returned to Yaqian. He made every effort to put into practice the sense of equality that he had gained during his years in Shanghai. Though his family continued to have household servants, he insisted that they call him by his personal name rather than by the title Third Gentleman.[6] He committed himself to dealing with farmers' problems. His essays and poetry during his Shanghai years had not indicated any special commitment to farmers; when Shen treated farmers in his writings, it was usually in a generic group of "laborers" that might include (as in the poem "Do You Dislike the Dirty?") farmer, lacquer worker, printer, cement worker, and factory worker.[7] Under this approach substantial numbers of his writings touch on the lives of farmers, but only three of his twenty-nine poems published in *Weekly Review* and *Awakening* until the fall of 1920 dealt specifically with the plight of farmers, and only one of thirty-three essays focused on the farm situation. Such a record does not indict Shen's motives for his role at Yaqian, especially given his rural upbringing and natural connection to the farm world, but it does indicate that—as for all radical May Fourth intellectuals in 1919 and 1920—rural revolution was not initially a compelling goal.

At Yaqian, Shen assumed the role of protector and supporter of the area's farmers, forging a strong personal link to his potential followers. He donned farmers' clothes (occasionally the water trousers worn by area fishermen) and, using the local dialect, talked with farmers about their living conditions.[8] He stopped tenants from working, gave them money, and encouraged them to go to the teahouse for refreshment. To tenants in difficulty, he gave generously.[9] Through this approach Shen was obviously trying to establish some greater rapport with the farmers. But this also appears to be Shen's conscious effort to actualize his prescriptive assumptions about solving China's problems set forth in his essay "He Really is You; You Really are I": there are no poor or rich; there is "no you, I, or he"; and "whoever under heaven is you, I, or he can be considered as one person joined together by love." In line with this way of thought and much to the dismay of his mother, who continued as the matriarch of the compound, he reduced the rent of his tenants, in some cases refusing to accept any at all.[10] Of him, a local history said, "Whenever farmers asked him, he would definitely help, exhausting himself to find ways of assisting."[11] When I asked his son Jianyun in the summer of 1993 to describe his father, without prompting he answered, "he was very kind to the masses, and he worked as a bridge to bring people together."

Shen's poetry from late 1920 through early 1922 especially reflects an understanding and sympathy with the frequent traumas of farm life. Not only did the farmers of the Southern Sands and Within the Dike face the cataclysm of raging rivers when there were floods in mountainous areas upstream, but they had to cope with the typical natural disasters faced by farmers in all cultures—flood, drought, and insect pests. In "Wind and Rain at the North Window," written at Yaqian in June 1921, Shen points to the world of nature (the mountain and the storm) separated from the world of man and to the stoicism of farmers having to deal with nature's caprices.[12]

> Black clouds touch the green mountain
> [Though] the mountain's appearance
>   depends on people who [see it],
> It is very much a pitiable place—
> And [the people near] do not diminish how it stands alone.
> A great wind suddenly blows up,
> Walking horizontally across the tree tops.
> Raindrops also strike horizontally;
> The sound of thunder following the lightning.
> The small child pulls its mother's skirt,
> Returns to the window, leaning his head
>   to listen to what is outside.
> The old and young of the household sit silently,
> [Seemingly] indifferent to the wind, rain, thunder, and
>   lightning moving in every direction.
> The green mountain does not know this place—
> As the faraway sky spits yellow light.

In such a frequently waterlogged world, problems of drought also dogged the farmer, especially in the heat of late summer. In "Water Wheels," written in August 1921, Shen examines the farmers' plight with insufficient irrigation water and with landlords.[13]

For two days it hasn't rained;
   I hear the sound of the water wheel.
For three days it hasn't rained;
   the sound of the water wheel is urgent.
For ten days, for half a month it hasn't rained;
The water wheels stand on end.
The east-flowing water has been turned to flow west.
For whom in this situation
   has such [great] energy been unloosed?
On the risk of offending the worthless . . .
Farmers!
At rent collecting time will they be able to take advantage
   in order to keep a few grains?

For his urban readers Shen appended an explanatory note to this poem further elucidating the farmers' predicament: "It doesn't matter what river or stream, they all have water wheels. The more wheels, the greater likelihood the water will be dried up."

The Yaqian Village School

In addition to his solicitude about farmers' agricultural and economic concerns and problems, Shen funded and established the Yaqian Village School, at which farmers or their children could enroll with no charge for tuition, books, or materials. Begun in the fall of 1920, it became first of all an educational center for those who had never had the opportunity to attend school. There were five different classes offered, some taught in the evenings for the benefit of local farmers. The school in the years from 1921 to 1923 had more than one hundred students.[14] In a number of his Shanghai writings, Shen had made clear his conception of education's central contribution to the new China: it unleashed the potentiality of individuals.

A wasteland, however huge, can be turned over by a hoe; a mineral deposit, however rich, can be dug out from the land by a hoe. We have a population of four hundred million; at least 99 percent of the wasteland and mineral resources in their minds has not been touched. What is the tool [to accomplish the goal]? Education.[15]

Again he argued, "Both ignorance and narrow-mindedness are obstacles to promoting civilization. Education is a good way of helping develop individual potentiality."[16]

In 1921 and 1922, the teachers were a small group of talented and idealistic graduates of the First Normal School in Hangzhou whom Shen specifically invited to Yaqian: Xuan Zhonghua, Yang Zhihua, Xu Baimin, and Tang Gongxian. With their participation in Shen's educational experiment following their contact with him during the May Fourth period, they were being linked closely to a man respected for his provincial leadership and famed for his New Culture writings. Such a connection could only bring advantages. From Shen's perspective, he was establishing a relationship with each as a patron-employer, one to whom they would owe gratitude for the opportunity to put into effect their ideals and to gain experience. Yang and especially Xuan came to play important roles in Shen's life, but the backgrounds of all these young adults shed light on the nature of the teaching at the school.

Xuan had been born in 1898 in Zhuji county, the son of a farmer who had owned six mu of paddy land at Zhonghua's birth.[17] But life became bitter for the family with ten children when income did not meet expenditures, and the land had to be mortgaged. Xuan was graduated from a village primary school in 1909 and an upper-level elementary school in 1913. In 1915 he entered Hangzhou's First Normal School, where he became known for his conscientious studiousness and his seriousness. He was on close terms with progressive teachers Chen Wangdao and Liu Dabai and the liberal principal Jing Hengyi. It is said that his peers respected him and tried to help him in his financial difficulties. Xuan became a leader in the Hangzhou Student Union in May and June 1919, leading student rallies, demonstrations, and strikes. During his time in Yaqian, Shen's relationship with Xuan became especially close. Cao Juren, another student who entered First Normal the same year as Xuan and Xu, remembered that "Xuan and Shen seemed to each other like one and the same soul. Even Xuan's handwriting came to be like Shen's."[18]

Yang Zhihua had been born in 1900 in Xiaoshan county, the daughter of a small landlord and silk merchant; the family had had connections to the family of Shen Dingyi for many years. Zhihua had been touched early on by progressive ideas, choosing to unbind her feet and seeking an education beyond Xiaoshan. She enrolled in the Hangzhou Women's Normal School in 1917 and, as a student, participated in the May Fourth demonstrations and the discussion of New Culture themes, influenced in her views by Chen Wangdao and Liu Dabai. It is clear that Shen saw Yang not only, or even primarily, as his daughter-in-law but also as his student and protégé. In 1919, as we have seen, Shen sent her progressive books and essays and brought her to Shanghai to work on the *Weekly Review*. Obviously aware of her talent and potential, Shen did what he could to politicize her. His invitation to the young mother to be a teacher at the Village School was part of that effort.[19]

Born in 1895, Xu, like Xuan, was a native of Zhuji county and entered the First Normal School in Hangzhou in the fall of 1915. In the May Fourth period he was elected as the Hangzhou student representative to the All-China Student Union meeting in Shanghai. After his graduation from First Normal in 1920, he served there as an adjunct teacher and organized and helped develop the Hangzhou labor movement. Tang, born in 1898, hailed from Suichang county in the southwestern part of the province. Also a First Normal student, he became with Xu and Xuan one of the key leaders of the Hangzhou Student Union.[20]

All four of the young teachers had all been closely involved in the May Fourth turmoil in the Hangzhou educational world.[21] The tempest over the essay "Against Filial Piety" in the *New Tides of Zhejiang* journal in late 1919 had led immediately to the journal's closing and the firing of four professors, among them Chen Wangdao and Liu Dabai, who had been associated with the journal. But the bloodletting did not stop there. In February 1920, when Principal Jing Hengyi was dismissed, students erupted in protest, their ire directed against Civil Governor Qi and provincial Education Minister Xia. Xuan, Xu, and Tang mobilized the resistance campaign. In response, authorities closed the school in mid-March. That action further mobilized students from the Hangzhou Student Union who believed that nothing less was at stake than the destruction of what had become known as the New Culture movement. A student union effort to present petitions at the provincial yamen led on March 27 to a military police attack and to bloodshed in the streets. This attack and the subsequent sending of military authorities to seal the school only fueled the student effort and fanned the flames all over the province.

Xuan, chairman of the Student Union's main policy-making council, took the lead in directing the continuing effort to oust Qi and Xia by trying to mobilize more of the province and even the nation. When the students attempted a protest march following a demonstration at the public athletic field along West Lake on April 21, a thousand military police blocked their way; in the ensuing melee more than eighty people were wounded. Once again anger ignited more opposition to the provincial hierarchy. In May the provincial assembly met to discuss the issues; in mid-June, they impeached Qi, who resigned the next day.[22]

Thus, the teachers who came to Yaqian had within the past year experienced the pain, frustration, and exhilaration of struggle against traditional conservative forces perceived as foes of the New Culture movement. They were filled with ideas of change and, on the strength at least of Qi's ouster, of the real potential of direct political action. In addition to the liberating and empowering goal of his school for individual farmers, the Yaqian Village School also became then a base for revolutionary activity. Teachers gave lectures in the classrooms located in Shen's compound in the village; Xuan Zhonghua taught an evening adult class.[23] The teachers visited farmers on their land and in their homes and investigated farm conditions; in private conversations they spread revolutionary ideas, propagandizing about antirent and antitax possibilities. They utilized customs in the area to popularize ideas about labor: on May Day 1922 they presented farmers at the school a kind of cake with the characters for "May Day commemoration." Their approach to the area's populace was pragmatic about and inclusive of other institutions in the area. Yang Zhihua noted that the Yaqian Village School had good relations, for example, with the relatively progressive staff of a nearby lineage school established by a local landlord.[24] There was, in short, little of the arrogance, dogmatism, or exclusivity that one might associate with recent graduates who had been engaged in a fervid battle against traditional ideas and ways.

A subsequent teacher at the school and another of Shen's protégés, Wang Guansan described visits that he and Yang made on an afternoon in the fall of 1922 to see students in neighboring villages. Visits to seven households revealed farm women who had a strong sense of the importance of education but who were constrained in their support by the realities of farm life. Wang and Yang were especially concerned about the high absence rate of young students. An older woman replied, "If they hadn't gone to chop wood and gather kindling today [and had gone to school instead], then we wouldn't have been able to cook. And there will be other days when they will have to do this." The distance also presented some difficulties for young children (this village was about two miles from Yaqian). Wang's conclusions on talking to the women was that rural education had to be structured so that farm children could take advantage of it and that old systems—even with such a common assumption as thinking in terms of "a year" of education—were not applicable.

Wang also described the great poverty of the farmers in this village. The inside of all thatched-roof farm homes, he said, were the same: black rafters, gray walls, a dirt floor, a kitchen table, a bench, farm implements, and amulets from the local temple. There was generally nothing on the walls; rather more well-off families might have several advertisements for brands of incense stuck on the wall. "The floors were covered with chicken shit; and people walked through it with their bare feet." Amid such conditions, the popular saying in the area: "Nothing to eat, nothing to wear—those things still go to the little king [*dianwang*, the name farmers in the area gave to landlords]!"[25]

The Origins of the Yaqian Farmers' Movement

A revolutionary process develops dialectically: like the events in Hangzhou in the spring of 1920, one act or decision becomes the context within which subsequent acts are carried out or decisions made, and those later acts, in turn, are reacted to or built upon. Such a process is unpredictable. There may be a continuous skein of events, each ratcheting up tensions and commitment, helping to create a snowballing effect; there may be acts that defuse tensions and diffuse commitment or that reorient developments. It is probably the case that the initial events in any revolutionary process do not seem to be so when they first occur. Certainly it is unlikely that Shen Dingyi could have imagined the effects of a request that came to him in April 1921. He had, to be sure, set out a context that was conducive to further change: his establishment of the Yaqian school and his publicly noted patronage of area farmers.

In that month, two Yaqian brothers, Li Chenghu and Li Chengjiao, both in their sixties, sought his help in recovering money still owed them for the previous year's rapeseed harvest by an unscrupulous merchant from the town of Anchang, five miles east on the Three River Plain. Six other households were affected by the merchant's actions. In this instance, the Li brothers and others needed the money for planting the new crop. Despite Shen's openness to the farmers in the vicinity, neither brother knew him, and Chengjiao initially sought out his own landlord to make the first approach to Shen. When Shen was apparently unsuccessful in getting the money from the merchant, he provided the necessary money himself, reportedly telling Li, "This money was not originally mine: it was yours—rent for farming our land. Therefore it is your sweat and blood. Count it as farmers helping farmers, not as my helping you."[26] Though this quotation first appears in a biography of Li Cheng-hu that was likely written by Shen himself in February 1922, this is not a case of revolutionary self-promotion; in essays and speeches in the first half of 1921, Shen had frequently set forth this sentiment.

Had the Lis' request not been followed by a more general problem in the area, it would be seen simply as a problem with one unscrupulous merchant. The problem was the rising inflation that was making life increasingly difficult. The Shaoxing newspaper *Yuezi Ribao* in 1922 noted the inflationary spiral that had continued to push up the cost of rice.[27] In late spring and early summer 1921, area rice merchants exacerbated the problem by arbitrarily raising prices. Most certainly on the basis of complaints from tenants, Shen encouraged farmers to confront a particularly notorious merchant in the town of Kanshan. It may have been this affair that led him to suggest for the first time the establishment of a farmers association. "One jute stalk is easy to break," Shen told some farmers, "but you can't break a bundle." Led by Li Chenghu, a group of farmers marched two miles to Kanshan, attacked the rice store, and continued the march to other offending stores there and in other towns. Along the way, the protest march drew more and more participants wanting to constrain rice merchants to restore preinflation prices.

There is no information whether in the face of destruction or threatened destruction the merchants lowered their prices, but the farmers' *perception* was that they had succeeded in the protests, striking a blow against a manipulative elite. Such a perception further inspired them to pursue other local issues, and Shen readily took the initiative. The Little West River, serving as the border between Xiaoshan and Shaoxing counties, was abundant with fish, but Shaoxing county elites (*guan-shen*) controlled the authority to raise fish there. Yaqian farmers decided to try to assert their interests in participating in fish-raising. When the Shaoxing magistrate came to the river to inspect the fish dikes, Shen met him and asked him to come to his home to meet interested farmers to discuss the issue. The magistrate, unable to say a word in self-defense, admitted to Shen that the position of the Yaqian farmers was well taken, and he agreed that the authority to raise fish in the river should be given by legal document to the farmers.[28]

These first stages in the farmers' pursuit of redress and achievement of what seemed sensible authority were perceived as successful and were attained without excessive effort or adverse consequences. The farmers were clearly profiting from the general power and prestige of their patron Shen. During the summer he was reelected to the third provincial assembly, the session of which would open in October; his rather cavalier 1918 vacating of the chairmanship of the assembly turned out not to be a significant obstacle to his reelection. The reelection itself only increased his local status and influence. The local history also suggests that the farmers' sense of success brought them the first taste of the allure of joint action.[29]

It was at this juncture that Shen ratcheted up the level of radicalism in his conversations with and speeches to farmers in the vicinity of Yaqian, becoming the first political leader in twentieth-century China to begin to talk of organizing farmers to challenge the power of the landed elite.[30] The premises of his movement he set forth in his first address at the East Mountain Temple, almost directly across the Grand Canal from Shen's residence.

I am not going to the cities where perhaps several thousands or tens of thousands may listen to my speech. I am going to the rural villages to Buddhist temple platforms where only a hundred or so farmers and workers come to listen. This is because you are my beloved [*qin'ai*] friends. You have built the earth with your hard work. Today I come to tell you: you use much hard work to build the earth but you eat all the world's bitterness. I hope to establish a law for you to escape this bitterness. However, this action is at base your own; therefore, you must understand and you must struggle.[31]

Shen always exhibited his identity with farmers. Whenever he spoke to farm groups, he wore the black felt cap popular in the area and the clothes of farmers, and he spoke in the dialect of the area. His message took on added power because of his renowned eloquence as a public speaker; his sonorous voice and use of clever and often earthy images gave him a charisma that reportedly could easily sway listeners to his point of view. Reports indicate that the farmers' reaction to Shen and his message was warmly enthusiastic.[32]

Whereas the earlier talk of associations had been in the context of farmer solidarity, in the late summer Shen began to define the enemy. At Kanshan's Dongqizao Buddhist temple on August 19, Shen chose as his topic "Who is Your Friend?" The answer was the workers, who wanted, he claimed, to join with farmers to make a "big stone" that would not easily be broken up; they did not want to make a "pile of loose sand." The key was joint action against the common enemy, the capitalist class, and the goal was that "the things of this world should all be returned to the possession of the laborers." Near the end of his speech he told the crowd, "I am a capitalist. [And yet] I've spoken these words.

But I am absolutely not a thorny water chestnut wrapped in lotus leaves—that will come piercing through. I certainly understand that I have eaten and worn things that I've received [through my being a capitalist], but they all came from the laborers' sweat and blood. I cannot [however] blot out my conscience." He welcomed any capitalist in the audience to come up to discuss the issues if he felt that Shen was wrong. But, said Shen, "I know they won't dare. I know they hide behind people's backs, and in secret they would like to pressure me to stop."[33] The use of the antagonistic rhetoric could not have been swallowed easily by landlords, who must have heard the rumors that swept out of Kanshan that afternoon. What was Shen up to? Was he a Bolshevik? Where would such rhetoric, such incitement lead? The heavens seemed to have responded in kind that evening—at least from the perspective of the landlords. The area was hit by incredible deluges, high winds, and severe flooding; crop losses were high as cotton plants were inundated and buried in mud. The Qiantang River ferry was halted because of the danger of its being sunk.[34]

On September 23 in the local temple at Hangwu Mountain, Shen spoke on "Farmer Self-Determination" to a reported audience of several thousand farmers from twenty to thirty area villages.[35] He used the reclamation of alluvial soil in the Southern Sands as an example of the predicament of the farmer.

When the Qiantang changes course and soil collapses in the east and rises in the west, when the muddy alluvium becomes grassy marshland, you can go out and use your strength to reclaim it. . . . But, on the one hand, you don't have the organization; [individuals trying to do it on their own] can't build a dike, and the situation fosters feuding and fighting. On the other hand, powerful landlords under the capitalist system act as follows: the Zhao family sets Zhao family pennants around several hundred or several thousand mu; the Qian family does the same. They go to the land office and register it: the Zhao family so much, the Qian family so much. All that you can do is become a household under the landlords' feet.

He condemned the landlords' contention that "to plant one year's crop you should collect one year's rent"—before the planting of the crop. While pointing to the devious greed of the landlord, Shen praised the farmers, whose "ability to produce is greater than the source of Qiantang River is distant." He called on farmers to join together and organize quickly and carefully, predicting that "one day the great landlords will surrender to you."[36] The farmers' response to Shen: "When we heard his speech, it was like seeing the sunlight."[37]

Shen spent August and part of September making speeches in the Southern Sands, in the vicinity of Yaqian, and in western and central Shaoxing county. His message was straightforward: join together and do not pay rents. Despite Shen's frequent "bull-in-a-china-shop" approach, he was also a clever politician. At a local temple in a village near Kanshan Shen was on a platform urging nonpayment of rents. In the village was a teacher and small landlord who opposed Shen's coming there to speak. The teacher had the great respect of the villagers who, in turn, urged Shen to desist so as not to offend the teacher. Shen's response: "Don't worry; I have a method." He asked the farmers to move a chair for the teacher to be seated and then he continued: "Today I will tell you what this teacher has taught me." And he recited the passage from the *Mencius* when Mencius sees King Hui of Liang: "The king said: 'You have not considered a thousand *li* too far to come, and must therefore have something of profit to offer my kingdom?' Mencius replied: 'Why must you speak of profit? What I have to offer is humanity and righteousness, nothing more.'" The teacher listened as Shen quoted other passages, clearly exhibiting himself as a master of the classics. The teacher was speechless as Shen won the day with the appropriateness of the message and the method.[38]

Not every "little king" remained silent in the face of Shen's challenges. Shen went to the local temple at Dayi, a few miles southeast of Yaqian, where he called on farmers to organize and strive for a 30 percent rent reduction. In the middle of his speech, one of the most powerful landlords in the region, Wang Yuanhong, strode into the temple and challenged Shen. "Third Gentleman is a fool! He's insane!" Wang warned the farmers about listening to Shen, saying that if they listened, they would eat great bitterness.[39] With his typical courage in the face of challenge by authority figures, Shen was not in the least cowed and continued to talk about why landlords did not deserve to receive any rent.

Shen had never shied away from confronting people with great status and power. As a mere nineteen-year-old magistrate in Yunnan, he had confronted the father of a provincial governor in a famous episode. Early in the century, the inhabitants of the Guangtong county seat defecated and urinated in a spot right outside the east gate. Walking was difficult since excrement was everywhere. Shen had the mess cleaned up, built a public toilet, and set up strict regulations to stop the traditional practices. When he went to inspect the area, he saw an old man squatting in the entrance of the gate to the city and shitting on the ground. Shen was furious. The man was the father of Governor Zhu Jiabao of Anhui province, a "local emperor" who lorded his connections over all and was known to be involved in corruption and pettifogging; on hearing of the regulations, he was going to prove that no young magistrate would change the town's customs. Shen sent runners to bring the man to him. Old Zhu resisted, screaming and shouting. Shen then gave the yamen clerks and runners orders to flog Zhu's buttocks. They were fearful, given the man's local power, and did not move. Shen grew even angrier. He personally went back to clutch Zhu, ordering the yamen employees to flog the man forty times with a flat bamboo cane. After the flogging, there was Old Zhu crying and shouting on the damp ground, not having believed that such a young magistrate would have dared to have the father of a governor beaten.[40]

August and September saw the spread in the popularity of the idea of a farmers association and the emergence of farmers in addition to the Lis who could lead the incipient movement. Chen Pusheng was a forty-three-year-old tenant farmer from a hamlet near Yaqian; he had made a meager living in the beginning of his career as a fruit vendor in Yaqian. He was an excitable man, who enthusiastically threw himself into the propagandizing effort. Like Shen, he was an excellent speaker; the two of them took most of the speaking assignments in the proselytizing campaign.[41] Shan Xialan, from Qianmei village near the town of Qianqing less than three miles from Yaqian, was a tenant farmer who had subsidiary occupations as a carver of pictures and figures and a smallpox vaccinator. A Christian, at least briefly, he was mercurial and perspicacious (sources indicate that he had a talent for being able to see through the falsities of people).

The Yaqian Farmers Association

The Yaqian Farmers Association was established on September 27 at a festive meeting at the East Mountain temple in Yaqian. The temple (which Shen had simply commandeered) and the area around it were crowded with throngs of enthusiastic and happy farmers; red pennants were flying; the air was filled with the sounds of slogans, music, and the explosions of long strings of firecrackers.[42] The main business of the day was the selection of six deputies to manage the association and the distribution of the association's declaration of principles and its regulations, which Shen Dingyi had drafted. Li, Chen, and

Shan, along with three other farmers (one of whom also hailed from near Yaqian), were the chosen deputies, elected for one-year, renewable terms. Three composed the council and three the executive committee. The council, headed by Li Chenghu, was to decide the association's agenda and settle policy disputes. The executive committee was to control the association's registration and records and oversee linkages that might be formed with other village associations. The regulations of which these are a part made it clear that the association stood in opposition to the landlords.[43]

In the association's declaration, Shen asserted that stance stridently.

Farmers support the strength of the greatest number of Chinese, paying for government expense, military expense, educational expense, and all sorts of proper and improper expenses in society. [All] depends on the farmers' sweat and blood as the source. In exchange for their sweat and blood, the farmers have gotten destitution, exhaustion, lack of education, and bitter suffering.

When there is a bumper crop, the landlord has it—the farmer has no part. When crops are bad, the landlord records in the rent book that they still have a debt for the next year. . . . Towns have pawnshops, assorted goods stores, rice and cotton stores—there's not one that does not try to skin the farmers and take advantage of that sweat and blood.

Generally the elites in this age of capitalism do not support the needs of our lives. The economic system they revere and worship produces our poverty as it produces their wealth and happiness. Farmers and workers are alike in this.

Our awakening is therefore our future. Our organization is our path for leaving the evil and moving to the relatively better future. To decide our fate is really to decide the fate of all the people of China. The whole wide country welcomes the splendid land we are making with our hoes and iron harrows. . . . Through the hoe used on the land the farmer dispenses power. Therefore, we must recognize that "the land is a tool through which farmers dispense power to nourish all human beings." Isn't this worthy of the farmers trying to protect?[44]

The declaration reiterates themes from his speeches at Hangwushan and Kanshan. Noteworthy are his dual linkages: landlord and merchant under the rubric of the enemy capitalist elites, with farmer and worker the impoverished victims. Especially frightening to the landlords in this declaration was the assertion that farmers dispensed power through the land for all others;[45] not very hidden are the implications that farmers are in positions of authority over the land with regard to the nourishing of all humans and that farmers might seize control of that resource. The association, the path to "the relatively better future," was Shen's creation of a new social form, whose significance he had become convinced of while in Shanghai, and it is likely that his suggestion that this action was related to the fate of all Chinese reflects on this path-breaking effort as a potential model for the future. The association would be the way out of the cesspool; Shen's use of "relatively better future" echoes "relatively clean outside the cesspool" from his earlier metaphor.

The chief agricultural aims of the association were the realization of a 30 percent reduction of rents; changing the measure of rental grain from a "large peck" containing seventeen catties to a "public peck" containing fifteen catties; eliminating a so-called cart-hire expense that the landlords required of the tenants; and doing away with the payment of rent before the crop was planted, installing instead a system where rent was paid on the basis of the harvest. But the association, as envisioned by Shen, had more varied and much larger aims. It proposed doing away with superstitions, sweeping away illiteracy, liberating women, opposing old-style education, and supporting the May Fourth emphasis on science and democracy. In order to begin to realize these general aims, the association threw out the temple's statue of the bodhisattva and simply took the temple and its courtyard as the office of the association. Over the protests of the head monk, who vowed revenge, it forced the monks to relocate to another temple. It promulgated the ideas that "women had the same qualities as men" and that "men and women alike receive the same education to direct their faculties." The association supported marriage by choice and forbade footbinding and ear-piercing.[46] On the arched memorial monument in Yaqian, the legend "Respect chaste women and filial sons" was blotted out and replaced by "Long live women's liberation." In addition a couplet was added:

> Beyond doubt in the Twenty-four Histories are written the
>   ethical teachings of those who eat people.
> Beneath this memorial arch there are the ghosts
>   of I don't know how many crushed women
>   who have been wronged.[47]

Interviews in the 1980s with area farmers indicate that in the beginning there were only a few farmers traveling to Yaqian from area villages, but the trickle of interest turned into a torrent within only a week.[48] On Saturday, October 1, so many people were coming to Yaqian to register as members of the association or to seek information about the establishment of their own associations that the Grand Canal and the Little West River were reportedly clogged with boats. Up to five or six hundred registered as new members of the association that day, receiving copies of the declaration and the regulations. Several thousand of these had been printed, but the supply was soon exhausted as the stream of interested farmers kept coming, many of them wanting to see Shen Dingyi.[49]

By this time, Shen was likely in Hangzhou, for the first session of the provincial assembly met on October 3. His work in initiating and giving life to the farmers association and in shaping its direction and guidelines was completed. As the association continued to develop during the fall, Shen played an important role in the assembly; we do not know how often he returned on what would have been roughly an hour and a half trip. In any case, he did not insert himself into the decisions and directions of the organization, allowing Li and the other deputies free rein.

During the next two months word of the organization and its goals spread rapidly across the southern coastal area of Hangzhou Bay. Shen had called the network of leaders into being through his patronage; now they would in turn serve as the nodes of other networks, which individual leaders would construct on traditional cultural forms. The interlinked waterways that knitted the Xiaoshan-Shaoxing plain together provided the vehicle for the expansion. Delegations of farmers boated to Yaqian, the center and the symbol of the movement, to learn organizational procedures and tactics; each day more than twenty farmers were registered and the names of their villages recorded. Farmers associations sprang up in eighty-two villages and towns in an area of 200 to 240 square miles: thirty-six in Xiaoshan, forty-four in Shaoxing, and two in Shangyu county, across the Cao-e River to Shaoxing's east. An estimated one hundred thousand farmers and their families became involved.[50]

What were the sources of the formation of these revolutionary associations? Many were established through ties to Shen and proximity to Yaqian. All but ten of the involved villages were within ten miles of Shen's home, and fully twenty-six (almost a third of the total) were located within a mile on either side of the Grand Canal between Yaqian and Qianqing. Involvement in the effort came from a variety of reasons. Chen Pusheng, as we have seen, heard about the movement and wanted to participate. Shen Zhengfeng, the association leader in Changxiang village, was related to Shen Dingyi.[51] Apart from Shen, links between Yaqian and towns and villages in Shaoxing came through social, economic, and labor networks. The Grand Canal directly linked thriving market towns to Yaqian. Marriage networks between lineages were well developed in the region. Many farmers in the Yaqian area traveled for part-time subsistence work to the cottage tinfoil industry in Shaoxing.

News of the association, its goals, and its founder spread through these personal connections.

Another indication of this dynamic is the clustering of association sites. Near the town of Keqiao about eight miles from Yaqian on the Grand Canal there were six associations established in towns and villages. Similarly, near the towns of Qianmei and Houmei, south and west of Qianqing, eleven associations were formed. The history of both the Keqiao and the Qianmei-Houmei associations points to another aspect of the rapid organizing, the active proselytizing by already committed members. Deputy Shan Xialan, the tenant-carver-vaccinator, organized these especially active associations. Chen Pusheng focused his organizational activity in villages to the west of Yaqian, near his home.[52] Both Shan and Chen had their greatest success in villages near their own native places. It is striking how often the men involved in the association are described as enthusiastic and excited.[53] Through November they had every reason to be, for there was great optimism about what they could accomplish in light of what had happened and in light of their patron. As a further indication of this developing organizational ethos and optimism, farmers in late November established at Yaqian an Alliance of Farmers Associations (*nongmin xiehui lianhehui*).

Calamity

Shortly after the alliance was formed, landlords in the vicinity of Yaqian marshalled more than eighty rent-gathering boats to be sent to tenants. To defend against them, the farmers association organized hundreds of farmers to meet the boats with anti-rent slogans and with rocks and stones. Many boats were sent away empty or half-filled after being attacked by stone-throwing tenants. There were at least two beatings of landlords who tried to insist on collecting the full amount of rent. One was a man named Gao who had been a police official and whose father was head of the Xiaoshan County Chamber of Commerce. Presuming that his status would awe tenants into complying, Gao was obstinate—until the tenants turned on him and he fled.[54]

An episode with a more serious impact on the movement occurred on December 8, when Zhou Renshou, the son of a large landlord from the town of Qianmei, brought a large group of supporters to Qingwu village to collect rents.[55] The Zhou family had refused to recognize the legitimacy of any farmers association, much less its authority to reduce rent payments. Association leader Shan Xialan, reportedly with some five to six hundred tenants, approached Zhou and asked him to go with them to some third party who could inform Zhou of the state of things. Zhou cursed Shan and the tenants; and with a sense of certainty that he would be backed up by Shaoxing officials, he ordered his subordinates to tie up the tenant leaders. With great anger, the tenants seized Zhou and beat him. He was able to escape and went immediately to the Shaoxing yamen to accuse the farmers association, call for an investigation, and have the instigators of the affair punished.[56] The incident served to escalate the growing tensions and to heighten the fears of the already concerned elites.

The reality of confrontation and potential violence thrust new decisions into the hands of the associations. Some figures, like ramrod Xu Meikun (b. 1893), a Socialist Youth League member and the Xiaoshan native who had spent the past two years as a Hangzhou labor organizer, counseled more active struggle.[57] But in the aftermath of the Zhou Renshou beating the vast majority of farmers association members favored peaceful demonstrations; they divided themselves between the county yamens in Xiaoshan and Shaoxing and went to kneel in petition for rent relief, actions that brought the Xiaoshan magistrate to order police beatings.[58] Some farmers were quite fearful about what might happen, asking Li Chenghu, "Is it possible that we are rushing to calamity?"[59]

The Zhou affair also prompted twelve Shaoxing landlords to meet with the magistrate at the county self-government office between December 10 and 17 to plan strategy to destroy the farmers associations, which they viewed as an increasingly serious threat. The words of one, Hu Shouchen, recorded later, provided the rationale for acting.[60]

Shaoxing farmers this year have had an abundant harvest; all the tenants can sing. The great number remain mutually peaceful—there are no differences. They are not scheming like those in neighboring Xiaoshan where farmers associations are spreading rumors. But it is slowly spreading to Shaoxing. It is being encouraged by the Communists. They cannot know what their antirent slogans mean. If there is abuse, it's not on the part of landlords; it's on the part of those who detain boats; it's on the part of those who have beaten good tenants who have still paid their rent. We simply can't bear those who would attack or cut off [traffic] at important points, not allowing rent boats to enter the area. This thing is small, but it's still spreading; we must control it to establish peace. We must punish the leaders of this evil in order to block the sprouts of chaos.

The decision was to ask the military to use force to repress the movement. Landlord Tao Zhongan was designated as the man to contact Sheng

Kaidi, the commander of the Third Brigade of the Zhejiang provincial forces, garrisoned in Shaoxing.[61] As a measure of the elite status of the group, Tao would still be among the county elite after World War II, serving then as a member of the second Shaoxing County Administrative Conference.[62]

The catalyst for military response came from a peaceful protest march and demonstration led by Shan Xialan on December 17 from Qianqing to the county seat to ask county authorities for relief. Shan had organized the Qianqing area associations, and they had been urged on by the labor organizer Xu Meikun. It was in that area that the outbursts against landlords Gao and Zhou had occurred. The Qianqing association itself flew an association flag, and members wore association symbols on their breasts.[63] More than a thousand participated in the march to Shaoxing, with the marchers extending almost a mile. Some carried incense, while others, more symbolically, carried rice straw that had been eaten by insects.[64] Keqiao police sent word to the county officials when the marchers passed the town so that the crowd was met at the west gate of Shaoxing by soldiers who prevented them from entering the city. Even though the effort was unsuccessful, it scared the elites and prompted their decision to strike the next day. A warrant was issued for Shan's arrest.[65]

It is also certain that a declaration from a group calling itself the Organized Farmers of Xiaoshan's Southern Sands was more frightening than any statement that had yet appeared.[66] Printed in the December 20 issue of Shanghai's *Republican Daily News*, it is likely that this outright call for revolution was circulated in the area by this time. Recounting the natural and social issues facing farmers in the Sands, the declaration specifically called Shen's late summer speech on peasant self-determination the beginning of the movement. It urged the farmers to organize the antirent struggle against the landlords. The cause of society's instability and inequity was the propertied class itself, and the declaration promised to fight "from this day forward" to break the power of that class. In the end, it admonished all those in the unpropertied classes to arise.

The crushing of the movement came on Sunday, December 18, as representatives of the Alliance of Farmers Associations met at the movement's temple headquarters in Yaqian to discuss strategy. The provincial government had dispatched by boat a company of soldiers led by Sheng Kaidi and sixty county police to the meeting hall. Just as lunch was about to begin, over one hundred soldiers carrying rifles with bayonets affixed surrounded the temple, in effect capturing the approximately hundred and thirty farmers inside the compound. In the vicinity around the temple were family members of those inside, some preparing food for lunch, others simply waiting and talking. Fearful about their fathers, sons, and brothers trapped inside, they yelled for help from others in Yaqian and to spread the word in nearby hamlets. In a very brief time an estimated thousand farmers lined up to confront the military and to demand the freeing of those men inside the temple. When the soldiers sensed that more time might embolden the farmers to resist military demands, they attacked the unarmed crowd with their bayonets, wounding three people. As farmers fled, the military ordered those inside the temple to leave; three people, two of them association leaders, Shan Xialan and Chen Pusheng, were arrested and taken to Shaoxing.[67]

Li Chenghu had been outside the temple welcoming people to the meeting when the soldiers arrived. Unnoticed, he escaped temporarily. Even though his son pleaded with him to go into hiding, he refused, and he was arrested in his field on December 27. He was unbowed before the magistrate who had earlier beaten petitioners, declaring, "I am a councillor of the Yaqian farmers association. I am one who proposed to organize the farmers associations. I am one who still proposes a 30 percent rent reduction."[68] The magistrate responded by placing Li in chains and fetters. Li died of illness in prison less than a month later, on January 24, 1922. Chen too became sick while in prison and died a month after his release from a sentence whose length is uncertain. Shan was released after three and a half years in prison and died sometime before 1949.[69]

In the aftermath of the Sunday crackdown, the provincial governor sent two civilian government representatives. The first was to investigate the case and see it to its conclusion: violators of the government policy were to suffer heavy punishment. The second came to announce that the rent reduction movement was unacceptable and illegal because it was detrimental to tax collection and disturbed the peace. His role was to symbolize to local farmers the force and presence of state authority; the provincial government was, in effect, saying to farmers that though they may have a supporter in high places, he did not have the power to effect the kind of change he had initiated. Announcements were posted in the two counties that the farmers associations were outlawed and leaders were to be arrested.[70]

The suffering went well beyond the individual plights of association leaders, for in the taking of the temple at Yaqian, the association registers with the names of all members and the leaders of the eighty-two organizations were seized. An estimated five hundred were arrested on the basis of the registers. The crackdown inaugurated a lengthy period of severe repression in which landlords more often resorted to government power for rent collection. Police were frequently sent to villages to collect sums of unpaid rent. In a village near the town of Guali, about three miles from Yaqian, for example, a tenant named Wang rented eleven mu of cotton land for eighty-four yuan annually. When Wang fell ill, his wife was unable to pay the entire sum. Three times the magistrate of Xiaoshan sent military police to collect the amount. Eventually the wife and child were forcibly hauled into court and held until the money could somehow be obtained.[71] In at least one other case, the Xiaoshan magistrate sent police to collect rent from recalcitrant tenants of the county assembly chairman, a further evidence of the alliance of officials and landlords.[72] In the weeks immediately following the crackdown, there were minor episodes of rent resistance, especially in Shaoxing county, often initiated by a single farmer, but they were simply briefly glowing embers in a dying fire.[73] The hope and optimism engendered in the process of the rent resistance movement had indeed rushed to calamity.

The Mystery of Shen

And what of Shen Dingyi, outspoken opponent of the socioeconomic status quo, who had initiated, incited, and organized the farmers' antirent and reform movement? From October into December, during the successful flurry of organizing, the beginnings of rent resistance, and its violent conclusion, Shen played the role of a powerful and active member of the Zhejiang Provincial Assembly. Though this assembly (likely as a result of his abdicating his chairmanship in the 1917–18 session) did not elect him as chair (he received only two votes), records show him as a key spokesman on many of the major issues, from assembly corruption to education to foreign relations to the plight of farmers.[74] Many of the values and themes that flowered in his late summer speeches and discussions with Yaqian farmers seemed still to animate him in the assembly.

In October and November, for example, Shen was the major spokesman for impeaching the assembly chairman and vice-chairman for vote-buying and corruption; he was supported by his earlier-established network of upholders of liberal parliamentary goals and procedures, among them notably Xu Zuqian and Ren Fenggang, joined by progressive lawyer Cha Renwei. Shen's long speech of October 15 appealed to law, moral authority, and especially anticapitalism. The insidious lure of capitalism was the source of the venality of politicians and warlords. "Since the industrial revolution, the world—even in desolate places—has been attacked by the principle of 'ready money.' There is no emotion, duty, or beauty that has not been progressively eroded by money. Money has become a kind of special human quality equal to others. Therefore, human qualities have been swept away. . . . The present assembly chairman is struggling with [the issue] of human qualities."[75] The assembly had been elected to uphold the new provincial constitution by controlling such venality. With this obvious corruption, he asked, how could the assembly act with good conscience? How could it, for the people, impeach other wrongdoing in the future? Shen called for disciplinary action. Though he had support among his network of like-minded assemblymen, his call fell on deaf ears. The only practical effect was to make enemies of powerful men.

In his first speech to farmers at Yaqian in the summer, he had spoken of his hope to establish a law for their relief. On November 6, Shen made an impassioned speech in the assembly on farmers' issues, particularly calling on the assembly to pass legislation on rent reduction. The occasion was his reaction to a letter written to the provincial government by local Xiaoshan-Shaoxing officials attacking the farmers movement as Bolshevist-inspired. Shen's speech called for the assembly to support the farmers.[76]

This is a severe case: farmers seek relief. . . . Nowadays if there is such a public request, it's criticized as Bolshevism. That is done to cow the effort. Unless the local officials make deputies of the producers' class, we will drive farmers to their deaths. The assembly must act. Here are the reasons.

First, the collapse of twenty to thirty thousand mu in the last ten years has created many farm refugees. This past summer and fall the area was hit once again by wind and rain, but landlords entered the area as usual to receive next year's rent, called "current rent." Farmers are compelled to come up with it even though it means that they'll not have enough food to eat. Their deaths continue—like the Kanshan farmer Li Wenxiao who was dunned by landlord Zhang Mingzheng for the last of his rent. Li had no alternative but to go to his relative by marriage Shen Jinsong to pawn clothes, hoping to get enough to pay the rent. But it wasn't enough and the pawnbroker wouldn't take them anyway. Li was so overwrought that he spat blood and fell down dead. This happened on October 20 in Kanshan township.

Furthermore in an area along the coast designated Ruren more than a hundred people have starved to death and more are dying—a tragic, ugly situation. Many more are not going to be able to avoid death in the coming year. Are we or are we not going to take responsibility for it?

Second, under these circumstances farmers have gone to Xiaoshan's government offices to seek relief. Xiaoshan's magistrate Zhuang Lunhan not only wouldn't hear them and take any responsibility, but he drove them away with police. On the one hand, he forbids them to petition for redress; on the other, he accuses them of instigating a Bolshevist movement. According to the eighth article in the constitution, people have the authority to petition officials: this is a government problem. Where did the name Bolshevism come from? What are its contents? What are its methods? Local officials don't understand any of this. Is it people coming to seek help from the local government? This assembly must act if the civil governor hasn't responded in eight days.

Again Shen was supported by his liberal constitutionalist associates, but again there was no practical action forthcoming, the assembly passing instead a meaningless directive to "protect the poor." His arguments in the assembly deliberations reveal clearly that he was continually aware of developments in Xiaoshan; but he did not apparently insert himself actively in the movement that he had promoted and supported.

One wonders about Shen's judgment and sense of morality as a leader and patron of society's subordinated. If he could have persuaded the assembly to support the movement, it would have been a revolution underwritten by the state. It is clear, however, that Shen, despite his considerable prestige in Hangzhou, did not have the power or support to establish programs that ran counter to the interests of the conservative assembly or governmental bureaucracy. Did Shen actually believe he could do so? If he did, he seems not much in touch with the realities of power. If he did not, was he simply staking out his position and the principles as he saw them?

And what of the more imminent issue of the likely reaction of officials to the rent resistance effort? Within the first ten days of November, well before the establishment on November 24 of the Alliance of Farmers Associations, it should have been clear that key officials would label and oppose the effort as Bolshevist. Was Shen blind to the potential tragedy that waited for those whom he had incited and encouraged? Certainly it is not that he was ignorant of the potent alliance of officials and landlords. Almost two years before, in the February 15, 1920, issue of *Weekly Review*, he had written a dialogue called "Elder Brother Doesn't Know." In it an elder and younger brother of landlord background discuss farmers and their problems, with the younger brother arguing for the landlord establishment, asserting that the plight of the tenant farmer is his fate.

Older: They work bitterly hard to grow the crops and give it to us to eat. We count this as conscionable. So—we completely eat what they have: is this conscionable?

Younger: Our father worked bitterly hard to earn what he did.

Older: Do those who plant the fields have sons?

Younger: Those who plant have many sons.

Older: They work bitterly to plant the fields; why don't they give what they grow to their sons?

Younger: They wouldn't dare give it to their sons.

Older: Why not?

Younger: If they gave it to their sons, they wouldn't have enough to pay all the rent.

Older: So, if they couldn't pay the rent, then what?

Younger: We can go to inform the officials.

Older: Officials only protect those who collect rents and do not see after those who plant the fields?

Younger: Naturally. The food and drink of the officials come from the taxes that we pay. Of course, they must protect us.

If he was intellectually aware of the political likelihood, why then had Shen misperceived the reality of the establishment's political power and its readiness to use it? Analyzing why something did not happen puts the historian on shaky ground, but if we are to begin to understand Shen and his world, some examination of the possibilities is essential. To some extent, he was blinded by contextual and personal assets. He may have concluded that despite the risks the times were right for experimentation. There was at the time no effective central government, and provincial politics were also in some disarray. The military governor, Lu Yongxiang, a survivor of the Anfu warlord clique, opposed the Zhili-clique dominated government. In the summer of 1921, he announced his support for a provincial constitution to serve as the first step to some sort of federation of provinces.[77] Zhejiangese elites, who had chafed under the control of the Beiyang military since 1917, eagerly supported Lu's sponsorship with a view to drafting a constitution in order to move toward more autonomy. Although the constitution was promulgated in September, it was never put into effect, and the fall of 1921 was spent in bitter recriminations among government and nonofficial elites in Hangzhou.[78]

During the constitutional debates, there were deliberations on a wide array of political and social issues; and Shen, involved as he was with important elite figures and in the assembly, participated in these discussions. The provincial political situation, in a word, seemed open for promoting change that might not be countenanced in a time of more central control and clear direction. Experimentation with new social and political forms in organizations composed of interest groups (e.g., labor, women, and student associations and a two-province conservation association) was evidence of the relatively free and developing sociopolitical situation. In the newspapers of the time the word "alliance" (*lianhehui*), referring to organizations, appears with frequency, indicating the organizational ethos of inclusion and signifying optimism about the possibilities of change. In such a context, an alliance of farmers associations might well fit the spirit of the times.

If Shen assumed that the times were conducive to new possibilities, he also had other resources to put him in good stead. His political reputation, and therefore his political capital, based upon years of progressive contributions in Zhejiang politics, was great. Despite having spent much of the family fortune in political causes, he still had sufficient funds to support political activity. His personal qualities—his magnanimity with friends and tenant clients, his interest in others, his courage and self-assurance, and his public speaking ability—were assets in gaining support and supporters.

But even with these assets, he seriously misjudged his opposition. This seems surprisingly naive given his decade-long leadership in provincial politics and his hard-nosed personal efforts to deal with Beiyang warlords in 1917 and 1918. It seems that fundamentally his misperceptions may have arisen from his fervid involvement in progressive intellectual circles in the early 1920s, particularly his immersion in revolutionary ideas in the Shanghai discussions that led to the founding of the Communist Party. It seems that as a proponent of change Shen presumed his authority and based his claims to legitimacy on ideas that seemed to hold an abstract truth for those involved in May Fourth circles. His speeches to the incipient farmers associations, his points before the assembly, and his poetry written in 1921 following the repression are filled with the language of individual natural rights, class, and revolutionary action. He thought, it seems, that he would be able to inspire class struggle in Xiaoshan and Shaoxing while he protected it and moved others toward its acceptance in Hangzhou, appealing all the while to a sense of self-evident right and compassion. The power of ideas and the ends he wanted to achieve led him to lose sight of the means that might be necessary to achieve them; the obvious ambivalence in his attitudes toward struggle—sometimes countenancing it while mostly condemning it and stressing love—may also have played a role in his not coming to grips with the implications of what he had begun.

There arises another troubling subsidiary question about Shen in this affair. Did he not feel an obligation to the farmers whom he had propagandized and who saw him as their highly respected patron? An obligation to warn about danger as the rhetoric heated up and the violence flared in early December? Or as a knight-errant joining the rent resistance battle by putting himself on the line with those he had so heart-wrenchingly described? Though Shen never spoke to the question directly, his actions and several writings after the crackdown and subsequent repression betray considerable guilt, anger, and sadness. Shen returned to Yaqian on hearing of the arrest of Li in late December, offering counsel and support to Li's family. After Li's death, Shen had his son Jianlong (Yang Zhihua's husband) draw a picture of Li for the family to keep. Shen had them bury Li on his land, and Shen wrote the inscription on the headstone. With Li's family having difficult times in subsequent years, Shen gave them money and a plot of alluvial land to farm. Shen followed up his assistance with many couplets and poems written in remembrance of Li and his sacrifice.[79] After Chen Pusheng's death, Shen also paid for the burial and a memorial stone.[80] For the farmers who had participated in the farmers associations, Shen remained a patron and leader, despite the fact that they had suffered and that (at least outwardly) he had escaped responsibility in the episode. Interviews in the 1980s with farmers who had been involved indicated that they continued to admire Shen and were moved by his concerned actions to alleviate their plight.[81] Networks suppressed in 1921 and early 1922 would emerge again in 1927 and 1928, with Shen once more playing a crucial role.

In a poem and brief essay that Shen wrote within a month after the crackdown, he clearly positioned himself with the farmers against the provincial establishment. They are worthy of analysis to indicate Shen's attitudes after seeing his project demolished. The poem, "After the Disbanding of the Yaqian Farmers Association," was written in late December.[82]

> A dog from Hangzhou city runs into the countryside to bark;
> A farmer with small eyes and hunger in his belly;
> The mice from government granaries as big as a peck.

[When there] is the reduction of rent,
    people open their mouths.
[When there] are military forces, people have no recourse.
[When there] are government deputies, people flee.
Iron chains and manacles block the future;
Proclamations of sealed doors block going out hereafter.
How is it that the state and official evilly make trouble?
And the well-to-do families are not willing to stop,
    not willing to stop:
A one-mu field will bring a picul of rent
    [so those who bring the] evil wind
    will not permit rent reduction.
Even as those who enter the association
    have broken with opium smoking.

No one can manage a gluttonous wolf or a starving tiger.
The phoenix, coming lower, folds its wings
    as it soars through the cold vast expanse.
Dawn comes, but the sun has not yet come:
Dreams fly no farther than the Qiantang.
I would rather it be a time to hope than to cast off reputation.
The stopping of tears and the sounds of feelings are
    absolutely no proof [that things are settled].
A capitalist night wind passed through Wuxu:
    all society mysteriously died.
The spirit is hidden; with whom do you speak?
The houses and gardens, close together
    for several ten thousand li,
A spreading sound interrupts the sound of crying:
Wild calls—the Heavens are not right;
The people's lives are like mole-crickets.
To cry out grievances should not exclude cursing
    when there is no other device.
Two characters—"Stupid farmers"—are how they're called.
Cut off the wolf's head; grind the bear with your teeth.

In cataclysmic language Shen depicts the clash between the farmers
with small eyes (i.e., with little demand for things) and with the capability
to change (giving up opium smoking) and the landlords and officials who
bring the evil wind of capitalism that spawns death in society. While the
farmer has to stave off hunger, the government officials grow fat. When
the farmers finally have a chance to open their mouths through rent
reduction, military forces and government deputies come to seal the
houses of those who have led the organizations and put them in chains
and manacles whenever they are seized. The phoenix in the second

stanza is likely a reference to Yaqian and its role in the movement: Phoenix mountain, just to the village's northwest, was the village's symbol: it brings dawn but not the light of a new day. The imagery here brings to mind the declaration of the Nansha farmers: Shen's speech a Hangwu Mountain had been, they claimed, like seeing the sunlight.

Then the tragedy: dawn but no sun—and that coupled with the reality that the dreams had been delimited to the east of the Qiantang. The last half of the second stanza is filled with images of turmoil and angry hope. The capitalist wind has killed society (a reiteration of his complaints in the assembly and in association speeches), has hidden the human spirit. Spreading "wild calls" overwhelm the sounds of weeping following the crackdown; they are signs that the order of the Heavens is amiss. When the people can only cry out their grievances, then even cursing becomes a weapon of the powerless. And yet, despite all their bitter suffering, the landlords and officials still call the farmers "stupid" and "ignorant." The last line raises once more the role of violence in the future. If "no one can manage a gluttonous wolf," then "cut off the wolf's head." "Grind the bear with your teeth."

In "Ignorance," written in early January, Shen deals with the label of "ignorant" given farmers by officials and landlords.[83]

The more than eighty farmers associations . . . have been officially disbanded, the associations' deputies jailed, their homes sealed. The official reports have said these things: farmers association regulations clash with current laws; their principles are really "destroy capitalism" through sentences like "The land is the tool through which farmers dispense power to nourish all human beings" and "The land over which the farmer labors is what this organization is designed to protect" and "This association's members are opposed to landlords; each year the members will freely decide on each year's rent." To put equality into effect, to put piecemeal freedom into effect—that suggests that there is only a small knowledge, that there has been no high degree of knowledge to correct the farmers' ignorance.

The Hangzhou Daily had an editorial entitled "The Origin of Farmers' Ugly Crimes." Its contents were really those of the official reports: "The leaders of this effort at base did not have much knowledge; they were in effect led by country bumpkins [ignorants]."

About this word "ignorant"—I don't know how many wrongs coming out of the blood, sweat, bitternesses, and tears of life are contained in this word.

At the end of this piece, in which are embedded several stanzas of poetry (some written by Liu Dabai), Shen indicates a hope for the future based upon the capability of the farmers.[84] Shen's opinions and ideals were not diminished in the calamitous aftermath of this movement; he seethed with righteous anger, optimistically hoping that the sun would soon appear.

Yet another mystery is how through all this Shen was able to escape responsibility and not be publicly accused or charged by authorities with fomenting revolution. He was clearly linked with the rent resistance movement in the declaration of the Nansha farmers in December, in the roles he and his school had played in the association movement from the beginning, and in his attacks on capitalism in the assembly, in speeches, and in the two writings just discussed. With angrily bitter tone and language, he was the foremost attacker of the landlord-official nexus. He must have known that the landlords of Xiaoshan and Shaoxing would perceive him as a traitor to their class, a dangerous radical, but Shen apparently believed that his local and provincial status would offer him protection. There apparently was no accusation lodged against Shen by the landlords. Twelve of them (likely those who had met with the Shaoxing magistrate to plan the crackdown) had planned to sign an accusation against him to be sent to governmental authorities in Hangzhou with a request for an investigation. One source suggests that Shen escaped because of recognition of his governmental influence and because of great fear about farmer reaction if he were charged and jailed.[85]

Another source suggests that the landlord action was blocked by Shaoxing elite Sun Deqing.[86] Sun was an old acquaintance of Shen dating back to the last years of the Qing. He had been involved with famed pre-Republican revolutionaries Xu Xilin and Qiu Jin at the Datong School in the county seat. Sun was an important figure in the Restoration Society and the Revolutionary Alliance; it was there that he had become acquainted with Shen. Sun served on the Shaoxing city council in 1911,[87] and the two found themselves on the same side with Lu Xun protesting against the excesses of Wang Jinfa, the military leader of Shaoxing in early 1912. But there is no record of much contact between the men after that time. Sources indicate that the two were friends. But Shen, as we have seen, shunned the societies formed by Sun to commemorate two of the Restoration Society leaders in 1915 and 1917. Furthermore, Sun's home town was located on the Cao-e River, not in an area greatly affected by the rent resistance movement. Sun had spent his years after the 1911 revolution in local charitable and cultural work that was largely apolitical.[88] If indeed it was Sun who was able to dissuade the twelve, the reasons for his support of Shen are somewhat mysterious. His sway over the landlords may very well illustrate among other things the great significance that active leadership in the events a decade earlier continued to have on political developments in the 1920s.

The Identities of Shen Dingyi

For Shen, 1921 was a pivotal year: he had come to believe strongly that the key to revolutionary change lay in the countryside among China's farmers. They, after all, were the most numerous social and occupational group; but even more, as Shen wrote, they "dispense power" through the tool of the land "to nourish all human beings." It was an idea whose time would come later in the decade, and Shen must be seen as the vanguard. His theoretical May Fourth thinking had matured into a practical emphasis on rural China as the arena in which to effect the changes in individuals and society that would bring about the new China. Shen most certainly saw himself as a revolutionary patron leading Chinese society to the light.

But "the facts that constrain personal identity are neither given nor determined by the subject. They are a matter of social construal, dependent on the context as well as the (often malevolent) motives of others."[89] Shen's actions in 1921 were providing evidence for others—local landlords, government officials, area farmers—to define and perhaps redefine him in the increasingly revolutionary context of the 1920s. The affair used up enormous personal political capital that Shen had accumulated since 1911. In the provincial arena his legitimacy as a leader was likely eroded, and it was not helped by his strong anticorruption attack on the assembly leadership. The Shen who would defy the outside warlords became the Shen who would defy any authority. He had also made many enemies among the landlords and county officials in Xiaoshan; he could expect little support from conservative elites who now labeled him a Bolshevist. The Shen who would represent their interests in the provincial assembly became the Shen who would destroy the system on which they survived and prospered. By these actions Shen was setting down a record that officials and local socioeconomic elites would use to shape their perceptions. These would have a constraining impact on his freedom of action and be a force shaping his future. Shen was indeed laying the groundwork for future difficulties. It was not only the rent resistance movement and its farmers associations that had rushed to calamity.

There is some evidence that Shen recognized and had second thoughts about the impact of his actions. In his poem "After the Disbanding of the Yaqian Farmers Association," he suggested that he still saw the future as a time for hope rather than as a time when, because of this episode, his reputation would be lost. A biography of Li Chenghu appeared in the February 7, 1922, issue of *Juewu*. It was almost certainly written by Shen, who was most knowledgeable about the details of Li's involvement and who was at the time writing regularly for the newspaper supplement. In it, there is an effort to distance Shen from the movement. The author has Li state directly to those farmers who had come to Yaqian in early October, many of them to see Shen: "You want to see the regulations; they have already been printed and we are going to give them to you; you want to see Shen, supposing that he began all this. In reality, this is completely our own undertaking; it is not at all something that Shen has done."[90]

If Shen accumulated any political capital in the episode, it was among the farmers. The Shen who was landlord master had become Shen the sympathetic and encouraging patron. But there was almost certainly great variation among the perceptions of tenant farmers. Some of them must have wondered about Shen's commitment to the effort and about his letting them "slowly twist in the wind." For them Shen the courageous actor had become Shen the coward who only spoke boldly. One farmer who had been moved by Shen in the beginning referred to him as "Uncle Word."[91]

While all farmers might understand the goals Shen had enunciated for the farmers associations, some must have been shocked by the full range of activities in which Shen had become involved in the locality. The ideas of cosmopolitan Shanghai and the May Fourth movement were not easily translated to the rural area of Yaqian. The images of Shanghai in Shen's writings—street demonstrations, automobiles, jazz, factories and the urban proletariat, New Culture debates, luxurious Chinese homes with maids and clinking champagne glasses—seem light years away from the collapsing alluvial world of rural poverty, of children scavenging the countryside for kindling, of floors in bare and bleak thatched-roof homes covered with chicken excrement, of families going from year to year always on the edge or over the brink of hunger. The contrasting worlds of these two arenas were illustrated by the reaction of locals to one Tong

Lizhang who came in February as a representative of the Shanghai Industry and Commerce Friendship Association to offer respects to Li Chenghu. He reported that when he inquired about the whereabouts of Li's home, the "rural people all stared, their visages full of fear." When he explained what he had come to do, they led him to Li's house, where, after meeting Li's son, Tong read written messages of commemoration and eulogy. "Those forty or fifty people who were standing around were very startled. [When] Tong explained the meaning to them, they were tongue-tied."[92]

For such people, the calls for feminist reforms that accompanied the associations and the feminist ideas discussed at the Yaqian Village School might be scandalous. When word got out that Shen had swum together with his daughter, son, and daughter-in-law at a nearby lake, for example, it caused great surprise in the area.[93] The casting out of religious images and the seizure of the Buddhist temple and its conversion to the headquarters of the farmers association could be upsetting not only to the affected Buddhist priests but also to committed believers. Shen the elite landlord assemblyman had become Shen the social radical, doing shocking things. Actions were giving Shen new identities—political, social, personal, revolutionary. As has been pointed out, identity is a "continuously changing" characteristic since it is "intrinsically associated with all the joinings and departures of social life."[94]

In the past these identities had come primarily from elites in networks, organizations, study groups, journal offices, the provincial assembly— that is, from men who were roughly equal in status and position with Shen. In the Yaqian movement Shen had established primarily patron-client and master-disciple ties to the farmers and to the Hangzhou students who came to teach at the Village School. He had established new networks: the small First Normal network growing out of his relationship with a few progressive students, the proliferating networks of farmers seeded by the small group of farmer leaders. In many ways these networks were likely to have a higher intensity and at the same time experience greater stress than networks of greater equality in the provincial assembly, study group, and discussion society, for they were based upon the inequality of superior and subordinate.[95] Shen had a paternalistic relationship to the network others, imparting wisdom, giving advice, nurturing; the others learned from and were indebted to Shen. In such a social situation, the patron-master would likely hold a greater expectation of loyalty on the part of his followers; in turn, clients-disciples would likely hold a greater expectation of deep commitment and moral example on the part of the leader. The chief difference between the farmers and the students was that the farmers would not grow out of their relationship of subordination, but the students-now-turned-teachers would. During the Yaqian movement that would not become a problem. But the dynamics of relationships between Shen and these Hangzhou student disciples would ultimately come to loom larger than those with the farmers and would come to change the course of his life.

CHAPTER FIVE

All Fall Down

Hangzhou and Yaqian, 1924–1925

Wild emotions drenched in wine:
In the heavens the stars sway.
On the earth the mountains sway.
In my hand the cup sways.

Vision is like chaotic lightning: there is no fixed point.
Thoughts are hard to maintain;
Hatred also is hard to maintain.
On all sides the vast expanse laughs; I draw the sword.
"Drunk" (Zui), 1922, at Xixing

At least into his late thirties, Shen had been a heavy drinker. It is said that his friends, aware of his large capacity for liquor, would encourage him to drink when he arrived for meetings.[1] In *Weekly Review* in November 1919, Shen claimed to have reformed partially in smoking (from a habit of smoking more than fifty cigarettes a day) and reformed absolutely in drinking: "I used to drink every day. These last three months I decided not to drink. On Double Ten, a very scholarly and nondrinking friend invited me to spend the day; I drank two cups. Afterward I thought that National Day really is a day of commemorating breaking the bonds of slavery. I really should not drink wine and become intoxicated—it is like going to another world."[2] It is this world that Shen describes in his poem "Drunk." Just as Shen linked a decision to stop drinking with national affairs, this poem can be taken as a metaphor for Shen's life in the mid-1920s when developments created a situation where, as in a drunken vision of chaotic lightning, the "fixed points" of his personal and political life toppled; his reaction in the case of his political life was to draw the sword.

Setting the Stage

Shen's "letter" to "comrades studying abroad" in the New Year's issue of *Awakening* in 1924 noted the deep revolutionary changes in the Soviet Union and argued that China must see itself as part of the world revolution. "We are in an increasingly precarious situation. . . . A revolution is essential. Neither a boisterous nor a romantic revolution is sufficient to remove [the] actual oppression [we face]. We must have organization; we must have a procedure; we must construct plans. We must not speak of long-term or short. In the most immediate future we must work. Regarding organization, there must be a very careful systematic structure." Shen's prescription for revolutionary success—building structures of organization, procedure, and plans—seems almost to contain an element of the contradictory when juxtaposed with his view of life as continual movement and change. In 1921, in an essay called "Questions about Life," Shen wrote

Is yesterday's Xuanlu [Dingyi] the same as today's? Yesterday's Xuanlu is definitely not the same as today's. Why not? Because Xuanlu himself knows that he cannot grow to age thirty-seven in one day; he must grow second by second. So the Xuanlu of a second before is different from the one now. He is growing every second. The real Xuanlu is in a state of change, absolutely not in a state of quietude. . . . We often hear people say that that person is conservative or that person is stubborn. In fact, it's wrong to say those things, for things you consider new today will already be old tomorrow. . . . The reality of life is in movement; without movement there will be no reality.[3]

Revolution is motion. Old systems are smashed; new systems sprout forth. Old patterns fall; new models rise. Old leaders are toppled; new leaders emerge. Old perceptions are discarded; new perceptions redefine reality. While artificial structures (organizations and parties) may facilitate revolution, the process of revolution is rarely kind to those structures. As Shen and others theorized about the proper organizations, procedures, and plans, various personal, professional, and political networks were among the most crucial structures of revolution. They grew naturally out of the Chinese soil of personal connections, expanding into interlocking and sometimes competing networks, always with the potential of continual flux. In his essay of moment-by-moment change and movement, Shen's perception of rapidly changing identities comes closer to the reality that Shen found in 1924 and 1925, when there seemed to be no stopping the shifts and turns that shaped the rise of revolutionary fervor.

Shen's involvement in the initial stages of the founding of the Communist Party had led to his leadership with Yu Xiusong in founding the Hangzhou Socialist Youth Corps in October 1920.[4] His anticapitalist writings and his patronage of rural revolution in the Yaqian movement also point to his Communist connections. Ruan Yicheng, the son of Ruan Xingcun, legal scholar and provincial assemblyman, remembered Shen's Communist involvement.

Several times I heard Shen lecture at the Zhejiang Provincial Education Association Hall on Pinghai Road. At that time he was infatuated with socialist and Communist theory. His body was slender and fine-looking; his eyes were clear and animated. Just entering middle age, he had a dark black mustache. I listened to his echoing voice, eloquent and quick-tongued in argument. His oration was extraordinarily rich and his persuasive powers strong: it could stir you up. Young students heard him speak and almost all fell for what he said.[5]

In the summer of 1922, the Communist Party decided, following the policies set forth by the Comintern, that its members could become concurrent members of the Guomindang; Sun Yat-sen had agreed to such a policy with a view to strengthening revolutionary potential and finding aid from the Soviet Communist Party.[6] Shen reportedly joined the Guomindang in late 1922, thus becoming a member of both revolutionary parties.[7] During this time he was also an active spokesman in the provincial assembly, espousing such causes as constitutional reform, regularized provincial administrative appointment procedures, and an antiwarlord plan for political reconstruction.

Though his actions in 1922 seemed to be focusing more on the provincial and national arenas, Shen always kept his eyes on the local arena as well. In each arena Shen maintained networks of supporters and like-minded individuals with whom revolutionary work might be accomplished. He continued to serve as mentor for his First Normal network. Yang Zhihua continued to teach at the Yaqian Village School, joined by new First Normal graduates like Wang Guansan with whom she made village home visits to students. Xuan Zhonghua, briefly at Yaqian in the momentous fall of 1921, had been chosen by the fledgling Communist Party to travel to the Soviet Union to be a representative at the Congress of the Toilers of the East in early 1922. First in Irkutsk and then in Moscow, he had become further enamored of the Soviet revolutionary model. In April 1922, Shen invited him back to the Southern Sands to edit a progressive journal that Shen was sponsoring in the town of Kanshan, the site of his anticapitalist "Who Is Your Friend?" speech the summer before. In taking on the editorship of *Responsibility*, published from late November 1922 until mid-March 1923, Xuan once again agreed to put himself in a close relationship with Shen. In the journal he, like Shen, espoused socialist revolution, with a stress upon the role of laborers and farmers.[8]

Assisting in writing for and editing the journal was former First Normal teacher and poet Liu Dabai, the close friend of Shen, who had served as secretary for the provincial assembly in 1917 and 1918, when Shen had chaired it, and who lived for several extended periods with Shen in Yaqian.[9] Participating also were Yaqian teachers Xu Baimin and Tang Gongxian who returned to the Southern Sands to help Xuan in this journalistic project. Several middle and elementary school teachers also participated—part of a group that published in a number of progressive Shanghai and Hangzhou journals. Many of them were also closely associated with the first modern labor organization in Hangzhou, the Zhejiang Printing Company Mutual Assistance Association, headed by Ni Youtian. Ni, a Communist labor organizer, had become acquainted with Xuan Zhonghua when Xuan taught adult night classes for the association in 1921. Xuan, in turn, had assisted Ni in further organizing Hangzhou printing workers. They had traveled together to the Soviet Union in 1921.[10]

Networks between laborer, farmer, and intellectual were clearly not simply a theoretical projection at this time. Added to the social "circles" or subcultures of a decade earlier were political activist networks reminiscent of those in the 1911 revolutionary period. While the 1911 variety had included lower-class figures in secret societies and the underworld, these united for the first time elites and socially legitimate nonelites, workers and farmers. As political, social, and educational networks linked, intertwined, and expanded, the revolutionary circles seemed to grow, connecting rural village, city, and metropolis. As Shen shuttled between Shanghai, Hangzhou, and Yaqian, and as he patronized, directed, and supported a variety of progressive efforts, personal and revolutionary allegiances were built up and expanded.

The Rise of the Zhejiang Provincial Guomindang

"On September 2, 1923," Shen later wrote, "I arrived at the center of world revolution."[11] Sun Yat-sen had named Shen to accompany Chiang Kai-shek to Moscow in the fall of 1923 on a mission to develop better relations between the leaders of the Soviet Communist Party and the Guomindang and to seek Soviet aid for military action in China's northwest with a view to defeating warlord Wu Peifu.[12] At the same time Michael Borodin, Comintern agent, came to China to begin his reorganization of the Guomindang. We know that Chiang was the key figure in the Chinese delegation, that he met with key Communist leaders including Lenin and Trotsky, that negotiations for military support went nowhere, and that, according to his diary, he began to feel disillusioned about the role of the Soviet Union as a model for China.

About the course of Shen's visit we know very little. One sometimes inaccurate biographer claims that Shen had lengthy discussions with Lenin about world revolution and became friends with Soviet leaders.[13] Certainly Shen's inability to speak Russian and his relatively short period of time in the Soviet Union would have hampered any such development.[14] Shen did relate that he was ill for over half a month after his arrival and admitted that what he gained through his investigation and research was very limited. His viewing of the changes wrought by the revolution were, he said, supplemented by conversations with Qu Qiubai, the Communist intellectual who had been in the Soviet Union from late 1920 until early 1923. Unlike Chiang Kai-shek, Shen was apparently not disillusioned by his stay in Moscow, for essays in 1924 indicated that he continued to see the Soviet Union as a model for China. He brought back a seedling which he planted in the yard of the Yaqian Village School, clearly a symbol of what he hoped would be the growth of a Soviet-style system in a new China.[15]

Less than a month after his return from the Soviet Union, Shen chaired a Guomindang meeting at West Lake in preparation for the first national party congress, to be held in Guangzhou later in January. Though the Central Executive Committee of the party had already chosen three delegates, among them Shen and Dai Jitao, the selection of three more was required.[16] One of them became twenty-five-year-old Xuan Zhonghua, Shen's very close friend and protégé in the First Normal network.[17] Shen's shifting relationships to Dai and Xuan would shape the revolution in Zhejiang Province over the next three years. Like Shen, whose journey to the Soviet Union had taken him out of the picture of Guomindang reorganization in the fall of 1923, Dai had also been on a mission for Sun Yat-sen. He had been sent to Sichuan Province in the fall of 1922 to help mediate a dispute between military factions and win support for his cause. Dai, despondent over recent ill health and perhaps over his probable ineffectuality in his assignment, attempted suicide on the way by throwing himself into the Yangzi River.[18] Though he was rescued, he failed in achieving the goals of his mission. His depression and his shrinking in the face of great odds, which gave rise to his suicide attempt, stand in sharp contrast to Shen's optimism and the considerable bravado with which he always approached problems.

At the Guomindang National Congress, which met from January 20 to 30 in Guangzhou, Dai was elected to the Central Executive Committee and the Central Political Council; he was also named to head the Guomindang propaganda department.[19] Shen was elected as an alternate to the Central Executive Committee. Their respective positions reveal their status and their main arenas of political action. Dai, with his longtime connections to Sun Yat-sen, was a key player in the national arena; Shen found his main arenas in the province and below. At the congress itself, the thrust of Sun Yat-sen's opening address surely resonated with Shen's own ideas: the need for a unified and cooperative party in the rebuilding of the nation. Shen had written repeatedly about the essential nature of human commonality, community, and cooperation to achieve that national goal. In relation to that community and cooperation, the policy of admitting Communist Party members into the Guomindang became an issue at the congress. Dai had opposed this policy so strongly that he had originally planned not to attend the congress; Shen, of course, was a member of both parties. The issue was temporarily put to rest when the delegates decided to retain the policy.[20]

While Dai remained in Guangzhou to carry out a variety of party functions, Shen and Xuan returned to Hangzhou to begin to establish the provincial and county party organizations. Shen's personal focus on careful organization in the Yaqian movement in 1921 had now been transformed in the wake of Borodin's party reorganization to a matter of party policy. For the next year and a half Shen and Xuan participated in two arenas (province and county), using two methods in their organizational work. One was to expand the pool of potential party members and leaders while laying a mobilizational context for revolutionary work through mass demonstrations and rallies. This was an inclusionary effort, facilitating the entrance into the party of the not-yet-converted by engaging them directly in public activities. The other method was to utilize party regulations and procedures to ensure that old and new party members were aware of what party membership meant and entailed, a process that often tended to turn on legalisms. This was an exclusionary effort, keeping the party membership for the party faithful. The use of both of these approaches in the revolutionary process would eventually drive Shen and Xuan apart.

Shen took the lead in announcing the new registration of party members that began on March 10 at the home of his nephew, lawyer Shen Xiaowen, in the New Market area, several blocks from the Lawyers' Association.[21] The reregistration of those members who had entered the party before the First Congress was necessary, Shen averred, because they were "simply men of talent coming together" whose comprehension of party ideology had not been questioned and who could until the present remain members simply through the payment of dues. Now party membership—"comradeship"—required three elements: (1) understanding, accepting, and carrying out party decisions and declarations from the First Congress; (2) submitting to party regulations; and (3) giving oneself physically and spiritually to the party. In his statement, Shen clearly specified that the individual worked for the party, which in turn worked for the nation: the key was sacrifice, not rights and privileges. Only with such an approach could the party "liberate the nation from the oppression of international imperialism and warlordism."[22]

With the establishment of the disciplined, carefully defined Leninist party that Borodin was constructing (as with the Communist Party established in 1921), the new party model of the 1920s became exclusionary rather than inclusionary. The old model had been the parliamentary parties in the first years of the Republic, a system discredited in the national and provincial arenas by 1924. The new model forced one to agree to accept, submit to, and give oneself to the party or not be reregistered. It therefore set up an institutional context that invited progressive exclusion: as the revolution of the 1920s proceeded, there would be frequent reregistrations in order for revised regulations and goals to be implemented. The reregistrations defined the players in the particular arenas of action. Even though the Chinese traditionally drew exclusionary borders around their immediate families, groups, and villages, the adoption of such a Western model, that insisted on strict impersonal regulations and disciplined enforcement of those regulations, seems a revolutionary departure for a culture where personal connections and the fluidity of the network were the social and political modus operandi. Yet it was simply a graft, implanted on the tree of Chinese approaches. Thus, who the party leaders were and the nature of their networks and factions became desperately important, for in effect they, and not the impersonal regulations, became the gatekeepers whose decisions allowed people in and forced them out.

One wonders whether there was any difficulty for Shen, whose political career had flourished amid the old party model and whose poetry and essays had consistently been inclusionary (e. g., "he really is you; you really are I"), to adapt to this model. Yet the key to the new system was the inherent institutional ethos also found in some of Shen's writings: that the party or at least some leaders of the party had a monopoly on the Truth; therefore to be a party member was to be imbued with a strong sense of absolute moral rightness and righteousness in dealing with the great issues of national survival and development. The very process of reregistration itself, in its assumption of the existence of an "opposition," eschewed approaches at compromise; it ostracized those who could or did not see the Truth—or those who were *perceived* as not seeing the Truth. Listen to Shen, for example, in "Sacrifice and Fish and Pork," written in September 1919:

Only when we can have a constructive plan and begin to develop individual potentiality can we save ourselves from the fatal danger. If someone does dare to oppose us or even prohibit us from doing these two things, he is trying to capture our hoe and prevent us from reclaiming the wasteland or digging out the mineral resources in our minds, which is the same as denying us our way of life. We will [then] have to . . . prepare for a greater sacrifice in order to protect our way of life.[23]

In effect, therefore, in revolutionary times the sense of political danger and the absolute political righteousness of the party as institution could outweigh the social institutions that generally provided for considerable fluidity and flexibility. In many cases those social connections and networks were damaged or even destroyed by the revolutionary political

institutions, but the opposite was true as well: the new political institutions could be undercut and reshaped by established social connections and networks.

The first meeting of the provisional provincial Guomindang bureau
was held on Sunday, March 30, at the Lawyers' Association, a fitting
meeting place given the long-time relationship between the pre-Borodin
provincial Guomindang and the Lawyers' Association. Accounts of the
meeting, attended by over eighty members and thirty guests, reveal the
composition of the leadership. Shen seemed in firm control, with the
majority of the nine-man provisional executive committee an amalgam
of two of his personal networks. Apart from Shen himself, two of the
remaining eight were relatives (Shen Xiaowen and Shen Erqiao) and four
were from Shen's First Normal School network. One had taught at
Shen's Yaqian School (Xuan); one founded the Hangzhou Socialist
Youth Corps with Shen in 1920 (Yu Xiusong); An Ticheng was their
classmate and Jing Hengyi their principal. Of the four alternates, Tang
Gongxian was a First Normal graduate, had taught at the Yaqian school,
and had helped edit *Responsibility;* and Ni Youtian, the printworkers'
leader, was a close ally of Xuan.[24] Shen, Xuan, and Yu gave the major
presentations, with Xuan reporting on the Guangzhou Congress, Xu
speaking on party regulations and registration, and Shen continuing for
over an hour on the history of the party, the meaning of the Three
People's Principles, and Sun's record and contributions. A newspaper
report noted (as was typical with Shen's oratory) that despite the length
of Shen's speech, "everyone listened with rapt attention" and (the
omnipresent cliché) "the applause was like thunder."

Shen was in demand as a speaker not only by the party but also by
some of the plethora of organizations that crowded the Hangzhou
social-political scene and that would become part of the revolution.
Because of his oratorical skill, student groups especially made numerous
requests for Shen to speak; student Gao Yuetian joined the Guomindang, he reported, because he was inspired by Shen's oratory.[25] A week
after the Guomindang meeting, Shen spoke to the Student Service Corps
on "We Must Strive to Serve the Youth," an attack on ancestor worship
and superstition. Earlier that day he had spoken at the request of the
Hangzhou Youth Advance Together Society to a group of over one
hundred on the topic, "The Nation Must Soon Prepare." The meeting
was attended by students, by representatives from newspaper offices
from the city, and by the representatives from two native place organizations, the Xiaoshan County Native Place Association and the

Dongyang County Workers' Native Place Association. The latter would become increasingly associated with the Guomindang.[26]

The two speeches, "We Must Strive to Serve the Youth" and "The Nation Must Soon Prepare," perfectly symbolize the fault lines appearing in the Chinese polity by mid-1924. The sociopolitical ethos of early 1924 Hangzhou was generally still inclusionary, expansive, and open—the continuing spirit of the May Fourth cultural revolution and its exhilarating social and political movements. Significantly, reporters noted that for a "youthful audience" the more exciting speech was in this individualistic strain. This fault line had given rise to shocks of earthquake-like import in the late 1910s and early 1920s and still had the potential to do so. But the other increasingly important fault line was the force of nationalism, and particularly an emphasis on actions that would contribute toward the building of a modern Chinese nation. Although national feeling could be stirred through public protests and demonstrations, the actions increasingly perceived as most conducive to nation building were directed and systematic: the establishment of parties and of an army. To be effective, both had to exclude those who for whatever reason were unsuitable. But it was not simply the institutions that were exclusionary; it was the goal itself. Working toward the building of a modern nation meant defining what that nation would be, putting a name on the end product, giving it a particular identity. Defining and naming exclude other possibilities. This fault line was much more dangerous and potentially deadly than the first because in addition to setting down firm limits and demarcations over policies and decisions, exclusion itself generates tension, anger, and violence and can build up an urge for personal revenge—a mix that helps create the personal tragedies of revolution.[27]

In the aftermath of the party organizational meeting, members were dispatched to cities and counties to organize party bureaus there. Jing Hengyi, for example, went to Ningbo to set up a municipal bureau in early April; the Hang county bureau was established in late April;[28] and Xuan Zhonghua organized the Shaoxing county bureau in June.[29] Shen's fellow provincial assemblyman from Xiaoshan, Sheng Bangyan, was sent to oversee the development of the Xiaoshan County bureau, but the area had been so prepared by Shen that youth, farmers, and local elites convened even before he arrived. On April 6 they met at Yaqian's steam launch dock, probably because one of the selected deputies—Shen Zhongqing, Shen's older brother—was manager of the Cheng'an Shipping Company, located there.[30] The other two deputies were Kong

Xuexiong, one of Shen's close county disciples, and progressive local self-government elite and First Normal graduate Qian Yizhang. The group settled on a local tea shop as a site for announcements and informal meetings.[31]

On April 12, the bureau took advantage of one of Shen's frequent trips home from across the river by having him speak on the topic, "Relations between the Military and the Farmers." The rainy day allowed many farmers from nearby villages to come hear Shen talk of them as natural allies of the military. When out-of-work farmers became soldiers, they could deal with local bandits, knowing their home areas as they did. Regular soldiers could then be used in dealing with "outer problems." Farmers could thus play an important role in the Guomindang revolution.[32] This presentation is interesting also for Shen's more positive picture of the military. His bitter opposition and denunciation of warlords and militarism in the 1916–17 and the May Fourth periods is missing. The reason: the context had changed. By 1924 there was a clear awareness on the part of both Guomindang and Communist Party leaders of the necessity of having a military force of their own to combat the force of the warlords. From the 1910s, then, there appears to be an acceptance of the expanding militarization of Chinese politics, as now civilian elite parties moved toward adopting the forms and the ethos of the men on horseback.[33]

The organization of the Xiaoshan county bureau was completed on May 18 with a meeting in the county seat.[34] Shen again was the featured speaker, discussing problems in the fight for the nation and calling for sacrifice and unity: "The work of our party is revolution; we can be successful. Our party's comrades are fighting for national freedom, for national plans for independence. We will very much have to sacrifice." He argued that those who joined the party must take on its ways, that narrow regional approaches must be dispensed with, and that the party must concentrate on youth to expand its membership. Of the seven provisional bureau deputies, two were long-time associates of Shen, Sheng Bangyan and Kong Xuexiong; two were members of the county assembly (one indeed was the chairman who three months earlier had called out policemen to collect his rent); one was principal of the county's Third Middle School; and one was a Beijing University graduate who would still be county Guomindang secretary in the late 1940s. The committee was thus composed of educated men from Shen's network and the established county elites. Shen's disciple Kong served as standing member of the committee; he sought immediate monetary support from

the provincial bureau, a request that would point to serious party difficulties.

By the spring of 1924, then, Shen had emerged as perhaps the most
significant party leader in the provincial and county arenas. Almost all
the chief players in party decision making in Hangzhou and in Yaqian
were members of his networks or associates of those members. He was
a man in great demand as a speaker. As a mark of his influence and status,
there was also the effort, apparently sponsored by the party, to establish
branch schools of Shen's Yaqian Village School; party member Wang
Guansan, who had taught at the school and was part of Shen's First
Normal network, was sent to investigate possible sites for these branches
around the county.[35]

Celebrations, Demonstrations, and the Rise of Revolutionary Fervor

As the organization of county bureaus continued apace
during the summer, many party members involved themselves in acts of
public remembrance, commemoration, and remonstrance. Mass rallies
and demonstrations were designed as part of the inclusionary strategy to
broaden the parties' revolutionary base and extend the revolutionary
appeal of the Guomindang and the Communist Party. They were the
means by which more people were inflamed with revolutionary zeal and
charged with party spirit. They show an aroused populace well before the
traumatic events of 1925. They also reveal in their organization and their
unfolding much about the developing revolutionary culture ritualized in
public space in Hangzhou and Yaqian in mid-1924.

The event that drew the largest Hangzhou crowds was a May Day rally
and demonstration planned and directed by the provisional Guomindang executive committee, with Xuan Zhonghua as chairman.[36] On that
Thursday factory, newspaper, and printing company workers stopped
their work by noon and gathered at the large athletic field by the
northeast shore of West Lake for a 1:30 rally. The site for the beginning
of all the major patriotic rallies in the 1920s was this athletic field in full
view of the lake and adjacent to the New Market area, in contrast to the
1917 rally to save Zhejiang for the Zhejiangese, which had been staged
at the enclosed First Theater near the train station. The area around the
train station had developed and taken its character from the city's first

wave of modern change, the construction of the railroad linking the city to Shanghai in the last decade of the Qing. The May Fourth period rallies bespoke a new world by permanently changing the focus of Hangzhou's political public space to grounds contiguous to the site of the former Manchu garrison, the destroyed political-military structure of the ancien régime, marked now by spatial openness and opportunity for recreation, physical activity, business, and political rallies.

There were reportedly over twelve hundred participants representing various known labor, political, student, and native place groups and over two thousand from groups whose names were unknown or who were simply residents of Hangzhou (*shimin*). Before the speakers' platform, there were four large flags with the characters *wuyi jinian* ("May Day Commemoration"); beside the platform were smaller pennants with various slogans setting forth workers' and national goals: "national revolution," "establish unions," "down with the warlords," "oppose imperialism," "make the eight-hour day a reality," "equal wages for men and women," "prohibit child labor," "emphasize factory safety and sanitation," "propertyless classes unite." Paper flags with the same slogans were distributed to individuals to wave as they rallied and demonstrated.

After Xuan opened the meeting with a description of May Day principles, the main speakers took center stage. Six men spoke on the general topic of uniting laborers in a movement to oppose imperialism. Reporters (as usual) noted that Shen's speech was especially moving and filled with indignation; the crowd responded with—what else?—"thunderous" applause. The other speakers were also Guomindang members: Ni Youtian; Zhang Qiuren, a disciple of Shen and a close friend of Xuan;[37] Chen Weilan, like Shen, Ni, and Zhang, a member of the party's provisional executive committee; Wu Xianqing, the wife of Xuan Zhonghua;[38] and Wu Zhiying, a silk entrepreneur intent on mechanizing the industry. After the speeches and three cheers for each of the slogans "Long live the workers" and "Long live the national revolution," the crowd lined up for the march through Hangzhou.[39]

The order of marchers is one indication of the status of the various groups and offers an introduction to some of the organizations that would play important roles in the coming revolution. Leading the way were 150 members of perhaps the most radical of the Hangzhou labor organizations, the Zhejiang Print Workers Club, organized in 1923 by Ni and Xu Meikun of Xiaoshan county. Its leaders had made close connections with teachers and students at the First Normal School; one of its teachers became the editor of the club's publication, *Qu River's Workers Tide* (*Qujiang gongchao*), China's earliest workers' publication. In its inaugural year the union had also led a strike against the Zhejiang Printing Company, a two-week affair that cost the company the rights to print the Zhejiang provincial gazette and other official publications, a loss that forced the company to close. Of all the workers organizations, the Club had the closest links to the Guomindang members giving the strongest support to May Fourth ideas.[40]

Following the members of the Club were two hundred representatives of the Hangzhou Workers Association, comprising a number of unnamed groups. This was likely an organization established in the spring by the Jin-Qu-Yan-Chu Association (JQYC Association), a political lobbying group representing provincial interior and hinterland counties (from the three least economically developed outer zones of the regional-systems model) that in the past had frequently been left out of the seats of power.[41] Directly behind the Workers Association and eventually linked to the JQYC Association was the demonstration's largest contingent, four hundred textile and craft workers of the Dongyang County Workers Native Place Association.[42] Evidence suggests that, in contrast to the Print Workers Club, these two associations operated more like paternalistic company unions. Wu Zhiying, one of the speakers at the rally, was an entrepreneur with close ties to the association; he may have been trying to maintain close control over the association at a time when his goal of increased mechanization had the potential for producing unemployment and consequent labor unrest.[43] Both organizations would come to play crucial roles in the revolutionary years ahead.

Fourth and fifth places went to individual factories—units followed by eighty members of the Hangzhou Youth Advance Together Society, the progressive group to whom Shen had recently spoken. Next came forty students from the Zhejiang Special Arts School, an institution that Shen sponsored and which he would head briefly as the principal in the summer and early fall of 1924.[44] Then came thirty members of the Socialist Youth Corps, followed by sixty representatives of the provincial Guomindang bureau. Bringing up the rear of the organized groups were the students from the women's sericulture school and the Eleventh Special Industrial School. Townspeople then joined the march as it wound its way through the main commercial and business district, moving from the New Market area until it reached the main thoroughfare running east to the train station, the demonstration's destination. Along the way the din of the crowd was punctuated by the shouting of the slogans that had been printed on the pennants at the rally. Once the train station was reached there were more shouts of the nationalistic slogans against imperialism and warlords and for the national revolution.

Several aspects of this May Day commemoration are noteworthy. Although the main organizers and speakers for the day were Guomindang members, they positioned themselves near the end of the parade, allowing the key labor organizations to lead the way. It was politically astute: their presence in the parade made it clear to all where they stood on the issues, but as they marched past the main businesses in downtown Hangzhou, they were not leading the way; they were not so openly challenging the capitalists. By allowing the laborers to lead the way they were also appealing to that class as a party that had the interests of labor in mind. The march also did not go past some of the key political and governmental buildings, but traversed the main east-west axis of modern Hangzhou that linked New Market, the symbol of modern commercial success, and the train station, the symbol from the early years of the century of modern change.

The first ten days of May provided progressive and nationalistic forces in Hangzhou two other opportunities for less massive commemorative meetings. At the May Fourth commemoration at the Education Association Hall on Pinghai Road in the New Market area, Shen and An Ticheng, both provincial Guomindang executive committee members, were the featured speakers.[45] On May 9, National Humiliation Day was observed also at the Education Association Hall. Sponsored by the Hangzhou Youth Advance Together Society and chaired by Xuan, the meeting featured speakers decrying the effects of imperialism. Among them were Communist and long-time Shen ally, Yu Xiusong, JQYC Association member Huang Weishi, and Wang Huafen, Shen's wife and "revolutionary helper."[46]

In mid-May 1924, then, the Hangzhou revolutionaries seemed unified. Laborers, students, journalists, educators, politicians from political and labor organizations with differing approaches and positions joined in expressing common nationalistic desires. Shen Dingyi was linked with all these groups through personal ties and direct networks and less directly through secondary links to associates of his direct connections. Shen himself through his identities as Communist Party member and Guomindang leader could be said to symbolize this unity in diversity. Though the First Congress in Guangzhou had raised among some of the participants the issue of CCP-GMD cooperation, it was not yet an issue in Zhejiang.

Shen did, in fact, at the insistence of party secretary Chen Duxiu, chair the CCP Enlarged Plenum that met in Shanghai from May 14 to 16.[47] That meeting, at which Chen wished to be relieved from the chair's duties so as to be able to speak more freely, also focused on the nature of the cooperation between the two parties. Zhang Guotao reports that though Shen was "normally quite garrulous in expressing his views, he became extremely courteous at the Plenum and ventured scarcely any opinion from beginning to end."[48] Whether Shen was beginning to have his own doubts and concerns about the issue (as Zhang explicitly claims), we cannot be certain. One source, his own memorial biography, re-counts an anecdote from that plenum meeting; its accuracy is subject to question given the desire of the authors to detail Shen's patriotic per-spicacity. Reportedly two Russians were present at the meeting. When talk turned to plans to destroy the Guomindang, Shen responded, "If the Third International has given the Chinese Communist Party orders to do away with the Guomindang, today there is nothing to stop de-ciding this by a vote." When the Russians heard the translation, they were angry, mumbling a few sentences. They asked Shen, "When you opened the meeting today, were there people who knew or not?" Shen answered, "Whoever is my friend knew." They were startled by his response, asking in return, "Do you mean to say that you didn't know that our meetings are secret?" Shen said, "Whoever is my friend is also my comrade." They said nothing else. The exchange allegedly deepened Shen's distrust of cooperating with the Communists.[49]

At Yaqian there would have been little doubt about the unity of revolutionary action. The May Day celebration at the rural village of Yaqian—without industrial workers—could be held because the popu-lace understood its meaning from the work of Shen and his First Normal teachers who sponsored its celebration two years earlier. This year Shen's school and Socialist Youth Corps (SYC) units planned the celebration. The SYC prepared printed materials and the newly formed GMD bureau issued reports that were passed out to boats coming to the steam launch dock. School children carried flags as they walked though the village in a "demonstration," singing labor songs along the way. SYC spokesmen gathered farmers together for speeches. The slogan of the day: "Work eight hours, educate eight hours, rest eight hours."[50] The Hangzhou May Day message had of necessity to be changed for Yaqian, but two points seem important. First, the day could be celebrated with any meaning at all only because of the previous work of Shen and his associates. Second, revolutionary institutions varied drastically according to arenas: in Hangzhou, labor organizations, high schools and colleges, and the rapidly growing Guomindang apparatus; in Yaqian, grade schools and the long-established SYC, dominant temporarily over the recently formed GMD bureau.

The Portent of the Collapse of Thunder Peak Pagoda

In September 1924, Zhejiang was pulled deeper into the vortex of national warlord factional politics. Zhejiang's military governor, Lu Yongxiang, was the only holdout in south central China against the Zhili clique of Wu Peifu. Tensions between Lu and Military Governor Qi Xieyuan in neighboring Jiangsu Province led to the outbreak of war on September 1, despite efforts to prevent it by the elites of both provinces.[51] Zhejiang was caught in a three-week war, fighting Qi to the north and the stronger forces of Sun Chuanfang moving up from the southwest. Lu fled Hangzhou on September 18, and Sun Chuanfang arrived in triumph on September 25. At 1:00 P.M., the exact time that Sun entered the city, the Thunder Peak Pagoda collapsed to the ground.

Built in the tenth century, the Thunder Peak Pagoda stood on a small hill on the southern shore of West Lake.[52] As a landmark, it was a spatial complement to the Baochu Pagoda on a ridge to the north of the lake. Originally a gray brick, in the sixteenth century it had been burned by Japanese pirates, destroying porches and balconies and turning the brick red. Nevertheless, the first of West Lake's so-called scenic views remained Thunder Peak "in the glow of sunset."[53] In addition to its contribution to scenic beauty, in the middle of the twelfth century there sprang up a story focusing on West Lake and Thunder Peak Pagoda that became one of China's most famous folk tales.[54]

The story of the White Snake was one of changing reality and dual identity, of overweening power and steadfast devotion. As a result of self-cultivation and the happenstance of swallowing a pill of immortality, a white snake living in West Lake was able to transform itself into a beautiful woman, Lady White. She met, fell in love with, and married Xu Xian, a pharmacist and dispenser of medicine. At one point early in their marriage, under the influence of sulphurated wine taken for a violent headache, she briefly lapsed into the form of the snake, "with mouth and fangs dripping with blood and slime," frightening Xu literally to death.[55] She had to revive him with a brew made from magic fungus stolen from Mount Kunlun. Their devoted happiness began to be shattered, however, with the appearance of a monk named Fa Hai, transformed from a turtle, who used black magic to enhance his powers. He ran afoul of Xu and Lady White when he unleashed an epidemic to impel more people to make heavier contributions to his temple; the epidemic, however, only brought more people to Xu's apothecary shop, for Xu's medicines were renowned. Fa Hai quickly became an enemy of Lady White; they engaged in stupendous contests of magical powers, battles that Fa Hai eventually won, in the process turning Lady White back into the White Snake. Then the monk built Thunder Peak Pagoda, "placed his gold begging bowl beneath the pagoda and imprisoned the white snake under it" for a period of twenty years.[56]

For the people of Zhejiang, Thunder Peak Pagoda conjured up a variety of meanings. Shaped in May Fourth ideals, Lu Xun's essays on "The Collapse of the Thunder Peak Pagoda" describe the pagoda as a prison that stifled the chosen identity of the White Snake and became a symbol of "the crushing burden of conventional morality over instinctual desire and love."[57] On a more popular level, over the centuries the pagoda had been a symbol of provincial protection because of its indestructibility at the hands of the Japanese pirates. Its sudden collapse, therefore, made the superstitious cluck their tongues, as they remembered the old saw that "when they should lose their liberty, Old Thunder Peak would fall down."[58] For many, this omen held a deeper reality than the likely reason for the collapse: over the centuries, pilgrims had chipped away at the structure's inner buttresses to obtain brick powder to mix with water as a remedy for stomach illness, a direct apothecary connection to the story of Xu Xian and Lady White.

Indeed, Sun Chuanfang's victory meant that Zhejiang would now be ruled as one of a group of provinces. The provincial autonomy that Shen had fought so hard to maintain in early 1917 and the figment of it that remained after that date was now completely swallowed up. Shen wrote a poem on the collapse of the pagoda, celebrating the historical existence and natural beauty of the pagoda and of drinking at dusk in its environs.[59]

Grief at the destruction of the great Thunder Peak Pagoda;
The hubbub of fleet horses clashing;
One cup, two cups, three cups—

Seated properly where the flood dragon
    respects and worships Shun.

The supernatural glory of the dawn,
    the clarity of the night star.
One hundred years, one thousand years, ten thousand years—
Till then people will be moved to write poems and to sing.

He saw the destruction of the pagoda as brought by the warlord scourge and the collapse as a metaphor for the destruction of much of China's most valued past by the era's militarism.

Though we have no record of Shen's commenting on the story of the White Snake, some resonance can be seen between the theme of the Snake-Lady's dual identities and the relativity of identity about which Shen often mused. Because identities are always relative to the social other and since identities vary across the range of family, social, and political possibilities without necessarily inviting contradictory guises, there was theoretically not any necessary conflict for Shen in choosing among his identities. But by the summer of 1924 Shen's actual persona was made up of a number of potentially competing identities. Communist Party member or Guomindang leader? Patron and teacher or party boss? Hangzhou provincial leader or Yaqian elite? Anchor primarily of which network—familial and native place? First Normal School? Provincial assembly?

It is most certainly at "times of social change and at critical decisions within the life course" that the "task of organizing multiple identities comes to the fore."[60] While the collapse of the pagoda had no direct relationship to Shen, it came at the same time that some of his own social and political supports began to be eroded and fall away, a process that necessitated Shen's more explicit definition of his own revolutionary identity. As in the case of the snake-lady, the process of identity formation was often compelled by outside forces. In such circumstances, which identities would come to the fore?[61] And why? What were the source and the dynamics of the making of social and political identity in a time of revolutionary flux?

No Fixed Point

In the summer of 1924, a process began among the Zhejiang revolutionary leadership not unlike that which had brought down

Thunder Peak Pagoda—the gradual but dangerous chipping away, here of good will and trust that undergirded networks and personal relationships. The initial irritant was the mundane problem of financial difficulties. From April through June, as we have seen, the party enjoyed great success in establishing county and municipal bureaus (in Hang, Xiaoshan, and Shaoxing counties and in Ningbo); deputies had also been sent to prepare for the formation of other bureaus (in Pinghu, Haining, Linhai, and Yongjia counties). The new bureaus (such as that in Xiaoshan headed by Kong Xuexiong) had generally asked for financial aid for the expansion of their work, and the provisional party bureau had responded positively. But in July the subsidy from the national party ceased at a time when a provincial debt of two thousand yuan had already been built up. Those in the provisional executive committee did not have the personal financial wherewithal either to pay the debt or continue subsidizing local bureaus.[62]

There was also growing discomfiture on the national level in both the CCP and the GMD about the working relationship of the two parties. Some CCP members, among them Chen Duxiu and Mao Zedong, questioned continuing the "bloc within" policy, while in the GMD old-line leaders like Zhang Ji and Xie Chi were growing increasingly distrustful of Communist goals. This unease had not directly affected the situation in Hangzhou, though Shen's chairing of the CCP Shanghai Plenum in May where the destruction of the Guomindang was discussed and his attendance at the Second GMD Plenum in Guangzhou in August where the issue was aired cannot help but have brought the relationship between the parties into sharper focus for him. If style of dress is any symbolic indicator of political position (as it has sometimes been in the People's Republic), then Shen had not yet taken a more conservative, traditional stance. A photograph of the twenty-one regular and alternate Central Executive Committee members at the August plenum (six of whom were also Communists) shows only two wearing Western-style suits and ties—Shen and fellow Communist Qu Qiubai; all the rest are wearing traditional Chinese dress. In addition, especially intriguing in light of the direction of Shen's own political inclination in the months ahead was what seems the symbolic placement of Shen directly behind a seated Sun Yat-sen. On the issue of party cooperation, the plenum complied with the position of Borodin that the "bloc within" policy should continue and recognized that Communists had special needs for secrecy and "special responsibility for the proletariat."[63]

In the middle of the Zhejiang-Jiangsu War in September, an incident occurred in Hangzhou on another National Humiliation Day, September 7, the date of the signing of the Boxer Protocol in 1901. There are reasons to suspect that the events of this day represent more of the cutting away of cooperation that had been seen in the demonstrations and commemorations of only four months earlier. The Zhejiang Provisional Provincial Guomindang Bureau organized the mass meeting, directed by Xuan Zhonghua, who had also chaired the May Day rally. The target was the corrupt presidency of Cao Kun, the National Assembly that had elected him, and the warlord regime of Wu Peifu that undergirded his regime. After the meeting six men led the crowd in a loud protest demonstration; five were the most important members and associates of Shen's First Normal network—Xuan Zhonghua, An Ticheng, Yu Xiusong, Wang Guansan, and Ni Youtian. The sixth was Cha Renwei, lawyer, journalist, longtime Guomindang member, and part of Shen's provincial assembly network. Efforts of the military and police to block the route of the demonstration were ineffectual as the marchers surged forward. When they reached Golden Sands Street, the pent-up anger against the Beiyang warlords and their regimes exploded in an attack on the family property of the Beijing government's Minister of Finance, Wang Kemin. Wang was seen as having caved in to French demands that the Boxer indemnity be paid in gold—an example of the unholy alliance between foreign imperialists and the warlord government.[64] The crowd destroyed the family's ancestral shrine and proceeded to take the ancestral tablets out of the compound in seven pieces and to throw them into West Lake, where they floated away.[65] It was a revolutionary act, symbolizing not only hatred for the warlords and imperialists but also considerable contempt for Chinese traditions.

Although all of the leaders of this demonstration were from the most progressive of Shen's networks, neither Shen nor any of his familial and native place networks participated; Cha was the single provincial assemblyman to join. Shen had long since returned from the Guangzhou plenum, but had apparently chosen not to involve himself in the Humiliation Day proceedings. Though the evidence is circumstantial, his absence in light of his continual participation four months before suggests that the relationship between Shen and the First Normal network may have begun to be strained.

Yet another obstacle for the party and for Shen was the effect of the war. Sun Chuanfang's victory and subsequent repression led to the arrest of key party members like Xuan and to the necessity of keeping party operations underground. Three members of the standing committee were forced to leave Hangzhou.[66] Sun's government suppressed party newspapers; *New Zhejiang*, edited by Cha Renwei, was stopped. Sun also closed the general branch office of the Shanghai-published *Republican Daily News*, which was managed by the provisional party bureau and which distributed copies to county branch bureaus.[67] In such a strained situation and beset by numerous practical, ideological, and social problems, the remaining leadership was also dogged by problems of jealousy in decision making.[68]

By October what party work was being done was by the provincial bureau's secretaries operating out of one room: party costs totaled only rent for the room and salaries for the secretaries. But there were not even enough funds to cover these expenses. In November, standing committee member and First Normal-linked An Ticheng advanced the money from his teaching salary so that the office could continue to be rented with the hope that progress in directing the affairs at the county level could resume. Although Shen was still the recognized head of the provisional party bureau, he did not involve himself in attempting to rescue the party from finance-caused oblivion; this further suggests his growing disaffection with the party's state of affairs. Even with the continuation of the office, subsidies to county bureaus could not be resumed. These bureaus further faced the reality that many of their responsible leaders of the summer had left their positions in light of the repression and harsh control of Sun Chuanfang.[69]

Whether from frustration with the situation in Hangzhou, the reality of the new regional warlord leadership of Sun Chuanfang, or new possibilities in the national arena of getting out of the warlord morass, in the fall of 1924 Shen seemed increasingly to focus on the national arena. From October 18 to November 4, he published a series of editorials on the national situation in the *Republican Daily News*. During this time, Feng Yuxiang had undertaken a successful coup against Wu Peifu and had invited Sun Yat-sen to go to Beijing to discuss the national situation. Suddenly, solving the national dilemma without recourse to a bloody civil war seemed possible. Sun left for Beijing on November 13. His willingness to go north further undercut the party; had he been successful, the laurels would have rested on his head, obviating the projected crucial role of the party in the unification of the nation.[70] Thus, his decision caused suspicion and chagrin in party circles. Shen was deputed to explain the thinking behind Sun's decision and to propagandize numerous political groups in Zhejiang. In this task throughout

December, Shen met with Sun Chuanfang and various organizations in Hangzhou and traveled to eastern Zhejiang where he met with county organizations.[71]

Before his departure, Sun had announced his plans for the establishment of a national assembly whose chief function would be the "unification and reconstruction of the country."[72] The assembly became the central focus of the Guomindang and CCP at the turn of the year. The formation in December of the Zhejiang Society for the Rapid Encouragement of a National Assembly suggests that, for all the problems that had troubled the party in the fall, the working relationship between the GMD and CCP members within the GMD was still viable. Not only were the seventeen people on the preparation committee a mix of GMD and CCP members, but the group included people from Shen's familial, First Normal, and provincial assembly networks.[73] The group was chaired by provincial assemblyman-bureaucrat and longtime Shen associate Mo Yongzhen, and the group met at the Xingwu Road law office of Shen Dingyi's relative, Shen Erqiao; but there were also key CCP-GMD members: An Ticheng, Huang Zhongmei, Shao Ji'ang, and perhaps Xuan Zhonghua.[74] It is no surprise that Yaqian village by early January 1925 had organized its own Rapid Encouragement Committee. Over and over again, movements and organizations in Hangzhou were replicated in counties that were linked to key figures in the capital, underscoring the practical political power of personal approaches and connections in the revolution.[75]

Drawing the Sword

In many ways the impact of the death of Sun Yat-sen from cancer in March 1925 on Shen Dingyi and his role in the Guomindang can be likened to the psychological impact of the collapse of Thunder Peak Pagoda on the people of Hangzhou and its environs. Like a landmark that offers direction, Sun had towered over the revolutionaries. He had increasingly become a focus of Shen's attention and admiration, from the time of his naming Shen to go to the Soviet Union in mid-1923 into late 1924, when Shen had become an apologist for Sun's Beijing trip. Now, like the fall of a landmark without which the site loses its previous identity, Sun's death had posed for the party and for Shen questions of identity and direction.

It is significant that the only reports of Shen's actions in the month and a half following Sun's death placed him in Yaqian, dealing with efforts to memorialize Sun. It is likely a measure of his disaffection from the situation of the provisional provincial party bureau that he did not participate in similar efforts in Hangzhou. On March 22, Shen chaired a Yaqian meeting to discuss preparations for commemorating Sun through renewed efforts to mobilize the masses.[76] The organizational meeting of the society to commemorate Sun was held in the hall of the Xiaoshan County Assembly on April 1, and throughout that month Shen was involved in the Yaqian memorial committee's efforts.[77]

On May 3, Shen left Shanghai for Guangzhou for the third GMD plenum, held between May 18 and May 25; it was the first attempt to set party policy after Sun's death. County party bureaus in Zhejiang had already begun to question the party's direction: the Jiaxing county bureau wrote to the provisional provincial bureau asking for discussion of the united front and questioning the import of the newly established Study Committee for Sun Yat-senism, formed by those opposed to Communist membership in the Guomindang.[78] The Guangzhou plenum heightened the anxieties of those who distrusted Communist motives, and yet again confirmed the policy admitting CCP members to the Guomindang and the continuation of the Political Council, a seven-man advisory council, dominated by Borodin.[79]

Shen made his final break with the Communist Party in the aftermath of Sun's death. A rather far-fetched report of Mao Dun claimed that Shen had been disenchanted with his membership as early as August 1923. He recounts that at a meeting of the Shanghai region Communist Party executive committee on August 5, Mao Zedong suggested that the Shanghai chapter of the Socialist Youth Corps moderate their criticism of Shen, Chen Wangdao, and Shao Lizi. The three had been denounced by some in the corps as opportunists. The party, on the other hand, wanted to blunt the criticism, for it felt that the three were too valuable to lose (they had already let it be known that they intended to resign from the party). A short time before, Shen had allegedly sent a letter to Chen Duxiu outlining his intent to resign. He said that at the time the party was formed, there had been a careful agreement that whenever party members were added, there had to be great attention shown to their quality: they must, Shen averred, be selflessly dedicated to the cause. Shen claimed, however, that after the party was formed, "it took too many party members, even hooligans, even those submissive to the White party." Mao Dun indicates that at the behest of the party he went to ask Shen to reconsider his proposed resignation. Shen did so and shortly thereafter left for the Soviet Union.[80] We know that his response to life in Moscow was highly enthusiastic, so this whole episode does not ring completely true.

By the spring of 1925, however, it was a different story. Shen's provincial power was ebbing away to assertive young Communists within the Guomindang; this in itself was a spur for Shen to act. Dai Jitao allegedly played a role in Shen's final decision to resign. If this is so, it must have happened at the Guangzhou Plenum in May. Dai himself suggests there were three reasons for Shen's decision: Communist Party opposition to a plan Shen favored to sponsor internal migration to Manchuria to relieve China's population problems; Shen's opposition to class struggle as a strategy; and Shen's belief that Communist Party members should not have dual party membership in the Guomindang.[81] For Shen the migration policy was something of an obsession. It fit closely with his opposition to class struggle. If population pressure could be relieved in this nonviolent way, it should also lessen the possibility of violent class struggle. But class struggle is at the heart of the Communist description of the march of history: on this there could be no compromise. The third reason—the "bloc within"—had been at issue at least since the First Congress in January 1924 and would become a major reason for the collapse of the united front. There is little reason to doubt that if these were not all the reasons for Shen's resignation, they were at least among the important ones.

In a short biography composed by the Memorial Committee after Shen's death, his allies gave two additional reasons for the resignation.[82] The first was that Shen opposed Communist strategy which saw the urban proletariat as the propertyless class that should be the major force in the revolution but which viewed farmers as small property holders who had little revolutionary potential. Shen believed by the end of 1921 that farmers should be the major revolutionary force in the construction of the new China, if only by dint of sheer numbers. In this sense, his ideas about rural revolution predate Mao Zedong's. The second reason was that Shen was at personal loggerheads with Chen Duxiu. This would not be surprising given Shen's desire for leadership and his knight-errant nature; others also had difficulty fitting into Chen's "patriarchy": it was the sole reason, in fact, that Chen Wangdao gave for his resignation.[83]

At the time when Shen resigned from the Communist Party, he was also making plans to wrest the provincial party structure from Communist Party members who had become leaders in the Guomindang.

The decision at Guangzhou to leave the "bloc within" policy intact had been the last straw. A 1926 Zhejiang party report that admittedly is unfriendly to Shen noted that from this point on, Shen was determined to destroy the provincial party bureau as it existed.[84] It is likely that Shen saw the continued leftist bent in the national arena as a harbinger of his being continually challenged for leadership in the provincial arena. The chief challenger was former personal friend Xuan Zhonghua, the especially committed Communist Guomindang member who held posts on the executive and standing committees in the Zhejiang provincial Guomindang and the secretaryship of the provincial Communist Party as well as posts in the Shanghai Communist Party. He had been active at the Fourth CCP Congress in January 1925, at which the CCP first specified a Right Wing, Left Wing, and Center of the Guomindang, "one of many Communist efforts to define the Kuomintang [Guomindang] in class terms."[85] Xuan, it was said, was grounded firmly in the spirit of the Fourth CCP Congress.[86] One wonders whether Shen's growing antipathy to Xuan and his former supportive network may indeed have had something to do with his own class background as landlord. Despite his identity of birth, he had constructed an identity from his commitment to social and political change. But Shen now found himself identified with the enemy by those very people who had taught at his school, propagandized farmers at his behest, and edited radical journals that he had begun. The revolution began to devour its own.

In determination and commitment, Shen and Xuan matched each other in their intensity. Anecdotes reveal much about their temperaments. In the winter of 1925, when Shen returned to Hangzhou to propagandize Sun's journey north, he threw a banquet for his friends, among them Xuan Zhonghua and An Ticheng. When the waiter brought the wine, he could not extract the stopper even though he used all his force. Shen then tried and also could not budge it, becoming increasingly angry. Finally he hit the neck of the bottle on the chair, saying, "Are you going to come out or not?" The neck of the bottle broke and wine spilled everywhere, soaking the clothes of those seated nearby.[87]

For his turn, Xuan, when admonished about risk taking in the face of danger, reportedly laughed, "What do you call danger? If we fear danger, why not return home to deal with your daughter's sons?" When admonished about his health, weakened by overwork and the effects of poverty, he replied, "Other people shed blood or suffer grinding difficulties in prison; how can I rest? What does being a little thin matter?"

A revolutionary who lived with Xuan and his wife in Shanghai remembered that "in the winter, they, husband and wife, only had one suit of cotton clothes; when one went out, he or she wore cotton clothing; the other covered his or her nakedness with a quilt."[88]

The May Thirtieth killings of Shanghai demonstrators on the orders of a British officer galvanized the anti-imperialist, antiwarlord fervor that had already been running at a high pitch for more than a year. Demonstrations of rage and revolutionary zeal swept the country. Though Shen had been in the forefront of antiwarlord and anti-imperialist activity in 1924, there is no record of his participation in the May Thirtieth Movement in any arena. Xuan, in contrast, was at center stage. The Shanghai local party committee sent Xuan to Hangzhou to work in the aftermath of the killings. On June 1, he spoke at a meeting of provincial education association chairmen; at the end of his speech, he reflected the sharp shift of the May Fourth Movement: "This time the struggle is absolutely not that of the individual—it is to sacrifice to save the nation." He called on students and those from all other circles to rise up and save the country, "to come to help our killed and wounded comrades in Shanghai." The Hangzhou Society for Student Assistance for Shanghai Comrades against Foreign Depredations was formed; it sponsored a huge rally on June 3, with more than ninety schools represented and an estimated thirty thousand people in attendance. The meeting produced a general demand that the government protect the national essence (*guoti*). During a protest parade that followed, participants shouted anti-imperialistic slogans.[89] On June 25 at yet another protest rally, chaired by First Normal graduate Han Baohua, an estimated sixty thousand participated.[90]

In the face of such massive nationalistic protests, Shen set his sights on establishing his firm control over the provincial party. He was aggressively moving away from an inclusionary approach, now a fleeting memory of more halcyon days, opting instead for a firm strategy of exclusion. Four days after the second rally in Hangzhou, Shen saw to the establishment of a full-fledged Guomindang bureau in Xiaoshan county, an institution that could sponsor a meeting in Yaqian that he would approach with drawn sword.[91] Of the seven standing members of the county party bureau at least five (and possibly all) were in Shen's personal network or had worked closely with him in local affairs. The same was true of the five alternate members. One of them, Zhang Liusheng, was as well a close friend of Xuan Zhonghua. These were the men who made arrangements for the Yaqian conference of the provincial Guomindang that began July 5, 1925. They were expected to follow Shen's policies and desires.

What happened at Yaqian depends on who reported the action. Shanghai's *Republican Daily News* gave what is probably the least biased and most factual reporting of the events. The Xiaoshan Guomindang executive committee and the Yaqian Village School's Self-Government Society welcomed the more than forty delegates from bureaus from throughout the province at 9:00 A.M. After both Dai Jitao and Shen Dingyi spoke, the whole assembly went to Phoenix Mountain, just to the north of Yaqian, to pay their respects at the tomb of Li Chenghu, farmer leader of the 1921 rent resistance campaign. Shen presided over the formal meeting that began at 3:00 P.M. He reported on the preparations for the establishment of a full-fledged provincial bureau and on the situation of the provisional bureau. Dai followed with a talk on the national revolution, detailing its history from the days of the Revolutionary Alliance and stressing the centrality of Sun Yat-sen's thought. He argued that party comrades were not doing as much as they could to bring about revolutionary progress, and he encouraged them to earnestly accept and uphold Sun's thought. The delegates discussed the specific techniques and methods that were most important in actualizing the goals of the national revolution.[92] The newspaper report's most interesting aspect is its disclosure of the ritual of paying respects to Li Chenghu. Its coming at the beginning of the conference clearly indicates how Shen ranked its importance for setting the tone of the conference. Whatever his positions relative to the specific party matters, Shen clearly had not departed from his ideas of class and social mobilization of four years earlier as a cornerstone of his social and political approach.

Though we have no account of the meeting from Shen's own hand, his 1928 memorial biography likely reflects his perspective. This account argues that the basic problem was the effort of Communist Party members within the provincial Guomindang to take or at least to curtail Shen's power. Their alleged technique was trying to gain control of the party's purse strings by controlling any monies coming from the party's Central Executive Committee for disbursement directly to county and municipal bureaus. Communist Party members within the Guomindang—as a group—wanted thereby to bypass the provisional provincial bureau that Shen controlled. In short, Communist activity was a power play against Shen, a reality that aped Communist efforts at the level of the party's central committee. This reality reportedly became clearer to Shen after Sun's death. The Yaqian meeting was therefore Shen's effort to stop the Communists' move for power and, with the help of central committee member Dai, to get the provincial party to commit itself to the ideas of Sun Yat-sen.[93]

To counter this view are two anti-Shen interpretations, by the major biographers of Xuan Zhonghua and by Zhong Baiyong, teacher at the Shaoxing Women's Normal School, whom Shen had asked to be one of the conference secretaries.[94] Both accounts depict the Yaqian conference as a naked display of Shen's thirst for power and his increasingly reactionary views. Since both accounts place this meeting in the context of the Western Hills conference still almost five months in the future, it is difficult to know whether their interpretation represented the view at the time of the conference or whether it has been added in retrospect in light of Shen's subsequent participation in the Western Hills meeting. Such anachronistic arguments raise questions about the historians' perceptions, interpretations, and, in Zhong's case, memory. Especially given Shen's reverence to Li Chenghu, which neither of his detractors even mentions, parts of their interpretation seem likely another case of events-yet-to-come disfiguring the reality of the past.

Xuan's biographers describe how Shen and Dai controlled every facet of the meeting. It was called on short notice so that the Communist Party members and the left-wing Guomindang members would not have time to prepare. It was held in Shen's home village, where Shen shaped the environment and structure of the meeting. Shen reportedly brought the delegates indiscriminantly into a common sleeping room, brought them together at the same hour to one dining hall, and even controlled their resting time. If the locations of struggle are not only real but also symbolic, then Shen's compelling the delegates to meet in his home compound and his control of space can be seen as "an active constitutive component of hegemonic power."[95] On the other hand, there were doubtless few if any inns, hotels, or restaurants in the small village for delegates to visit, and if the meeting had a schedule, the rest time of the participants would obviously be controlled.

While the anti-Shen sources agree on the general outcome of the meeting, they offer substantially different pictures of the meeting's dynamics and tenor. The biographers lambast Shen's dictatorial organizational style, but they find Dai to have been an especially slick operator, putting forth a very friendly demeanor, gathering everyone to hear his old stories, and even singing Japanese songs. Given reports of Dai's general laconic style, this activity does seem forced and strained. The alleged point of these techniques was to befriend delegates so as to make them easier to win over to his point of view. But the leftists were no fools, according to the biographers; they met every argument head-on and gave no ground even when Shen allegedly tried to stop every speaker who disagreed with him.[96]

Zhong's account depicts a far more rancorous meeting, with Dai playing a very different, abrasively challenging role. It should be noted that Zhong is far from an impartial historian; he had worked closely with Xuan Zhonghua when Xuan had organized the Shaoxing County GMD bureau and from that experience had noted his "youthful arrogance and passion." Zhong claims that the conference was a three-day affair attended by sixty party cadres. Although it was directed by Shen, Dai Jitao dominated the first two days with talks on the thought of Sun Yat-sen, describing himself as Sun's foremost disciple. Zhong claims that Dai told the delegates that after hearing his exposition, they were to return to their counties to organize societies to study Sun's thought. Zhong describes the delegates' response as amazement. That incredulity turned to anger, however, when Dai allegedly launched into a description of Sun as the inheritor of the orthodox morality of Yao, Shun, King Wen, the Duke of Zhou, and Confucius, and called Marxism incompatible with the central directing principles of the GMD: the eight virtues of loyalty, filiality, benevolence, love, trust, morality, harmony, and peace. Zhong does not use direct quotations from any extant versions of the meeting's presentations; we do not know his sources or if the account is largely from his own memory. Certainly the views represented Dai's current feelings: he had written them in his books that summer. Whether he would be so blatantly unpolitical in a politically charged meeting where he and Shen were trying to pick up support for their position is another question. Whereas the account of Xuan's biographers makes Dai a wily politician, Zhong's account makes him an apolitical ideologue. Whatever the truth of the matter, it is clear that he upset a number of delegates. Zhong reports that the more they heard, the angrier they became, filling the air with shouts for Dai to stop talking.[97]

Shen, according to Zhong, did not speak until the last day, when he addressed the conference on the incompatibility of Communism with the national spirit of China. He did not stir up the ire that Dai had unleashed. Xuan Zhonghua emerged as the chief spokesman against the positions of Dai and Shen.[98] The meeting ended quite suddenly, according to Zhong, when Xuan turned the tables by using Sun Yat-sen against them. He charged them with obfuscating the meaning of Sun's teachings and of turning their backs on his legacy and his important policies decided at the First Congress.[99] He argued that the so-called Sun Yat-sen Study Societies would undercut the party organization, and he made it clear that he would take the issues to the Guomindang Central Party bureau in Guangzhou. Allegedly, Shen, on seeing the great anger of the crowd, abruptly announced that the meeting was concluded.[100] Because none of the sources at the time that are sympathetic to Shen provide any details of the meeting other than to say Shen made known his opposition to the "Communist element," we are left in a quandary. But in light of the tendencies of Shen's detractors to have subsequent events color earlier reality, especially the foreshadowing of the Western Hills meeting or even Xuan's eventually taking the issues to the Second Congress, it is difficult to determine the truth of what occurred in Yaqian in early July 1925.

All sources do agree that the issues reportedly sparking the most fire were the party's positions on class struggle and the continuation of the "bloc within" policy. Shen had a record of inconsistency on the issue of class struggle. He clearly recognized the inherent conflict between classes and occasionally pointed out the *necessity* of violence. In "Poems and Labor," he had written, "there isn't even an inch of land in the world where the laboring class can live happily. When there are both classes existing in the world, the laboring class, which creates the wealth for the world, will never progress if they don't overthrow the robbing class."[101] And yet at the same time Shen championed an empathetic love, harmony, or benevolence *(renai)* between the landlord-capitalist class and the masses. This emphasis on community based upon a common humanity was evident in the essay from November 1919 where he argued that "there are no poor people; there are no rich people; there is no [difference between] you, I, or he; and whatever under heaven is [called] you, I, or he can all be considered as one person joined together by love [*ai*]."[102] Such an outlook matched landlord Shen's own *perceived* personal history of responses to farmers and workers. In Shen's relativist thinking, his own natal class identity as landlord could not fix him permanently as a member of the "robbing class": his actions superseded his class name, giving him his existential identity. His *renai* approach, from his perspective, had been and would continue to be constructive. From the viewpoint of the provincial Communist Party members, however, dispensing with the idea of class struggle was forsaking the very core of Marxist thought. The issue of the "bloc within" was really at the heart of Shen's sponsoring the Yaqian conference. His experiences had brought him to the point of viewing the Communists within the Guomindang as devious and power hungry—the mirror image of the view those members had of him; thus he now opposed allowing Communist Party or Socialist Youth Corps members to join the Guomindang. Xuan bitterly opposed this change.

The provisional provincial party bureau's special instructions to party branches after the conclusion of the meeting promulgated Shen's positions.

The Three People's Principles are the ideology to save the country; it links the revolutionary classes; it recognizes that to save the country, the future of the revolutionary forces must be based on our party organization. "People's livelihood" [*minsheng*] is the central focus of history. "Empathetic love" [*renai*] is the great morality of "people's livelihood." The wisdom of knowing "human-heartedness" [*ren*] and the courage to put it into action actualizes the Way [*tao*] of empathetic love. These principles allow us to know thoroughly revolutionary and antirevolutionary elements. They are not attributes belonging to class, but of knowledge and awareness [*jue-wu*]. . . . About the ills of society and the incipient class struggle, our party will strive mightily to call each class to become aware, to use revolutionary methods, to put into operation the national institution of the Three People's Principles, to defend against the harm of class struggle, and to eliminate the difference in classes.[103]

But the "victory" won at the Yaqian meeting was pyrrhic. If the conclusion of the meeting was as Zhong described, then the victory was angrily self-proclaimed. Even if the conclusion was that Shen and Dai won the day because they were able to convince the majority of the delegates,[104] Xuan and others in Shen's First Normal network did not yield to Shen; they simply ignored him and worked to set up their own party apparatus. In sum, while the Yaqian meeting was the first open confrontation between Shen and those who had become his opponents, it settled nothing. It only confirmed and deepened the mistrust and dislike that each side had of the other. For Shen the debate and the actions of those who had once been his disciples proved that he was right in his earlier estimation of them. For the First Normal network, the conference had been a case study in the arrogantly authoritarian style of Shen and in his retrograde ideological stance. On his return boat trip to Hangzhou, Xuan was reportedly warned by one of his friends about opposing Shen, who despite the events at Yaqian was still the most powerful figure in the provincial party. "You and Shen have had some cooperation; people say it is very difficult to break you and Shen up." Xuan's alleged response: "I am for revolution and cooperation with

Shen. Shen can encourage me to join the CCP; however, he can in no way compel me to leave. If he dares oppose the revolution, then I will oppose him."[105] Like the establishment of the Leninist party, the process of revolution brought an exclusionary dynamic spawned by the changing and developing definition of both the revolution and the opposition.

In many ways what had happened at Yaqian was the result of a year long's drift apart, at the time an almost imperceptible separation of once very close allies. The enervating frustrations over financing the party, the controversial trip of Sun to Beijing and Shen's strong support of it, and the radical symbolism of the September Humiliation Day actions and the May Thirtieth Movement—all gave rise to perceptions and fears, some of which may have had elements of truth to them, that began to erode the mutual trust of the strong network on which Shen had relied to do his work and his bidding. This erosion underscores the fragility of networks, especially in revolutionary times. But even more, the confrontational Yaqian meeting had the effect of polarizing the delegates into hardening factions and blowing up the earlier temporary evidences of suspicion and distrust into a permanent reality. In the process of revolution, the Yaqian conference produced a new level of polarized perceptions and expectations about "the opposition" as it shaped or enhanced new identities for the delegates in the revolutionary days ahead. In such a situation, as in deciphering polarized historical accounts, it was difficult to tell what was image and what was reality. What was not difficult to tell was that if the goal of the meeting had been to achieve consensus for the making of revolutionary progress, then it had been a case of all falling down. Shen's First Normal network was not only dead, but he had turned it into an active personal enemy.

As a measure of the extent of hostility among the revolutionaries in the summer of 1925, longtime associate of Sun Yat-sen Liao Zhongkai was felled by an assassin in Guangzhou on August 20. Shen, in Shanghai at the time, wrote the following couplet, speaking of righteous revolutionary commitment and undoubtedly reflecting his own sense of heroic exceptionalism.

> One must be a mediocre man if no one is jealous of him.
> In the roily rigors of life
> How could he find the peaceful time
>   to ask surcease from trouble?
>
> If one can do something exceptional even if he has to die,
> It is like the sun;

The brilliance of the light comes completely
    from his righteousness.[106]

The killing of Liao, one of those who continued to work cooperatively
with the Communists, was a bloody exclamation point to the rising
intraparty feuding. When party conservative Hu Hanmin was implicated
in the crime and sent away from Guangzhou on a "mission" to the Soviet
Union, Shen joined Dai Jitao and Shao Yuanzhong (a Zhejiangese
journalist in Shanghai) in sending a telegram decrying Hu's temporary
exile.[107]

After the collapse of the Thunder Peak Pagoda, provincial officials and
nonofficial elites raised ten thousand yuan to restore the old landmark.
As another measure of the times, the funds were seized by the warlord
government of Zhejiang for military use, and it was reported in the fall
of 1926 that there was no hope of regaining the money.[108] Similarly, the
death of Sun Yat-sen had led to a situation where, without fixed points,
the party was drawing swords. It is hard to see how there could have been
any hope of restoring the revolutionary unity and sense of inclusion that
had once existed.

CHAPTER SIX

The Black Star
Hangzhou and Yaqian, 1925–1926

I know that ultimately for the Chinese people the name is more important than the deed.
        "Is the name or the deed more important?"
        (Mingyi zhong? Shishi zhong?), 1919

The mystery of Shen Dingyi from the Yaqian conference until his murder three years later is made particularly difficult by the polarization that burgeoned at Yaqian and that increasingly colored Chinese politics in unremitting shades of invidious red and treacherous white. For the detective, who must face the continuing interpretive problems of identity and perception in efforts to reach some sense of the reality of the times, these years, like the Yaqian conference, provide the added problem of reconciling opposing descriptions of historical actions and events. And always there is the name ascribed by the opposition, a name defining social role and one's relationship to the political environment. The action of naming is, like the process of revolution, exclusionary. In a culture where social role and relativity are the base, one's social name helps to create a perception that in turn often becomes reality.

Take the name "politician," often linked with "venal" in the period when pecuniary alliances with warlords frequently included bribery and graft. Rumor had it that money was a reason for Shen's 1925 shift in party policy. A 1926 report of the left wing of the party suggests that it was a subsidy of a thousand yuan from Dai Jitao that permitted Shen to hold and host the Yaqian conference.[1] One negative biographer claims that Shen was attracted to the networks of Dai and other party conservatives because of the possibility of long-term financial support.[2] Given the desperate state of party finances, this interpretation might seem to take on some credibility. But unless one believes that Shen was motivated by the simple thirst for additional power that would come— only temporarily—from a subsidy, it strains credulity to believe that Shen would cast off all ideals and many personal relationships for a relative pittance. His tirades of the May Fourth period against the allure and destructive nature of money are clearly on record.[3] These charges are just the kind one would expect in the effort to cast Shen as just another venal politician. Hear the words of Xu Meikun, Communist Party member embittered by Shen's actions and rumored to have had an affair with Shen's wife Wang Huafen: "Shen was an opportunistic politician; he was involved in all sorts of movements, but his goal was always himself."[4]

Or, link the name politician with "arrogant," "unfair," and "unjust." Reportedly when elections were held in September 1925 for the January 1926 Second Guomindang Congress, Shen lobbied hard first for himself and then for his nephew Shen Xiaowen. In discussing the election of delegates, Shen allegedly said something like, "If one deeply understands Zhejiang's politics, economy, culture, and education and you talk an hour or two and there is no repetition [of his qualifications], then that is the man to be elected." Thereupon, he volunteered himself. Xuan Zhonghua's reported response: "I agree with Comrade Shen about his qualifications; however, if we are going to elect a perfectly fair and just person, we must pay attention to that person's impartiality."[5]

Also reported (from the opposition) was Shen's high-handed actions when Shen Xiaowen was not elected a delegate. When he became aware that Xiaowen would fail, he allegedly refused to open the remaining ballots, thereby nullifying the election. When others tried to prevent this action, he stuffed the ballots in his pockets and walked out.[6] There is no corroboration of this incident from impartial sources; indeed, given the polarized situation, there is likely not such a source. Certainly Xuan's call for impartiality was nothing more than a plea for his position. The obvious result of such reporting was to shape a particular image of Shen that then has been accepted by various later writers.

Or, take the name Shen allegedly applied to Xuan before the Yaqian conference: "tool" of the Third International. "He receives the direction of the Third International; do not believe him."[7] For a party trying to cast off the hold of outside imperialistic powers, the image conjured up here is obviously one of submissiveness to an outside power. For party members who shared Shen's images or whose images Shen was trying to shape, the name brought with it a powerful reality.

Or, finally, take the terms "left" and "right" that began to be bandied about with increasing frequency. The Communist Party had not always had a right-wing Guomindang as a target. At the Second Plenum of the Communist Party Central Committee in February 1924, resolutions had in fact warned that "Communists should not categorize those [Guomindang] members who were cool to them as 'Rightists' nor treat them disrespectfully, as this would only create a Right Faction."[8] Policy resolutions adopted at the meeting and at the spring Socialist Youth Corps meeting, however, prompted several Guomindang members to impeach the Communist Party as a party seeking to destroy the Guomindang from within.[9] While the August 1924 and May 1925 Guomindang plenums had seemingly settled the issue with a decision to continue the "bloc within" policy, the polarizing events of 1925, especially following the assassination of Liao, led to frequent Communist attacks on the "right" Guomindang.[10] Not only did the Communists apply the name of right wing to its opponents, but it also supplied its definition: "counter-revolutionary and subservient to imperialist interests."[11]

In addition to their arising in pointedly antagonistic rhetoric as a brush to tar opponents, the reality to which these terms pointed is particularly fuzzy and fluid. They are, of course, relative to one's own position at any particular time. Even the Communist Party, which first used the label, changed its description of the nature of the right wing several times from the summer of 1925 to the summer of 1926. The right wing did not have an independent, discrete meaning: instead it was determined by the Communist Party's reactions to various political contingencies in a fluid revolutionary situation. Those who designated individuals and institutions "right" or "left" intended the terms to connote whole complexes of particular conservative or liberal ideological and sociocultural views. Because of the constellation of historical meanings associated with these terms, those designated "right" or "left" took on primarily an ideological identity. This implication was exactly what the Communists intended in the turbulent world of revolutionary politics, for only then could its political opponents become ideological (not merely political) enemies and it could use its imputations of counter-revolution to expand its power within the party against powerful veteran allies of Sun Yat-sen.

The Provincial Battleground: County and Municipal Bureaus

Shen had been weakened on the provincial level but was still a dominant force. He installed in the provincial bureau supporters from Jiaxing and Wenzhou. Political polarization has left historical accounts which are contradictory about many actions relating to this bureau. For example, anti-Shen sources claim that Shen removed from the provincial party executive committee Yu Xiusong, of the First Normal network and cofounder with Shen of the Hangzhou Socialist Youth Corps, and replaced him by his kinsman Shen Erqiao.[12] Pro-Shen sources, however, say that Yu simply resigned his post because of his plans to travel to the Soviet Union.[13]

It was, however, in the local party bureaus that the struggle between Shen and his erstwhile First Normal network raged. A meeting in September of the Shanghai-area Communist Party committees advised Xuan, who had now become the node of the First Normal network, that there "should be extensive progress in local areas in order to mobilize and link county and municipal party bureaus against the right-leaning movement of Shen."[14] For Shen such a strategy was a direct challenge, an attempted cooptation of his major arena of action, the locality. Not only had he always retreated to the locality (his native place) for support or solace, but much of his work had been in other local county and subcounty arenas. As we have seen, at least from the point of his confrontation with Wang Jinfa over local control in the 1911 period, Shen paid special attention to the locality and its possibility as a base for social and political change. Sun Yat-sen had made Shen his propagandist in the local arenas of eastern Zhejiang in late 1924. Shen's "victory" at Yaqian had come through his links to delegates from some of these areas. Shen had no choice but to try to meet the challenge. The provisional provincial bureau made closer connections to those bureaus that were friendly, propagandizing them about the dangers of continued collaboration with the Communists. Shen and his allies pointed out the power of Borodin and the mistake the party's central committee was making in continuing the "bloc within" strategy. According to leftist opponents, all this made Shen and his allies—and here another name—"running dogs of the imperialists." Mao Zedong claimed they "really are doing the work of imperialism because their work fits the needs of imperialism" by undercutting the national revolution.[15] The 1926 report of the left asserted that those local bureaus hostile to Shen were the objects of Shen's destructive malice and his attempts to subvert them through the use of monthly subsidies (the source of which, given the general poverty of the provincial party, is not disclosed).[16]

The Western Hills Episode

In 1926, at the Shanghai congress dominated by the Western Hills group, Shen gave the major report on the earlier Western Hills "plenum."[17] In that speech, he set forth the political context which prompted the coalition. He argued that the Soviets had discovered that the Chinese national revolution was not Communist but actually marched under the banner of the Three People's Principles; thus, their decision to destroy the Guomindang. Borodin's power was the instrument of that destruction, and the initial weapon was financial control of party formation and development. All financial requests, Shen claimed, had to pass Borodin's scrutiny. Borodin had proposed that the level of financial support of local organizations should be based upon the extent of revolutionary work being accomplished. Though Shen agreed this was logical (*bu cuo*), in practice Borodin meant the extent to which a given local institution was controlled by Communist members of the Guomindang.

The immediate context for the organization of the Western Hills group was growing disputes between the authorities of the Whampoa Military Academy and the Central Executive Committee of the party. Articles in the Communist publication *The Guide* (*Xiangdao*) began to refer to left and right factions of the Guomindang, an ominous development indicating the Communists were trying to stimulate such a split. The sending of Hu Hanmin to the Soviet Union and Borodin's hounding of conservative Zou Lu, head of Guangdong University, out of Guangzhou also seemed to indicate the need for opponents of the increasingly powerful role of Borodin and the Communists to join together. Thus, the meeting in front of Sun's coffin outside Beijing from November 23, 1925, to January 4, 1926.[18]

It is clear that Shen saw identity as something to be constructed, but it is also bestowed by others. For some Shen's social identity as politician and rightist matched their perception of reality, but others in the party saw him on the other pole of the political spectrum as a Communist. Since he had been involved in the discussions that led to the founding of the Communist Party, Shen's identity for some was shaped and fixed by that historical role. When, in the fall of 1925, Shen made a commitment to action in the national arena, this perception had immediate repercussions. On November 19, four days before the opening of the Western Hills conference in Beijing, Shen and Dai Jitao, who had traveled to the capital together, were kidnapped from their hotel, held, and beaten by ultraconservative Guomindang members who believed that Shen was a Communist agent out to subvert the meeting.

Shen's participation with this group in the national arena from November 1925 through April 1926 is an involvement that had drastic and permanent implications for his image and his future. Still shrouded in mystery, the motive for his participation in what has traditionally been seen as a meeting of the ultraconservative right wing of the Guomindang is somewhat puzzling. On its face, it might appear as though Shen had cast aside his long record of being in the forefront of liberal and at times radical ideological causes. But the proceedings of the conference and of the Western Hills-dominated Second Guomindang Shanghai Congress (March 29 to April 10, 1926) give little evidence of being dominated or even marked by substantial attention to ideological issues.[19] Though without question many Western Hills adherents were conservative, there was sufficient ideological differentiation in the group to cast doubt on the assumption that ideology served as its primary basis.

The group was more bound together by specific political grievances at a particular historical moment than by long-held conservative ideological commitments. Outrage at Communist actions and the power of Borodin in party matters sparked the holding of the conference and produced its significant decisions: to oust Communist members from the Guomindang, to dismiss Borodin as a party adviser, to abolish the Political Council (controlled by Borodin), and to suspend Guomindang leader Wang Jingwei for six months. Important also in the group's formation was a variety of personal connections, networks, and arenas of action and commitment that both brought the Western Hills adherents cohesion and paradoxically contributed to a lack of it.

A study of the Western Hills participants' various connections (friendship, native place ties, kinship and marriage ties, shared voluntary political associations, political patron-client ties, and shared political experiences) reveals two networks. The network to which Shen belonged (with Dai Jitao, Shao Yuanzhong, and Ye Chucang) was linked by common native place and professional background and by individual friendships (Dai and Shen; Dai and Shao). They had a more tolerant political stance on the issue of Borodin and the "bloc within." This network, which I will term the moderates, had met with longtime Guomindang revolutionary Wu Zhihui on November 18; they agreed that there should not be a unilateral break with the Communists and that Wang Jingwei not be impeached. This moderate proposal reportedly enraged the fervent anti-Communists at the conference and may have precipitated the physical attacks on Dai and Shen the next day.

All men in this network left the conference early, though Shen, Shao, and Ye played not insubstantial roles during the conference. Shen drafted many of the policy documents and organizational procedures and regulations at the meeting.[20] But in many ways, this network was peripheral in the Western Hills group in terms of organization and ultimate commitment. Dai left Beijing after suffering the beating even before the meeting began. Shao and Ye were seen even by the Communists as men who could be brought back within the Guomindang headquartered in Guangzhou. On their return to Shanghai they met with Communist leaders Chen Duxiu, Zhang Guotao, and Cai Hesen in conciliatory discussions.[21] The left wing's continued negative reaction to Dai, despite his declaration that he wanted nothing to do with the Western Hills group, would likely have come from aversion to his writings. The continued castigation of Shen likely stemmed from the strong hatred the Zhejiang contingent had developed for him. The Communists also probably saw Shen and Dai as turncoats, as they were involved early on in the formation of the Communist Party but forsook it for the "extreme right." One other noteworthy aspect of this network was that the main arena of political action for three of the four—Shen, Shao, and Ye—was not the national stage but the provincial and local arenas. Though all three had periods of action in national politics, their chief focus was below that level: Shen in Zhejiang and Yaqian, Shao in Zhejiang, especially Hangzhou; and Ye in Jiangsu. In the political fluidity of the era, various propelling or constraining forces in the arenas of individual actors were significant elements shaping the intensity and durability of political commitment.

The core network of eleven men in the conference was composed of two clusters, one linked by friendship and voluntary political association (the initiators of the meeting and longtime Sun Yat-sen supporters Zou Lu, Lin Sen, Zhang Ji, Xie Chi, and Deng Zeru); and the other by the same bonds with the addition of native place (the central Yangzi) and former allegiance to the revolutionary Huang Xing (Shi Qingyang, Ju Zheng, Shi Ying, Tan Chen, Mao Zuquan, and Fu Rulin).[22] While there were multiple links between the men within each cluster, the clusters were joined by single-stranded links. Men from these two clusters signed the initial letter to Wang Jingwei setting forth the necessity of separating the Communists from the Guomindang. This network had the clear majority power in defeating the position of the moderate network. Though both networks shared a strong fear of and consternation about the increasing power of Borodin and the Communists, each person came to the conference with different motivations—personal pique at recent political directions in Guangzhou, friendship with other conference participants, ideological conviction, nationalistic resentment of Soviet interference in the Chinese revolution.

The sources for Shen's participation in the Western Hills meeting appears to have been a combination of personal connections, his immediate political experiences in Zhejiang, and his political fears about the future of the revolution. Connections to Dai Jitao, with whom he traveled to Beijing, seem important in this regard. Their personal friendship, forged in Shanghai in 1919 and 1920, Shen's support of the party ideology set forth by Dai in the summer of 1925, and Shen's possible indebtedness to Dai for the money to hold the Yaqian conference in July 1925—all linked Shen to Dai. Even more important was that the Western Hills conference came at an important juncture for Shen in his leadership of the party in Zhejiang. He entered the national arena as he was being increasingly challenged in his main provincial arena by the organizational successes and growing influence of Communist members in the party. Shen's participation may well have been prompted by his sense that his dilemma and struggle in Zhejiang were part of the same trial the party center was facing and that a national solution was necessary before the revolution could proceed.

Telegrams from Zhejiang in support of that meeting came mostly from eastern Zhejiang, counties that would have had closer relationships to Shen and his allies, though one from Jiaxing, a bureau that had been organized by Xuan, is striking in its description of the problem of name and deed:

Since Sun died, there has been no discipline in party principles. The party splits are complicated. There are many designing followers. From outside the party, people borrow the party's name, secretly putting into effect Communist reality. . . . They use one or two selfish people to monopolize party affairs. Several days ago Jiaxing Standing Committee member Gu Zuozhi on his own authority under the name of the party sent a telegram opposing the party. His behavior was incorrect; his tactics were mean and base.[23]

The Eastern Hills Meeting

If the Yaqian conference had been a declaration of war between Shen and his opponents, the Western Hills conference brought the groups into full-scale battle. On December 7, Communist members of the provincial Guomindang—all of them former members of Shen's First Normal network—cast off their registration with the provincial party bureau. Provincial bureau executive committee members Xuan Zhonghua, Yu Xiusong, and An Ticheng and alternate members Ni Youtian and Tang Gongxian wanted to have nothing more to do with Shen's party.[24] Five days later the provincial bureau took the redundant action of ousting these five Communist members and four additional ones, including Wang Guansan, another of Shen's former allies. At the same meeting the bureau agreed that the Western Hills conference represented the party to which it would owe allegiance.[25]

Having left Shen's party, the First Normal network took the struggle to the localities. On December 15 the chairs of ten county and municipal bureaus met at Eastern Hills Park in the town of Zhashi in Haining county, contiguous to Hangzhou to the northeast.[26] Only two counties did not send delegates, Xiaoshan and Pujiang, although also conspicuously absent was the municipality of Hangzhou. These three bureaus remained in Shen's camp and supported the Western Hills conference.[27] Xuan Zhonghua chaired the Eastern Hills meeting, which denounced the Western Hills group and established the Alliance of Zhejiang's County and Municipal Party Bureaus. This alliance would seize the authority of Shen's provisional provincial bureau and would organize a provincial party congress in order to finally establish a full-fledged provincial bureau. Under Xuan's guidance, the alliance sent a telegram to the Central Executive Committee of the party, reporting on their actions and on Shen's "villainy." The Eastern Hills meeting was a dramatic effort to undercut Shen's provincial power. But although the alliance was composed of representatives of most of the local bureaus, many of those local bureaus also had partisans of Shen and the Western Hills meeting. By early January these partisans were forming Sun Yat-sen Study Societies or trying to seize power over the alliance in local party bureaus.[28] Shen's strongest support came from Hangzhou and Xiaoshan bureaus composed of relatives (like nephew Shen Xiaowen and fellow lineager Shen Erqiao) and disciples and friends (like Wang Nayin, Chen Bodun, and Xu Panyun).[29]

The presence of a substantial local and provincial opposition to the Western Hills meeting also likely gave the national Western Hills group pause about trying to build up the Zhejiang-Jiangsu-Shanghai region as a base from which to attack the party center in Guangzhou. When the 1926 Second Guomindang Congress met in Guangzhou from January 1 to January 19, it decided to keep the three "great" policies (*san da*): to continue to uphold Sun's links to the Soviet Union, to maintain the alliance with the Communist Party, and to focus on farmers and workers. The congress declared that the Western Hills meeting was illegal and blamed the Western Hills group for reactionary behavior that was destroying the national revolution.[30] Xuan gave the report on Zhejiang provincial party matters at Guangzhou; on the basis of that account, the Second Congress ordered the dissolution of Shen's provincial party, approving the transfer of authority to the alliance.[31] After the congress, the alliance made plans to establish the provincial bureau in a new location, on Headhair Lane in central Hangzhou, far removed from the area of West Lake, in what might be called the cultural and educational district. With this decision, Shen found himself in clear opposition to the party establishment.

Never one to shrink from battle, Shen met his opponents head-on. On January 23, he and his allies opened an All-County Conference of the Chairs of Guomindang Standing Committees. The conference decided to support the purge of Communist members called for at the Western Hills meeting and to blunt the formation of the so-called full-fledged bureau by the alliance.[32] Just as the Xuan faction declared Shen's faction illegitimate on the basis of the decisions of the Guangzhou Congress, so Shen's faction found Xuan's illegitimate because its alliance structure had never been mentioned or envisioned in the teachings of Sun Yat-sen.[33] Though Shen did not chair the January 23 meeting, key associates—provincial executive committee members Shen Xiaowen, Shen Erqiao, and Chen Lianchai—presided over the decision making. Wang Huafen, his wife, was made head of the Women's Department of the provincial party.[34] Six weeks later she was named editor of the *Women's Weekly* by the Western Hills Central Executive Committee.[35] Thus, in early 1926, Shen, his relatives, and his networks dominated one wing of party life in Zhejiang and extended their influence as well into the right-wing party beyond the province.

But their political dominance in the province had at the very least been halved; the assertions of another group that it had the *name* of the rightful party could not be the object of appeal to some higher authority for, with Sun gone, there was none. Just as the party under Xuan Zhonghua, recognized by the Guangzhou Congress, had established a new party headquarters, so did Shen, at Little Cart Bridge, remaining unlike Xuan's group in the New Market area.[36] The work of Shen's party was to purge the Communists through the reregistration of party members, in effect once again renaming the party pure and faithful through the redefinition of party objectives and the forceful use of party discipline. Shen's group denoted their opponents with an epithet that had no relationship to the political realities: "reactionary elements" (*fandong fenzi*), while they were defined by Xuan's group as the "antirevolutionary elements" (*fan geming fenzi*),[37] names that defined both opponents as opponents of revolutionary progress.

Though the Western Hills meeting had called for the purge to be accomplished by early spring, the specific procedural details of the purge did not reach provincial party leaders until May.[38] All the while sharp hostility existed between the two groups, each wanting to purify its party and each refusing to recognize the other as a legitimate political institution. The work of revolution had turned into a game of mutual exclusion where the only goal seemed to be destroying perceived revolutionary competition, not eradicating the warlords and imperialists. Such a pass had been reached because the imminent denouement of the revolutionary process held out the promise to revolutionaries of realizing their personal ambition; because the logic of revolutionary exclusion had made revolutionary purity and commitment increasingly significant criteria; and because perception, image, and ideology had begun to fracture existing personal and political networks, often ironically fixing individuals in a perceptual mold at the same time as the flux of revolution grew even more turbulent. Creating bêtes noires at such times becomes an easy task.

The Context of Revolutionary Struggle

The alliance, decrying the "illegal" January conference of Shen's group, on March 6 opened the First Zhejiang Provincial Party

Congress. Asserting its identity as the rightful provincial party, it elected its executive and control (*jiancha*) committees and general secretary. They were all former members and associates in Shen's networks. Xuan Zhonghua and associates Pan Fengyu and Ding Qimei were standing members of the executive committee. Cha Renwei, lawyer, provincial assemblyman, and Shen ally, was one of five control committeemen. Wang Guansan, teacher at the Yaqian Village School, was the general secretary.[39] They prepared themselves to combat their former patron and associate.

A year before, Sun Yat-sen, the arbiter of party disputes, had still been alive. Now as the anniversary of his death approached, both factions, claiming to be his political heirs, set out to commemorate his death. Upholding the memory of the party's founder was one way of retaining legitimacy for the commemorators; this, it would seem, was especially important for the party faction headed by Xuan, for Shen's group had made the writings and will of Sun hallowed since the Western Hills meeting. Reports indicate that it was indeed Xuan's faction that initiated a commemoration, inviting various organizations and associations to participate. Proposals from local bureaus also came to Shen Xiaowen, Dingyi's nephew, who emerged as the day-to-day provincial leader of Shen's faction; Xiaowen reportedly encouraged suggestions for the proper commemoration. Each faction's awareness of the plans of the other promoted stiff competition.

News reports indicate that Shen's faction planned jointly with the Provincial Education Association, the Hangzhou General Chamber of Commerce, the Lawyers' Association, and over ten other established institutions. Their proposed ceremonies were titled a "requiem assembly" (*zhuisi dahui*) to differentiate it from the "commemorative assembly" (*jinianhui*) of Xuan's faction. While Xuan and the left had theoretical legitimacy from the party, the participants in the requiem assembly reveal clearly that in the wider context of provincial politics Shen's faction had the greatest legitimacy. Reportedly about nine hundred attended the meeting, at which handbills and flags were distributed and Cai Yuanpei, Zhejiangese educator and a central party deputy, lectured. Those who participated directly and those who sent memorial addresses and couplets were from the governmental, educational, and economic elites. A report of party developments given by Shen's faction indicates that the faction used the success of the requiem assembly to recruit supporters from student and labor organizations that had originally favored Xuan's faction.[40]

The reasons for their participating with the Shen group are obvious. Shen Dingyi had been a provincial leader since 1912; many governmental leaders, bureaucrats, and nonofficial elites had worked with him or been associated with him to some degree. The long-term connections that Shen had built were stronger than those that the First Normal network had been able to establish, especially given their being a generation younger than Shen. In addition, Shen Xiaowen was a leading lawyer in the capital and in the Lawyers' Association. Once again, the context gave meaning; within the context of the Guangzhou party center Shen's status was greatly reduced, but within the context of provincial politics his status was dominant relative to Xuan's.

Not only was there the competition between the two groups over the popularity of their respective rituals, but subsequent reporting of the events took on the aura of a public relations battle. Shen's adherents claimed that the commemorative assembly for Sun sponsored by the Xuan group attracted only several dozen people to the public athletic field along West Lake. Described as a pathetic event at which handwritten—not printed—handbills were distributed, the "assembly" was alleged evidence of the poor public reception of Xuan's faction.[41] In contrast, Xuan's partisans, although not commenting directly on the ceremonies for Sun (a revealing fact in itself), claimed that several thousand people attended their commemorative assembly. After the meeting at the public athletic field, a military band reportedly led a parade with the likeness of Sun carried before the marchers. As they passed the gate of the Educational Association, where the requiem assembly was being held, there were loud shouts of "Down with the Western Hills faction" and "The direction of the revolution goes left."[42] Xuan's supporters in addition claimed that very few people were attracted to Shen's faction or his cause.[43]

Shen's connections to provincial elites and (perhaps) the relatively better reception his faction received among nonparty members point to a troubling question regarding the strategies that he and his associates would countenance to defeat the other side. Xuan's partisans allege that during their early March party congress, Shen was secretly informing the provincial warlord authorities about the meeting and the whereabouts of Xuan and other radical leaders.[44] During this period, Xuan follower Han Baohua was getting secret reports of government plans from Liao Xunpu, Civil Governor Xia Chao's top secretary. Xuan and his network became aware of plans of Military Governor Lu Xiangting to arrest and execute Xuan and Guomindang left leader Song Yunpin. Both fled to

Shanghai while the March congress was yet in session. Xuan's group assumed this was the result of Shen's group colluding with the warlords.[45]

Several points are important here. Shen was, first of all, in Shanghai during this period; if there was informing, it was not done by Shen himself, although it may have been sanctioned by him.[46] Second, the threat of government pressure did force Xuan to go briefly into hiding, but this repression against perceived radical forces was not a new development. The provincial government under Sun Chuanfang since the fall of 1924 had become increasingly repressive. Under Military Governor Lu Xiangting the closing of newspapers and the arrest of editors became commonplace in the early months of 1926. In early February Song Yunpin, editor of the *Zhejiang People's Daily* (*Zhejiang minbao*) was ousted for "red propaganda." On March 23, longtime Shen provincial assembly ally Xu Zuqian, editor of the *Hangzhou Daily* (*Hangzhou bao*), was arrested for reporting information on government activities; the paper was closed. On the very next day yet another Hangzhou newspaper was closed and its editor arrested for printing news on warlord activities. The retaliations after the arrests were not light: Xu, longtime respected provincial leader, received a prison sentence of fourteen and a half years.[47] Thus, Xuan's intimidation by the government may not have been caused necessarily by an informer, either Shen or Shen's clients.

Certainly, if Shen were now collaborating with warlords, whom he had tried desperately to keep out of the province in 1916 and 1917 and against whom he had written dozens of essays from 1919 through 1924, it would be a measure of the considerable desperation he was experiencing in trying to combat his opponents. The charge that he was cozying up to warlords certainly rankled him and those around him. The unnamed authors of his commemorative biography tried to turn the tables on Xuan and his partisans by claiming that the Communists, not Shen, had advocated collaborating with the military overlords. It seems on its face to be a far-fetched claim, the introduction of which raises the suspicion that there may have been some truth to the charges of Shen's collaboration.

In the summer of 1925, when the Zhejiang Party Conference [the Yaqian conference] was opened, Communist faction leader Xuan Zhonghua brought to Shen Chen Duxiu's personally written letter to discuss linking up with Sun Chuanfang. Shen loudly cursed Chen Duxiu: "Has Chen lost his senses? Whether we are GMD or CCP, how can we link up with a warlord? We are the revolutionary parties. They cannot fathom our depth and cannot presume how to deal with us. If we have to join them, they will know the limits of our force and will not fear us." However, later at the Second Party Congress in Guangzhou, Xuan in the middle of the meeting informed on Shen, saying that Shen was in the process of linking up with Sun Chuanfang. This kind of planting of false goods and false implications was a common CCP trick.[48]

We cannot, however, finally exclude the possibility that both sides may have been willing to work out temporary alliances at various times with warlord regimes. Angus McDonald's picture of the alliances and coalitions in Hunan between both the Guomindang and the CCP and military and civilian powerholders points to the rationale and reality of such united fronts.[49] Shen's faction did find itself on the same side as warlord authorities regarding the press. It contended that coverage of the activities of Shen's faction in many Hangzhou newspapers (whose reporters or editors were linked to the party's left wing) was distorted and rumor-filled; some editors had claimed that the meetings of Shen's faction were not even newsworthy. At one point in March, Shen's factional spokesman even tried to become what today we would call a "truth squad," pointing out errors and omissions in the press coverage of both factions.[50] As for the possibility that the warlord regime was targeting Xuan's faction for repression, Shen's faction did not immediately have a response: "Even though the opposing faction isn't loyal to our party, they have been a revolutionary element. Thus, when warlords suppress it, what should be our attitude? Our bureau will hold a special meeting on this topic."[51]

The county and municipal bureaus were the trophies to be won in the factional struggle. The reports of those allied with Shen detail the battles in terms of blue and white (the white sun in the blue sky of the Guomindang flag) versus red. A few bureaus, like that in Shen Dingyi's own Xiaoshan county, were purged relatively easily. Most bureaus saw major struggles before they were described as "pure" blue and white. Shaoxing county, for example, had many people in opposition to the Western Hills meeting, but the party bureau began the purge early on the instructions of Shen Xiaowen. Xiaowen went to Shaoxing to instruct members in the reorganization, lecturing on the Three People's Principles as the party's standard. Reportedly as a result of such patronage, by the spring of 1926 the number of "blue and white comrades were many," a situation found also in Yongjia, Lanqi, Changhua, Taishun, Tiantai, and Ninghai counties.[52] However, other bureaus—Ningbo, Haining, Jiaxing, Linhai, and Haimen, some of which had been established by Xuan Zhonghua—continued to be fought over: "their color was not yet manifest," in the language of the report.[53] Each struggle had its own cast of actors and its own dynamics.

In addition to the personal involvement of key personnel from the provincial level, Shen's faction encouraged the formation of extraparty organizations that could participate in popularizing and leading the purge. The dual strategy of Shen's faction was to seize Sun Yat-sen's mantle and to lift high the banner of anti-imperialism: thus the founding of its two main subsidiary organizations. The Society for the Study of Sun Yat-sen's Thought was not only intended to purify party thought but to induce nonparty people to enter the party and study Sun's vision for a modern China. The Foreign Affairs Alliance (*waijiao xiehui*) championed the nationalistic cause of China vis-à-vis the imperialists, taking on the Soviet Union most directly. Other organizations also played supporting roles for Shen's faction. The Uniform National Language Society was devoted to standardizing Mandarin as the national language; Shen's partisans saw it as efficacious in getting their principles understood and in the realization of nationalism. The Society to Encourage Compulsory Education was formed under the auspices of Shen Xiaowen before the Western Hills meeting, and it put its energy into the opening of new schools in early 1926. Finally the Provincial Education Association and the Society for the Encouragement of the National Assembly, two older organizations that sided with Shen, often collaborated with his faction.[54]

The contexts of provincial and local politics and party were not the only important contexts for the party struggle. Perhaps even more significant were the social turmoil and economic uncertainty that swirled around the historical actors, forcing them to react to everyday problems and make decisions about mundane issues. The economic situation in Zhejiang was not good. The government had wrestled since 1912 with the reality of revenue insufficient to equal needs.[55] As the province was brought into the whirlpool of warlord politics in 1917, the financial situation only worsened. Dragged into two wars in 1924, Zhejiang experienced further economic dislocation. Between 1924 and 1926 Hangzhou saw an inflationary spiral that increased the price of rice by one quarter and the price of vegetables by half.[56] Rising prices contributed to hoarding that further exacerbated the problem.[57] Workers suffered from low wages, long working hours, and poor factory conditions; the numbers of farmers losing their land were increasing, which only swelled the number of urban poor. It is little wonder that major provincial cities were swept by unrest and strikes; among the most significant were the strikes of Shaoxing tinfoil workers and Hangzhou printers and soy sauce workers.[58]

The largest strike erupted among the Hangzhou silk textile workers in mid-March 1926.[59] The silk factories employed weavers (*zhigong*) and assistants (*banggong*). The initial strike was an effort of some five thousand assistants from four factories to raise their wages an additional three cents (*fen*) for each foot of silk produced. Though there was a clear division of labor between the weavers and the assistants, the work was mutually dependent; thus, when the assistants went on strike, the weavers could not work. When factory managers refused the wage increase, the workers petitioned governmental officials, to no effect. The strike grew, eventually affecting more than ten thousand workers. Rumors swept the city that Shanghai Communists were coming to take an active role in the unrest; fears and a nervous government prompted factory owners and managers to join together.[60] The government responded to the confrontation with police repression. In street clashes, ten were injured and several dozen arrested.[61]

This socioeconomic unrest cannot help but have played into the worldview of the Xuan faction: it was a case study of capitalists, bureaucrats, and politicians—the ruling class—crushing the already beaten-down working class. According to reports, the Shen faction under Shen's nephew Xiaowen tried to play a role in building support among the workers and ending the strike. On the outbreak of the strike Xiaowen went to the affected factories, allegedly warning factory managers about precipitate actions and at the same time discussing assisting workers with the Dongyang County Workers Native Place Association.[62] After the strike was put down, the Shen faction undertook to make closer connections to key labor organizations, to let them know its concern. Since 1924, Shen himself had had connections to the Dongyang County Workers Native Place Association and some of its leaders. In addition, talks now took place with the Machine Weavers and Seamsters Union, the Print Workers Union, and the Musicians Union to try to link them to the Shen faction.[63]

That this was not simply a cynical political strategy for Shen should be remembered. Much of his poetry and many of his speeches from the May Fourth period on dealt with the hardships and tragedies of laborers. His poem "To Hear of the News," written at Yaqian after the massacre of railway workers by the forces of warlord Wu Peifu in February 1923, indicates Shen's depth of feeling.

> After the violence, terrified and dizzy,
> Very sorrowful, heart broken. . . .

The boundless blue skies call to stop the autumn wind,
Sparks wildly flash in the eyes.

Killed innumerable people,
Killed innumerable bodies,
Stolen innumerable lives. . . .

There on the stage snap the fingers now;
Again carry the load—there is no stopping on the road.
Northwest winds and clouds; southwest smoke and rain.

How many things are contained in the breast?
What cannot be contained is also what must be contained.[64]

In addition to the economic and social distress and turmoil that served as backdrop to the continuing party struggle, two events in mid-March served to heighten revolutionary outrage and raise more questions about the direction of the Guomindang. For Shen and his partisans, they were significant contextual elements for the Shanghai Second Guomindang Congress (the Western Hills congress). The first was the massacre of forty-seven students by Beijing police on March 18 as they were demonstrating against Japanese demands on the Chinese government.[65] Yet another evidence of the deadly combination of warlord brutality and imperialist depredation, the killings became a much discussed and condemned tragedy. The second, on March 20, occurred in Guangzhou, when military academy commandant Chiang Kai-shek used the mysterious predawn approach of a Communist-commanded gunboat to Whampoa Island as the pretext for a coup against Communists in the Guomindang.[66] As the Shanghai congress opened on March 29, the meaning of that event was unclear but filled with promise for Shen and other like-minded party members, for it gave evidence that powerful others besides the Western Hills group were willing to take on the Communists.

The Shanghai Congress

The Zhejiang delegation to this alternative party congress was composed of Shen and some of his closest comrades in the provincial party leadership. His nephew Shen Xiaowen, an increasingly important figure in Hangzhou, was probably second in importance to Dingyi; certainly as a family member, Xiaowen had the closest personal connections to Dingyi. But Xiaowen had begun to make a name in his own right in various political organizations and campaigns. Also from Hangzhou was party leader Wang Nayin, the man who would travel with Dingyi on the day of his assassination; the men, a generation apart in age, were obviously close friends. Kong Xuexiong, from Dingyi's own Xiaoshan County, had been a strong supporter of Dingyi, a close friend, and a leader of the Xiaoshan County Guomindang. Shi Bohou was the principal of the Fifth Provincial Middle School in Shaoxing with close native place ties to Shen. These five all hailed from the Hangzhou and Shaoxing region. (We do not know the native place or the connection to Shen of the sixth provincial delegate, Wei Jun.)

For Shen Dingyi, the Shanghai congress ironically marked both the high point and the end of his participation in the national arena. Undoubtedly his renown as a compelling speaker led the Western Hills group to select him to give the lengthy report on their late 1925 meeting. After his report, Shen continued to be a frequent spokesman at the congress, providing an index of his ideas at a crucial juncture in his career. He emerges as strongly against the Soviet Union's influence in the Chinese revolution, as focused on the socioeconomic problems of rural China, and as hot-blooded and impetuous.

During the first session the delegates debated the congress's stance toward the March 18 massacre, desiring to notify party bureaus of the party's official line. Given the anti-Soviet thrust of the meeting, it is not surprising that there was considerable sentiment about placing blame on the Soviets. After all, the Japanese demands that had prompted the student demonstrations came after Russian-supported warlord Feng Yuxiang had mined Tianjin harbor as a way of protecting himself from Japanese-supported warlord Zhang Zuolin. Shen (along with several others) argued that "this tragedy is really instigated by the Russians; however, we cannot send telegrams blaming Russia. If we do so, it will become fodder for Communist propaganda." Thus the consensus was to blame the warlords, pointing out their crimes against China.[67]

More important was the disposition of the congress to Chiang Kaishek's coup. Shen's March 31 speech in this regard and his statements in debate on April 1 reveal his attitude to the Guomindang, the Communists, the ongoing party purge, and the revolution. Shen saw Chiang's actions as the preemptive suppression of an incipient Communist rebellion against the Guomindang leadership. "But we still want to understand the reasons for the episode. It is really complicated. We have known for a long time of the parasitic life of the Communist faction in our party. They have all sorts of political and military plans—already in

complete detail. . . . [Thus] what has happened at Guangzhou is not
accidental and doesn't relate only to Guangzhou. It relates to the whole
party."[68] Thus Shen set the stage for rationalizing the purge and for
laying to rest criticism that the purge was in fact the breakup of the
Guomindang.

Whenever our party institutes a purge, the average person will interpret this
as the Guomindang breaking up. This is in reality a great error—because the
Guomindang and the Communist Party are completely different. When you
mix together two different parties, of course you will not have good results.
And naturally when the party undertakes a purge, there will be a separation.
This is not our party's self-destruction. We must join together and strive
mightily to seek our party's freedom. . . . If it's not free, we comrades must
struggle [to make it free].[69]

How should the party make itself free? And where should it struggle?
Shen's brash proposal followed.

Guangzhou was our Chairman's place of struggle for many years. It was the
place where our comrades came forward with hot blood. . . . Now is it
conceivable that our comrades cannot go to risk their lives and that in risking
they cannot succeed? Therefore, I propose that this whole congress at this
time should move immediately to Guangzhou to convene. If we wither and
pull back from the front and we wag our tails, begging for food from the
people, then we are not revolutionary. We must now take the whole congress
to Guangzhou. If this means death, it is better to die in Guangzhou.

Most speakers who responded to the proposal were skeptical about
its feasibility; there appeared to be too many practical difficulties, and
counterproposals were made about relocating the congress in May or
June after necessary preparations were made. But Shen was unbowed.

Our party has had several times in its history when disloyal outsiders assumed
the name of the Guomindang. In 1915 and 1916 corrupt officials and
bureaucrats paraded themselves as Guomindang members and shook the
party. Now the Communists do the same thing, and the party is shaken. We
want very much to clarify things and see the blue sky and the white sun on
our flag already obscured by black clouds. We want to scatter the clouds and
to see the heavens and the sun.

And in response to yet more discussion of the practical obstacles of
moving to Guangzhou:

It is natural to be anxious about going, but I think there's too much
willingness to be anxious. Isn't our party built by the accomplishments of

people? If we don't go to Guangdong, how can we show our revolutionary spirit? There was a comrade who reported on an article in the *Shenbao;* from it we can see that in Guangdong there are many comrades who will welcome us. If they don't, they're not our comrades. We shouldn't refuse to go because of people who are not our comrades. We will see that there are many comrades who will welcome us and fight bravely forward.

As for each person's excuses for not going—like, we don't have ships—I assume these are not real problems. I was a member of the Communist Party but now I have cast it off and joined the Guomindang. If we hold to the right of the individual to make his decision, we all fear going to Guangdong. If we keep paying attention to the individual, how will there ever be a revolution?[70]

Despite his passionate arguments, Shen did not persuade the convocation that an immediate move was the proper course of action. Ultimately the congress decided to send special deputies to investigate the possibilities of a move. Shen and Xie Chi were the unanimous choices of the delegates to serve. In the end neither ever went, for the hopes of the Shanghai congress about being treated as equals with the Guangzhou party central were stillborn.

At the congress, Shen took an active part in the deliberation of two other issues—the stance the delegates should take on relationships with the Soviet Union and the Communists, and the proper position on farmers and the land issue. On the first, Shen argued that a hard-line position against the Soviet Union was necessary "to wake them up" so that they can "change their behavior toward us."[71] He did not support any sort of permanent break. Shen's attitude to Communists in general retained some flexibility: his evaluation of their cause depended on the context. "The Chinese Communist Party," he said, "does not fit our country's spirit (*qing*). However, elsewhere—in England, America, and Japan—it is necessary to bring up class struggle. Communism wants to destroy imperialists and in that objective they are one with us."[72]

On the farm issue, the delegates agreed that the ultimate solution for the land problem was nationalization, but there were differing opinions on policies to be chosen before achieving that end. There was confusion over the option of colonizing Manchuria as a way of relieving the pressure on land south of the Wall. Shen argued that if farmers were not more secure they would not join the revolution; colonization would help to enhance their livelihood and security. Colonization did not detract from the revolution. He declared, "We want revolution, a complete people's revolution, standing firm for the position of every worker and farmer."[73]

Much discussion turned on the necessity of promoting the "awakening" of the landlords to stave off class struggle. Shen argued, "If we want to block class struggle, must we not advise farmers as they plan for their development? Now it seems every landlord finds farmers associations detestable. We must bring landlords to the realization that farmers organizing associations is necessary. We are absolutely not saying 'Down with landlords.' We are only proposing farmers associations, hoping to bring an awareness to the landlords."[74] Such a policy would lead to the merging or blending (*diaohe*) of classes and avoid the destructive class violence that many at the congress feared would be the bane of nationalism and the vehicle by which more imperialist depredations would be visited upon the country.

Shen's major contribution in debate and as a leader at this conference clearly showed that he had emerged as among the forceful elite in this branch of the Guomindang. The delegates' respect for Shen and his contributions is illustrated by a seconding speech, by one Xiao Yi, to Shen's nomination to go to Guangzhou. "The choice of Shen is very good because he understands previous history. No matter whether it's farmers, workers, or merchants, he respects them. Even though he was a Communist Party member who joined the Guomindang, he has been a very important force in our party since he joined. Moreover, he is very knowledgeable about the Guangdong situation."[75] The respect that Shen enjoyed from the group was further evidenced in his election to the three-man Standing Committee of the Central Executive Committee of the "Western Hills party" at the CEC's meeting in mid-April. Shen received the highest number of votes—seventeen—with the other two, Xie Chi and Zou Lu, longtime associates of Sun Yat-sen and the organizers of the Western Hills meeting, receiving ten and eight votes respectively.[76]

Three days later, on April 16, Shen asked for a leave of absence because of an illness.[77] Though in the Republican period "illness" was often a euphemistic cover for political dismissal, failure, or ostracism, there is no reason to suspect that here, given Shen's acclaim at the conference. In addition, Shen's career had been punctuated by illnesses, some serious, some not. This time the unnamed illness was lengthy, possibly serious. By the time Shen had recovered—not until the late fall or early in 1927—time and events had seemingly passed him by; the Northern Expedition had changed the political landscape. His meteoric appearance on the national stage was over in a matter of six months, the apparent brilliance of his contribution extinguished quickly. He returned to Zhejiang as a deputy to the provincial party bureau, where he played a role only in the background, leaving his personal network of fellow provincial delegates at the Shanghai congress to play the active roles in the party faction.[78]

The Summer of Their Discontent

For both branches of the Zhejiang Provincial Guomindang, the summer of 1926, which saw the beginnings of the Northern Expedition in Guangdong, was a period of eating bitterness. The bleak prospects growing out of the bitterly partisan excesses of mutual purging seemed to be reflected in the inhospitable and destructive forces of nature. Hangzhou and neighboring counties, including Xiaoshan, endured a number of days of heavy wind and rain in early July that turned land into swamp and brought suffering to thousands.[79] But by mid-August, the drought was so severe in Hangzhou that motors were used to draw river water into the city canals for relief.[80]

Shen's faction met from May 10 to 13 in Hangzhou to make preparations for the establishment of a purged provincial party congress. Attended in the end by twenty-six delegates from county and municipal bureaus, the gathering elected an executive committee with a standing committee composed not only of Shen's closest allies from the Hangzhou-Shaoxing area (Wang Nayin and Kong Xuexiong) but also of men from the interior of the province who had become active in the purge.[81] There were some problems in determining which county bureaus had been properly purged and whether the new bureaus had to have a certain number of members before they could be recognized.[82]

But the major problem for the Shen faction of the Zhejiang party was the continuing and demoralizing reality of insufficient funds. Revolutionary activity faded into the background as the day-to-day concern became the emptiness of party coffers and worries over whether future activities were even possible. It seemed to be a never-ending problem. The purge had increased expenses early in the year; even with two hundred yuan from the central party apparatus, by lunar New Year in mid-February the bureau was three hundred yuan in debt. It was successful in borrowing an emergency loan in that amount from an unnamed source in order to clear the accounts by the traditional New Year's date, but by late March the situation had reached such a pass that the bureau's only secretary and clerk had to be laid off. In May, before the provincial congress, party leaders estimated that they needed at least 150 yuan per month for the next two months to cover rent and electricity, stationery and printing costs, postal expenses, miscellaneous expenses, and monies for preparing for the provincial party congress. Added to the monthly expenses, the emergency loan pushed the indebtedness to 600 yuan. Various other expenses—costs for the commemoration of Sun Yat-sen and the continuing purge—increased the total another 50 yuan.

There was no alternative but for the party's leaders to chip in on their own. For May and June, Shen Dingyi, Shen Xiaowen, and Shen Erqiao were each to contribute twenty yuan per month and Chen Lianchai, ten yuan per month.[83] That amounted to less than half of the projected needed amount and did not even begin to deal with the accumulated debts. There were no other sources to tap; the bureau's only recourse seemed to be to petition the central Western Hills Guomindang for help, but a letter from the Central Executive Committee in late June said that it could not help with funds.[84] Such financial straits promised what looked to be no future at all.

If Shen's faction was threatened by an increasingly rapid death by penury, Xuan's faction faced continued repression by the military regime of Sun Chuanfang. While Shen's party had met in May to prepare for a provincial party congress, Xuan's had held its own provincial party congress. More than one hundred attended the meeting at which former Shen allies—Xuan, Cha Renwei, Ding Qimei, Pan Fengyu, and Wang Guansan, among others—were elected deputies. But Sun Chuanfang's heavy hand dogged this faction's every move, just as it had threatened Xuan and others after the March meeting. With the beginning of the Northern Expedition in July, the military repression became even more severe. In August Sun's military police closed the Xuan faction's office on Headhair Lane, arresting several in the process; Han Baohua's government spy gave enough warning for party documents to be hidden before the crackdown.[85] The Shen faction's bureau, responding to a query from the Shanghai Guomindang about a newspaper report of the closing, assured the Shanghai bureau that the closed bureau "must be the Communist faction assuming the name of the party bureau."[86] The left-wing Guomindang had become in the thinking of Shen's group simply "the Communist faction"—the name once again creating reality.

Even though Xuan's Headhair Lane office had been closed, reports indicate that from April to October Xuan's faction, directed on a daily basis by Pan Fengyu and Wang Guansan, was active in expanding bureaus into counties of what would be the core zones of development.[87] The reports of Shen's own people indicate that their rivals had been very successful in organizing in the localities; one reason seemed clear: Xuan had the funds that Shen lacked.[88] Shen knew, it is said, that the "Communist faction" was controlling each level of the party bureaus and that it saw itself and was seen by the party central as directing the orthodox Guomindang. The knowledge that the success of the Northern Expedition would come with the Xuan faction controlling the party bureaus cannot but have made Shen disconsolate. When the two factions came together in a united front in December 1926 with the imminent approach of the Guomindang armies and the need for revolutionary solidarity at that crucial juncture, Shen's biographers talk of the "necessity of temporarily bearing the pain of cooperation," of something they were "temporarily obliged to do." Xuan's group dominated the new "unified" party bureau; and when they directed the process of registration for the new party bureau, Shen was not even allowed to register as a party member. On the whole, his memorial biography stated, "it was a bitter situation about which little could be done."[89]

What is striking is the rapidity with which Shen fell from positions of substantial power to being unable even to register in the party that he had helped found and that he had headed. By his albeit short-lived involvement in the national arena of the Western Hills effort, he had seemingly lost not only his provincial base but his local base as well. Part of this defeat can be attributed undoubtedly to Shen's arrogance, his certainty of his own right position, his fear of not being in control, and his manner of dealing with others. But as, or even more, significant were the vagaries and contingencies of revolution and the bitter partisanship growing out of personal, ideological, and political animosity—all shaped by a host of perceptions and misperceptions, some unconscious, others consciously created and maintained. Shen's dream of revolutionary leadership had seemingly turned into a desolate nightmare; he had lost the power to impose names and thus to define reality by his challenge to the Guangzhou party and then by the siege of illness.

The experiences of Shen in 1925 and 1926 can be analogized to the images of a poem, "Star and Sea," that he wrote in 1922. In it, the shining star can be seen as a metaphor for Shen's leadership and elite status at the beginning of the period; the clouds—which make the reflections of the star in the sea disappear and even raise the possibility that the star itself has become black—are the changing environment and context that shattered Shen's status and destroyed his leadership.

The stars and clouds in the firmament!
You borrow a star cluster to become your shining star.
When the cluster becomes yours, its light then sees you from afar.
It sees you bathed in the great sea.
The sea also displays the mind to bathe you.
Why doesn't the sea envy your shining star in the heavens?

Clouds come, separating the stars and the sea.
The sea becomes intensely black—is it possible that the star is also black?
The wind comes, blowing the sea up into waves:
The starlight in the sea is swaying in disorder!

The wind passes, the clouds receiving its influence.
The sea also returns to its former state, submerging a star.
The star still shines clear and bright
While the earth as before sees the star.[90]

The question for Shen as the Northern Expedition neared Zhejiang in the late winter of 1927 was whether, as in the poem, the clouds would pass and he would once again return as a shining leader.

CHAPTER SEVEN

A Dangerous Time

Hangzhou, 1927

Ahead I don't see the village;
Behind I don't see the city.
Vast indeed is the space between heaven and earth.
Besides a few piles of dried bones, there were only the remains
  of a dead man—no one to rely on, to depend on.

Terribly lonely.
Intensely clear and cold,
Icy cold.
Piercing wind blows: my blood is hot, but the marrow all
  congealed!
Who will bring me peace in this journey?

Is it conceivable that sunk in this pile of bones there was a life?
Moreover you cannot ask him "what about the anxiety, what
  about the evil."

To pull oneself together, to be roused to action, to make a
  striking advance!
Advance and advance again.

A higher road. A lower road.
What I pass are nothing but resentful sounds, hateful sounds,
  despairing sounds—
  the sounds of killing.
Many pits on the road are filled with blood.
How much will it take to fill those pits?

Advance and advance again.
A beam of light from my forehead passes through my body to the
  sole of my foot.
A dream! Awake! Is it false? Is it true?

"A Youthful Dream"
(Yige qingniande meng), 1920

It was the time for which Shen and Xuan and others had maneuvered for several years: the turning point in the struggle to free China from warlords and imperialists—the moment of revolution. As such, it was a time of danger, for no one could know how the revolutionary tides would shift and who would ride the waves to power and who would be swept out to defeat and perhaps death by riptides that could not yet be felt.

The Nationalist army took Hangzhou on February 17. By early March there were an estimated 100,000 Nationalist troops in the province, a source of potential instability or at least social edginess, given the fact that many soldiers were "outsiders" coming into others' native places.[1] They came to make a revolution, a sure formula for economic uncertainty. Rising prices and rice shortages heightened the growing political agitation; rice stores were destroyed in Hangzhou and in neighboring towns and cities.[2] The General Labor Union (GLU), a major political actor allied with the left Guomindang, tried unsuccessfully to get the provincial government to sponsor meetings for it and the Hangzhou General Chamber of Commerce to deal equitably with the rice prices.[3]

Xuan Zhonghua, now Shen's nemesis, had become at age twenty-eight one of the key political figures in the province. Trying desperately to maintain political power in the hands of the left Guomindang as a vehicle for sustaining Communist power and fearful about the rising power of Chiang Kai-shek, Xuan had made every effort to facilitate cordial ties with Chiang and the forces of the Northern Expedition. In November 1926, he had journeyed to Nanchang to meet Chiang and make arrangements for the establishment of new provincial political institutions.[4] He had arranged for Communist groups to propagandize along the two routes of the army in the province. While he undertook propaganda work in Wenzhou and Ningbo, Wang Guansan returned to Hangzhou for party planning, and Pan Fengyu traveled to meet the troops entering Zhejiang from Jiangxi.[5]

When the provincial Guomindang bureau was established in late February in the old Provincial Assembly building, all but two of the eight people on the executive committee were Communists. While the situation was not quite so favorable to the leftists in the three provisional governmental organs, the left Guomindang and their Communist allies were still in a very good position. Of the seventeen men serving on the Guomindang Central Political Conference, the Political Affairs Committee, and the Finance Committee, the breakdown was two Communists, five members of the Guomindang left, five who were former Zhejiang political leaders, and five squarely in the camp of Chiang Kai-shek. The Communists dominated the Guomindang left; and at least three of the Zhejiang political leaders, Chu Fucheng, Shen Junru, and Wei Jiong, had connections to or had worked with the Communists. In March two of the strongest of the Chiang camp, Zhang Jingjiang and Chen Qicai, had not yet arrived in Hangzhou. Thus, the strength of the left and its potential allies in the government and the party was substantial in the exhilarating days following the success of the Northern Expedition.[6]

But Xuan, who was elected to the provincial party's executive committee and its standing committee in late February, was beginning to discover, like Shen before him, that without strong support in the national arena a strong provincial base might prove to be no base at all. He was dismayed to learn of Chiang's appointment of Zhang Jingjiang, a central figure in Shanghai's powerful Zhejiang financial clique, supporter of Sun Yat-sen, and since 1916 chief patron to Chiang, to head two of three key government leadership posts.[7] A native of Zhejiang, Chiang had long connections to many Zhejiang elites, who made up the group of former provincial leaders as well as the group securely in his camp. Most had been involved in the anti-Qing efforts before 1912; many still saw the essence of the revolution as bringing the revolution of 1911 to a successful conclusion, as political action rather than major social and economic change. Most had not been active players in the province for two decades, acting instead in the national arena. Now they appeared—almost as interlopers—receiving the fruits of revolutionary success in the province without having endured the provincial struggles that had so consumed the lives of Xuan and Shen and their networks.

Xuan therefore had to be concerned that rightists and perhaps even Shen and his group might emerge from the revolutionary flux to lead the new provincial party and government, thereby turning his own success after years of struggle into ashes. On March 10, he chaired a meeting of representatives from the provincial and county bureaus to maneuver against a reborn right wing. At the opening of the meeting he pointedly said, "The general situation before us is that there are many elements seeing the point and coming to attach themselves to the revolution. This is a very dangerous time. If we do not have resoluteness to continue the fight, our party may be destroyed. The loss of the 1911 revolution is a precedent."[8] For both the Right and the Left, then, the 1911 experience was the memory, the base line against which the events unfolding in 1927 was viewed: for the Right, an unfinished dream; for the Left, a forbidding nightmare. Xuan announced plans to enhance the "struggle power" of county and municipal bureaus and to hasten progress in developing more party activities.

While in the surrounding countryside the major revolutionary activity concurrent with the success of the Northern Expedition was the formation of farmers and women's associations, in Hangzhou, amid the growing evidence of an incipient battle over party and government authority, it was the almost manic establishment of labor organizations.[9] The *Zhejiang People's Daily* reported that "all sorts of Hangzhou labor unions have been established, like spring shoots after a rain, angry sprouts growing in luxuriance."[10] By mid-March there were reportedly more than ninety unions in the city with about 150,000 members. The leftist GLU struggled to seize these sprouts for its own, sponsoring a meeting of about 450 representatives of these unions on March 14.[11]

Since the strike of the Hangzhou silk workers in the spring of 1926, Shen and his associates had made overtures to a number of labor organizations; Shen had long been linked to the Dongyang County Workers Native Place Association, which had formed the nucleus of a more general union, the Workers' Association, founded in 1924. Branch units of this organization, which incorporated at least textile and construction workers, were subsequently founded in a number of Zhejiang counties.[12] It was transformed in the middle of March into the Workers' Federation, an umbrella organization of at least thirty-one unions. The Federation had the support of many workers (it claimed more than 100,000) in varied unions, among them, textile workers, shippers, carpenters, ironworkers, tinfoil makers, and construction workers. The initial impetus for its formation was the unexplained refusal of the GLU to accept certain unions (carpenters, barbers, shoemakers, painters) as members.[13] There were also other grievances about management policies and practices of the GLU that gave rise to a competing organization. Secret decision making, relatively high GLU fees, restrictions on labor unions participating in GLU elections, and violent tactics in labor disputes were some of the charges leveled.[14] The Federation favored more conservative political positions. The spring labor organizing, thus, offered both a labor and a political alternative to the GLU.[15] Later charges that the Federation was only a front organization set up to serve as the instrument of the right wing to challenge the GLU overlook the background to the Federation's formation; it is a case of seeing history only in light of what happened at the end of March.[16]

Although provisional government committees had been meeting since late February, the formal establishment of the provisional government did not occur until March 25. Despite the initial party and government makeup, which was favorable to the left, the power, as in the provincial crisis of a decade earlier, ultimately lay in the hands of the military. It was not so much that the division commanders of the Northern Expedition in Zhejiang were in Chiang's camp. More crucial for the situation in Hangzhou was the appointment of a strongly antileftist Whampoa faction leader, Zhang Lie, as head of the Zhejiang Public Security Bureau. That office emerged as a garrison for anti-Communist, antileft efforts. Under the increasingly strict control of the military police, the provincial government in late March and early April, in the words of Chu Fucheng, "had duties but no power."[17]

Near the end of March, after Shanghai had been conquered, it was clear that Hangzhou political tensions centering on the polarized labor scene were rapidly coming to a head. On March 27, a strike for higher wages broke out at Hangzhou match factories; the workers were openly supported by the GLU even though the match workers union had joined the Federation.[18] That same day the GLU issued a list of thirty-nine work-related and political demands (e.g., "factory foremen cannot prohibit workers from participating in patriotic demonstrations").[19] Xuan upped the political ante on March 28 by sending a demand to the provincial government, in accord with a provincial party bureau decision, that the Hangzhou Public Security Bureau dissolve the Federation.[20] The party was thus asking the military to dismantle the military's potential rightist ally. This request precipitated the chain of events that would lead to Xuan's death. Shen Dingyi would become one beneficiary of the events, although he did not play any role in them; the historical record does not specifically disclose his whereabouts, though evidence points to his having been at home in Yaqian.[21]

What happened in response to Xuan's request is disputed by Left and Right.

Left. Late in the afternoon of March 30, allegedly with the support of government authorities, members of the Federation marched in a demonstration to the headquarters of the GLU with the purpose of provoking hostilities with an attack. In the ensuing fifteen-minute attack by Federation members, more than fifty people were wounded, several fatally. Military police stopped the violence.[22]

The *Eastern Times (Shibao)* in Shanghai corroborates this general description of the nature of the episode.[23]

> *Right.* Late in the afternoon of March 30, the Federation, in protest of the GLU's demands for its dissolution, began a peaceful and orderly demonstration march. When they reached the vicinity of the GLU headquarters, GLU pickets were standing along the streets and in every intersection, holding various kinds of weapons; others were on roofs. Suddenly those on the roof began pelting the marchers with bricks and tiles as the pickets attacked the marchers, fatally wounding three and injuring some fifty others.

This version is corroborated by reports from the Eastern News Agency (*dongfang she*) and an independent eyewitness who claimed that the marchers had no weapons nor had they prepared in any way to defend themselves.[24]

An uneasy calm prevailed the next day as troops from the Public Security Bureau patrolled the city in the wake of an early morning GLU demonstration at the West Lake Athletic Grounds. Xuan left for Shanghai to report to the Communist Central Committee on the increasingly dangerous situation; Wang Guansan, general secretary of the Zhejiang Guomindang, was dispatched to Wuhan to report to the Guomindang Central Committee.[25] At the end of March Zhang Jingjiang came to Hangzhou. He did not go, however, to the provincial government offices, but holed up at the Xinxin Hotel at West Lake, where he had talks with key figures such as Ma Xulun; he refused to receive visitors from the Left. Tensions mounted as banners of street demonstrators denounced Zhang ("Down with the imbecile—old and useless Zhang Jingjiang") and Ma ("Down with the Western Hills faction"). Though Ma had not been at the Western Hills meeting, he had associated himself with the group since the spring of 1926.[26] The day following the street demonstrations, Zhang, Ma, and Cai Yuanpei went to Shanghai where Ma allegedly reported his account of the demonstrations and banners directly to Chiang Kai-shek.[27]

Xuan returned to Hangzhou within several days. By April 8, two battalions of Nationalist troops were transferred back to Zhejiang from Jiangsu. On the evening of April 10, deputies from the provincial and

Hangzhou municipal Guomindang bureaus met to discuss emergency plans amid a general sense that things were about to happen; they contacted Chu Fucheng and Shen Junru with the promise to remain in communication with them. That night the provincial government head, Zhang Jingjiang, having returned from Shanghai where he was most surely apprised of Chiang's planned Shanghai coup, announced the institution of martial law.

Monday, April 11, dawned foggy with a light misty rain; the fog did not lift the entire day. The military struck as people were headed to work: it was the beginning of the purge of Communists and the Guomindang Left.[28] Just as the military had triumphed over the civilian constitutional culture in the 1910s and early 1920s, now the military was smashing the revolutionary civilian culture of the left. The Public Security Bureau dispatched military police to the provincial party bureau, the GLU, the Student Union, the municipal party bureau, and the offices of the *Republican Daily News*.[29] Provincial government offices were sealed with signs prohibiting entrance.[30] When 4–11 (as the purge in Hangzhou is known) began, Xuan was at home asleep. Pan Fengyu, on his way to the Guomindang office, saw the troops blocking the door and stopped his rickshaw short of being seen. He hurried to Xuan's house nearby, roused him, and urged him into immediate hiding, but, according to his biographers, Xuan realized the danger of staying in Hangzhou and wanted to go to Shanghai to relate the extent of the emerging "White Terror" in the Zhejiang capital. Hangzhou-area Communist Party members who had not been arrested agreed with Xuan and arrangements were made to protect him. On April 14, he took off his glasses, removed two false front teeth, and donned the clothes of a railroad worker. Protected in Hangzhou by three Communist friends, he boarded alone a Shanghai-bound freight train at the Liangshan Gate station, farthest from the main sections of the city.

The freight train stopped at Longhua to unload before proceeding into the city. Longhua was one of the main military garrisons in the region and was the site of a prison that Chiang was using for Communists and leftists. Fearful of being detected if he remained on the train, Xuan got off to walk into Shanghai. It is said that he had almost reached the International Settlement when a Guomindang secret agent arrested him. His captors were reportedly ecstatic to catch the head of the Zhejiang Communist Party and a key member of the Shanghai regional party bureau. Yang Hu, the Shanghai (Song-Hu) garrison commander, was brought in to interrogate Xuan. But Xuan was belligerent and refused to give any information to his captors. In their hagiographies, his First Normal associates put properly revolutionary last words in his mouth. But we do not in truth know what he said before his execution late on the night of April 17. In less than a month he had gone from provincial leader to his death at age twenty-nine.[31]

His bitter antagonist Shen had nothing to do with Xuan's death, but he would later be blamed for it. Almost thirty years later, Yang Zhihua, the former disciple of Shen married briefly to his son, put it simply if wrongly and anachronistically: "It was Shen who caused Xuan's death."[32] An historian of the 1980s claims that Xuan died (in April) as a result of the purge Shen led beginning in July![33] The Communist Party has never forgiven him for this and other "crimes"; even those who had once been his disciples remembered him with a cold hatred.

The Purge

Shen bore the wrath of the Communists in large part because he became in July the director of the purge of Communists from the provincial Guomindang. The first wave of purging had come in April and May; arrested in the initial sweep were thirty-two provincial, county, and municipal left Guomindang and Communist party members.[34] Xuan's 4–11 alerter, Pan Fengyu was arrested, as were Chu Fucheng, Shen Junru, and Cha Renwei.[35] The first list of those targeted by the Public Security Bureau included Shen's defunct First Normal network, the young men whom Shen had brought with such hope to the Yaqian Village School and the rent resistance movement in 1921.[36] In addition to Xuan, two of the other male First Normal graduates who had taught at the Yaqian Village School, Xu Baimin and Tang Gongxian, were both arrested in the purge. Xu was held until 1932; on his release he left the party. Tang was held until 1937, dying several months later.[37] In less than six years the revolution had destroyed three of the first four teachers at Yaqian Village School, this provincial May Fourth generation falling before the military and political might of their elders, those who been cheated out of revolutionary spoils in the aftermath of 1912. One has only to note one of the early civic rituals of the new regime to see where it was rooted: elaborate ceremonies on May 18 marked the eleventh anniversary of the death of Chen Qimei, 1911 revolutionary, patron of Chiang Kai-shek, and uncle of two of Chiang's closest supporters.[38]

During the April purges and into June, Shen was in Xiaoshan. A number of his personal network—the poet Liu Dabai, his nephew Shen Xiaowen, and Shi Bohou—emerged in early May as bureaucrats in the provincial education ministry.[39] But Shen does not appear in the provincial arena until June 20, when he attended the founding meeting of the Zhejiang Guomindang Reorganization Committee as a special deputy. Serving with Shen was his lineage kin, Shen Erqiao, and serving as secretary to the committee was Shen's young protégé and Hangzhou native, Wang Nayin.[40] By early July, Shen was chosen to be chief deputy of the subcommittee on the farmers' movement.[41] It is clear that he and his group were able to seize the opportunity of the new regime to parlay it into their political advantage.

The party's Central Purge Committee appointed the provincial purge committee on June 11; all its members except Shen held government posts in the new regime.[42] In many ways Shen's appointment is surprising. He had antagonized the right with his early membership in the Communist Party and the left with his participation in the Western Hills group. Indeed, just as in Beijing in November 1925, some among the right who now held the reins of power protested Shen's appointment to the purge committee, this time with a telegram instead of a beating. "Because Shen has a Communist 'tint'," the telegram read, the appointment should be withdrawn "in order to safeguard the party and the country."[43] But there was no reneging from the center. It was likely Shen's experience with and knowledge of many of those now being sought that made him a promising candidate for the committee, and anyone who had listened to his positions after the summer of 1925 understood his animosity toward the Communists and their view of how to change society.

The Zhejiang Party Purge Committee first convened on June 23; by all accounts Shen was first among peers in directing the continuing purge. Chaired by famous educator Jiang Menglin, who gave an opening address on the purge's crucial importance for the revolution, the inaugural meeting featured remarks by Shen. Though this is not likely the complete account of Shen's talk and though the elliptical nature of what is recorded presents some lack of clarity, it still gives insight into his thinking as he entered a dangerous, risk-filled episode in his life.

Today we are establishing the Purge Committee with the goal of purging the antimovement elements: the Communists, the local bullies and evil gentry, corrupt officials, and opportunists. At this time, it is difficult [to handle] the Communist element, for [much of] it has already run away.

However the local bullies and evil gentry and the corrupt officials are like a kind of monarchical restoration; they have run into the party for cover. Therefore now the purge must be of two kinds. . . .

Now let's first talk about Communist Party behavior; it's really no different from that of imperialism. It makes use of high school students and workers as their tools. They use moments of tragedy [for their own ends] and to cast light on [their idea of] national revolution—and then call it class struggle. The recent general strike cost more than two million yuan—where did it come from? It is raised from the people of the country and overseas comrades who contributed. Moreover, the Communist Party, according to their own announcements, took possession of 470,000 yuan. This kind of self-aggrandizement—is it not the same as that of the imperialists?

The Communists opposed our policy of colonization [in Manchuria]. They [now say] that they only support the policy of moving 200,000 to the Northeast; how, in the end, is it different from what we have advocated?

Formerly it was the warlords' guns; hereafter it will be the Communists' wooden sticks. . . . Therefore the Communists must be purged.

The oppressive and evil local bullies, evil gentry, and corrupt officials have the same character. Though an old presence, they are like a new illness. They were old illnesses; now as a new illness, they are difficult to treat. Moreover, we must protect against an old illness. Therefore a purge is better than an inoculation. This purge must get the support of the masses and then we can have excellent results. How can it get the support of the masses? It must come from [persuasive] party announcements.[44]

Although Shen talks of two targets for the purge, it is obvious that in his view, the Communists should get the most attention. Warlords and imperialists were the bêtes noires of the Nationalist Revolution; Shen identifies the Communists with both (though his reference to the 470,000 yuan is unclear). If the revolution would have any success against these two proclaimed enemies, Shen was saying, the Communists must be ousted. Shen's suggestion that the local bullies, evil gentry, and corrupt officials were like the restoration of the monarchy seems much like his 1919 depiction of warlord soldiers as "emperor's cells" and "shrunken shadows of the emperor."[45] Though in his emphasis, Shen feared these elements less than the Communists, the reality of the period of his direction of the purge (officially from June 1 through August 31) was that the local bullies and evil gentry became the chief target, many Communists having already been arrested or, as Shen said, "run away." As a group to be purged, local bullies and evil gentry were much trickier to deal with than Communists. One either was or was not a member of the Communist Party, but what defines one as a local bully or an evil gentry? That is defined only by others in the community; for a culture where, at least Shen thought, "the name is more important than the deed," such defining, while it may go on continually, becomes dangerous during revolutionary purges. As he spoke of local bullies and evil gentry, it is unlikely that Shen would have believed that within less than a year he would be defined as such by some even on the purge committee to whom he was speaking.

Shen's wish to get the support of the masses through party announcements seems naive. Yet he attempted to begin to realize this hope in a press conference two days later with reporters from newspapers in Hangzhou and Shanghai. At the meeting Shen set forth "the ideas behind and the principle of the purge in a very thorough way." He called on journalists to assist in the work of the purge and to help in its reporting to rectify the mistaken views of the average person in society.[46]

The purge committee also issued periodic public announcements to popularize its actions. In mid-July, for example, it declared, "The Communist Party took advantage of the farmers and workers. In the movement for stirring up the national revolution, they injured the people and misled the nation: their crime is the same as that of the warlords."[47] How effective these strategies were in shaping people's minds cannot be known. Such public relations efforts indicate the committee's clear understanding of the political dangers that a purge perceived as a White Terror could unleash. For Shen himself to be seen as the main leader of the purge placed him in considerable danger as a target for those that the purge itself targeted. There is no indication that Shen was ever concerned for his safety. He approached the purge with a conviction that it had to be done to save the revolution. About dissent from a revolutionary consensus he had written in 1919 that "in ten years, we'll be able to know what's the best way to go. When we all know what we want, no one will dare to dispute us. If there is someone who dares oppose us, then everyone must within their noses make grunts of disapproval and dare to think that each one of those who oppose must tie themselves up and ask forgiveness."[48]

The committee took a very serious and strict view of its work, establishing not only a team of detectives but also a small secret investigative unit; it remained in close contact with and directed county purge committees.[49] It was extraordinarily hard-working, hearing and discussing hundreds of individual cases round the clock; sometimes sessions lasted through the night, concluding only at dawn.[50] In late July, the committee received the cases of several hundred local bullies and evil gentry sent from county bureaus. The work load included remaining on top of any possible Communist subversion: as anti-Japanese sentiment flared in July and August, rumors flew that Communists would try to use patriotic agitation to disrupt Guomindang plans; the committee sent telegrams to each county bureau to be vigilant about stopping "the sprouts of chaos."[51]

Not only was Shen a key figure on the purge and reorganization committees, but he also appeared to have been completely rehabilitated as a provincial leader. He was a key figure at public ceremonies marking the twentieth anniversary of the death of feminist martyr Qiu Jin; he was one of the noted figures at a rally in mid-July against the deployment of Japanese troops in Shandong province.[52] Ruan Yicheng, son of famous Hangzhou lawyer and judge Ruan Xingcun, recalled that the summer of 1927 was the point when Shen's party and governmental power was at its height: "in many policies of state all [that was needed] was one word from him. Zhejiangese referred to him as Shen 'Gefu' (every deputy)."[53] It was a remarkable comeback in his career; he seemed finally to have overcome the heavy burden that his Western Hills involvement had created for his approval by centrist and some leftist Guomindang members. The poem with which this chapter began, "A Youthful Dream," reflects the sharp shifts and changes in Shen's own career, from the despair and loneliness of being the outsider to the resoluteness and hope of advancing as a leader.

Illnesses, however, continued to bedevil him. Whether the cause was overwork is not known, but by late July newspapers noted that he had returned to Yaqian because of illness.[54] He returned to Hangzhou sometime in August, when a Shanghai newspaper noted that "he put forth great effort to carry things out; he is very well known for working hard."[55] But he had to return home again on August 31 "because of a foot disease and a severe case of dysentery," illnesses that lasted until late September.[56] Illness had taken a toll on Shen. His photograph as member of the purge committee shows him dressed (ironically) in military style uniform; when compared to the photograph taken only three years earlier at the Guomindang plenum, Shen seems to have aged markedly. Illness seemed to strike him when he was at the peak of his political power and possibility—as in the spring of 1926 when he seemed to emerge from the Shanghai Western Hills Congress with enhanced standing in the national arena. Even during his periods of illness, however, he remained active, lecturing, for example, on July 31 at the Xiaoshan party lecture hall on the Guomindang and education.[57]

Before he left for home in July, Shen submitted to the central party a detailed description of a special institution he designed to deal with the rehabilitation of those who were purged but whose record did not indicate incorrigibility. Called the Self-Examination Institute (*fansheng yuan*), this organ prefigures the reeducation schemes adopted by Mao and the Communists in Yan'an. As his creation, it is a good indicator of his thinking at this time in the revolution. The Institute

is the place where the thought of the revolutionary movement is promulgated, where the wrong thinking influenced by the Communist Party, leftist thinking, and narrow individualism [is changed]. Those things that would not be conducive to the principles and methods of the Three Principles of the People, that would make one abandon the idea that the Three Principles of the People are applicable around the world, that would obstruct the goals of the Guomindang in carrying out the revolution [are done away with]. Thus we set up the Self-Examination Institute. For those who have the opportunity to participate, it is a fundamental indication of our party's benevolence (*ren-ai*). It is a place to build anew one's future.[58]

Headed by a director, the institute had the qualities of a prison, a hospital, and a school. The director was most like a warden, making weekly reports to the Zhejiang provincial party. There were two programs, common (*putong*) and special (*tebie*), to which one who had been purged might be assigned depending on the nature of the individual as judged by the purge committee's investigation and judgment. Before being allowed to enter, the purged had to get a guarantee from a prosperous firm that would take responsibility for the costs involved. For the common program, the shortest time for the reeducation was three months. For the special, there was no time limit. Each program was composed of three courses: "overseeing" (*jianguan*), which included superintending and managing the individual; "guiding into truth" (*jiaodao*), which included information on the national and provincial situation; and "general matters" (*congwu*), which included business and accounting matters and public health. Each individual was isolated and could be transferred to the other program depending on the report of the director. For the individual to be released, the guarantor had to pay for the costs incurred in the program.

Depending on one's perspective, the scheme was indeed benevolent, as Shen claimed (for it kept away the dire alternatives of long prison terms or execution), or it was a malevolent effort at thought reform. Certainly self-examination was a time-honored Confucian practice, but Shen's pointing out that the institute was a prison and a hospital as well as a school adds qualities of force and psychological pressure that can be disconcerting, even though there is no description of psychological techniques to be applied other than isolation. The director had enormous power in hiring the teaching staff, in being the official who reported to the provincial party, and in deciding the fate of purged participants.

Two other interesting points were the course of study and the requirement of a guarantor for the costs. The third course, general matters, seemed to be an effort to inculcate ideas of general citizenship with practical, almost vocational skills. This course was educational in the traditional school sense. The specific inclusions strike one as somewhat odd. One wonders whether the public health emphasis grew existentially out of the cholera epidemic that raged throughout Hangzhou in July; similarly, the inclusion of accounting might stem from another concern of Shen's at that time.[59] The requirement for an economic guarantor would seem to have limited the participants to the wealthier or to those more socially and politically elite, for the connections required to get the guarantor would seem to preclude people from the laboring classes. Despite the fact that this scheme would not add to government expenditures, this bias toward the elites seems strange for Shen, who had so consistently made efforts to support the underclasses.

There is no record of the functioning of the institute except for the circumstantial fact that suggests its effectiveness: later the institution and system were imitated in Hunan, Hubei, and Shanxi provinces. We have no clear sense of how long Shen headed the institute, but after his service, he maneuvered to have named as his successor one of his personal network, Qian Xiqiao from Xiaoshan county.[60] As in almost every policy during this revolutionary time, perceptions and interpretations are polarized. Those sympathetic to the Communists castigate Shen for the institute; one historian in the 1980s says, "The point was to get arrested Communist members and progressive youth inculcated with anti-Communist thought. . . . The damage was great, and Shen has to bear the blame for initiating it."[61] Those sympathetic to the Guomindang see the institute as a boon to the revolution in Zhejiang; one historian in the 1970s notes it as a symbol that Shen led the purge without a sense of retribution. "The result was that Zhejiang had no executions and no outbursts. If the Communist leader Xuan Zhonghua had not escaped and been arrested by Longhua soldiers, he would not have been executed [in Zhejiang]."[62]

Because so many cases came before the purge committee, its life had to be extended briefly into September. The number of those purged is not clear, although it was clearly in the hundreds. At one point the purge committee asked the government to require that military prisoners be sent elsewhere so that the entire military prison in Hangzhou could be used for the purged; the government refused the request.[63] At times the pressure on prison space was so great that suspected Communists were simply let out on bail. When the purge committee was closed down in early September and there were still many cases to be heard, it organized a special court with five judges to deal with the remaining cases.[64] In at least one important way, the purge under Shen was milder than in many provinces. No one was executed in Zhejiang under the purge committee in the summer. This record is in sharp contrast to the days in April when 932 were executed and to the late fall of 1927 and early 1928, when a new wave of bloodier purges swept the province.[65] Shen must get some of the credit, but from those purged he would obviously get none.

On September 3 at the Hangzhou train station there was a "Purge the Government" rally sponsored by "city residents" (*shimin*). It attacked six men whom it named in slogans that began "Down with. . . ." The men were Mayor Shao Yuanzhong, Shen Erqiao, Shen Dingyi, and conservative government leaders Ma Xulun, Jiang Menglin, Jiang Shaomou. All the men had been involved in the purge, either on the purge or the reorganization committee or both, and the name of the rally points to animosity over the purge and its extent. The site for this rally is striking: as we have seen, most Hangzhou political rallies in the 1920s began at the West Lake Athletic Field and then moved out into street demonstrations. This location suggests that leaders of the "city residents" may have been railway workers, some of the closest allies of the Communists and one of the most active organizations in the now defunct GLU. Their opposition to those involved in the purge would hardly be surprising. The Public Security Bureau sent troops to disperse the rally.[66] Shen was in Yaqian at this time nursing his health; there is nothing in the record to indicate that the animosity he had helped stir up in some sectors was disquieting to him.

Cause Célèbre: Shen and the Case of Kong Jirong

In 1921, at the time of the rent resistance campaign, Shen had written a poem, "Swallows Fly," that had celebrated freedom and rejoiced in the possibility of sweeping away barriers.

> Swallows fly in the sky where they meet no obstacles.
> In the air there are no barriers;

Flocks come and go.
People come and go alone—
Everywhere oppressing or suffering oppression.

To break the oppression
Freedom must [be] what the heart is most fond of,
What is worth paying the absolute price for—
In order to sweep away the great net.[67]

Between 1921 and 1927, Shen's world had changed, and with the changing contexts, so had his identities. The openness and inclusivity of the early years had been sharply narrowed by political events, by shattered personal networks, by fear of being passed by as the revolution proceeded, by loss of political control, and by being refused registration in the party he had headed. Firmer political control is what he and others had sought in the purge; adherence to one way of thought is what Shen had sought in the Self-Examination Institute. In the summer of 1927 yet another episode revealed this harsher side of Shen even as it paradoxically pointed to the continuing closeness and humanity of Shen as patron to people in his native place.

Kong Jirong was a wealthy, seventy-year-old manager of a Hangzhou cosmetics store. He was determined to gain the glory that would come by serving as an official. He was very well acquainted—and thus had important connections—with Chen Qicai, the head of the Zhejiang Finance Ministry. Though Chen allegedly tried to use Kong's age as a way of dissuading him, Kong was obstinate and determined. Chen thus appointed him as the Xiaoshan County Cocoon Tax Bureau Chief, a seasonal appointment: the bureau operated during the spring and summer, closing each year after silk cocoons were taxed. Perhaps as a check on the elderly man, Chen appointed as Kong's assistant Jin Runquan, the manager of the Hangzhou branch of the Bank of China; but after Kong went to Xiaoshan, Jin introduced a man as Kong's assistant, one Xu Yaoting. The Xiaoshan bureau had for many years been known for its corruption. Xu, working either with Kong's approval or on his own but with Kong's knowledge, demanded bribes of merchants in return for reduced tax bills.[68] At his trial Kong's testimony showed him to be a bumbler: he clearly did not understand the economic situation of the cocoon firms as a background for the collection of the taxes: "All this I didn't know; you'll have to ask the accountant." He also revealed little sense of morality; even though he knew about the bribery at the time it was going on, he said at his trial, "I did not recognize this as corruption."[69]

Shen did. Just as farmers had come to him in 1921 with accusations against certain rice merchants, so did those connected to the county cocoon firms bring word of the bribery. As in 1921, Shen acted forthrightly by setting out himself to investigate the case. He went to each cocoon hong in the county and discovered that the piculs of cocoons sold and the amount of tax taken in did not correspond. He quickly uncovered the widespread corruption and referred the case to the government, which sent an investigator of its own.[70] But Shen was unwilling to let go of this case. Ruan Xingcun, the judge with whom Shen would wrangle, chalked Shen's subsequent action up to his "liking to grasp for authority." Whether that is a fair assessment, it is likely that Shen reacted in the same way as in the purge and the self-examination plan.

Put simply, Shen wanted Kong executed for corruption as an object lesson under the new regime. One can imagine that Shen's experience with the shifting tides of revolution had made him wary about the continual redefining and the relativity of morality; his attitude clearly suggests that he hoped that the new regime would demand a new standard. A Guomindang historian in the 1970s argued that Shen took this position because "he hated evil as an enemy."[71] Kong was brought before Ruan for an initial hearing, with the judge telling Shen that Kong should be turned over to the courts, which could hear and deal with the case. Shen said that the criminal code under the new regime had not yet been promulgated, that the court's judgment would be lenient and thus insufficient to use for a revolutionary government to show as a warning. Ruan declared that if the law were not followed and a man was killed, he would resign his post; moreover, he warned, it would be a crime to kill a man based solely on an accusation. Shen was adamant, demanding in the short term that Kong be sent to a lockup for prisoners awaiting trial and kept in custody there without bail. The clash was between Shen the powerful political figure and the judicial system. When Ruan urgently telegraphed Wuhan for instructions, there was considerable consternation. It finally sent a regulation promulgated in Guangzhou in 1926 that had not yet been brought forward for use. It stated that the crime of corruption could draw the death penalty once the amount involved reached a thousand yuan; in Kong's case the amount was nine hundred. Following the reception of the ordinance, Ruan organized a special court to hear the case.

The special trial was held on July 25 in the provincial government yamen. Shen's seizing on the case and, through his demands, personally making it a test of the nature of Guomindang leadership had created a cause célèbre. More than two hundred people were present, including such party and government figures as Ma Xulun and Jiang Menglin. Shen was ill in Yaqian. There was no doubt about the outcome, as there was documentary proof of the corruption. A number of people testified, including Kong's son, who affirmed his father's moral probity.[72] The only suspense came in the sentencing, which was delayed until mid-September. Then Kong was sentenced to twelve years in prison, while others involved received three to five years.[73] For some, Shen's persistence in this case seemed inappropriate. They pointed to Kong's age and Shen's brashness. In the end, Kong became ill and died in prison. Especially after his death, it is said that many blamed Shen for the severity of the sentence; as with the death of Xuan Zhonghua, such a charge was a non sequitur, for Shen had nothing to do with the sentence, even if his initial insistence and claims might have had some subsequent impact on the judge's thinking. In the end, Kong's death did not come until after Shen's in the fall of 1928.[74] Whatever Shen's initial motives for justice and his concern for the people of his native place, the perceptions that Shen stimulated for some in this episode were of arrogance, lack of benevolence for a rather pathetic old man, and dogmatic inflexibility. None of them marks of the swallows.

Tenants and Landlords

By early September, the committees that had brought Shen and some members of his network to considerable power in the province, the purge and reorganization committees, had been dismantled. There seemed little likelihood that Shen would be called upon again in the provincial arena. But the shifting revolutionary currents in the national arena provided him yet another chance. When the Northern Expedition took the lower Yangzi valley in the spring of 1927, the Guomindang was split into three groups: the left at Wuhan, an amorphous right (the remnants of the Western Hills group) in Shanghai, and Chiang Kai-shek and his supporters at Nanjing. Political victory for the party could not come until there was a compromise or until one group achieved sufficient power to be able to chart and lead the course of the government.

In early September a compromise was effected with the establishment of a Special Central Committee; such a body would transcend the difficulties posed by having two rival Central Executive Committees, one elected in early 1926 in Guangzhou at the regular party congress, the other elected in the spring of 1926 at the Shanghai Western Hills-sponsored congress.[75] Though the Special Central Committee was to be a compromise organ, when the composition was announced, the Western Hills group controlled about 40 percent of the committee (as compared to about 25 percent who were supporters of Chiang and far fewer who supported Wang Jingwei).[76] It is interesting that the power of the Western Hills group on the national scene was greater in the fall of 1927 than in the past because the faction had been able to establish links with military forces, major opponents of Chiang, the so-called Guangxi clique. It was this heavily Western Hills-dominated Special Committee that appointed Shen (along with He Yingqin, Jiang Menglin, Cai Yuanpei, and Jiang Bocheng—all conservative supporters of Chiang) as Special Officer (*tepaiyuan*) to the Zhejiang provisional party bureau. It also appointed Shen's political network as the provisional provincial committee (Wang Nayin, Shen Erqiao, Kong Xuexiong, Xiao Mingxin, Jiang Shaomou, Jiang Jiannong, Wang Zhaofan, Zhou Xinwei, and Liu Guanshe).[77] To a man, all were personal supporters of Shen. A decision in the national arena over which Shen had no control had catapulted him into a position as one of the most powerful men in the provincial government. Given the fact that Shen had had nothing openly to do with the Western Hills group since he left Shanghai in April 1926, his return to provincial power through his Western Hills connections seems high irony, though he had at the time, it should be remembered, been elected to the three-man Standing Committee of the Central Executive Committee with the highest number of votes.

The despair of the previous year was farther and farther behind him. Shen entered upon his new position with excitement and aggressive optimism. His speech to the provincial committee on October 9 was forceful and assertive.[78] He told his network members that "you have dismissed your own concerns and come to take on the most dangerous and troublesome of the country's problems. Our whole party is plowing the fields for the masses; each party member provides the implements for the advantage of the masses." He dismissed those who were questioning the legality of the formation of the Special Central Committee and by extension his and his network's appointments, pointing to a precedent in the party in 1925. The majority of his talk focused on party organization and functioning in the local arena rather than the national and provincial. And the forward-looking lines of "A Youthful Dream" seemed the catchword. "To pull oneself together, to be roused to action, to make a striking advance! Advance and advance again."

The main advance came in promulgated regulations concerning farm rent and the relationship between tenants and landlords. Reprising his 1921 role as champion of the farmers, in September 1927 Shen drafted the Regulations for Farm Rent that a joint conference of the Zhejiang provincial party bureau and the Zhejiang provincial government announced publicly and put into effect.[79] Without Shen's own leadership and without his men on the central committee, it is not likely that these regulations would have been adopted. Their centerpiece was a 25 percent reduction in rent, with the ultimate goal being rent that would be no more than 40 percent of what was harvested. Playing a critical role in the administration of this policy was the local farmers association.

Long a spokesman for reduced farm rents, Shen had early on championed farmers associations in the 1921 movement. In the immediate aftermath of the success of the Northern Expedition, mass organizations composed of farmers, workers, merchants, and women sprouted up all over the countryside. Leading the provincial way was Shen's home county and his home township; by early May the associations were formally established at Yaqian's East Mountain Temple, now renamed Sun Yat-sen Hall.[80] Though there is no direct documentation indicating that Shen was instrumental in this early development, he was in Yaqian at the time; given his record of support for these associations and their establishment first in his native village, it is probable that he was the guiding force in their founding. When the rent regulations were announced early in the fall, the Xiaoshan government, party, and farmers association acted quickly to put the procedures into place.[81]

Despite the percentage stipulations regarding rent, there was considerable flexibility in the regulations, which led to confusion and disputes between landlords and tenants. The rent targets for each year were to be achieved not for individual farmers but for an area (county, township, or village) on the basis of the projected crop yield. It was the job of the farmers association to estimate the average yield of the area chosen as a base; if the area had no such association, the party bureau would draw district lines and conduct elections of farmer representatives who would calculate the estimate. By early November, a joint provincial party and government clarification (that set forth more detail about the actual workings of the new rent procedures) noted the problems that had developed: "progress has varied a great deal; standards have not been clear because of variable conditions; methods have varied, giving rise to contention between landlords and tenants; and the party and the government have been at odds."[82] This last assertion points specifically to difficulties between the provincial party committee, dominated by Shen's network, and the more conservative men in the government, like He Yingqin and Jiang Menglin.

The basic problem was not the plan's details but the fact that for the first time the government, led by the party, was taking income away from landlords and giving it to those who cultivated the land. In imperial times and during the Republic up to this point the government had had a vested interest in the tenants' paying their full share of rent as demanded by the landlord, for the landlords had always claimed that their payment of taxes (on which the government operated) depended on their tenants' payment of rent. Landlords were bitterly angry; once again a policy effort led by Shen Dingyi was costing them money; and this was much worse, for in 1921 they had the force of the government behind them to crush the rent resistance movement. Now the government was siding with their tenants, whom they frequently demeaned with such epithets as "rent chicken," "rent goose," and "rice feet."[83]

In late October one Huang Qingceng of Xiaoshan, denoting himself only as "citizen," cabled the Hangzhou government about the 40 percent rent target; he said, "We fear there's going to be trouble. We ask the government to reopen this issue and ask the abolition of this announcement."[84] Others went beyond sending telegrams. He Bingcao, a *juren* degree holder, principal of a school in Linpu town, and longtime community leader, organized the Property Owners' Alliance to collect the rents that landlords claimed were due. His organization was suppressed.[85] But the Xiaoshan county bureau reported to Hangzhou that "local bullies and evil gentry" were forming such alliances in many areas, blocking the progress of revolution.[86] Landlords were refusing to follow the rent regulations not only in failing to reduce their rents but also in other ways. The regulations set down a clear, three-level procedure for arbitration in active disputes between tenants and landlords; it was to be handled by committees of party and government figures. Reports in December indicated that many landlords were taking their tenants directly to judicial officials and the courts; the government sent out orders that judicial officials were not authorized to deal with these cases.[87]

Concurrently with these increased tensions and even struggle between landlords and tenants on the local scene, the national context was changing rapidly. The Special Central Committee compromise had broken down. Wang Jingwei had never accepted the compromise, and there were rising shouts of opposition from the supporters of Chiang Kai-shek. In late November Chiang supporter Chen Guofu led a Nanjing rally celebrating victory over a military opponent that turned into a demonstration against the Special Central Committee. Violence erupted; three people were killed and over seventy injured. Chiang blamed the Western Hills-controlled Special Central Committee for this "massacre"; his animosity to the Western Hills group was fueled by their "alliance" with the Guangxi military clique.[88] In early December preliminary meetings were held preparing for the party's Fourth Plenum; because there were no Western Hills members on any of the committees that came out of the Second Congress at Guangzhou, the Western Hills group was effectively frozen out of the potential for power.[89] The days of provincial power for Shen and his network were numbered.

In these chaotic times in the national, provincial, and local arenas, there was also a rise in reported Communist activities throughout the province.[90] Calls in November for the suppression of Communists and increased military and police surveillance were the first steps in what is usually seen as a second purge, which would run into the new year.[91] Tensions were building in the party and the government in Hangzhou. Party and government leaders met in joint session on December 16 to try to deal with the tenant-landlord situation and the new Communist threat. Although Shen had played little role in the late fall in what looked like the unraveling of his rent-reduction policy, he was present at the December 16 meeting. It is clear that he was unhappy with the drift of events and decisions.

The joint meeting pointed its finger at what it considered the cause of the turmoil: the farmers associations. It claimed,

although all farmers associations have been established and are under party direction, in reality there are not enough personnel for [directing] or financial resources to pay for such direction. As it is, the county farmers associations are not paying enough attention to the district associations under them. People in the countryside generally don't understand those who are in charge of the national revolution; they don't see that the farmers associations are the building blocks for local self-government. Therefore local bullies and evil gentry take the farmers associations as [structures for] a rampage of wild animals. And the local hoodlums and vagrants take the associations as their instruments to seek the status of local bullies and evil gentry and substitute for them. The situation is extraordinarily easy for them to be used by Communists.

We have to rectify the farmers associations. We must drive out the hoodlums and vagrants; we must punish the local bullies and evil gentry; we must direct the farmers associations. The first step is to investigate all the farmers associations in the province. . . . We must have this completed by January 31, 1928.[92]

The interpretation is remarkable for completely leaving out landlords. In this view, rural society seems to be completely made up of tenants, local bullies and evil gentry, hoodlums and vagrants, and Communists. It is clear that the conservative government forces both in the province and at the center had had enough of the social experimentation that had begun to challenge the power of landlords and cause struggle between classes in the countryside. On January 1, a declaration of the party and government stated that "the latest governmental principles are to put into effect the liberation of the farmers by reducing rent by 25 percent. But tenants get an inch and desire a foot. This leads to the greatest confusion."[93] Ten days later two party leaders, Jiang Menglin and Jiang Bocheng, asked the provincial government, and received its agreement, to order the cessation of all mass organizations, including the farmers associations.[94] In terms of its relationship to the already mobilized masses, the Guomindang revolution was lost even before Chiang began his final drive to Beijing.

There is no record that Shen spoke at the December 16 meeting; although given his combative and outspoken nature, it is hard to imagine that he did not. He spoke loudest the next day with his resignation from all his provincial party posts, saying he was willing to be a party man but no longer a party official.[95] Shen was surely aware of the changes in the national arena and that as Chiang solidified his power in the party, he and his faction would dole out the seats of power in the center and in the provinces. Shen, exceptionally able but never completely trusted, could not remain. By the end of January, the provincial party committee composed of Shen's network was also history. The legacy of the Western Hills episode was a stigma that Shen could not in the end overcome. As an indication of how this stigma permeated provincial politics, the house of Shen Erqiao, at which Shen and others of his provincial Guomindang frequently met in the fall of 1927, was popularly known as the "Western Hills Zhejiang Garrison."[96] *I know that ultimately for the Chinese people the name is more important than the deed.*

There are signs from early in the fall, however, that Shen was thinking about new possibilities. As Shen was performing his provincial tasks in Hangzhou—being chief speaker at a large Double Ten rally, participating in other political demonstrations, serving as chair of a preparatory committee for a provincial Party Affairs School, conferring with He Yingqin on the Self-Examination Institute, and participating at provincial party meetings—his eyes were beginning to turn back to Yaqian and the locality that had always seemed to him to have significant revolutionary potential.[97] He understood the direction in which the supposed revolutionary currents were flowing, a direction at odds with his own view of the importance of the countryside and the crucial nature of the mass organizations that he believed had to be at the heart of the revolution. When he left that cold mid-December day, he would never again return to the provincial arena as a major player. The break was clear and dramatic. Perhaps the dangerous time had passed. Perhaps the cycles of lonely despair and zealous action that marked his revolutionary years would at long last cease with his return to his native place.

CHAPTER EIGHT

The Representative of the Masses

Yaqian, 1928

The frosty air spreads across the heavens;
The hibiscus has abandoned the earth;
The wutong tree's one leaf is hanging on moss.

Raise your eyes to look at the autumn wind.
It blows among everyone haggard from grief.

This dry, yellow, withered, exhausted earth
Only has the chrysanthemums daring to fight
    the spirit of destruction by blossoming.

You were born in this season.
I was also born in this season
To lead the people by the hand to look at the chrysanthemums.
                    From "Chrysanthemums" (Ju), 1920

Shortly before he initiated the 1921 rent resistance movement, Shen wrote a short story entitled "Gu Laotouzi's Secret History."[1] Gu was an old man when he moved to Goose Creek Village, a hundred-household community marked by poverty. He quickly built up his reputation as one who helped financially strapped families with needed amounts of money, though the source of his benevolence remained a mystery. At one point Gu's household had a guest, a monk whom he had known earlier.

Gu asked, "Brother, what have you done these past four years?"
    The monk answered, "Fourth Brother, our plans to achieve a lot have not been successful. It's been 'east a scale, west a scar'—only broken traces.

These traces not only cannot have an impact on society, but, linked together, they are too many bitter fragments that do not help to increase the reputation of our great temple."

Gu then asked, "Have you changed your way of thinking?"

The monk responded, "No, I have not changed my way of thinking, but I generally feel that the tactic we've used is too weak and will not produce sufficient results."

Gu said, "We must find another method to succeed. . . . The so-called 'another way' is most assuredly not finding another person to take the lead. Instead it's something we must stir up ourselves. You're a monk—everybody recognizes you as a monk and calls you a monk. You do your duties at a small temple. When you take care of your duties (e.g., repairing bridges or roads or building a pool or pavilion), you must collect subscriptions. . . . Is it possible that the subscriptions are not able to be enough to do what needs to be done? . . . What I want to do will produce more than enough. I have spoken about repairing bridges and roads; so we can begin by doing that. The road from Goose Creek Village needs repairing; I've already proposed it—it will take more than nine thousand yuan. So that you won't have to come alone to collect subscriptions, I will come along."

The monk said, "So, tomorrow and the next day, I'll come to pass a subscription book."

Gu responded, "Good!"

In no more than half a year, the road from Goose Creek Village to the town was repaired and very level. Everyone said, "It's an accomplishment of a poor monk raising subscriptions."

Before the road was repaired, in the town there were thefts at two of the large pawn shops—totalling ten thousand yuan. Everyone in confusion remarked, "This money should have been taken earlier to repair the road; isn't it all to the good?"

Taken as an allegory about Shen's attitudes in 1921 and also his grand experiment in the first eight months of 1928, the story of Gu and the monk tells us much about Shen and his reaction to the political realities of revolutionary strategy—and to frustration. Frustrated by the lack of success in the revolutionary undertakings over the preceding years, Shen could see the small successes only as "bitter fragments." And yet, like the monk, all the Guomindang revolutionaries seemed able to do was to continue what they had perfected—a cyclical process of unifying, factionalizing, purging, and reregistering, each time in a more exclusive party than before, always dependent on and controlled by power from the center; but because of the political feuding, jealousy, and violence, the center, as Shen indicated, was ultimately "powerless."[2] Continuing to do what it had always done was no way to bring about the desired results of the revolution. Shen believed that he had to stir up a new way;

the goals of building the nation and of greater social equity could be achieved through building on the locality.

The Vision

Shen had talked openly about his local strategy since at least his October 9 address to the provincial party committee. At that time, he had said, we must go out among the masses and train them ourselves, working closely with them, and using their energies in order to build a new China from the bottom up.[3] Shanghai's *Republican Daily News* reported that "Shen Dingyi is so determined to build on a strong local base that he has decided to send cadres to each district's branch bureaus to investigate methods of organization in order to solidify the base and to assist in their rectification."[4] After his resignation from the provincial party posts in December 1927, Shen said, "From now on, as I use my party qualifications, it will be to dig deeply among the masses, to plant the ideas of the Three Principles of the People in so firm a foundation that they cannot be pulled up, and to instill among the masses a trust in party leadership. It is important to do this at a time when the masses are still not really able to achieve active leadership in the movement. I must work at training them. We really cannot countenance delaying. If it takes ten years, it will be well worth it."[5]

He sponsored and taught at a Party Affairs Training Institute for Xiaoshan county's second and sixth district branch bureaus, three sessions that ran from October 1, 1927, to February 10, 1928; his wife, Wang Huafen, headed the institute.[6] Following Sun Yat-sen's conception of the pattern of revolution, national unification brought about by the Northern Expedition should be followed by a period of party tutelage of the people, training them for self-government. Shen and Wang's institute tutored about two hundred enthusiastic youths for the express purpose of leading Shen's experiment at local self-government.[7] Newspaper reports in November 1927 had noted that he was busy planning the Yaqian self-government system. Shen would build on those institutions left from the revolutionary flurry of 1921—the village school, the public athletic grounds, the newspaper reading room; he would expand the area to be included from the provincial road north to the Kanshan dike; and he would build a branch bus station at Yaqian to facilitate transportation.[8]

At the center of his plan was mobilization of the area's farmers. In his "Regulations on Farmers Associations in the Period of Political Tutelage," Shen's first regulation was that "the adult farmers in every village should be members of the farmers association."[9] In Shen's opinion, a prerequisite to reconstruction following the bloody years of warlord struggle and national unification was imbuing the masses with power.[10] To make a difference, mass power had to rely on organization, and farmers, composing 80 to 85 percent of the population, would assume the largest mass power in associations. "Agriculture is the country's foundation. In actuality, to realize the liberation of the lives of Chinese farmers, agricultural production must develop positively. No matter what the politics or the aspects of the nation's people, if we do not look at the farmer as the main strength, then not only will the political system lose its base, but the economy will lose its strength, and even the whole nation's people will lose their footing."[11]

Shen's clearest rationale for his experiment came in a speech on February 6 at a preparatory meeting in Yaqian for township and village self-government.[12] Shen noted that any seeds of self-government among the Chinese people had seemingly been crushed by the boulder of four thousand years of autocracy under the emperor system. "When the emperor was overthrown, the boulder was broken up into innumerable pieces that became the warlords, evil gentry, and local bullies." Barely acknowledging the local self-government movement of the late Qing, Shen suggested these bodies were "no more than lichens on the rocks and were absolutely not sprouts of self-rule coming from the masses." Politics, Shen averred, has not been the concern of the farmers, the workers, the merchants (all of whom seem only concerned with their immediate economic fortunes), the educational institutions (concerned only with their own announced courses of study), and women (most of whom "are among the working people whose lives are as slaves"). Shen ironically recalled his own poem by concluding his initial point with "Whatever has to do with politics certainly does not enter youthful dreams."

But now, he declared, this customary aversion to politics had been challenged by "the thunder of revolution," an inexorable force "that will not allow the masses to hibernate again." Shen talked of the difficulties that remained among revolutionaries themselves, before even considering the problems with "enemies" of the revolution: the occupation gap and consequent different goals and approaches of the farmers, workers, and merchants; the class gap between the educated and the masses; the gender gap that thrived on the exalting of males and the diminution of female worth; and the personal "evil customs" of jealousy and the mutual subversion of efforts by revolutionaries striving to emerge on top. A revolution was necessary to break down these boundaries. This Shen is more like the Shen who wrote "Swallows Fly," the May Fourth Shen who seemed in his returning to Yaqian to be freed from the boundary-building, exclusionary mentality that had so defined politics in the period following the death of Sun Yat-sen.

What kind of revolution? Here Shen seemed to pull back slightly from his aversion to violence and from his calls for benevolence that had marked his political rhetoric since the Yaqian party conference in July 1925. "Revolution," he says, "is not a busy market. It must use social force to spur along social progress. The scope of negative destruction must be limited to the little that must be destroyed, but it is not the destruction of society itself. In the present, the reconstruction of society itself is like the beginning joining together of a nebula. This is a kind of new self-governing bright star." A bright star, giving light of its own. In the 1922 poem Shen had written of a black star that was simply a function of its environment. For Shen local self-government had clearly taken on the quality of a beacon. It was, he said, "the foundation of political work by which the Chinese people will save themselves."

Finally, he argued that the evil customs of the past, "the control of old thought," would be cast off through the effects of the new mass organizations and the self-government bodies. Changes in society and politics would precede changes in thought and culture. In this point as well as in the emphases on mass mobilization, the centrality of the countryside, the countenancing of violence for social change, and the criticism of the landlord-capitalist class, his views seem much more the May Fourth leftist than the perceived Western Hills rightist. Just as Shen believed that the social and political contexts could help shape thought and culture on the level of the polity itself, so it could be said of Shen the person that the shifting social and political contexts of the 1920s' revolution helped to shape and reshape and reshape yet again his own views of what the revolutionary goals should be.

Inaugurating and Explaining the Experiment

For all his musings in poetry and essays about the role of context in the workings of human affairs, Shen apparently did not see that the context for the experiment was not good. The view from Nanjing and Hangzhou was colored by the red lenses of Communism redux in the struggle between landlords and tenants. Newspaper reports from November to February are filled with accounts of provincial tenant threats, resistance, and violence against landlords. Tenant disputes, stimulated in some cases by farmers associations, became symbols in an increasingly violent and polarized atmosphere. For leftists, the disturbances were clear examples of the tyranny of landlords as local bullies and evil gentry; for rightists, they were symbols of the dangers of instability inherent in any tenant protests. Increased security forces and occasional periods of martial law in various cities brought hundreds of arrests throughout the province, some of which were followed by public executions in Hangzhou. Rumors of the Red peril were rife around provincial cities as labor unrest also began to spread. As we have seen, in early January the central party's Special Provincial Deputies (Shen had been one until his resignation) had asked the provincial party to stop the activities of mass organizations. The political climate of the winter was a bitter mix of fear, suspicion, and paranoia.

Yet it was at this precise moment that Shen inaugurated his experiment in rural self-government in a symbolically inflammatory way. He announced a commemorative service for Li Chenghu, leader of the rent resistance movement in 1921, to be held on the sixth anniversary of his death on January 24.[13] As far as we know, there had been no previous commemorations of Li's death in the intervening years. Given the context, this ritual remembrance of a man whom government authorities and local elites saw as a lawbreaker and disturber of the peace, who served as head of the first farmers association in the province, was bound to be seen by authorities as a symbol of defiance, an assertion of an alternative and opposing vision of sociopolitical strategy. Furthermore, the immediate county context of Shen's dramatic announcement was a meeting of representatives from county farmers associations called by the party for the purpose of reining in aggressive associations under the direction of the party bureau.[14] Why Shen chose to assume symbolically the position of political and social opponent at the beginning of his project is difficult to imagine. Whatever his thinking, the act is consonant with Shen's brashness and devil-may-care attitude before authority and authority holders.

If Shen's ritual remembrance potently symbolized opposition to the authorities, it also served as a powerful symbol to area farmers, who reportedly had held a large reception for him shortly after his resignation.[15] Shen was appealing to their memory of his serving as patron and supporter during the heady autumn of 1921. Essentially, he was renewing his connection to his farmer followers in his role as local leader and the director of a new experiment. That they responded positively is almost certain. The Shanghai journalist Lin Weibao, who visited the tombs of Li and Shen in 1935, reported that Li's son directly linked the 1921 movement with Shen's project in 1928: the Yaqian Farmers Association was established in 1921, he said, but its most active days came in 1927 and 1928 when many important self-government proposals were adopted.[16]

The political challenge for Shen was to establish his legitimacy as a *loyal* opponent to party and government, after having so directly linked himself to a rebel tenant at a time when the domestic peace was being destroyed by masses of rebel tenants. This he tried to do through his speeches to key self-government association meetings, through communication with national and provincial party leaders, and through the agenda of the whole project. From the very beginning Shen had sought to place his self-government experiment in the context of the ideas of Sun Yat-sen and therefore of Guomindang goals. He cannot have been unaware that others would remember the last time he had undertaken an initiative in the Yaqian countryside or the fact that he had once been a not unimportant member of the Communist Party. The fact that Shen continued to keep alive the mass organizations from early January when they were shut down for over three months by the provincial party likely only raised questions in paranoid and/or cynical minds of provincial party leaders.

Thus the conclusion of Shen's major speech in February to the Yaqian Village Self-Government Association.

Therefore we are beginning to actualize the plans for political tutelage and local self-government set forth by the Guomindang Chairman Sun Zhongshan. We will begin to realize the hard work of Guomindang members. The seeds of political thought latent among the people from of old will then gradually expand, . . . must grow and give forth sprouts.

To make the experiment of Yaqian village self-government is to follow the legacy of Sun Yat-sen.

Shen asserted his ideological legitimacy as the upholder of the doctrines of the founder of the Guomindang. Sun's canonical legacy, the Three Principles of the People and the directives for effecting them, became Shen's legitimizing base for setting up an alternative line from that of the current leadership in Nanjing and Hangzhou.

He continued to hammer home his rationale for action in the June 8 speech at the time of the establishment of the East Township Association.

If we want to understand the township's self-government organizational system, we must first understand the village self-government regulations. In putting local self-government into effect, our leader Sun says, "If a rural village has twenty or thirty [square] li, then it can establish a self-government organization." To organize a self-government organization is to "mass-ify" the party and, more precisely, to transform the ideology of the masses. We want to bring each of the mass organizations together. The Communist Party separates people. It schemes to cause each class to struggle against the other, to kill each other. Our Guomindang unites the classes. People must come together to live; the more you come together, the greater your strength, the stronger your level of production. The purpose of self-government is to unite the classes and do away with class struggle, to bring the people together in the close relationship of politics and the economy. Together they can come to manage their own affairs to build and improve the principles of society.[17]

He spoke these words to his supporters, but they certainly reached those in the party in Hangzhou. Shen also specifically addressed the provincial and central party committees in several letters that placed his strategy in the context of party rhetoric.

[What I am doing is] expanding the methods of putting into effect local self-government as set forth by our Leader, for which task all party comrades should actually work. The general regulations clearly set down the district's branch party bureau as the basic organization. The party furthermore frequently rouses comrades to exert themselves in work at lower levels, using words like "foundation," "lower levels," "organization," and "work." Isn't it appropriate to try to figure out how to proceed [in such undertakings], how to progress—or else this becomes just empty talk. . . . As for methods of putting local self-government into effect, the model is good, our plans are careful and strict, and they are deeply congruent with the country's spirit. They will heal the people's ills; they can allow scholars to apply deep thought to constructing the foundation of our country that will not be destroyed for ten thousand years. No policy is better than this: to train Guomindang members and build the nation. We cannot delay in planning for this foundation.[18]

The self-certainty and assuredness that Shen had exhibited throughout his adult life was clearly communicated in this letter: "No policy is better than this."

He tried in various speeches and writings to stanch the possible charges that he was leaning to the class struggle position of the Communists. He contended that revolution was a necessity to get the masses, "scattered like sand," to join in common endeavor. Revolution, he argued, must employ force to spur along social progress, but the resulting destruction must be as limited as possible.[19] In essence, Shen was positioning himself between the current line from Nanjing (which distrusted local initiatives) and the Communist ideal of struggle, always asserting emphatically his ideological and practical justification from the highest authority in the party. In these speeches and communications, he linked himself as directly to the Guomindang and its values as he could, all the while remaining silent about his specific allegiance to the provincial and national party regimes. It was a case, to play upon a later phrase, of using the Guomindang flag to oppose the Guomindang.

In one other communication with the government in Hangzhou, Shen tried to show how his self-government regulations could fit together with the policies of the new regime regarding localities and their government structures.[20] A biographer says that Shen invited eleven party and government leaders, including Dai Jitao and Zhu Jiahua, to serve as organizational deputies; but apparently they did not respond.[21] Clearly Shen hoped for assistance from Hangzhou and perhaps even Nanjing, at the very least for official recognition of the experiment. In the end there was no sanction from Hangzhou or Nanjing to proceed. Shen recorded in February: "It is begun after the sanction of the county party bureau."[22] Kong notes that "after the high point of revolutionary fervor had decreased and calm was established, [the mass organizations] felt the emptiness of the [party] decision [not to provide assistance]. Looking up hopefully for what they sought, there was no assistance. Therefore they turned their heads and knew that they would have to help themselves."[23]

The Shape of the Experiment

Another strategy Shen employed was to emphasize the reform agenda of the self-government effort, practical in its appropriateness to area needs. This approach attracted local support, and because of its potential for solving local problems, some of which might otherwise have required provincial assistance, it was calculated to win some measure of approval from the provincial authorities. Shen argued that the prerequisite for reconstruction was imbuing the masses with power, but that, to make a difference, mass power had to be structured in effective organizations. By the spring of 1928, the Xiaoshan mass organizations that Shen would use as a base for the self-government system had been flourishing for almost a year. By the summer there were farmers associations with an estimated 30,000 members: Yaqian had the largest, with 2,830 farmer members; the smallest totaled between 800 and 900. Merchant associations were located in eleven sites with about 2,000 members. In addition there was a construction workers union (in one site, with 350 persons), a communications union (in one site, with over 150 workers), a union for unskilled laborers (in one site, numbers unknown), and a women's association (in eight places, with about 500 women).[24]

Their importance lay in their serving as parent bodies to the self-government organs. The self-government committees drew their membership from the mass organizations, with farmers associations contributing the largest number of representatives. Regulations stipulated that all matters of procedure and questions about institutional regulation be taken to the Mass Organizations Council for a decision. Most importantly, the expenses of the self-government association were covered by the mass organizations, with the largest sum coming from the farmers associations.[25] For the Yaqian village self-government association, for example, the farmers associations of Yaqian and Xinlinzhou (a contiguous hamlet) each picked up 35 percent, the construction workers union 8 percent, the merchants association 12 percent, and the women's association and the village school 5 percent each.[26] Since one of the key powers in directing and overseeing a subsidiary organization is that of the purse, it is clear that the real direction of the self-government bodies came not from the party but the mass organizations.

The initial scope of the experiment was the Yaqian village self-government district, an area of about sixteen square miles with a population of more than ten thousand. It was a homogeneous district with an economy based only on agriculture. Reports indicate that word of the self-government effort spread rapidly. Villagers in nearby areas clamored to become involved, hoping to take advantage of the presumed benefits that Shen's movement would bring. In early June Shen brought together a joint conference of leaders of branch Guomindang bureaus to discuss the establishment of a much larger self-government association, the East Township association. Here again he stressed the crucial theme that party members must understand that their role was to serve the people by working among the masses. The establishment of the East Township association would not come until January 1929, but then it included all of the alluvial area known as the Southern Sands, roughly one-third of the county. The association would comprise fifteen village self-government districts, and Yaqian would be the center, as it had been in the 1921 rent resistance movement.

At their greatest strength, the people working in the various self-government activities for the Yaqian village district and the East Township association (most probably party members) numbered more than 250. Shen himself distributed assignments for the daily work, which consisted primarily of groups of workers holding organizational meetings with area villagers. In the evenings workers often led small group training sessions that Shen frequently attended. Reports described the workers' fervent excitement as they set out to build a foundation for a new China; they were, it is said, all moved by Shen's enthusiasm and spirit.[27]

An outside visitor during the summer detailed the self-government scene at Yaqian. "Walk here, there, everywhere, you can see signboards denoting so many self-government bodies and mass organizations. On the entrance at the rather large house hangs the sign, 'Village Dormitory.'" In an announced public opening, Shen had given his home to society, renaming it the "Village Dormitory." It housed the village school, the East Township branch of the Xiaoshan Education Association, the Tiger Spring Reading Room, and the Guomindang branch bureaus of the First and Second Districts.[28] "Entering the house, you can find several dozen youths writing essays, taking down accounts. Three or five sit under the big tree discussing party principles. Eight or ten surround a table where there are laid out the plans for work. They are busy, but their faces all show contentment. They are living a political life; each is lost in thoughts of plans and policies. You ask them something and they tell you everything they know and are doing."

Shen seemed in essence to be reliving the glory days of 1920 and 1921, when he returned from Shanghai and made his close ties with the First Normal students who came to teach at his school. Now his closest confidantes were men from his party network who had composed the provincial party committee from October through January—Kong Xuexiong, Jiang Jiannong, Wang Nayin, Xiao Mingxin, and Zhou Xinwei. He had been their patron in the years since 1925, and they worked for him now without salary.[29] He had other new disciples now, the mostly local party men who went through his training institute to become self-government leaders, young enough to be his sons, half his forty-four years and less. But the excitement and enthusiasm they reportedly shared must have made this one of the happiest periods in his life. People who saw him knew that he was in his element. "Shen lives with the young men in the dormitory and even exceeds their fervor about building a new life. In the dormitory, you can often meet many farmers, with short pants and bare feet, holding long cigarettes in their mouths. Placidly and naturally they discuss the problem of the alluvial land and how what will soon be submerged in the stream can be saved. No matter what they come to discuss, Shen always speaks with them." While in 1921, in the early days of the rent resistance movement, Shen had adopted the outward symbols of dress and local dialect as a bond with farmers, in the 1928 effort he worked closely day after day with farmers. In this regard, the cogent anthropological analysis of the Potters suggests that Shen's strategy went to the heart of local values. They claim from their work in Guangdong that in rural villages "work is the symbolic medium for the expression of social connection," that "work affirms relationship in the most fundamental terms."[30]

Shen will speak with you about the experience and plans of putting self-government into effect. He is always completely full of and even overflowing with ideas—he never seems tired. In speaking with one person, he will use the vigor and tone as if he were talking to several dozen people—that sense of earnest purpose, that clear-sounding and bright tone. When he talks to you, you believe that those words come as a true report straight from the heart; it is not propaganda.

He will talk to you two or three hours, and you will forget that you're tired. You listen to him as he distinguishes the advantages and disadvantages of a small matter: for example, how to dig a small channel whereby water from a mountain stream can be drawn to a certain place to irrigate a dry paddy; or what kinds of techniques a kindergarten teacher can use to teach children to like cleanliness. You perhaps can object to his excessive triviality, but you must admire his attention to details. You see him stimulated to a high degree of excitement when talking about overthrowing the local bullies and evil gentry. You see him leap up and suddenly issue forth in speaking about how you take local self-government from such a small area and expand it to the whole province and country. You could really mistake him for a youth from a thatched hut.

The two most important initial steps in actualizing the self-government plan were census taking and land surveying. Census taking began in February with more than fifty investigators finishing the census of the sixteen-square-mile Yaqian village district in ten days (a total of 10,355 people in 2,490 households). But when the census was extended to all of East Township in July, the effort was hasty and slipshod, and Kong Xuexiong, one of Shen's Guomindang network and historian of the self-government experiment, admits that the information gained was never adequate for reconstruction work.[31] Similarly, the much more difficult and time-consuming process of land surveying, including sketching detailed maps of villages and countryside and investigating and recording the landlord and tenants of each plot of land, was completed in only a part of the Yaqian village district. Such maps and registers would have been able to clear up difficulties in assessing taxes and rents. As Kong points out, it is a pity that later, when the self-government experiment was stopped, the Guomindang provincial government did not even use what had been compiled.[32]

What then was the agenda of the East Township Self-Government Association? Though it is unnecessary to analyze the scope of efforts in great detail, an overview sheds light on the comprehensiveness of Shen's project and therefore on his grasp of the issues. In addition to the establishment of various institutions (hospital, orphanage, and education society) and offices (conservation, surveying, sanitation, forestry, and public cemetery), there were also many initiatives undertaken to solve social, environmental, economic, educational, and political problems. Short-lived initiatives focused on road construction, insect control, and the establishment of workhouses.[33] Four initiatives outlived Shen to greater or lesser extent: conservation projects, educational and sericultural reform, and the introduction of credit and retail cooperatives.

The early establishment of the conservation office underscores its preeminent importance for East Township; the very future of the land in the township depended on effective halting of the erosion of alluvial soil by Qiantang river currents. Not less than 83,000 acres of rich East Township farmland had already collapsed into the river. In June 1928 representatives of the township's mass organizations met with the self-government association, representatives of the provincial Reconstruction Ministry, and the Qiantang River Engineering Office to set forth plans to deal with this environmental and human tragedy by building jetties to protect the land.[34] They decided on a plan to float a 500,000-yuan East Township River Control Engineering bond to mature in three years. The mass associations' representatives seemed willing to levy taxes to help solve this critical problem. Alluvial land outside the sea wall would be taxed forty cents per mu; inside the sea wall, twenty cents. The special tax would make up the interest for the bond repayment. The provincial government also contributed one-third of the costs of construction. Shen, though he likely participated in the joint conference, did not live to see any results. Work began in December 1928; forty-seven jetties were eventually constructed, reportedly to great benefit. The river, however, would continue to bedevil East Township, to the present day.

Two major reform initiatives came in education and in sericulture. Shen's first local initiative in 1920 had been the Yaqian Village School, but the Southern Sands area as a whole had been slow in establishing educational institutions. As it now took over control from the county education office, the self-government association gave the locality a greater say and therefore more interest in developing schools. It faced an immense task: in the first school term of 1928, the whole township had only thirty-two elementary schools with 1,930 boys and 234 girls—this in an area with an estimated 30,000 school-aged children. The unrealistic association goal was to move toward the achievement of mass education with a total of three hundred schools each with one hundred students.[35] Such a plan could not have possibly been realized with local resources. Even the much more conservative goal of having each of the fifteen village districts establish two new schools was not achieved.

The self-government association sought centralized control over schools to monitor the teaching. No spirit of experimentation and of May Fourth liberal thought here: teaching ideas opposed to party, party line, or nationalism was not permitted.[36] The association also sought to establish a teacher-led Children's Society (*ertong hui*) in each school. Calling the children "leaders of the future revolution" and the eventual "effectuators of the Three Principles of the People," the association intended each children's society to build self-government spirit and increase self-government awareness. The focus of the organization would be on such activities as music, art, gardening, work methods, exercise, swimming, and sanitation work.[37]

The third longer-surviving self-government initiative was in sericulture reform. East Township had for many years been a silk-producing area, every year in the early part of the century producing about three million yuan from cocoon and silk production. But by the 1920s farmers' conservative practices had led to sharp declines in production. The first step of the self-government association to turn the industry around was to improve the quality of silkworm eggs and thereby raise the quality of cocoons. Shen reportedly began to advocate use of better quality eggs in 1927.[38] He was most certainly aware that experiments in Hangzhou in 1926 had produced the first generation hybrid silkworm eggs: the hybrids "require[d] a shorter period of feeding than pure breeds; the time of their sleep and awakening [was] more uniform; and they produce[d] better silk, both in quality and quantity."[39] Traditionally East Township had bought its eggs from Cheng county in the southeast of what had been Shaoxing prefecture. Though Cheng county had the largest number of cocoon hongs in Zhejiang, its product was not of the highest quality, though for farmers concerned about prices the cost of egg sheets from Cheng was among the cheapest in the province. Again Shen had to convince farmers that their best interests depended on paying a higher price for better eggs.[40] The self-government association in the spring of 1928, certainly with Shen's advocacy, decided to push the sale among East Township farmers of four thousand sheets of better quality eggs (in 1929, the number shot up to 45,000 sheets). To make the higher costs more palatable, the association also sponsored a cocoon-selling cooperative to facilitate sales of cocoons. In the spring season of 1928, East Township farmers harvested over 37,000 catties of cocoons, with the sale price of better cocoons a third higher than that for those produced from Cheng county eggs.[41] Though there were other plans in the whole reform effort, by 1933 the East Township sericulture industry had been destroyed by the economic depression.

The fourth major initiative of the association was the establishment of various cooperatives. The first, headed by Shen, was established in July 1928, a Yaqian credit cooperative with lending and savings functions. A detailed report by the Yaqian Village Self-Government Association in May had pointed to the need for such a cooperative. Giving specific figures on the amount of unhulled rice produced on the farms in the district per adult and the cost of living per adult, the report showed that each year the district came up over 4,500 piculs short of what it needed to live on.[42] Such a situation necessitated borrowing to be able to continue with the next year's crop. The Yaqian credit cooperative, initially joined by over three hundred persons, loaned over a thousand yuan the first year and over six thousand the second. By 1930, its membership was up to 540. Other towns followed in setting up credit cooperatives. The original self-government association plan called for each village self-government district to organize such a cooperative and for all of East Township to establish a central cooperative or its own bank to help build up the economy. There were several retail cooperatives, including the silk cooperative, and in Yaqian a vegetable sellers' cooperative and a cooperative for straw hat makers. Given the fact that most of the successful cooperatives were at or near Yaqian, it seems clear that Shen's strong support of the idea of cooperatives made the difference. But by the mid-1930s the cooperatives were gone.[43]

Problems, Politics, and Perception

As the proponent of a specific program not adopted or even approved by the national or provincial party, Shen had made what seem credible claims to legitimacy and embarked on a constructive strategy to build a base of support and contribute to his locality. There were, however, several problems that militated against the success of his experiment. Of great importance was his lack of material resources. Without provincial party or government approbation, he could expect no support from these sources. While the self-government association received, according to the regulations, "direction and oversight" from the relevant branch bureaus of the Guomindang, the county party and its branches provided no financial assistance.[44] With his family fortune exhausted, he could no longer provide the financial backing that had once been possible.

It is not that self-government expenses were great. Temporarily there were local government funds for the construction of jetties and dikes and activities dealing with sericulture reform. Since most of the workers were trainees, they lived in Shen's compound and were not generally paid salaries; the only main expense was food. To help deal with this expense the Yaqian Farmers Association (but none other) collected and then contributed 300 to 400 catties of rice, which served as more than enough rations for a year for the self-government workers. Plans were originally made to survey the land and afterward levy a tax based on land value; this tax, which would have been above and beyond the land tax remitted to the government, would have served to meet self-government expenses. However, as Shen's experiment was aborted by his death, there was insufficient time for the surveying, which was completed only for part of the Yaqian self-government district.[45]

Even though the financial pressure was not then severe, financial demands and worries continued to dog Shen and the self-government movement, just as they had in 1925 and 1926 during his struggles over the direction of the provincial party. Much of Shen's June 8 speech before party leaders from East Township branch bureaus dealt with the reality of the money situation.

Now, no matter who it is, he thinks that if he doesn't have money, then he can't do things. Every person thinks that if he has money, then things are good. . . . [This kind of thinking] leads to official corruption and warlords selling the country. A joke applies here. An adult asked a child, "Where does your food come from?" The child answers, "From my mother's mouth." One answers, "From inside the rice bowl." Another says, "From inside the rice container." The food in the mouth comes from the bowl which comes from the container. Today's officialdom only wants more money. Wanting more money, they come to the government to get it: the government becomes the rice container.

Now let me raise the real issue. In recent days the self-government surveying team, because their work is very taxing, want a higher salary; they want money from the self-government association; they see the association as the rice container. The self-government association responds to them: you must ask the households in East Township. Those who survey are certainly township people; those who pay out money are also township people. If they can pay out sufficiently, then it's good to increase the salary.[46]

There is no record of whether the salaries were increased, but Shen's position is clear: if the people wanted self-government and the advantages that it would bring, they had to be willing to pay for it. He said, "We want to solve the problem of people's livelihood, and it is linked to popular sovereignty. Self-government expense must be shouldered by the people—it should, in fact, cause them to increase production."[47] What effect such a tax policy would have had on the support Shen was receiving is unknown because his death came less than three months after this proposal.

The absence of material resources was not, however, Shen's prime problem. It was clear from the beginning that the provincial and national party bureaus were not going to allow Shen's experiment to go unchallenged. Shen and his wife, Wang Huafen, had played important roles in the Xiaoshan county Guomindang bureau since its reorganization in September 1927.[48] Even before Shen's announcement of his project, the county bureau had, however, begun efforts to rein in the actions of particularly obstreperous farmers associations.[49] Such action coincided with provincial government efforts to curtail the actions of mass organizations, the very groups upon which Shen depended in his project. Less than a week before Shen's February 6 founding of the Yaqian Self-Government Association, the provincial party executive committee, which had been composed mostly of Shen's supporters, was disbanded upon the arrival from Nanjing of reorganization deputies.[50] By mid-April, the provincial party bureau had been purged of Shen's supporters and replaced by men loyal to the increasingly important CC clique.[51]

From that point on, Shen's base, like the township's coastal land, was increasingly undercut and eroded by the national and provincial party, with their control of material resources and monopoly of political power. In late May the new provincial party bureau appointed two of its supporters to serve as directors of the Xiaoshan county party bureau.[52] In June, as Shen's project began to experience financial difficulties, the county party bureau organized under its control farm associations (*nonghui*) in each township, obvious antagonists to the existing farmers associations.[53] The most devastating blow came when the county bureau fell under control of the CC clique in early July; by the middle of that month, it began a party reregistration to weed out undesirable or inappropriate members.[54] As Shen saw his base in the Xiaoshan party bureau—which had been the sole sanctioner of his project—threatened and seized and his resources diminishing, his rural reconstruction project seemed to be in some peril.

During this rapid decline in overall position, he maintained great prestige in the local arena. He was not only active in Yaqian, but played several roles in the county on permanent committees. He headed the Xiaoshan County Reconstruction Committee, a position in which he drew up the main principles for county reconstruction; they were never put into effect.[55] He was on the committee superintending the partial reclamation of Xiang Lake, a reservoir south and west of the county seat, and prime mover of the establishment of a school in the lake area.[56] He was a county deputy on the Committee on Funds and Property.[57] He also participated in various other public meetings not connected to the East Township Association. On August 9, he attended a meeting in the county seat on the procedures and details of county financial management.[58] The next day he traveled to the town of Linpu with Wang Huafen and Kong Xuexiong for the establishment of an educational association for the southern third of the county; Kong chaired the meeting, but it was Shen who was the featured speaker.[59]

At this same time in Nanjing (August 8 to 14) the Guomindang's Second Central Executive Committee was holding its Fifth Plenum. It was the Fourth Plenum in early February that had effectively ended the power and role of Shen and his network and brought to power the CC clique. Since that time, the Northern Expedition had successfully accomplished the goal of seizing Beijing; military leaders had met in early July before Sun's coffin in the Western Hills to report as much. The role of the Fifth Plenum then was to plan for the future following the military unification. The most contentious issue became the question of centralization versus some retention of local power; although the hotly contested issue reportedly "almost ended the meeting," the proponents of centralization carried the day.[60] It was a strategy that could not have looked kindly on Shen's experiment. For the national party, this meeting inaugurated the period of political tutelage, something Shen had begun six months earlier on a much different scale and with a completely different approach.

Context, Identity, and Perception in Revolutionary Political Culture

Shen tried to mobilize the farmers of the Southern Sands (East Township) in the rent resistance effort of 1921 and the self-government and mass organization project of 1928. In neither episode did Shen accurately gauge his opposition's power or understand the nature of the response to his actions. His idealistic appeals for legitimacy, in the first instance to natural rights and in the second to the thought of Sun Yat-sen, could not affect or sway the reality of his opponents' political power. The naivete of this intellectual activist who had stood up to warlords and party leaders seems striking.

In almost every respect, Shen's position seemed ironically stronger in the rent resistance movement than in his rural reconstruction effort. In the first, Shen still held a nonbureaucratic provincial position and substantial prestige, while in the second his only political sanction came from the county party bureau. In the first, Shen still had substantial personal financial resources, while in the second these had been exhausted. It seems clear that by any objective measurement of resources and strategy Shen was a greater threat to the establishment he opposed in 1921 (fomenting a rent resistance rebellion) than in 1928 (initiating a rural reconstruction project). And yet the reaction against him was much stronger in 1928: seizing control of the county party, Shen's political base, and undercutting the farmers associations and other mass organizations, Shen's social base.

What accounts for the difference? In part, it was because Shen had been able to remain in the background in the first episode. But it was the political context that was crucial. In the first instance, the context was more conducive to success: the less polarized political scene and the spirit of the May Fourth era which invited greater experimentation and questioning provided a more open atmosphere for maneuvering. In the latter, the continuing political purges in the violent search for a new political state unity created a tension that invited suspicion and distrust of any challenge and that stifled the possibility of dissenting alternatives. The role of political opponents thus became fraught with greater risk.

At any time the perceptions of political actions can become more significant than the actions themselves, but in the context of rising paranoia over challenges to authority, perceived identities can quickly harden into an immutable reality.[61] It is especially in such situations that one's identity, "the symbolic screen through which [one's] world is ordered and organized, is constantly under strain."[62] If "enmity lies in the eye of the perceiver,"[63] what party leaders perceived may not have had much to do logically or empirically with what Shen was actually doing. Shen's speeches conveyed a deep-seated conviction that he was doing the party's work; he did not apparently believe that his rural reconstruction plan would be perceived as such a threat. Kong Xuexiong argues repeatedly that Shen was indeed a loyal party supporter. Logically, the issues between Shen and the party leaders should not have created insurmountable difficulties. Kong alludes to the likely flash points between the opponents. The party apparently argued that Shen's experiment did not actually have a proper ideological base in Sun's Three Principles of the People: Shen's assertion that he was effectuating Sun's legacy obviously challenged the party leaders in their role as keepers of the ideology.[64] They attacked him for what would become known in later times and in the affairs of another party as "commandism." They criticized him for his dependence on the untrustworthy mass organizations, a dependence which the party believed had to be rectified in the summer of 1928.[65]

But it seems likely that Shen's symbolic linking of the rural reconstruction plan to the earlier rent resistance was the serious, and perhaps fatal, miscalculation. That ritual of remembrance for Li Chenghu was the party leaders' first perception of Shen's goals. As word of Shen's experiment spread widely, visitors came in increasing numbers to see the changes in the township. Many of the reviews were favorable. In late June a group of government officials returning to Hangzhou from Shaoxing stopped at sites in East Township to visit self-government villages and the headquarters of the farmers association and to ascertain the progress of sericulture reform.[66] Other visitors left with comments like "The local self-government experiment [is flourishing] like a potted plant," indications of its effectiveness.[67] One newspaper report in mid-August called Shen "the representative of the masses."[68]

But, Kong Xuexiong noted, the more people came, the more distrust of his goals increased.[69] Visitors obviously came with preconceived perceptions of Shen and his work. Whether these perceptions were challenged or enhanced by the visits likely depended on the outlook of the visitor. At a time when enemies were everywhere and the "revolutionary" aims of the party leaders not yet realized, Shen's alternative strategy of rural reconstruction complicated the political situation and in its dissent threatened the leadership. Given the transcendent goal of state unity as an expression of nationalism in the revolution, it is perhaps not surprising that the leaders reacted as they did.[70]

Kong Xuexiong argues that people understood neither Shen's aims nor his enthusiasm. In the case of the East Township experiment, rumor became the medium of cognition and seized on symbols or perceived symbols of a man building a power base in order to plan a revolt. A photograph, taken of a rack for equipment of the township fire-fighting brigade, was interpreted as a gun rack for a growing township militia rumored to number twenty thousand. Workers, sighted on Phoenix Mountain near Yaqian quarrying stone for memorial stelae, were rumored to be building a military garrison.[71] Such rumors created new identities for Shen, transforming him into the "commandist," specifically into the infamous symbolic category of the late 1920s: a "local bully, evil gentry," who had pretensions for power in a larger arena. Shen's personality did not encourage those on the outside to see past the rumors. As self-assurance shaded into arrogance and his sense of his own ability led to arbitrariness, Shen eroded the possibility of greater sympathy among party leaders.

In sum, it seems clear that perception of Shen's identity was more significant than the reality of the threat. Shen's eroded resources could not have mounted a credible challenge to the party at any level: at most his self-government experiment had collapsed into a symbol of his opposition. It seems that the party leadership willingly chose to perceive the nature of Shen's actions as conspiratorial in order to undercut an opponent they felt they could not trust or manipulate.[72] Those in authority, with their control over the key resources of power, seemed unwilling in this episode to understand or countenance any alternative from those they wanted to perceive as disloyal. At least in this period of threats to the leaders' goals there apparently could be no loyal opposition; Shen's effort to offer himself and his self-government strategy as such was doomed from the start. In the increasingly antirevolutionary political culture following the Guomindang victory—where conformity to authority (in the name of supporting the nation and the revolution) was the standard for political judgment, where rumor with its imaginative unpredictability was an important political medium, and where political enemies (Communists and the bully-gentry amalgam) were perceived and identified in all guises and places—misperceptions, both conscious and subconscious, were a continual possibility. In Shen's case, like those of many others in these turbulent years, this paranoiac mix was destructive and ultimately deadly.

CHAPTER NINE

Scenarios

Steeled by a thousand hammers, by ten thousand chisels
  before I emerge from the mountain,
I am not afraid of the fierce, raging fire.
I am not afraid
  if my bones are powdered or my body crushed.
I only want to leave clarity and honor among the people.

Yu Zhongxiao, Ming dynasty
Epitaph of Shen Dingyi

Death, death, death
Stumbled and fell, terrified the city,
Tread over the resentment of the common masses—
Blood road, road of life.

"Death" (Si), 1922

The hail of bullets had left Shen a bleeding, dying heap on the bus platform. As the heavy rain continued to pelt down, some of those who had fled when the shots rang out probably returned; almost all of them likely acquaintances of Shen, they would naturally have gathered round the body. Shen's network comrades now involved in the self-government effort, Jiang Jiannong and Zhou Xinwei, heard the shots and the commotion from the self-government office and arrived quickly, helping to carry the body to the party and self-government office. They dispatched a special car to Hangzhou to report on the events. On receiving the news, Wang Nayin sent two doctors to Yaqian.

Someone ran to the Village Dormitory to get Wang Huafen and Shen's oldest son, Jianlong. Years later his second son, Jianyun, ten at his father's death, remembered that he too was at home when he heard the news. Policemen had arrived at the bus station before Shen's body was removed. Lying by the corpse on the ground was a printed name card of one Lu Baozhang of Cheng county; it was the only tangible clue at the crime scene. The police immediately alerted police departments in the nearby towns of Kanshan and Keqiao. Police from both Kanshan and the county seat came to Yaqian, hoping to surround and slay the killers, not knowing of their escape.

Shen's body was then carried to his home, his clothes soaked in blood from the multiple wounds. The Xiaoshan hospital was sent a telegram; the head doctor, accompanied by the county magistrate, arrived about 10:00 P.M. After the doctor's examination, the family prepared the coffin; the corpse was dressed at 6:00 P.M. on August 29. "Comrades from far and near who had worked with Shen," his associates, and his household were painfully grieved and outraged. Telegrams to the central and provincial governments, to relatives, and to friends informed them of the death and that the body would be placed in the coffin at 1:00 P.M. on Saturday, September 1.[1]

Over the next four months at least eight men in Shaoxing and Cheng counties were arrested as suspects in the assassination. All were eventually released for lack of evidence. More than a year later, a young laborer surnamed Xing from the Harbin Shipyard in Manchuria arrived in Hangzhou. A native of Cheng county, Xing gave secret testimony to the head of the Shen Dingyi Memorial Committee, reporting a conversation he had had with a fellow unskilled laborer at the shipyard, a man surnamed Qian, also from Cheng county. Qian had said that "a person came to me last year and offered thirty thousand yuan to kill a man. After I killed him, I received only ten thousand yuan. The day after the killing, I went to Shanghai, read about the murder in the newspaper, and saw Shen's picture. The newspaper said that he had been a good man. Because of this, I felt very guilty. Because the newspaper promised a reward for the murderer, I had no one to turn to—and therefore, I came to Manchuria."

After the Memorial Committee received the report, it corresponded with the Harbin authorities to get the suspect extradited to Hangzhou. However, as an investigation by Zhejiang authorities began, the murderer, who had by this time confessed, met an unexpected and unexplained violent death in prison. In his initial statement, he had said only that a landlord from the Xiaoshan-Shaoxing area had solicited the murder; he implicated no one else.[2] In the end, no one was ever tried for the killing.

The Assassination:
Evidence and Key Questions

Eyewitness accounts of the crime were not much to go on, offering only very general descriptions of the killers: both around the age of thirty; one very thin, bald on top, with short hair around. Bystanders remembered that the assassins had spoken with the accents of Cheng and (its neighboring) Xinchang counties; together with the name card found at the murder site, this bit of information gave the police an initial area to target their investigation.

The general police and press opinion as the investigation progressed was that the assassins were well-trained marksmen. Their shots fired at twenty feet were deadly accurate; no one else, including Song who was standing next to Shen, was wounded in the slightest. The implication was that they were clearly professional hit men, that the killing was not the work of individuals who had been personally disgruntled or aggrieved in dealings with Shen. The assassination was obviously well planned; one killer is sufficient to eliminate an unarmed victim. Here two men carrying three guns had ridden with their victim since the River Bank bus station and had ever so deliberately moved in for the kill. The savageness of the attack indicated they were taking no chance that he might live. In addition, their escape seemed extraordinarily easy and indicated a carefully considered plan. If they had been less thoughtfully prepared and had moved against Shen at the far busier River Bank station, successfully eluding pursuers would have been far more difficult. In 1993, Shen's grandson, Zhongliang, called it "a well-organized murder."

Before considering the various suspects behind the murder, key questions about the events of August 28 must be asked. How did the two assassins waiting at the River Bank station know when Shen would return from his visit to Moganshan? Could they have simply been waiting indefinitely or perhaps appearing at the station when Yaqian-bound buses were due to depart in the late afternoon? Or were they informed that day about the probable time of Shen's arrival? The latter possibility takes on credibility when it is remembered that sources suggest it was not at all certain that Shen would return to Yaqian on Tuesday. He had been pressed by Zhou Bonian to remain at the resort, but had chosen not to do so. It seems more than likely that an informant had notified the killers about Shen's schedule, a probability that makes it unlikely that these men were acting on their own. Where might an informant have been? There seem to be three possibilities. Someone at Moganshan had passed the word; that might have been someone at the resort or at the steam launch embarkation point from which Shen and Wang Nayin traveled to Hangzhou. Or someone at the Imperial Arch Bridge where Shen and Wang disembarked on the north side of Hangzhou. Or someone at the Qiantang River Ferry station at Windy Mountain Gate in the town of Jianggan. Though, at this point, it was only a relatively short time before Shen would get to the Qiantang's eastern bank, he was held up by a very unusual temporary imposition of martial law whereby eastbound travelers had to pass through a police search.

There is also the question of the men's identity in relation to Shen. If the testimony of Qian from Cheng county is to be believed, then the killers did not know Shen. But other sources suggest that the men were acquainted with Shen. Some reports indicated that the killers talked with Shen before getting on the bus; his son in 1993 even said that he had been told that Shen had bought food for the men at the bus station. Witnesses later reported that the men had tried to sit near Shen on the bus. The key question, of course, is, if he knew them, what was the nature of their acquaintance?

One problem in trying to solve Shen's murder is that there are too many possibilities. In the midst of the revolution, he had made many enemies in his national, provincial, and local leadership in the last dozen years of his life. The Shanghai newspaper *Shenbao*, reporting on Shen's death noted that "Shen's natural disposition was that he made arbitrary decisions on his own and that he was continually in disagreement with people."[3] But it is worth exploring the possibilities suggested by commentators at the time; there is always the possibility, of course, that the murderer was someone who has not been speculated upon. But this exploration will help us determine as best we can who was likely responsible for Shen's murder and can provide further insights into politics and society in the 1920s.

Scenario 1: Murder as Personal Revenge

The suspect: The head monk from East Mountain Temple in Yaqian.[4]

The motive: Revenge for Shen's seizing and dispossessing the monks of the temple.

The evidence: Circumstantial. The monk's threat to kill Shen and the monk's seizure of the temple after Shen's death.

Credibility. East Mountain Temple was the largest of many temples in the Yaqian area, its buildings and property extending over ten mu. It was located almost directly across the Grand Canal to the south of the Shen family's compound. In 1921 when he was establishing the Farmers Association and beginning the rent resistance movement, Shen proposed taking the temple and changing it into the association's headquarters and a site for other public meetings. Imbued with May Fourth fervor about the wastefulness and futility of superstition, Shen decided simply to do so. The temple was seized, the monks were evicted (moving to another Yaqian temple), and some of the Buddhist images and temple equipment were destroyed. Other temple materials were later moved, registered, and housed in what was announced as a fine arts exhibit.

In the raucous fall of 1921, the association met at the temple and received the hundreds of visitors there who boated to Yaqian for guidance. It was both the center of the rent resistance movement and the site of the military's crushing of the movement. The monk, who even before had the reputation of mental instability, continued to lash out at Shen, letting him know that he could sooner or later expect revenge and that he wanted to see Shen die. There were occasional outbursts of such rhetoric throughout the 1920s. From late 1921 until early 1928, the temple was frequently used as a public meeting site; the proximity of the temple to Shen's home was of great convenience. After 1925, the temple was called Sun Yat-sen Hall, and it was here that first the Yaqian Self-Government Association and then the East Township Association were established. Other area temples were also used for self-government offices, but they functioned jointly as Buddhist temples and association offices, in most cases after the associations had helped in renovating the temples.

In 1927 word leaked out that the monk had accumulated two thousand dollars as "hit" money to hire someone to kill Shen. After Shen's death, the monk immediately moved back to the former temple and refused to leave. Police arrested him in early September, forbidding him to stay in Sun Yat-sen Hall; he was not charged in the murder. While the monk may have indeed had a motive to kill Shen and had not only threatened repeatedly and perhaps built up a fund to hire a killer, the professional nature of the assassination would seem to argue against the involvement of this monk. Two thousand dollars was a relatively small sum for hiring two men who had the expertise to coordinate the affair. Enraged though he might have been at Shen, the monk should be removed from the list of suspects; the fact that he had not acted to carry out his threat for almost seven years raises the question, why act now? His move back to the temple was simply opportunistic.

Scenario 2: Murder to Forestall Economic Deprivation

The suspects: Cheng county silkworm merchants.[5]

The motive: To eliminate Shen, who more than anyone else was responsible for the East Township policy of stopping the purchase of Cheng county silkworm eggs, which eventually led to large financial losses for the Cheng county merchants. While only four thousand sheets of better quality eggs were purchased in 1928, the merchants feared that the policy would end their longtime, profitable relationship with area silkworm producers.

The evidence: The name card found at the scene of the crime was of Lu Baozhang from Cheng county; the dialect spoken by the murderers was that of Cheng and Xinchang counties, according to eyewitnesses; the visit to Xiaoshan earlier in the summer of a Cheng county merchant who threatened Shen for advocating sericulture reform.

Credibility. At the time investigators assumed that the name card belonged to one of the assassins. Speculation was that he had given it to Shen on the bus and that when Shen was fumbling for his ticket in the moments before the assassination, it had fallen to the ground. That possibility seems odd: why would an assassin offer his name card to the intended victim? Whether Lu Baozhang from Cheng was, then, one of the assassins cannot be determined; there is no record (whoever he was) that he was ever found. While the use of Cheng county dialect seems at first glance to point to the assassins' place of residence as Cheng county, the reality is less clear, for many migrants to the newly formed alluvial lands near Yaqian hailed from the relatively poor counties of Cheng and Xinchang and thus spoke that dialect. Thus, while circumstantial evidence suggests a strong connection to Cheng county, it is not a necessary one.

The motive would be a rather strong one for Cheng silkworm merchants. Competition between silkworm egg suppliers in Zhejiang was intense; the trade in 1927 was estimated at several million dollars a year. Silkworm egg suppliers in Cheng, Xinchang, and Yuhang counties competed to try to get their eggs out on the market first in order to sell all their egg sheets. Cheng and Xinchang counties normally produced about three hundred thousand sheets per year; and there were about eight hundred people involved in the process.[6] While a drop of four thousand sheets sold to East Township farmers in the summer of 1928 would not be a large decrease, the drop of forty-five thousand in 1929 obviously had a huge impact. Cheng county had the largest number of cocoon firms in the province (fifty-nine); with an economy based relatively more strongly on the silkworm egg business than that of any other county, Cheng merchants and the economic health of the county depended on continued sales to those areas that had purchased eggs in the past.[7]

Eggs from Cheng were sold from approximately the end of April until late May. Shen had reportedly spoken in 1927 about the desirability of area farmers purchasing hybrid and improved strains of eggs. With the establishment of the farmers associations and the Yaqian Village District Association, organizations to define farmers' interests and shape long-term goals, joint action in deciding how many new egg sheets to purchase was more possible. Such possibilities of community decision making and joint action underlay Shen's strong desire to establish mass organizations.

In early summer after the spring silkworm season came the visit of the menacing Cheng merchant, threatening Shen for his role. Other silkworm merchants also tried to undercut the policy and future plans in that direction by playing on the financial fears of township farmers: why spend more per sheet of silkworm eggs when there will not be any greater return? Reportedly there were a number of disturbances in East Township spawned by these efforts. We do not know how many of the incidents, if any, may have been incited by Cheng natives now resident in East Township and with strong connections to people involved in the egg production in their native place; but some tensions were likely raised over the issue.

In sum, there was substantial hatred of Shen among those in the silkworm industry and an understandable desire to be rid of him and the threat to their economic profit. Modern scientific changes, in this case the development of hybrid strains of eggs, posed the same kind of challenge to the established system in Cheng county that revolution posed for the political and social system. As he had through most of his adult life, Shen unfearingly offered challenge upon challenge to those in power. Might his challenge to the Cheng merchants have been his undoing? They would have had agents in the area to whom they could turn, natives of Cheng living in East Township who could have known Shen. They would have had the financial resources to offer large sums to hire the killers. They would have had the contacts on transportation routes and at ferry and steam launch hubs to convey Shen's whereabouts to the killers. If the killers were from Cheng, the silkworm merchants were a likely suspect.

But the evidence is not compelling. While it is said that the character of the people from Cheng is fierce and overbearing and that the county has a tradition of contentiousness,[8] there are in this scenario simply too many assumptions based on tangential possibilities; they "could have had this" and "might have done that," but how likely were the this and the that? Why spend thousands of dollars to kill Shen when there was no reason to suspect that he alone was making the egg sheet decision? His associates were clearly supportive of the policy. It would likely be (and it was) continued even after his death. While they should remain on the list of suspects, it seems only a remote possibility that they hired Shen's killers.

Scenario 3: Murder from Vengeance and Fear of the Future

The suspects: Xiaoshan landlords.[9]

The motive: Revenge against Shen for the 1921 rent resistance movement and his leadership of the 25-percent rent reduction campaign and fear of what the East Township Association and the mass organizations portended for their future.

The evidence: Circumstantial. The confession by Qian from Cheng county shortly before his untimely death in jail included the allegation that a Xiaoshan-Shaoxing area landlord, one Wang Yuanhong, hired him to commit the murder. Reports came also from Lai Ajin, a boatman from the town of Changhe, west of the county seat, that he had carried messages between three landlords surnamed Lai, Fu, and Zhou in the vicinity of Changhe and three East Township landlords, surnamed Jin, Fang, and Wang, the last of whom might well have been Wang Yuanhong.

Credibility. That many landlords in Xiaoshan hated Shen was common knowledge. They saw him, as the idiom literally puts it, as a "nail in the eye."[10] At the same time that the landlords' anti-Shen conspiracy was supposedly taking shape, the Changhe landlords were trying to deal with rent protests that had been fomented by Communist Party members. With Xiaoshan county having at this time the largest number of Communist Party members of any county in the province, this kind of social unrest threatened to get out of hand.[11] To landlords challenged repeatedly by Shen's work in the past and faced by social disruption in the present, it was quite logical to see that Shen's project and promotion of tenant issues would likely only foment more trouble: in the words of the January provincial party and government declaration, "Tenants get an inch and desire a foot."

Then there were reportedly the inflammatory rumors (always the rumors) that Shen was planning to put forward some land redistribution scheme, that he had in fact already drafted the applicable regulations.[12] Such talk did not seem out of line with what Shen might have promoted. In his June 8, 1928, speech in Yaqian, for example, Shen noted that "when we have achieved society's reconstruction, we can then destroy the system of private ownership and thereby attain the aim of people's livelihood."[13] There is no information in any source indicating that Shen had ever drafted such a plan. But as it is clear over and over again in the 1920s, rumors and what people wanted to believe were more important and compelling than the reality.

In any case, on the basis of their attitudes toward Shen and their fears of what the continuing action of such a determined proponent of rural reform and perceived radicalism might portend, the landlords are credible suspects. They had the wealth to pay for the killing; and a conspiracy of at least six (such as is suggested by the boatman) would undoubtedly have had access to enough networks to know of Shen's plans and deal with matters of timing and the escape of the killers.

We also have the name of Wang Yuanhong, large landowner and businessman from the village of Dayi, very near to Yaqian. In the fall of 1921, Wang, it should be remembered, had shouted accusations of idiocy and insanity at Shen while Shen spoke at a local temple to encourage the establishment of farmers associations; then Wang had issued an ominous warning to the farmers about continuing to listen to Shen.

Shen and Wang were almost certainly not on good terms after the episode. Chen Gongmao, who worked in the Xiaoshan Guomindang bureau, reported in 1982 on the mysterious Qian who was killed more than a year later in prison after naming Wang as the person who had hired him. But when asked about this accusation, Wang Huafen, Shen's widow, said, "Wang Yuanhong and Shen [Dingyi] have been in closely associated families for generations. Ordinarily the feelings between them are by no means bad."[14] Her statement is certainly no ringing endorsement of Wang's innocence; the word "ordinarily" (*pingshi*) is troubling, but it is clear that Shen's widow was not ready at least publicly to suggest that landlord Wang was involved.

Yet Wang, in fact, was arrested for the murder in the fall of 1928, more than a year before Chen says he was implicated by Qian; thus there are discrepancies with the sources—Chen does not appear to have all his facts accurate; at least the chronology is incorrect.[15] A Xing (the man who reportedly first notified the authorities about Qian) and a Qian first appear in newspaper accounts in February 1929; and then they appear as part of a five-person conspiracy—along with Wang—in the murder plot.[16] Wang was an extraordinarily "connected" member of the Xiaoshan financial elite. In early December 1928, communications came to the Hangzhou government from every merchant establishment in every town in Xiaoshan and Shaoxing counties asking for Wang's immediate release. The government responded that there were still suspicions about Wang and that the investigation would continue.[17] But eventually he was released, as were all the suspects.

So what do we make of this? The reports of the conspiracy by Boatman Lai were investigated by Shen's memorial committee, composed of his provincial committee and East Township network. They found nothing to support Lai's charges.[18] The intriguing figure remains Wang Yuanhong. Might he have masterminded the assassination? Possibly. If that is the case, an important question concerns the timing. Why at the particular time after Shen's return from Moganshan? There seems to be no good reason why Wang would have selected this time and method (a long bus ride for the assassins before the attack). He lived only a mile or two from Yaqian; Shen could have been cut down any number of times—and closer in time to some of his actions or speeches that were more offensive to Wang.

A more likely possibility is that Wang was the middleman who willingly hired the killers for some higher authority. If we are to believe the gist of Chen's story, Qian was allowed to live until after he implicated

Wang; then he met his mysterious death. While Wang and perhaps other landlords may have been involved, we must wait to examine the last two suspects before trying to render a judgment.

Scenario 4: Murder as Political Revenge

The suspects: The Communist Party or individual Communist Party members.[19]

The motive: Revenge for Shen's perceived "double cross" of the party at the Yaqian Conference in 1925 and Shen's involvement with the Western Hills group; revenge for Shen's perceived role in the death of Xuan Zhonghua; and most of all revenge for Shen's leadership of the provincial purge in 1927, the White Terror.

The evidence: None.

Credibility. Though the Communist Party and individual Communist Party members seem to have one of the strongest motives for eliminating Shen (and they undoubtedly rejoiced after the killing), there is nothing in the record to link them to the crime. The Shanghai Guomindang newspaper, the *Republican Daily News*, speculated that the crime was committed because of political jealousy and resentment that the farmers of East Township were following Shen rather than Communist leadership. "This hateful act is congruent with typical Communist Party action."[20] Congruency does not mean actuality.

The fact is that the provincial Communist Party, having in the previous sixteen months gone through three purges, two of them bloody and all three costly, was largely demoralized and practically defunct. County efforts at Changhe in the spring of 1928 had been suppressed by the military; the county party would not rebuild a base of any sort until 1929.[21] Shen was certainly no long-term threat to Communist fortunes; everyone could see that the former head of the purge had been purged himself and that there was little likelihood that he would—at least in the foreseeable future—hold any power whatsoever in the provincial government or party. As hateful as he was, he had become ignorable, a man whom time had, from the Communist perspective, seemingly passed by.

If one still wanted to adhere to the interpretation that the Communist Party or individual Communists committed the crime as a kind of explosion of pent-up revenge, there are a number of questions that would have to be answered. Given the state of the party, why would its leaders decide to spend monetary and human resources to kill Shen when there were much higher priorities for their very survival? Is it logical to assume they would have made the effort at this time? Why in late August 1928 and with the common bus ride to Yaqian? Why not at any of the frequent public meetings Shen attended? Why not closer to the time that Shen left the provincial government after his association with the purge? If we assume that Communist Party members themselves committed the act, would they have had the contacts all along the route to Moganshan to notify the killers of Shen's schedule? Why would they have hired professional hit men (this assumes the police were right in their judgment)? If the act was one of political revenge, wouldn't the avenger want society and the world of revolutionary politics to know that the party or its members were responsible?

In sum, in addition to the fact that there is no evidence, the hypothesis that the Communists killed Shen seems to be found wanting for contextual and logical reasons.

Scenario 5: Murder to Forestall Political Success or Potential Rebellion

The suspects: The Guomindang or Guomindang party members.[22]

The motive: To end the career of a troublesome and unpredictable charismatic leader whose successes in East Township and with the mass organizations ran counter to the party line; to prevent Shen's reappearance in the national arena as a spokesman for the Western Hills faction; to prevent Shen from building a base that could be a launching pad for renewed political success and provincial position.

The evidence: Circumstantial, but compelling.

Credibility. There is a high degree of probability that the Guomindang, at either the national or the provincial level, ordered the assassination of Shen Dingyi. Of the five major suspects in this case, only two, the landlords and the Guomindang, had a motive—fear of what he might do in the future—that called for Shen's elimination as soon as possible. The main question is which level of the Guomindang, the national or the provincial, was more likely responsible.

It is clear that neither the national nor provincial party trusted Shen. A central party inspector investigated the Xiaoshan county bureau in late November 1927; in late January 1928, a Zhejiang government team investigated the Xiaoshan Farmers Association.[23] In late May 1928, the provincial party appointed two "directors" to be assigned to the Xiaoshan party branch.[24] Shen's ritual remembrance of Li as the inaugural act of his project and his insistence on the power and role of mass organizations in Xiaoshan while they were outlawed throughout the province; his maverick self-government experiment at a time when the watchword from the center was centralization; his June 8 statement about "destroying the system of private ownership"—all seemed radical at a time when "radical" was anathema because it flowed in the same stream as Communism. Thus, the party acted to purge the Xiaoshan county bureau of all Shen influence in the summer. Shen's pleas for assistance, recognition, and sanction for what seemed to him the carrying out of Sun Yat-sen's guidelines for reconstruction and political tutelage went for naught. And then there were the rumors of a plan for the redistribution of land and of the mountaintop garrison and many guns and Shen's training a self-defense force of twenty thousand farmers. The garrison and self-defense force rumors were enough to brand Shen with the sobriquet "local bully, evil gentry," an enemy of the Guomindang government.

A few days before his death Shen reportedly received two letters, one from Zhang Jingjiang, provincial party chairman, soon to be named Zhejiang governor, and close personal ally of Chiang Kai-shek, and the other from Si Lie, former provincial civil commissioner. Both letters admonished Shen not to be too radical, outspoken, or extreme. They warned about the current tense situation (presumably the Red scare) and cautioned him to be alert for the unexpected. Shen's reaction to the letters? He did not heed the warnings at all.[25] All the reasons to act against Shen, increasingly perceived as a radical or as a "local bully and evil gentry," were in place. All that was needed was an event or action to trigger Shen's murder and remove for once and for all this thorn in the side of the current regime.

The event or action that seems to emerge as key and which helps to uncover yet another particular motive for and perhaps the agent behind the killing is Shen's trip to Moganshan. There are a number of puzzling questions that emerge from the sources about this trip. First, why did Shen go? His biography, written by the Memorial Committee, says that on August 25, the day before he left, he read in the newspaper that Dai

Jitao, whom he had not seen for three years, was staying at the resort. Shen thus decided on his own to go in order to discuss methods of expanding self-government. But when Dai had lectured in more convenient Hangzhou in January before a crowd of roughly three hundred, Shen had not bothered to go seek Dai out.[26] Other sources, including Kong Xuexiong's history of the East Township Association published in 1934 and Shen's son Jianyun in 1993, contend that Shen did not choose to go to Moganshan on his own but was summoned there.[27] Since Kong was an intimate friend of Shen and because Jianyun would be expected to relay the story that had been passed down in the family, their version is important.

What difference does it make whether Shen went on his own or was invited? If he went on his own, there was no formal meaning to his visit. The memorial biography may have wanted to free Shen from any hint of going to Moganshan for suspicious political reasons; it was written while Shen's murder investigation was still ongoing, and it implies that any untoward Guomindang political assumption about the trip would be incorrect. If he were, on the other hand, summoned to Moganshan by key party leaders, there was a formal political meaning to his visit: could this have been a follow-up of the Zhang and Si letters of a few days before? Was the party attempting to stress its warning through the words of old friend Dai Jitao? And, in light of Shen's "radical" activities, how would Dai have reacted to what Shen told him, recorded in the memorial biography as Shen's "last revolutionary viewpoint." "The revolution which originally rose in people's hearts has not been satisfied. Because the situation was [originally] unsatisfactory, we had to have a revolution. But the present unsatisfied nature of people's hearts means that there must be another revolution."[28] It was not a way to silence fears about radicalism.

But there is yet another piece to the Moganshan puzzle. Reliable sources list four men whom Shen met at the resort: Dai Jitao, Zhang Ji, Zhu Jiahua, and Zhou Bonian. None of Shen's biographical sources, however, lists a fifth Guomindang leader who was at the sanitarium with his wife from August 23 to 30. He was Li Jishen, Guomindang Central Executive Committee member and currently head of the Guangdong provincial government.[29] He was also closely linked to the Guangxi clique and from the fall of 1927 to men in the Western Hills faction.[30] It is not as though Li was not associating with the other four; when Li left the resort, he was accompanied by Dai.[31] While it is possible that Shen and Li may not have talked at length, neither apparently did Zhang and Zhu have much intercourse with Shen, yet they are mentioned in the accounts nevertheless.

Why was Li left out? It appears that sources close to Shen wanted to make it appear that there was no relationship between Li's presence and Shen's going to Moganshan. Not mentioning Li's presence was the easiest technique. But if there was complete "innocence" in Shen's trip to the resort, why not mention Li? The suspicion inevitably emerges that Shen's biographers were involved in trying to cover up something, if only to squelch any questions that might be raised about Shen's intentions. We have seen that at the time of the Special Central Committee the Western Hills faction was in league with the Guangxi clique. Reportedly in the summer of 1928 rumors began recirculating of anti-Chiang ferment among the Guangxi clique. Li's visit to Moganshan corresponded with that of Zhang Ji, a leading member of the Western Hills group who had just become chair of the Central Political Council in Beijing. Is it possible that Li or Zhang was the person who summoned Shen to Moganshan to discuss the possibilities that may have existed to replace Chiang? Might Shen have been considering a return to action in a higher arena? Or had it been his decision alone to go to Moganshan, and was the presence of Li and Zhang just a coincidence?

Whatever the facts, two Xiaoshan county natives, one a Guomindang member in the 1920s and the other a Communist Party member, suggest that Shen's going to Moganshan at that moment was the critical act leading to his assassination. Chen Gongmao, who worked in the Xiaoshan County Guomindang bureau, wrote in 1981 that Shen's trip stirred up the Western Hills–related suspicions of Chiang Kai-shek, who would likely have been notified of Shen's visit by Dai Jitao. Their trip to Moscow in 1923 had brought Shen and Chiang into contact for the longest period in their lives, but their relations were never good. Chiang was repelled by the tendency of the Western Hills group in general to speak of itself as the older generation of anti-Communists. Shen was a striving, ambitious man; Chiang disliked him and never accepted him as one of his group, always treating him distantly and indifferently. The possible connivance of Shen with Li and Zhang, added to what he had likely been hearing from close confidant Zhang Jingjiang about Shen's actions in East Township, was enough, this scenario goes, to push Chiang into a decision to order Shen's assassination.[32]

Xu Meikun, the Communist labor organizer who had worked with Shen in the rent resistance campaign in 1921, basically presents the same story, though with more detail and some factual errors. Xu's account was first written in 1957; he amended it in 1980. He puts different people at Moganshan than were actually there during Shen's visit. Instead of Li Jishen, he names Li Shiceng; and instead of Zhang Ji, he names Zhang Jingjiang. Xu writes that "at the secret conference at Moganshan they planned to overthrow Chiang and make Zhang Guomindang chairman. Chiang recognized that Shen was conspiring with Li and Zhang . . . and therefore ordered He Yingqin to find a way to kill Shen. He Yingqin ordered Military Affairs Minister Jiang Bocheng to send an assassin. These circumstances I heard from the assassin himself when we were in prison together at that time."[33] There are sufficient factual errors in Xu's remembered record to question these allegations. I do not base my conclusions on it; but it is interesting and thought provoking in light of my interview with Shen's son in the summer of 1993. The names that were mentioned by Shen Jianyun and others of the household after some hesitancy were He Yingqin and Dai Jitao.

Certainly the course of the afternoon of August 28 becomes more understandable if we see both the ruling central and provincial Guomindang as responsible. Someone at Moganshan, presumably Dai Jitao, would have let someone in the Hangzhou government know Shen's schedule. The temporary imposition of martial law at the ferry station was most unusual; after all, the Communist threat was supposedly incoming agents to the capital city, not people trying to leave, but it makes sense if we see it as the result of an order to the police from some authority. The reason: the assassins, based in the capital city, had already crossed the river from Hangzhou, but there was some concern on the part of government officials privy to the conspiracy that Shen had hidden a weapon on his person.[34] Thus the search was set up to confiscate the weapon to make certain that Shen was unarmed when the killers struck. If Guomindang authorities were responsible for the killing, it would also help explain the easy escape of the assassins. Suspicious in this regard is the fact that there was only one policeman at the Yaqian police bureau when the assassination occurred; all the rest were out on "public duties."[35] The story of Qian the confessed murderer who fled to Manchuria and then met a mysterious death in prison before he could be extradited to Zhejiang also becomes more compelling, for if party or governmental authorities were involved they would have had the goal and the means of silencing Qian permanently. The arrest of Wang Yuanhong, perhaps the middleman in the killing, would have been necessitated by his being fingered as a suspect. With Wang and the authorities in collusion, he could be held for a time for propriety's sake and then freed, his secret remaining hidden.

The generally cold post-assassination actions of Guomindang national and provincial leaders contribute to the suspicion that they may have been culpable; at the very least they revealed that Shen was strongly disliked. Only two provincial party-government representatives (and they, Jiang Menglin and Cheng Chenjun, not highly important) went to Yaqian to pay their respects to Shen, although the government did contribute toward the funeral expenses.[36] Dai Jitao, who had been such a critical person and supposed friend in Shen's party development, did not come, though he was in Hangzhou on August 30. His name did appear with Chiang Kai-shek's on a pro forma list of a memorial society.[37] Shen's associates and family noted with some anger that when Chiang sent a funeral scroll, included in it was the ambiguous phrase "to cause the evildoer to be slain."[38] The provincial party leader Zhang Jingjiang did have a stele erected at the assassination spot, but there were no encomiums or even words recalling Shen's accomplishments, only the stark characters for "the place where Mr. Shen Dingyi died."[39] Interestingly, the only party reaction that could be considered warm in its praise came from Li Jishen. Asked in an interview for his reactions to Shen's death, Li responded, "Shen was one of our party's senior members; his death breaks up the revolutionary family. He had successes in the party and the country and most recently in his management of the Xiaoshan local self-government. His contribution in effecting revolutionary work is honorable. After I heard the news, I could not contain my grief."[40]

The Shen Memorial Committee petitioned the Central Committee proposing a state funeral and the organization of a special court to handle Shen's case because of its gravity. Chiang immediately rejected both requests, in the latter case saying that it was a simple murder case and that ordinary courts should handle it.[41] The provincial government initially acceded to the request that the East Township Self-Government remain as a permanent memorial to Shen; but by mid-1929 the government was moving to change it, and the whole project was shut down at the end of 1929. From that point on, the party and party spokespersons acted as though Shen had never existed. In 1929, when the provincial government under Governor Zhang Jingjiang opened the West Lake Exposition and established the Memorial Hall of the Revolution, the provincial party bureau under the control of Chen Guofu and Chen Lifu rejected out of hand the proposal of the Shen Memorial

Committee that Shen be included as a martyr.[42] In the lengthy definitive official study of the 25-percent rent reduction effort in Zhejiang Province published by the Central Political Institute in 1935, Shen is not even mentioned.[43]

Thus, it seems likely that Shen's involvement in the Western Hills episode for six months (from November 1925 to May 1926) not only destroyed his national and provincial careers but that the continuing perception of Shen as a Western Hills partisan may also have been the proximate cause of his murder. It is also likely the cause of the subsequent obliteration of his memory as a key player in the national, provincial, and local arenas during the revolution of the 1920s. Shen's second son wrote in June 1993, "They put the hat of the extreme rightist counterrevolutionary Guomindang on his head, and there was no scientific analysis of the specific situation. Every coin has two sides, but they didn't view and resolve the issues in objective perspective."[44] Shen's son, to be sure, has an interest in the interpretation of his father's record, but in light of the facts of the time he seems to be right on target.

In conclusion, we must also remember the impact of Shen's past Communist record, his organization and promotion of the 1921 rent resistance movement, his emphasis on mass mobilization, and his self-government project on the perceptions of landlords and Guomindang leaders. Distrust of Shen's objectives by the provincial party and by landlords had created powerful animosities; if the landlords were involved, it would have been most likely the case that the provincial party was able to turn to networks of aggrieved "little kings" to arrange the killing. Even if they were not involved, it seems clear that the perception of radicalism was also involved in Shen's demise. It certainly seems to be the case with Shen that "the dramatic quality of [his] life [and death flowed] from the endless negotiations of identities as [he] attempted to appropriate identities that other [did] not bestow [and] others attempted to bestow identities that [Shen did] not appropriate."[45] *The sad and ironic fact is that Shen seems to have been killed because he was perceived as too radical and as too reactionary at the same time by the same party.* Shen could not be defined in 1928. Sixty-five years later: "We don't know whether he was a good or a bad man," the Communist official said that June day on Phoenix Mountain. In the China of today Shen still cannot be defined.

CHAPTER TEN

Shen and the Chinese Revolution of the 1920s
A Postmortem

The Chinese revolution of the 1920s, like any revolution, was a process of defining goals, of identifying ends. For its protagonists, antagonists, hangers-on, and even spectators, its political and social convulsions meant the necessity of constructing or reshaping social and political identities and relationships in a multiplicity of spatial contexts with their own processes and dynamics. For the revolutionaries, constructing both the identity of the revolution and their own identities was an integral process. The early stages of the revolution, in which its enemies were defined and identified, carried an inclusive dynamic that joined together many with differing political and intellectual persuasions in the antiwarlord, anti-imperialist crusade. (The "bloc within" was a prime example.) The ethos was that of the more tolerant, open, and experimental May Fourth period.[1] For personal identities, based at least partially on political, social, and ideological commitment, this inclusive revolutionary stage allowed considerable fluidity, multiplicity, and experimentation with what looked to be insubstantial political costs for identity shifts and changes.[2] But since, as the mystery of Shen reveals, personal identity is not only chosen by the subject but is also bestowed by history and society, one can rarely escape the effects of identity choice and bestowal at any stage.

In the mid-1920s, when indicators began to point to the possibly imminent success of the revolutionary movement, the revolutionary process became increasingly exclusive rather than inclusive. By 1925 the revolutionaries had to begin to look beyond common enemies and define firmer goals because of the promise of their own military power and the contingencies of Sun's death and the May Thirtieth Movement. Boundaries were drawn that delimited the party's current goals (the party line) and identified supporters of that line through the vehicle of successive party registrations. Only after that time did the degree of politicization and polarization become a malevolent scourge as the May Fourth values and dynamics that had given rise to the revolution were submerged in the drive toward political and ideological uniformity. In such a politicized context, personal identities interpreted by others tended to become fixed, to be fitted and stereotyped into named social and political categories, thereby making alternative identities and inter- pretations less possible.

Shen's charge that for the Chinese the name is more important than the deed focuses on this aspect of political culture. Shen's death and the reaction to him since provides a case in point. More than perhaps many Chinese elites during the early Republic Shen moved easily and fre- quently among various arenas, utilizing approaches ranging from jour- nalism to party organizing to rent resistance to chairing provincial as- semblies to party purges to self-government projects—in many cases challenging authority with a notable flare. He was a landlord who led a rent resistance movement and encouraged the mass mobilization of farmers and workers; a young magistrate who had the father of a gov- ernor flogged; a provincial assemblyman who upbraided the military governor of the province; leader of a breakaway Western Hills Congress who urged readiness to die by going to fight for position in Guangzhou; leader of a conservative Guomindang faction that had been read out of power but who persisted in struggling back; establisher of a self- government experiment that dared those in power with new approaches and ideas.

"We don't know whether he is a good man or a bad man," said the official on Phoenix Mountain. Why? Look at his names in the list above: landlord, magistrate, provincial assemblyman, Western Hills leader, leader of conservative Guomindang faction, elite leader. They are all, as was said during the Cultural Revolution when farmers blasted open his grave, black elements. Then look at the deeds: led a rent resistance movement and encouraged the mass mobilization of farmers and work- ers; had the father of a governor flogged; upbraided the military gov- ernor of the province; urged readiness to die by going to fight for position in Guangzhou; persisted in struggling back; dared those in power with new approaches and ideas. The color of the deeds is red. If the measure of a man's record were his deeds, there would have been little question, given the values of Maoist Chinese revolutionary culture, that Shen would be a "good" man, who perhaps would be judged like others (specifically Mao himself) as having made mistakes (in Shen's case, the 1927 purge).

As it has applied to Shen and more generally, modern Chinese political judgment has tended to place more value on identity through the noun than through the verb. Perhaps that has traditionally been the case: after all, the aim of the Confucian rectification of names was to use the name as the standard and to bring action into proper congruency with it. But in the increasingly politicized twentieth-century Guomindang and Communist world, social categories like class and role (local bully, evil gentry) and political categories like party or faction have become almost all-powerful determinative nouns. The verb, like the revolution itself, is process and change; the noun defines and limits the process by attaching it to a particular movement, event, or person. In the unpredictable flux of revolution amid the full range of social connections and interactions, even as Shen's own views and approaches changed, his social and political identities were continuously changing. But in the great complexity of revolutionary change, the human mind brings order by naming and holding to that name as the key to the identity of the other. The sense of "once-named, always-known" becomes the easiest way for individuals to order their world; though it is certainly possible, it then becomes extraordinarily difficult to change the key. Any verb attached to the noun afterward can be explained away as the exception, rationalized as deviant action from the expected, charged up to devious manipulation and opportunism. If the revolution was continuous change and Shen's identities (like those of all involved actors in the revolution) were continuously developing in relation to changing contexts, then to hold to one perception of identity, especially those bestowed by the name of organizations and structures (the Guomindang, the Communist Party, the Western Hills faction, the First Normal network) and by the name of class (landlord), was very likely to distort reality. If we seek to avoid repeating that error and to understand more accurately the dynamics of the Chinese revolution and the contributions of its major actors, we must strive to analyze their personal and social identities and the change and evolution of those identities in varying social and political contexts; and we must understand their perceivers' changing assumptions, goals, and contexts as well.

In the analysis of social identity and the 1920s revolution itself, this study has focused on issues of social connections and networks, of place, and of process. In this culture, where all social reality is relational and where social connections are the vehicle for achieving one's goals, the personal network has always been an important social and political structure; in the revolution of the 1920s, it performed a variety of important functions. Networks readily served as political resources; effectively cultivated and used, they were important bases for success. The men in the Baoding and Zhejiang military networks of the 1910s could depend on their respective networks for physical and moral support. Shen's First Normal network came to Yaqian to teach and proselytize among the farmers, and in the beginning of Guomindang efforts in 1924, they remained the people to whom he could turn for assistance and support. Shen's provincial assembly network participated in the political discussion society in 1917, giving Shen and others in the assembly needed support; and it continued to serve as a support for Shen's unsuccessful initiatives in the assembly in the fall of 1921. Shen's provisional executive committee network went to Yaqian in 1928 to serve as unsalaried workers in the self-government experiment.

The successful use of networks as a resource depended on their durability and intensity, which in turn were based on a variety of factors. Family, personal friendship, and native place ties almost always added great strength to the strands of connections in a network. Networks based on these local cultural forms were generally stronger, more resilient, and longer lasting than those formed in higher arenas; these attributes also made the network a more general resource, able to adapt and react to a variety of needs.[3] Provincial arena networks incorporated local networks in network coalitions that retained strength from the local bases but were weaker and more easily sundered than those in the village, microregion, or county. In this arena, school ties, alumni connections, and work experiences, relatively less strong connections than those in the locality, were particularly important. The national arena generally saw the least durable and intense networks. Though they were often linked by some strands of friendship, native place, school ties, and work experience, coalitional networks at the national level were most often formed to attain particular political ends. Ad hoc political networks like the Western Hills coalition might endure afterward, but their intensity tended to be weak. Existential revolutionary struggle could be a very potent tie, as between Xuan's First Normal network and Hangzhou labor organizers, but it could also erode networks, as it did with Shen and his First Normal network. Those that developed from memories of shared revolutionary struggle in the 1911 period also tended to be weaker and more ephemeral, since memories of each network member diverged, shaped as they were by individual experiences, by personality, and individual consciousness.

Networks provided identity, defining and interpreting individual members; social identity came in large part by association.[4] To participate in Shen's First Normal network or his provisional executive committee/East Township network was to link oneself to others who shared an identity in that linking, especially in relation to Shen, the network node. It also provided an indicator of one's identity to others, who perceived the network in a certain way and saw the individual members in that framework. As we have seen, the meaning of the network as perceived by network outsiders may have had little relationship to the actual meaning; Shen could never cast out of others' minds (if indeed he wanted to) his being part of the Western Hills network, even though the meaning of Shen's inclusion was far different from the perception. This was especially the case during revolution, when roles changed and allegiances shifted. As networks defined identity, they also legitimized or delegitimized. Becoming part of a strong network or linking oneself to a network whose node was a powerful person could bring social legitimacy and prestige. The networks of Chu Fucheng in the late 1910s or Shen in the early 1920s or Xuan in the mid-1920s put their members into proximity with key political leaders of the time with all the attendant advantages. On the other hand, Shen's association and subsequent identification with the Western Hills network in the end politically delegitimized him and ruined his political effectiveness.

Space and place were also significant contexts and components of revolutionary action and of social identity. Analysis of the relationships among spatial arenas in the polity in the 1920s revolution—national, provincial, and local—reveals differences from those at the time of the 1911 revolution. That difference was based on the political meaning and role of the locality. The 1911 revolution in Zhejiang was a two-stage process, with the key event for provincial politics taking place at Hangzhou; as Hangzhou went, so went the province. When a series of coups somewhat haphazardly occurred at county seats and market towns, they were largely spontaneous and were not directed from Hangzhou.[5] The two-tiered hierarchy of revolution was clear. In the 1920s revolution, the key events occurred in the localities. Local party bureaus were organized and purged and participated in revolutionary acts through the direction of men from Hangzhou; the localities became the battleground between left and right for party support; and they welcomed and supported the

Northern Expedition as the two routes wound their way to Hangzhou. What happened in Hangzhou was, then, determined in large part by struggles in the localities. The key to succeeding there was the linkages made by party cadres to local party members and the establishment of networks of supporters. The model is much more that of horizontal connections and networks than of hierarchy. The increased degree of integration and interdependence of the higher level arenas and the locality—at least in the core zones—over that of fifteen years earlier is noteworthy.

Thus localities became much more a part of provincial and national movements than in the 1911 period, when they seemed more discrete and could almost go their own way. Province and nation now reached penetratingly down to the locality. This greater interconnectedness of localities with provincial and national arenas is a measure of revolutionary organization, ideological approach, and modern transportation and communications. Such interconnectedness meant new political realities. Whereas in 1916 Zhejiangese talked of protecting the locality from the threat of the nation, by 1928 the locality (East Township) itself had become a symbolic threat to province and nation. By the 1920s if one had ambitions for political power, it was not enough to legitimate one's power in what seemed the most relevant arena. Shen's strong provincial base was not enough for him to prevail in the province as he might have in the 1910s; the changed context made province and locality more crucial units in the equation of national power. On the other hand, Xuan's strong support in the national arena of the party was also not enough for him to prevail in the province without a broad base of provincial support.

Particular space is extraordinarily significant for personal identity. "The paramount importance of local origin in defining personal identity" is clearly evident in crucial roles taken by native place in this account.[6] Protesters in the 1917 provincial crisis used native place, specifically their common identity as Zhejiangese, as the basis of their resistance to Beiyang forces. Native place was one of the most significant sources of all local, provincial, and national networks. Native place was the focus of Shen's work, identifying him with the Southern Sands, East Township, and Yaqian.[7] For all of the importance of native place, existential identity is finally relative to particular spatial settings.[8] In Shanghai, Hangzhou, and Yaqian, the three main arenas of Shen's actions, his identity varied considerably. Revolutionary thinker, journalist, Communist, Western Hills spokesman in Shanghai; provincial leader, party organizer, ally of labor unions, and Guomindang purge director in Hangzhou; and, in Yaqian, patron of farmers and students, antilandlord landlord, and progressive reformer. Changing political contexts and discourses in Shen's arenas of action propelled different and sometimes apparently contradictory aspects of his identities to the fore. Though Shen might evidence similar identities in each arena, the morphology and meaning of the full range of identities varied according to each contextual arena.

The mystery of Shen reminds us that specific spatial locations, often laden with symbolic import, became places of political meaning that contributed to the dynamics, the process, and the actors' understanding of the revolution. This study has focused only on some of the most obvious places of political import and thus is primarily suggestive of the necessity of paying more attention to space in studies of the revolution. It is also important to note that the meaning of particular space or place, like the interpretation of personal identity, is relative to the perceiver. Shen's observations of life on the streets of Shanghai's French Concession (especially those near French Park, where wealthy Chinese and foreigners drove past women workers, where shiny cars startled beggars and prostitutes) informed much of his prose and poetry and contributed to and enhanced his strong sense of the problems brought by class separation, imperialism, and Chinese not yet aware of the light. Others of different class or gender or party or inclination might obviously have conceived of this space in starkly different ways. Similarly, the West Lake Athletic Field became for political progressives the appropriate place for initiating significant popular political rituals and for rallies from the May Fourth period on: a place encompassing the ideas of political nationalism and change, the modern value of physical activity, and the newness of spatial openness to West Lake. To others, that same space might suggest, for example, the simple delights of recreation (to tourists) or dangerous radicalism (to conservatives) or a threat to public order (to the city's public security bureau). The demonstration parades launched from there all tended to follow the same path, winding their way past the Military Governor's offices (symbolically situated in the New Market area), past the shops and stores of old and new merchants, to the train station on the eastern edge of the city—a ritualization of political space.

But it is the dramatic episodes at Yaqian that most clearly reveal the politically hegemonic import of place in Shen's world. There in 1921 in his home compound and in the East Mountain temple, within several

hundred feet of the compound, he initiated the rent resistance movement; farmers came to Shen and his native place in a massive pilgrimage
to register and learn of the plans of the movement. The locus of political
power was clear. In the crucial Guomindang meeting in July 1925, Shen
made his home compound the site of the showdown with the growing
leftist provincial opposition; he controlled the space in hegemonic fashion, though ultimately he could not transform his spatial control—which
was deeply resented by the opposition—into clear political domination.
In 1928, he turned his home compound into the Village Dormitory,
bringing his workers into his very household, symbolically affirming his
role as fellow worker but more importantly underlining his role as
powerful patron. These three episodes at Yaqian all underscore Shen's
acute awareness of the political import of space, as do his theatrical calls
at the Shanghai Western Hills Congress to move the site of the meeting
immediately to Guangzhou in order to dramatically challenge the Left
through spatial proximity and what might be called "in-your-face"
bravado.

Revolutionary and social identity obviously varied across time. In a
personal sense, Shen's identity in 1928 as important political leader with
resources and connections paled in objective comparison with his identity in 1921 and 1925, yet that too was relative to the perceiver: his
identity perceived by the Hangzhou government was far different from
that perceived by his self-government workers, who hung on his every
word. In the revolution itself, perhaps the sharpest change in identity was
that of the military from the perspective of civilian elites. The military
had come into the social arena as legitimate actors with their role in the
1911 revolution, but the actions of Yuan Shikai and his successors had
turned the hopes of civilian elite constitutionalists on their head. Ex-
coriated by Shen and others for feeding on the marrow of Chinese
society, the military quickly came to be identified as a scourge that had
to be removed. But the experiences of Sun Yat-sen in trying to establish
linkages to warlord armies showed the parties that military power of their
own would be necessary to succeed in their goals. Whereas in 1917 Shen
and others worked mightily to prevent the entry of the military from the
outside into the province, in 1927 Xuan and the Guomindang worked
just as strongly to bring and welcome outside military forces into the
province. Shen himself was recorded as speaking positively about the
military. The civilian constitutional culture with its twin emphases on
process and law had been co-opted and destroyed within a decade by a
military ethos riding the tide of revolution.

This study of individual choices and actions in the life and death of Shen Dingyi offers a portrait of revolution as a melange of the dramatic and the humdrum, the momentous and the mundane. The process of revolution included not only the spark of powerful ideas to confront China's problems, the adoption of revolutionary and military approaches, and major turning points in the revolutionary road, but also the day-to-day enervating problems of struggling to finance even basic party and individual needs, the seemingly endless meetings and party registrations, the time-consuming ordinary work of making connections and establishing or enhancing the relationships in networks, organizing bureaus, offices, and associations and making certain that they were operating—all marked by individual jealousies and petulance, inopportune illnesses, deadly mistakes in perception, naive decision making, and quixotic commitments. With the exception of a handful of strikingly dramatic events—the entrance of Beiyang forces into Zhejiang, the rent resistance movement, the death of Sun, the May Thirtieth Movement, the Yaqian conference, the Western Hills conference, the Northern Expedition—what is striking is the slow, incremental nature of the revolutionary process. Each step led to the next, sometimes with little direction or awareness or sensibility about where things were headed.

This process shaped the revolution even as it helped shape personal identity.[9] Take the formation of Shen's First Normal network. During Shen's tenure as chair of the provincial assembly, he was watchful of the needs of education in general, but he paid special attention to the First Normal. First Normal teachers and students obviously knew of his solicitousness. During his editorship of the *Weekly Review*, he began corresponding with them after they sent him questions. From their perspective, he was a progressive scholar with growing reputation; they journeyed to Shanghai to visit and discuss issues. They read his essays and poetry; progressive as they were, they undoubtedly heard of the cell meetings in Shanghai. They were aware of his being cofounder of the Socialist Youth Corps in Hangzhou in the second half of 1920. He too knew of their outstanding leadership work in the Hangzhou Student Union in 1919 and 1920. There had to have been something of a mutual admiration. Thus, now as patron, he invited them to teach at the Yaqian Village School, a venture that led to the founding of the network and to the special friendship for Xuan. This was the stuff, slowly evolutionary, of which the revolution was made.

Or look at the dissolution of the network. Shen's and Xuan's attendance as provincial delegates at the Guomindang's First Congress in

1924 after both had visited the Soviet Union was followed by a series of successful party-led rallies. But work at building the organization of the party led to frustrations: not enough money, different ideas on strategy, perhaps questions about why either Shen or members of the network did this or that. The First Normal members also found themselves in other networks, especially those involved in Hangzhou labor organizing; members of these other networks (like Xu Meikun) had reservations about Shen as an opportunistic politician. Rumors spread of Shen doing thus and so; rumors reached Shen's ears about Xuan saying this and that; and the first inklings of mistrust began to erode the relationships. As one scholar of networks has said, "The network of relations that sustains [the network] is always changing."[10] This slow and incremental deterioration played out day by day until the momentous meeting at Yaqian—though those at the meeting could hardly have told how momentous it was at the time.

For the thing about being in the process, of course, is that no one knows the end results. That is one of the main problems with autobiographies of Shen's contemporaries from the 1920s. Each historian was at work trying to bestow an identity on Shen: for, as it has been said, "the discourse of history . . . is simultaneously a discourse of identity; it consists of attributing a meaningful past to a structured present."[11] Li Da, Mao Dun, Gao Yuetian, Chen Gongmao, and Xu Meikun all saw Shen and the 1920s from the vantage point of the 1950s, 1970s, and 1980s and their own agendas in a "structured present." They knew what Shen would never know: the end results of the events of the 1920s; and their knowledge shaped and colored their pictures of the man and his times. A journalist has recently said it best: "Perhaps the most difficult thing for the historian to recapture is the sense of what, at a given historical moment, people did *not* know about the future."[12] For if they did not know about the course of rural revolution under Communist leadership, how might they have defined Shen, leader of the first rent resistance campaign, first to mobilize farmers into mass organizations, and founder of one of the first efforts to establish a rural self-government movement based upon the masses?

One must analyze the long-term forces and patterns that came together to help produce the Chinese revolution of the 1920s. But ultimately the men and women of the time produced it through their leadership and reactions to the existential crises that presented them with the choice in the first place of whether to act and, if so, how to act. For the revolution, like Shen's life and death, could have gone in many different directions, flowed in many different channels. What seems often most important in the choices people made is not their reactions to warlordism and imperialism, to anarchism and Marxism, to nationalism and provincialism, that is, to the "big" issues that provided the general context for the choices that had to be made in the 1920s. Rather, what emerges as crucial in many cases were their reactions to contingencies: Sun's death, Shen's illnesses, Dai Jitao's beating in the Western Hills, the beating of the son of Landlord Zhou by farmers. And crucial in almost every case were their reactions to proximate events, not long-term trends or background contexts: Shen pushed by May Thirtieth fears to press for the Yaqian conference; reactions of each side to the Yaqian conference and the Western Hills meeting; Xuan's asking the government to abolish the newly formed Workers' Federation in the rapid rush of events in late March 1927; Shen's journeying to Moganshan after being summoned or after reading about Dai's presence there in the newspaper.

To play the historical game of "what if?" with one question is to see not only the significance of proximate causes but also the open-ended possibilities of the revolution, based as it was on personal choices and individual actions. Given the likely catalyst for his murder, what if Shen Dingyi had not *chosen* to journey to Moganshan in August 1928? For him, it was one of countless choices he had had to make during the revolution. But this choice meant death, Shen's final exit from the revolutionary drama. Such personal existential choices by countless participants produced the ultimate direction and shape of the revolution.

Notes

Abbreviations

MR   Minguo ribao (Republican Daily News)
SDX   Shen Dingyi xiansheng shilue (A brief biography of
       Mr. Shen Dingyi)
XP   Xingqi pinglun (Weekly Review)

Introduction

1. Wang Weilian, "Shen Xuanlu yu gongchandang," p. 158.

2. Lin Weibao, "Yaqian yinxiang ji," pp. 73–74.

3. See, for example, essays in the spring 1991 issue of *Daedalus* that focus on issues of Chinese identity: Vera Schwarcz, "No Solace from Lethe: History, Memory, and Cultural Identity in Twentieth-Century China"; David Yen-ho Wu, "The Construction of Chinese and Non-Chinese Identities"; and Myron Cohen, "Being Chinese: The Peripheralization of Traditional Identity." Note also *Self As Person in Asian Theory and Practice*, edited by Roger T. Ames with Wimal Dissanayake and Thomas P. Kasulis. In late February 1994, the annual symposium of the Center for Chinese Studies at the University of California, Berkeley, took "Chinese Identities" as its theme.

4. The phrase is Liz Bondi's in "Locating Identity Politics," p. 97. Although Bondi's essay examines identity in the context of contemporary feminism, her phrase captures well the production, yet the indeterminacy of identity in Shen's case.

5. Ira Lapidus, "Hierarchies and Networks: A Comparison of Chinese and Islamic Societies," p. 42.

6. See, as examples, the centrality of networks in Mary Rankin's analysis of elite managers in Zhejiang province in the late Qing in *Elite Activism and*

Political Transformation in China; networks as part of his cultural nexus of power in Prasenjit Duara, *Culture, Power, and the State*, p. 16; and the network as opposed to social and economic hierarchies in Kenneth Pomeranz, *The Making of a Hinterland*, pp. 277–80. Note also the introduction by Gary G. Hamilton and Wang Zheng to Fei Xiaotong, *From the Soil*, pp. 27–33; and Ambrose Yeo-chi King's essay, "Kuan-hsi and Network Building: A Sociological Interpretation."

7. Bei Dao, "Note from the City of the Sun," as translated in David S. G. Goodman, *Poems of the Democracy Movement*, p. 29, and quoted in Jonathan Spence, *The Gate of Heavenly Peace*, p. 370.

8. Chie Nakane, *Japanese Society*, p. 1.

9. Sociological psychologists define identity as "a definition that emerges from and is sustained by the cultural meanings of social relationships activated in interaction." See Andrew J. Weigert, J. Smith Teitge, and Dennis W. Teitge, *Society and Identity*, p. 31. Note Mary Rankin's argument that "leaders were defined by their combined social and institutional networks," *Elite Activism and Political Transformation*, p. 228.

10. Elizabeth J. Perry, "Strikes among Shanghai Silk Weavers, 1927–1937," p. 317. In the same volume, note Marie-Claire Bergère's comment that "in China, institutional interplay not only did not exclude personal relations but often merely reflected them." See "The Shanghai Bankers' Association, 1915–1927," p. 24.

11. See, for example, the work of Henri Lefebvre, *The Production of Space*, and that of Edward Soja, *Postmodern Geographies*.

12. G. William Skinner, "Marketing and Social Structure in Rural China" and "Regional Urbanization in Nineteenth Century China."

13. Robert Darnton, *The Great Cat Massacre*, p. 23.

14. Graham Peck, *Two Kinds of Time*.

15. Leo Ou-fan Lee, "In Search of Modernity: Some Reflections on a New Mode of Consciousness in Twentieth Century Chinese History and Literature," p. 121.

16. R. Keith Schoppa, "Contours of Revolution in a Chinese County, 1900–1950."

1. Death in Yaqian

1. *Shenbao*, August 24, 1928.

2. *Shenbao*, July 17 and August 11, 1928.

3. Carl Crow, *The Travelers' Handbook for China*, p. 108, and Eugene Barnett, "As I Look Back: Recollections of Growing Up in America's Southland and of Twenty-Six Years in Pre-Communist China, 1888–1936," p. 3.

4. This account is based upon "Shen Dingyi xiansheng beici jingguo."

5. Ruan Yicheng, "Shen Xuanlu," part 2, p. 18.

6. Gao Yuetian, "Shen Dingyi xianshengde yisheng," part 2, p. 11.

7. "Shen Dingyi xiansheng beici jingguo," unpaginated.

8. *You Hang jilue, xia juan*, p. 4a.

9. See the description in Ruan Yicheng, *Sanju buli ben Hang*, p. 2.

10. Chen Gongmao, "Shen Dingyi qiren," p. 45.

11. *Shenbao*, August 11, 1928.

12. See the notation by Harry A. Franck made in 1925 in *Roving through South China*, p. 41.

13. Interview with Shen Jianyun, June 9, 1993, in his home in Phoenix Village in the town of Yaqian in Xiaoshan county.

14. *Shenbao*, July 2, 1928.

15. Wang Weilian, "Shen Xuanlu yu gongchandang," p. 159.

16. Shen, "Yige qingniande meng" [A youthful dream], *Juewu*, April 1, 1920.

2. One's Native Place

1. Gao, "Shen Dingyi xianshengde yisheng," p. 7.

2. Liu Dabai, "Zeng Shen Xuanlu qilu sishou," p. 49.

3. *MR*, September 9, 1916.

4. For separate student and worker native place associations in Shanghai, see Bryna Goodman, "New Culture, Old Habits: Native Place Organization and the May Fourth Movement," pp. 84–89. See also Mary Rankin's comments on sojourning from occupational migration, *Elite Activism and Political Transformation*, pp. 76 and 79.

5. Ruan Yicheng, "Xianjun Xunbo gong nianpu," p. 14.

6. *SDX*, unpaginated. For purposes of these notes, I have numbered the pages starting with the title page. This citation is on p. 7.

7. *Yaqian nongmin yundong*, 1987, p. 111. Chen Juemu claims that Shen financially helped support Liu during their stay in Japan; "Liu Dabai xiansheng zhi shengping," p. 49.

8. *SDX*, p. 7.

9. Kong Xuexiong, "Dongxiang zizhi shimo," p. 330.

10. Gao, "Shen Dingyi xianshengde yisheng," p. 5.

11. Ibid., p. 13.

12. *SDX*, p. 7.

13. *XP*, December 7, 1919.

14. Gao, "Shen Dingyi xianshengde yisheng," p. 5; see also *SDX*, p. 14.

15. *SDX*, pp. 2–5; Gao, "Shen Dingyi xianshengde yisheng," pp. 5–7.

16. Gao, "Shen Dingyi xianshengde yisheng," pp. 6–7.

17. *XP*, December 7, 1919.

18. Benjamin A. Elman, "Political, Social, and Cultural Reproduction via Civil Service Examinations in Late Imperial China."

19. For an excellent discussion of the common Chinese culture, see Myron Cohen, "Being Chinese: The Peripheralization of Traditional Identity," pp. 114–25. For more on the cultural integration of late imperial China, see Evelyn S. Rawski, "Economic and Social Foundations of Late Imperial Culture," pp. 3–33.

20. *Shibao* and *Shenbao*, *passim*.

21. R. Keith Schoppa, "Politics and Society in Chekiang, 1907–1927," chaps. 2 and 3.

22. Ge Jing'en, "Xinhai geming zai Zhejiang," p. 98.

23. Mary Backus Rankin, *Early Chinese Revolutionaries*, pp. 119, 137, and 204–5.

24. Ibid., pp. 30–47.

25. Anselm L. Strauss, *Mirrors and Masks: The Search for Identity*, p. 45.

26. Chen Xieshu, "Shaoxing guangfushi jianwen," p. 107, and Lu Xun, *Selected Works*, 1:415–16.

27. *Shibao*, December 3, 8, 1912. The elites were the two vice-presidents of the provincial assembly, the two most important leaders of the Hangzhou General Chamber of Commerce, and two regimental commanders.

28. *XP*, June 8, 1919.

29. For a detailed account of the 1911 period, see Schoppa, "Politics and Society in Chekiang," chap. 2.

30. Yao Zong, "Xinhai Zhejiang geming shi buyi," pp. 8–9.

31. Ge, "Xinhai geming zai Zhejiang," p.122.

32. These generalizations are based upon a day-by-day reading of the *Shibao*, the *Minlibao*, the *Minguo ribao*, and from 1916–17 the *Zhonghua xinbao*, as well as the following sources: Zhang Xiaoxun, "Zhejiang xinhai geming guangfu jishi," pp. 118–24; "Zhejun Hangzhou guangfu ji," pp. 131–45; Chu Fucheng, "Zhejiang xinhai geming jishi," pp. 114–121; Zhong Liyu, "Guangfu Hangzhou huiyilu," pp. 89–103; Xu Bingkun, "Hangzhou guangfu zhi yede yici guanshen jinji huiyi," pp. 165–66; Ge, "Xinhai geming zai Zhejiang," pp. 91–126; Lai Weiliang, "Zhejun guangfu Hangzhou he chiyuan Nanjing qinli ji," pp. 152–60; Lai Weiliang, "Xinhai gongchengying Hangzhou qiyi ji," pp. 67–74; Lu Huanguang, "Xinhai Zhesheng guangfu qianhouzhi junzheng cangsang," pp. 8–9; Lu Gongwang, "Xinhai geming Zhejiang guangfu jishi," pp. 114–17; Ma Xulun, "Guanyu xinhai geming Zhejiang shengcheng guangfu jishide buchong ziliao," pp. 47–57; Ma Xulun, "Wo zai xinhai zheyinian," pp. 170–79; Si Daoqing, "Zhejun shibaniande huiyilu," pp 76–93; Xi Daoqing, "Xinhai geming Hangzhou guangfu bieji," pp. 144–47; and Li Zhengtong, "Xinhai geming yihou shiliuniande Zhejiang zhengju," pp. 147–58.

33. See the discussion of aspects of network durability in J. Clyde Mitchell, "The Concept and Use of Social Networks," esp. pp. 20–29.

34. Lu Gongwang, "Xinhai geming Zhejiang guangfu jishi," p. 112; Ge, "Xinhai geming zai Zhejiang," p. 112.

35. Ma Xulun, "Wo zai xinhai zheyinian," pp. 178–79.

36. *SDX*, pp. 6–7.

37. *XP*, June 15, 1919.

38. Weigert, Teitge, and Teitge, *Society and Identity*, p. 30. Such an approach should certainly not be taken to preclude the development of relationships within parties and organizations, but I would hypothesize that basic personal linkages pulling on traditional cultural connections would generally have greater strength and durability.

39. For Liu, see *Gendai Shina jimmeikan*, p. 337. For Xu, see *Gendai Shina jimmeikan*, p. 782; also see *Shibao*, November 14, 1912; March 3, May 16, 1914; July 27, September 28, 1920.

40. Newspapers were primarily political vehicles; many young Chinese intellectuals became editors to set forth their views and proselytize for their positions in publications, many of which were ephemeral.

41. See Marie-Claire Bergère, *The Golden Age of the Chinese Bourgeoisie, 1911–1937.*

42. Xiang Shiyuan, *Zhejiang xinwen shi,* p. 43.

43. *Geming renwu zhi,* 4:14–15; *Zhejiang renwu jianzhi,* pp. 43–44.

44. Xiang, *Zhejiang xinwen shi,* p. 91.

45. Ibid., p. 84.

46. Zhejiang was traditionally divided into units designated as Zhexi (western Zhejiang) and Zhedong (eastern Zhejiang). This traditional division was not an accurate geographical expression of the reality of the division, for only the three northern prefectures were labeled western Zhejiang, while the prefectures east of the Fuchun and Qiantang rivers were called eastern Zhejiang. In this account, I dispense with the traditional designations and use the appropriate geographical descriptions.

47. *Xinhai geming Zhejiang shiliao xuanji,* 360–63, 453–58. Initially Shen was not drawn any more closely to the Guomindang, the later incarnation of the Revolutionary Alliance, than to the Restoration Society. Almost from the beginning of his career, Shen eschewed parties that polarized the scene, choosing or creating his own alternative. In early 1912, Shen had formed a decidedly reformist Citizens' Radical Party (*gongmin jijindang*) in Shanghai. Combining morality with nationalism and civic duty, its purpose was to "cultivate righteousness [*zheng*] and extirpate the wrong [*fei*]; to transform selfish interests into public consciousness; to understand and lead the whole nation; and to fulfill the citizen's duty." Shen saw the Guomindang as a fellow party with which his Radical Party might cooperate. In the provincial and national assembly elections in late 1912, some members of Shen's party won alternate seats in the legislature. But the Citizens' Radical Party was limited to Shanghai, and the hold of the Guomindang on Zhejiang was so strong that Shen was unable to expand it there. With little likelihood that it would survive, funds dried up. After Shen participated in the second revolution, Yuan delivered the coup de grace by dissolving the party.

48. Gao, "Shen Dingyi xianshengde yisheng," p. 5.

49. *Xinbian Zhejiang bainian dashiji,* pp. 143–44. See also "Sun Zhongshan zai Hangzhoude yanshuo," pp.1–6, and "Sun Zhongshan Hangzhouzhi xing," pp. 149–55. Sun lodged in the Qingtai Number Two Hotel, described in a tourist manual of the time as "spacious and beautiful." See *You Hang jilue, xia juan,* p. 30a.

50. For a description of the garrison and its relation to the city, see Pamela Kyle Crossley, *Orphan Warriors,* p. 248, n. 84. See also Barnett, "As I Look Back," p. 104.

51. For information on the modernizing changes, see *Gesheng guangfu,* p. 153, and *Returns of Trade and Trade Reports,* 1914, p. 822. See also *Shibao,* February 21, March 19, 1914.

52. *Shibao,* December 13, 1915.

53. Ruan Yicheng, "Xianjun Xunbo gong nianpu," p. 15. Ruan was the first person to buy land in the New Market area for a residence.

54. This important symbolic meaning of the New Market space does not exhaust the array of possible political, social, and economic spatial meanings this area had for various types of people or for individuals. For discussion of the multiple meanings of space, see Michael Keith and Steve Pile, "Introduction, Part 1: The Politics of Space."

55. Lu emerged as both military and civil governor in May 1916. He seemed more progressive than many military figures, consulting readily and heavily with civil officials and civilians in times of crisis. A lower-level degree holder and member of the Restoration Society, Lu had been instrumental in the planning for the 1911 Hangzhou coup and had served as Zhu's chief of staff at Nanjing. Described by a journalist as "strong-spirited" and well versed in military affairs and foreign language, he had cast wide political and social nets. He had been a friend of 1911 revolutionary Tao Chengzhang and others of Tao's fellow Restoration Society members. He had worked closely with Zhu Rui and the Nanjing Academy group, not burning bridges to other military groups. A native of eastern Zhejiang, he had made an excellent record as defense commissioner of Jiaxing and Huzhou prefectures in northern Zhejiang. As a balance, he had taken political stands on issues of importance to his native prefecture, shoring up local support and building up local political obligations. See *Shibao*, June 27, December 6, 1913; February 21, 1914; and May 12, 1916.

56. *Minlibao*, December 8–10, 1912. See "Sun Zhongshan zai Hangzhoude yanshuo," p. 1, and "Sun Zhongshan Hangzhouzhi xing," pp. 149–51.

57. "Sun Zhongshan zai Hangzhoude yanshuo," pp. 3–4.

58. *MR*, September 6, 1916.

59. *Shibao*, April 14, 1915; May 6, 1916.

60. *MR*, September 7, 1916.

61. *MR*, September 9, 1916.

62. These committees are found in *MR*, September 21, October 16, 1916.

63. *Shibao*, January 22, 1913.

64. See also George Yu, *Party Politics in Republican China*, pp. 76 and 97, for an overview of the party situation in the aftermath of revolution.

65. For Chu, see Schoppa, *Chinese Elites and Political Change*, pp. 58, 93–94, 146, 147, and 179.

66. At the first plenary conference on April 22, 1917, Acting Chairman Chu Fucheng reminded those in attendance: "This is a political organization that studies local reform [*xingge*]." *MR*, April 24, 1917.

67. *MR*, December 9, 1916. There are no extant records of these discussion meetings.

68. A specific profile follows: There is background or occupational information on 51 of the 69 available names (75 percent) of the members. The most important unifying aspect of the group was its participation in the 1911 revolution; almost half of those on whom we have information (47.1 percent) had joined or led the revolution in their native place or in Hangzhou. Twenty-two (43 percent) had been members of the Restoration Society, the Revolutionary Alliance, or the Guomindang. Their memory of revolutionary success snatched from their arms and their hopes for a fulfillment of revolutionary goals were motivating factors in the formation of the organization. Thirty-four (67 percent)

were currently members of the provincial assembly or were upper-level bureaucrats in the Zhejiang government; nine others (17.6 percent) had served in earlier provincial assemblies. They were thus men grappling with the chief political problems of the day. Ten (almost 20 percent) held traditional civil service degrees, while fourteen (27.5 percent) had attended schools in Japan. At least ten were educators, and there were at least six lawyers and six journalists in the group.

69. See my *Chinese Elites and Political Change*, pp. 168–74. Not all elites in this organization from the inner core zones were necessarily progressive, and not all progressive provincial elites joined this organization. As is obvious, people join organizations for a wide variety of reasons. Connections to those who were already members might provide incentive to join; indeed, recommendation by three established members was a prerequisite for a new member's joining the society. There were close friends in the organization. Examples were Ren Fenggang and Xu Zuqian, and Wang Wenjing and Huang Zhenmin. On Wang, see Zhang Rentian, "Yi Guangfuhui Wang Wenjing," pp. 85–90. There were various personal networks, such as the many linked to Chu Fucheng. There were alumni networks such as that of Japan's Hōsei University that composed one of the most stellar in Hangzhou politics, in which some joined the discussion society and others did not. In addition to Chu Fucheng, there were Chen Shixia, vice-chair of the Qing Provincial Assembly and dean of the Zhejiang Law School; Xu Ren and Ruan Xingcun, partners in Hangzhou's earliest law office and cofounders of the Zhejiang Law Association; Shen Junru, second vice-chair of the Qing Provincial Assembly and head of the provincial Education Association; and Tong Hangshi, journalist, law professor, and member of the National Assembly. Of these alumni, only Shen and Ruan did not join. See the following for information on the Hōsei graduates: for Chen, Rankin, *Early Chinese Revolutionaries*, pp. 215, 216, and 223, and *Shibao*, December 25, 1909; for Xu, see *Gendai Shina jimmeikan*, pp. 780 and 781, and *Shibao* January 19, 1912, and December 13, 1919; for Ruan, his *nianpu*; for Shen Junru, Rankin, *Early Chinese Revolutionaries*, pp. 200 and 215; for Tong, Xiang, *Zhejiang xinwen shi*, p. 73.

70. *MR*, October 29, 1916.

71. *MR*, September 22, October 9, 1916.

72. *MR*, October 23, 26, 29, 1916.

73. *MR*, December 6, 1916.

74. *MR*, December 22, 1916.

75. Li Zhengtong, "Xinhai geming yihou shiliuniande Zhejiang zhengju," pp. 151–53; and *Shibao*, December 28, 1916.

76. Li Zhengtong, "Xinhai geming yihou shiliuniande Zhejiang zhengju," p. 152.

77. *SDX*, p. 8.

78. Chen Gongmao, "Shen Dingyi qiren," p. 40. The reactions of both sides following the initial confrontation indicate clearly that the Baoding perception of the antagonism was closer to reality than the Zhejiang position, that is, Xia was the plotter whose goal was greater power for himself. While Lu quietly accepted the defeat of his personnel shift, Xia acted highhandedly. An open

telegram from the people of Jiaxing argued that Xia had actually opposed Fu's appointment because Fu would bring to light Xia's personal accumulation of funds. (*Shibao*, December 30, 1916) As if to corroborate this account, on the day of the attack and strike, Xia took many chests of money hidden at the police department and deposited them in the Bank of China. That evening he dispatched his chief military aide to the newspaper offices to censor news reports; he sent another aide to Fu with fifty thousand yuan in paper currency as a bribe not to interfere; and he sent a third to Lu himself, reportedly offering him one hundred thousand yuan if he resigned and named Zhang Zaiyang as his successor. Lu reportedly refused the money, saying that he would name Zhang if he had to do so. Li Zhengtong, "Xinhai geming yihou shiliuniande Zhejiang zhengju," p. 152.

79. Si Daoqing, "Zhejun shibaniande huiyilu," p. 85.

80. *Shibao*, January 4, 1917, and Chen Gongmao, "Shen Dingyi qiren," p. 39. Before the 1911 revolution, Yang had been instrumental in establishing Zhejiang's New Army; he had been serving most recently as defense commissioner in the Shanghai area.

81. *Shibao*, January 6, 1917; see also *North China Herald*, January 6, 1917, p. 11.

82. Li Zhengtong, "Xinhai geming yihou shiliuniande Zhejiang zhengju," p. 153.

83. *MR*, January 4, 5, 1917. Here Shen used the traditional designation of Zhexi and Zhedong.

84. *MR*, January 5, 1917.

85. Ibid.

86. *Shibao*, January 18, 1915.

87. *MR*, November 29, 1916.

88. *MR*, January 7, 1917. The meeting's executive committee members were chosen to petition the government to countermand the original order: there were twenty representatives from the nine prefectures, eleven from the commercial circles, one from scholarly circles, five journalists, and three from the Political Discussion Society.

89. Ibid.

90. See the similar point made by Goodman, "New Culture, Old Habits," pp. 100–101.

91. Despite his illness, Shen called a special meeting of the provincial assembly on the night of the rally to discuss the situation.

92. *MR*, January 11, 1917.

93. *Zhejiang bainian dashiji*, p. 140.

94. Li Zhengtong, "Xinhai geming yihou shiliuniande Zhejiang zhengju," p. 153.

95. *Zhejiang renwu jianzhi*, p. 92.

96. *Shibao*, February 13, 1917.

97. *MR*, October 18, 1916.

98. *Zhejiang bainian dashiji*, p. 140.

99. *Shibao*, April 6, 1917; *Zhonghua xinbao*, April 13, 1917.

100. *MR*, April 12, 1917; *Shibao*, April 22, 1917.

101. *Shibao*, April 8, 9, 1917.

102. See his poem, "Toushi yihoude 'mao'" [The cat after stealing the food], *Juewu*, November 8, 1921.

103. *SDX*, p. 5, and Chen Gongmao, "Shen Dingyi qiren," p. 38.

104. *XP*, October 26, 1919.

105. *XP*, August 17, 1919.

106. *XP*, June 8, 1919.

107. *XP*, August 31, 1919.

108. Lu Xun, "The Misanthrope," pp. 176–96.

109. *Juewu*, February 22, 1920.

110. Howard L. Boorman, ed., *Biographical Dictionary of Republican China*, 1:71.

111. *Zhonghua xinbao*, June 16, 1917.

112. *SDX*, p. 9.

113. Ibid.

3. Awakening

1. Chen's comments were printed alongside Shen's essay.

2. For an exploration of this idea tied directly to social networks, see Jeremy Boissevain, "An Exploration of Two First-Order Zones," pp. 125–148.

3. *All about Shanghai and Environs*, pp. 55–57.

4. C. E. Darwent, *Shanghai: A Handbook for Travellers and Residents*, p. 71.

5. Pan Ling, *In Search of Old Shanghai*, p. 93.

6. See publishing information on each issue of *XP*.

7. *XP*, August 24, 1919.

8. Darwent, *Shanghai: A Handbook for Travellers and Residents*, pp. 74–75.

9. Pan Ling, *In Search of Old Shanghai*, p. 79.

10. Ibid.

11. Darwent, *Shanghai: A Handbook for Travellers and Residents*, p. 80; see also *All about Shanghai and Environs*, p. 185.

12. Pan Ling, *In Search of Old Shanghai*, p. 89.

13. See the description of Yuyang Lane in Ren Wuxiong, "Guanyu Yu Xiusong lieshi," p. 76.

14. "Huibo" [Ripples], *XP*, June 6, 1920, reprinted in *Xuanlu wencun*, pp. 204–14.

15. *SDX*, pp. 5–6.

16. Yang Zhihua, "Yang Zhihuade huiyi," p. 25.

17. Herman Mast III and Willian G. Saywell, "Revolution Out of Tradition: The Political Ideology of Tai Chi-t'ao." See also Boorman, *Biographical Dictionary of Republican China*, 3:200–205.

18. Mast and Saywell, "Revolution Out of Tradition," p. 77.

19. Ibid., p. 78.

20. Ibid.

21. Herman Mast III, "An Intellectual Biography of Tai Chi-t'ao from 1891 to 1928," p. 46. Mast notes (p. 45, n. 46) that Marius Jansen in *The Japanese and Sun Yat-sen* "cites a Japanese Foreign Office intelligence report that [D]ai was almost always at Sun's side."

22. Boorman, *Biographical Dictionary of Republican China*, 3:180; Pan Ling, *In Search of Old Shanghai*, p. 78.

23. Mast, "Intellectual Biography of Tai Chi-t'ao," pp. 50–51.

24. It is possible that they first became acquainted in early 1912 in Shanghai when Shen was organizing his Citizens' Radical Party. Shen had been involved during the revolution with leading Shanghai revolutionary figure Chen Qimei. After Dai was pulled into Sun's orbit, Dai developed connections to Chen and other Alliance leaders, like Zhang Jingjiang. See Mast, "Intellectual Biography of Tai Chi-t'ao," p. 26. The two could have been introduced in this context. During Shen's exile in Japan, he was not in the circles of Sun Yat-sen and his Chinese Revolutionary Party; it is not likely that Shen met Dai there. The other possibility was that they met in May 1918 before Dai left for Wuxing or, since Dai reportedly stayed in Wuxing until May 1919, on a short trip back to the city.

25. *XP*, August 17, 1919.

26. For Shao's biography, see *Zhejiang renwu jianzhi*, pp. 115–17.

27. For Ye, see Boorman, *Biographical Dictionary of Republican China*, 4:27–29. Ye had edited *Minlibao* [*People's Stand*] in Shanghai in 1912 and 1913 and *Shenghuo ribao* [*Life Daily*] in 1913 and 1914. The son of a poor merchant, Ye had received a classical training at local schools. In addition to his journalistic career, he taught at a girls' school as well as at Fudan University and was a prolific writer of fiction.

28. For the outline of events in Shanghai following the May Fourth incident, I have relied on Joseph T. Chen, *The May Fourth Movement in Shanghai*, especially pp. 75–190. See also chaps. 2 and 3 in Jeffrey N. Wasserstrom, *Student Protests in Twentieth-Century China: The View from Shanghai*.

29. Chen, *May Fourth Movement in Shanghai*, pp. 85–86.

30. For a description of the role of the Boy Scouts, see Jeffrey Wasserstrom, "The Evolution of the Shanghai Student Protest Repertoire; or, Where Do Correct Tactics Come From?" pp. 124–25.

31. *XP*, June 15, 1919.

32. *XP*, December 28, 1919.

33. *XP*, June 22, 1919.

34. "Shanghai bagongde jianglai" [The future of the Shanghai strike], *XP*, June 15, 1919.

35. Yang Zhihua, "Yang Zhihuade huiyi," p. 26.

36. Qian Gengshen, "Shen Dingyi xiansheng," pp. 62–63.

37. Yang Zhihua, "Yang Zhihuade huiyi," p. 26.

38. More evenly treated over the seventeen-month period were themes of family and feminism, the New Culture movement, and Shen's general views of life and society.

39. Yang Zhihua, "Yang Zhihuade huiyi," p. 26.

40. For the Korean situation, see "Suibian tan" [Random talk], *XP*, June 15, 1919; and "Xue" [Blood], *XP*, September 21, 1919; on the French gov-

ernment policy, see "Qingkan minzhuguode xin falu" [Request to see a democracy's new laws], *XP*, July 27, 1919; on European and United States governments, see "Suibian tan," *XP*, July 13, 20, 1919; for the labor conference, see "Suibian tan," *XP*, August 17, 1919.

41. "Mingyi zhong? Shishi zhong?" [Is the name or the deed more important?], *XP*, August 24, 1919. Shen's use of this imagery came more than three years before Lu Xun's image of waking the sleepers in the iron house which appeared in his preface to *Call to Arms*.

42. "Gua yu Rihuo" [Watermelons and Japanese goods], *XP*, September 14, 1919.

43. "Suibian tan," *XP*, August 10, 1919.

44. *XP*, November 23, 1919.

45. *XP*, June 15, 1919, reprinted in *Xuanlu wencun*, pp. 117–19.

46. Margery Wolf, "Women and Suicide in China," p. 118.

47. Christina Gilmartin, "Mobilizing Women: The Early Experiences of the Chinese Communist Party, 1920–1927," pp. 144–45.

48. Gao Yuetian, "Shen Dingyi xianshengde yisheng," part 2, p. 8. In 1981 Mao Dun reported a bizarre episode from the summer of 1923, when Shen allegedly tried to resign from the Communist Party because he claimed that Yang had been kidnapped and taken to Shanghai. Mao Dun provided an explanation, which puts Shen in a very socially and culturally conservative light and is quite at odds with the feminist views he had come to hold. He recounts that a young Communist Party and Socialist Youth Corps member named Wu, an acquaintance of Yang, was a guest in Shen's home; Yang wanted to hear about the educational situation at Shanghai University. Wu described the university; and when he left Yaqian, Yang went with him and enrolled in the university. Shen allegedly believed that Wu had kidnapped her. According to his account (as reported by Mao Dun), when Wu was at his home, he gave evidence of a love interest in Yang, who remained friendly but did not reciprocate Wu's interests. She asked about Shanghai University "much like you'd ask directions from someone on the road." But then she disappeared. Shen claimed that she was a victim. Mao Dun acknowledges that Shen knew Yang's marriage to his son was a bad one, and yet there was this kind of "guess and finger-pointing." See the account in Mao Dun, *Wo zouguode daolu* [The road I travelled], reprinted in *Yaqian nongmin yundong* as "Mao Dunde huiyu" [Mao Dun's recollections], pp. 78–79.

The implication is that Shen was interested in Yang's remaining in his Yaqian home because of his own interest in her. This story flies in the face of what we know about Shen at this stage of his life and it lacks logic. To prove or disprove the kidnapping allegation would only require contacting Yang, who obviously of her own will enrolled in the university. This seems likely to be part of the Communist campaign to tar Shen's name by allegations of immorality.

49. From February to April 1921, Shen edited in Guangzhou a journal, *Laodong yu funu* [Labor and women], that focused on labor and women's liberation. See *Wusi shiqi qikan jieshao*, 2:539–41; 3:647–50.

50. *XP*, August 3, 1919.

51. "Wo zuo 'ren' de fuqin" [The meaning of fatherhood], *XP*, December 7, 1919.

52. Yeh Wen-hsin, "Middle County Radicalism: The May Fourth Movement in Hangzhou."

53. Ma Xulun, *Wo zai liushi sui yiqian*, p. 77.

54. See the accounts of the closeness of the First Normal students to Shen in Xia Yan, "Dang wusi liangzhaozhong dao Zhejiangde shihou," p. 733, and in the same volume, Ni Weixiong, "Zhejiang xinzhaode huiyi," pp. 738–39. See also the account by Cao Juren after the death of Shen in *Juewu*, September 3, 1928.

55. Cao Juren, *Wo yu wode shijie*, p. 173.

56. "Wo zuo 'ren' de fuqin" [The meaning of fatherhood], *XP*, December 7, 1919.

57. *Juewu*, September 6, 1920, reprinted in *Xuanlu wencun*, pp. 143–45.

58. Interview, June 9, 1993.

59. *SDX*, p. 14, and Gao Yuetian, "Shen Dingyi xianshengde yisheng," p. 13.

60. *SDX*, p. 15. The phrase "revolutionary helper" is the language from Shen's memorial biography.

61. Wang Weilian, "Shen Xuanlu yu gongchandang," p. 159, and Gao Yuetian, "Shen Dingyi xianshengde yisheng," p. 10.

62. Ruan Yicheng, "Shen Xuanlu," part 2, p. 19; see also Wang Weilian, "Shen Xuanlu yu gongchandang," p. 159.

63. Ruan Yicheng, "Shen Xuanlu," part 2, p. 19.

64. Wang Weilian, "Shen Xuanlu yu gongchandang," pp. 159–60.

65. According to the interview, Wang taught in the Yaqian Village School during the People's Republic. She apparently suffered a mental breakdown during the last years of her life; she died in 1988.

66. *Juewu*, June 6, 1920, reprinted in *Xuanlu wencun*, pp. 204–14.

67. *Juewu*, October 14, 1920.

68. *XP*, October 10, 1919, reprinted in *Xuanlu wencun*, pp. 130–31.

69. "Suibian tan," *XP*, June 8, 1919.

70. "Suibian tan," *XP*, July 20, 1919.

71. "Shei shi shuai? Shei shi di?" [Who is the leader? Who is the enemy?], *XP*, September 28, 1919.

72. *XP*, November 23, 1919.

73. "Jieshao 'gongdu huzhu tuan'" [Introducing work-study mutual aid groups], *XP*, December 21, 1919; and "Gongdu huzhu tuan" [Work-study mutual aid groups], *XP*, February 8, 1920.

74. See Hans J. Van de Ven, *From Friend to Comrade*, p. 59; C. Martin Wilbur and Julie Lien-ying How, *Missionaries of Revolution*, pp. 442–43; Arif Dirlik, *The Origins of Chinese Communism*, pp. 203–5; Chen Shaokang, Luo Meiling, and Tian Ziyu, "Li Hanjun," p. 119; Shao Lizi, "Dang chengli qianhou yixie qingguang," p. 61; and Mao Dun [Shen Yanbing], "Huiyi Shanghai gongchanzhuyi xiaozu," p. 46.

75. Yang Zhihua, "Yang Zhihuade huiyi," p. 26.

76. Wilbur and How, *Missionaries of Revolution*, pp. 442–43.

77. Dirlik, *The Origins of Chinese Communism*, p. 161.

78. Chen Gongpei, "Huiyi dangde faqi zu he fu faqin gongyingxue deng qingguang," p. 564.

79. Gilmartin, "Mobilizing Women," p. 145.

80. Yang Zhihua, "Yang Zhihuade huiyi," pp. 25–26.

81. For Chen, see *Zhejiang renwu jianzhi*, 2:181–82; for Shi, see the same volume, pp. 257–58; for Yu, see the same volume, pp. 256–57. This biography says that Yu's native place was Zhuji county.

82. Ren Wuxiong, "Guanyu Yu Xiusong lieshi," p. 76.

83. Boorman, *Biographical Dictionary of Republican China*, 1:242–43. The mélange of socialist, ill-formed Marxist, and especially anarchist ideas that prevailed in the Shanghai area has been described persuasively by Dirlik in *The Origins of Chinese Communism*.

84. Chen Shaokang, Luo Meiling, and Tian Ziyu, "Li Hanjun," pp. 109–16.

85. Yang Zhihua, "Yang Zhihuade huiyi," pp. 25–26.

86. Shi Fuliang, "Zhongguo shehui zhuyi qingniantuan chengli qianhoude yixie qingguang," p. 71; and Chen Gongpei, "Huiyi dangde faqi zu he fu faqin gongyingxue deng qingguang," p. 564. There were others mentioned as well. Mao Dun mentions Zhou Fohai, who was in Japan until 1921; Shi reported that Shen Zhongjiu was involved but Chen Gongpei says this was an error; Li Da says that Wang Mingzhai was involved, but he was translator for Voitinsky; and Yang Zhihua mentions Shen Zhongjiu and Liu Dabai.

87. Mao Dun, "Huiyi Shanghai gongchanzhuyi xiaozu," p. 47, notes that Shen attended every meeting of the discussion group during the summer of 1920.

88. Ibid.; Shao Lizi, "Dang chengli qianhou yixie qingguang," pp. 61–62; and *Zhejiang renwu jianzhi*, 2:159–60. Zhang, like Shao, had been active in Shanghai May Fourth activities.

89. Boorman, *Biographical Dictionary of Republican China*, 2:328.

90. Li Da, "Zhongguo gongchandangde faqi he diyici, dierci daibiao dahui jingguode huiyi," pp. 6–18 (originally published in 1955), and in the same volume, "Zhongguo gongchandang chengli shiqide sixiang douzheng qingguang," pp. 50–55 (originally published in 1959); and Wang Huiyu, "Jian dang chuqide yixie qingguang," pp. 76–78.

91. Chen Wangdao, "Huiyi dang chengli shiqide yixie qingguang," p. 20.

92. Wang Huiyu, "Jian dang chuqide yixie qingguang," p. 76.

93. Bao Huiceng, "Gongchandang diyici quanguo daibiao huiyi qianhoude huiyi," pp. 303–4; and in the same volume, Xu Zhichen, "Guanyu Yuyangli liuhaode huodong qingguang," p. 58.

94. Ren Wuxiong, "Guanyu Yu Xiusong lieshi," pp. 76–77.

95. Xu Zhichen, "Guanyu Yuyangli liuhaode huodong qingguang," p. 58.

96. Mao Dun, "Huiyi Shanghai gongchanzhuyi xiaozu," p. 46.

97. Wang Huiyu, "Jian dang chuqide yixie qingguang," p. 76.

98. Bao Huiceng, "Gongchandang diyici quanguo daibiao huiyi qianhoude huiyi," p. 312.

99. Qian Gengshen, "Shen Dingyi xiansheng," p. 62.

100. Yang Zhihua, "Yang Zhihuade huiyi," p. 26.

101. Li Da, "Zhongguo gongchandang chengli shiqide sixiang douzheng qingguang," pp. 51–54.

102. Yu, *Party Politics in Republican China*, p. 76.

103. For a discussion of various aspects of self-identity, see Chad Gordon, "Self-Conceptions: Configurations of Content," pp. 115–36.

104. Weigert, Teitge, and Teitge, *Society and Identity*, p. 31.

105. Li Da, "Zhongguo gongchandang chengli shiqide sixiang douzheng qingguang," p. 54.

106. Lee Feigon, *Chen Duxiu: Founder of the Chinese Communist Party*, p. 196; see also the report of Yuan Zhenying in Dirlik, p. 249.

107. Yang Zhihua, "Yang Zhihuade huiyi," p. 26.

108. Li Da, "Zhongguo gongchandangde faqi he diyici, dierci daibiao dahui jingguode huiyi," p. 7; and "Zhongguo gongchandang chengli shiqide sixiang douzheng qingguang," p. 52.

109. Shao Lizi, "Dang chengli qianhou yixie qingguang," p. 68.

110. Ibid., p. 69. Shao notes also Chen Wangdao's unwillingness because of his scholarly, quiet research temperament, and Shen Zhongjiu, who had socialist thoughts but would not participate.

4. Rushing to Calamity

1. Schoppa, "Contours of Revolution in a Chinese County."

2. "Tanjiang pianying" [Traces collapsing into the river], *Juewu*, May 6, 1923.

3. *Xiaoshan xianzhi, fulu*, p. 1.

4. *Xiaoshan xianzhi*, 23:8–9.

5. See, for example, *MR*, April 22, 1921; May 16, 1922.

6. *Yaqian nongmin yundong*, 1985, p. 69.

7. *Juewu*, March 25, 1920.

8. *Yaqian nongmin yundong*, 1985, pp. 76–77.

9. Ibid., 1985, p. 69; *Xiaoshan xianzhi, fulu*, p. 2.

10. *Yaqian nongmin yundong*, 1985, pp. 76–77.

11. *Xiaoshan xiangtu zhi*, cited (without giving page number) in Yang Fumao and Wang Zuoren, "Zhongguo xiandai nongmin yundongde xian-sheng," p. 31.

12. Written on June 20, this poem was published in *Juewu* on June 26. It is likely, although we cannot be certain, that Shen is describing Phoenix Mountain.

13. *Juewu*, August 8, 1921.

14. Yang Zhihua, "Yang Zhihua tongzhi tan Xiaoshan nongyun," p. 6.

15. "Xixing yu yurou" [Sacrifice and fish and pork], *XP*, September 7, 1919.

16. "Jingzheng yu huzhu" [Competition versus mutual aid], *XP*, July 13, 1919.

17. The most extensive biography of Xuan is Zhao Zijie, Xu Shaoquan, and Li Weijia, "Xuan Zhonghua." The information in this paragraph comes from pp. 79–83.

18. *Juewu*, September 3, 1928.

19. Gilmartin, "Mobilizing Women," pp. 144–46, and letter to the author dated October 4, 1991.

20. See the brief biographies of Xu and Tang in *Yaqian nongmin yundong*, 1987, pp. 113–14.

21. For accounts and memoirs of the May Fourth movement in Hangzhou, see the following. *Wusi yundong zai Zhejiang*, in *Wusi yundong huiyilu*, vol. 2, see Xia Yan, "Dang wusi liangchaozhong dao Zhejiangde shihou," pp.730–36; Ni Weixiong, "Zhejiang xinchaode huiyi," pp. 737–39; Fu Binran, "Wusi qianhou," pp. 742–48; Shi Fuliang, "Wusi zai Hangzhou," pp. 755–756; Jiang Danshu, "'Fei Xiao' yu Zhejiang diyi shifande fan fengjian douzheng," pp. 757–62; finally, Yang Fu, "Wusi shiqi Makesi Liening zhuyi zai Zhejiangde chuanbo."

22. Zhao, Xu, and Li, "Xuan Zhonghua," p. 86.

23. *Yaqian nongmin yundong*, 1985, p. 27.

24. Yang Zhihua, "Yang Zhihua tongzhi tan Xiaoshan nongyun," p. 6.

25. Wang Guansan, "Jiating fangwen ji," pp. 45–46, reprinted from the short-lived journal *Zeren* [Responsibility], December 15, 1922, published under Shen's sponsorship at the town of Kanshan.

26. *Yaqian nongmin yundong*, 1985, pp. 37–38.

27. *Yuezi ribao*, March 27, 1922, quoted in Yang and Wang, "Zhongguo xiandai nongmin yundongde xiansheng," p. 30.

28. *Xiaoshan xianzhi, fulu*, p. 2.

29. Ibid.

30. Angus McDonald notes that Changsha intellectuals in the 1917–19 period had spoken of the necessity of peasant participation but that "until 1923, the peasant movement in Hunan was merely a gleam in the eye of intellectuals." See *The Urban Origins of Rural Revolution*, p. 217. For accounts of the later efforts of Peng Pai at organizing farmers, see Fernando Galbiati, *P'eng P'ai and the Hai-Lu-feng Soviet*, and Robert Marks, *Rural Revolution in South China*. Both Galbiati and Marks put Peng's decision to organize farmers in mid-1922. See Galbiati, Chap. 3, and Marks, p. 173. See also Roy Hofheinz, Jr., *The Broken Wave*.

31. *Yaqian nongmin yundong*, 1987, p. 13.

32. Ibid., pp. 4 and 13.

33. "Shei nide pengyou?" in *Yaqian nongmin yundong*, 1987, pp. 14–16.

34. *MR*, August 23, 1921.

35. "Nongmin zijue," in *Yaqian nongmin yundong*, 1987, pp. 17–20. There is a discrepancy in the sources for the date of this speech. *Xiaoshan xianzhi* says it was given on August 1; *Yaqian nongmin yundong*, 1987, citing the November 1921 issue of *Laodong zhoukan*, puts the date at September 23.

36. *Yaqian nongmin yundong*, 1987, p. 20.

37. *Yaqian nongmin yundong*, 1985, p. 36.

38. Ibid., 1985, pp. 69–70.

39. Shi Dazhong and Wang Siniu, "Shen Shuyan lai Dayi, Qianqing hao-zhao jianzu," p. 101.

40. *SDX*, pp. 5–6; Gao Yuetian, "Shen Dingyi xianshengde yisheng," part 1, p. 6.

41. *Yaqian nongmin yundong*, 1985, pp. 6 and 74–75.

42. Yang and Wang, "Zhongguo xiandai nongmin yundongde xian-sheng," p. 31.

43. *Yaqian nongmin yundong*, 1985, pp. 32–33.

44. Ibid., 1985, pp. 30–31.

45. *MR*, December 21, 1921.

46. Yang and Wang, "Zhongguo xiandai nongmin yundongde xian-sheng," p. 32.

47. Sun Xilu, "Shen Dingyi yi liang shi," cited in Yang and Wang, "Zhong-guo xiandai nongmin yundongde xiansheng," p. 32.

48. Zhang Ruisheng, Ping Liusan, Weng Ashun, et. al., "Doumen, Gaoze dengcun jianzu qingguang diandi," p. 102.

49. *Xiaoshan xianzhi, fulu*, pp. 3–4; and *Yaqian nongmin yundong*, 1985, pp. 7–8.

50. *Xiaoshan xianzhi, fulu*, pp. 1, 3–4; see the map at the beginning of *Yaqian nongmin yundong*, 1987. See also Cheng Hanchang, "Zhongguo xi-andai nongmin yundong zuizao fasheng yu heshi hedi?" pp. 55–57.

51. *Yaqian nongmin yundong*, 1985, p. 29.

52. *Xiaoshan xianzhi, fulu*, p. 4; *Yaqian nongmin yundong*, 1985, pp. 73–74.

53. Shao Weizheng, "Yaqian nongmin xiehui shimo," p. 465.

54. Ibid., pp. 465–466.

55. Shi and Wang, "Shen Shuyan lai Dayi, Qianqing haozhao jianzu," p. 101.

56. *Yuezi ribao*, December 12, 1921; *Xiaoshan xianzhi, fulu*, p. 5.

57. Xu Xingzhi (Xu Meikun), "Dang chengliu shiqi Zhejiangde gongnong yundong," pp. 38–43; *Yaqian nongmin yundong*, 1985, p. 9.

58. *Xiaoshan xianzhi, fulu*, p. 5.

59. *Yaqian nongmin yundong*, 1985, p. 80.

60. *Yuezi ribao*, December 19, 1921.

61. *MR*, December 31, 1921; *Yaqian nongmin yundong*, 1985, p. 13.

62. *Shaoxing xian xingzheng dier xingzheng huiyi tekan*, p. 16.

63. Yang and Wang, "Zhongguo xiandai nongmin yundongde xian-sheng," p. 33.

64. *Yaqian nongmin yundong*, 1985, p. 73.

65. *MR*, December 21, 1921.

66. *Yaqian nongmin yundong*, 1985, p. 36.

67. *Xiaoshan xianzhi, fulu*, p. 5; *Yaqian nongmin yundong*, 1985, pp. 13–14; *MR*, December 21, 1921.

68. *Yaqian nongmin yundong*, 1985, p. 40.

69. Ibid., pp. 40, 73–75.

70. Ibid., p. 14.

71. Ibid., pp. 15 and 80.

72. *MR*, February 10, 1922. For more on the state involvement in rent collection in Jiangnan, see Kathryn Bernhardt, *Rents, Taxes, and Peasant Resistance*, pp. 165–72.

73. See the articles from the *Yuezi ribao* reprinted in *Yaqian nongmin yundong*, 1987, pp. 150–58. These articles date from December 15, 1921 to April 13, 1922.

74. See the coverage in *MR*, October 7, 8, 9, 14, 17, 26, 29, 31, November 7, 1921.

75. *MR*, October 17, 1921.

76. *MR*, November 8, 1921.

77. R. Keith Schoppa, "Province and Nation: The Chekiang Provincial Autonomy Movement, 1917–1927."

78. R. Keith Schoppa, "Shen Dingyi in Opposition, 1921 and 1928."

79. *Yaqian nongmin yundong*, 1985, pp. 42–45, 71–72.

80. Ibid., p. 75.

81. Ibid., pp. 68, 76–77.

82. Ibid., pp. 62–63.

83. *MR*, January 13, 1922.

84. He also pulls the reader out of the Xiaoshan-Shaoxing arena by analogizing the situation with that of the Washington Conference, meeting on Pacific issues from November 1921 to February 1922. There, the analogy goes, China loses out to capitalist Japan and the West, called, like the Yaqian farmer, "ignorant," the world's "bumpkin."

85. *Yaqian nongmin yundong*, 1987, pp. 8–9.

86. *Yaqian nongmin yundong*, 1985, p. 68.

87. *Shibao*, June 8, 1911.

88. Zhu Shunzuo, *Shaoxing xianren zhi*, 1:113–14.

89. Robert C. Solomon, "Recapturing Personal Identity," p. 14.

90. *Yaqian nongmin yundong*, 1985, p. 39.

91. Shi and Wang, "Shen Shuyan lai Dayi, Qianqing haozhao jianzu," p. 101.

92. *MR*, March 4, 1922.

93. Gao Yuetian, "Shen Dingyi xianshengde yisheng," part 1, p. 7.

94. Gregory P. Stone, "Appearance and the Self," p. 94.

95. On network content, intensity, and durability, see Mitchell, "Concept and Use of Social Networks," pp. 20–22, 26–27.

5. All Fall Down

1. Gao Yuetian, "Shen Dingyi xianshengde yisheng," part 1, p. 8. Gao reports that although Shen did resume drinking, he did so with considerable self-control.

2. "Xuexiao zizhide shenghuo" [The life of school self-government], *XP*, November 2, 1919. Shen claimed also to have reformed absolutely in gambling and visiting prostitutes.

3. *Juewu*, January 5, 1921.

4. Editors of *Zhejiang gongren yundong shi* say that only Yu established this organization and not until April 1922 (pp. 51–52). It is not supported with documentation and contradicts other accounts. See, for example, Chang Kuo-t'ao, *The Rise of the Chinese Communist Party*, 1:128.

5. Ruan Yicheng, "Shen Xuanlu," part 1, p. 5.

6. Wilbur and How, *Missionaries of Revolution*, pp. 45–57.

7. *SDX*, p. 9.

8. *Wusi shiqi qikan jieshao*, pp. 468–469.

9. Chen Juemu, "Liu Dabai xiansheng zhi shengping," pp. 49 and 53. Chen says that at Yaqian Liu and Shen wrote new style poetry together.

10. *Wusi shiqi qikan jieshao*, p. 467; see also Zhao, Xu, and Li, "Xuan Zhonghua," pp. 87, 89–90. For an account of the labor activities of the print-workers, see *Zhejiang gongren yundong shi*, pp. 46–48.

11. *Juewu*, January 1, 1924.

12. Wilbur and How, *Missionaries of Revolution*, pp. 87–88. See also the brief description in Tony Saich, *The Origins of the First United Front in China*, p. 193.

13. Wang Weilian, "Shen Xuanlu yu gongchandang," p. 159.

14. See Chang Kuo-t'ao, *Rise of the Chinese Communist Party*, 1:191–201, for a description of Chinese students in the Soviet Union in 1922.

15. The tree, unlike the system, was still flourishing in 1993.

16. That Dai represented Zhejiang at the Congress seems at first surprising since Dai's family had emigrated from Zhejiang in the eighteenth century and had lived since that time in Sichuan; but Dai's closeness to Sun likely insured his official standing as a delegate.

17. *MR*, January 8, 1924.

18. Mast, "Intellectual Biography of Tai Chi-t'ao," pp. 169–171.

19. Boorman, *Biographical Dictionary of Republican China*, 3:201.

20. Wilbur and How, *Missionaries of Revolution*, pp. 97–100.

21. *Qingdang shilu*, p. 211. Shen often stayed at Xiaowen's home when he was in Hangzhou. In 1923, Xiaowen had served briefly as principal of the Fifth Provincial Middle School in Shaoxing with Liu Dabai as dean of studies. See Chen Juemu, "Liu Dabai xiansheng zhi shengping," p. 53.

22. *MR*, March 8, 1924.

23. *XP*, September 7, 1919.

24. *MR*, April 1, 1924.

25. Gao Yuetian, "Shen Dingyi xianshengde yisheng," part 2, p. 9.

26. *MR*, April 4, 9, 1924.

27. On the defining of the revolution, see John Fitzgerald, "The Misconceived Revolution: State and Society in China's Nationalist Revolution, 1923–26."

28. *MR*, April 9, May 10, 1924.

29. Zhao, Xu, and Li, "Xuan Zhonghua," p. 97.

30. *MR*, May 7, 1924.

31. *MR*, April 15, 1924.

32. Ibid.

33. See the discussion of the militarization of politics in this period in Edward A. McCord, *The Power of the Gun: The Emergence of Modern Chinese Warlordism*, pp. 308, 312–15.

34. *MR*, May 21, 1924.

35. *MR*, April 22, 1924.

36. *MR*, May 2, 1924; Zhao, Xu, and Li, "Xuan Zhonghua," pp. 97–98. The events were planned in an April 22 meeting attended by representatives of the Guomindang, an organization called a Labor Alliance, the Dongyang Workers' Native Place Association, the Print Workers' Club, the *Zhejiang Republican Daily*, and the Youth Advance Together Society.

37. See Wang Weilian, "Shen Xuanlu yu gongchandang," p. 159.

38. Zhao, Xu, and Li, "Xuan Zhonghua," p. 100.

39. *MR*, May 2, 1924.

40. Xu Xingzhi, "Dang chengliu shiqi Zhejiangde gongnong yundong," pp. 38–39. David Strand in *Rickshaw Beijing* notes that printing workers in Beijing were also the first to "establish ties with radical politicians and labor organizers" (p. 165).

41. For a discussion of this group, see Schoppa, *Chinese Elites and Political Change*, pp. 175–81.

42. Jean Chesneaux, *The Chinese Labor Movement, 1919–1927*, p. 365.

43. Schoppa, *Chinese Elites and Political Change*, pp. 182–83.

44. *Zhejiang bainian dashiji*, p. 183.

45. *MR*, May 6, 1924.

46. *MR*, May 11, 1924.

47. Chang Kuo-t'ao, *Rise of the Chinese Communist Party*, 1:342–43. See also an account of that plenum in Wang Xueqi, "Yijiuersinian wuyue zhonggong zhongyang kuoda zhiweihui shuping."

48. Chang Kuo-t'ao, *Rise of the Chinese Communist Party*, 1:342. Part of Shen's reticence here may have stemmed from his having to chair the meeting.

49. *SDX*, pp. 15–16.

50. *MR*, May 5, 1924.

51. Schoppa, "Politics and Society in Chekiang," pp. 225–29.

52. *You Hang jilue*, p. 26a.

53. *Zhejiang bainian dashiji*, p. 184.

54. Lu Yichun and Ye Guangting, *Xihu manhua*, p. 164. There are many variations in this folk tale; I have used two tellings of the tale, cited in the next footnotes.

55. The phrase is from "Legend of the White Snake," p. 24.

56. *West Lake: A Collection of Folk Tales*, p. 64. In another telling, Fahai was commissioned and sent by the Buddha "to judge and punish the White Snake for her sins." See "Legend of the White Snake," pp. 29–33. According to this version, the twenty years were a period for the White Snake's meditation in which "that purity of mind and body necessary to the attainment of immortality" could be attained" (p. 37).

57. Leo Ou-fan Lee, *Voices from the Iron House*, p. 119.

58. E. H. Clayton, *Heaven Below*, p. 32.

59. Gao Yuetian, "Shen Dingyi xianshengde yisheng," part 2, p. 13.

60. Weigert, Teitge, and Teitge, *Society and Identity*, p. 58.

61. Mitchell has noted that the "multiplexity of relationship" in networks "leads to a strain towards inconsistency in behavior," "Concept and Use of Social Networks," p. 47. Such an argument might help explain the many identities attributed to Shen: inconsistencies of behavior within and between networks of which he was a part gave rise to or enhanced certain identities.

62. "Zhejiang sheng dangbu baogao," p. 424.

63. C. Martin Wilbur, *The Nationalist Revolution in China, 1923–1928*, p. 19; Wilbur and How, *Missionaries of Revolution*, pp. 105–6.

64. Boorman, *Biographical Dictionary of Republican China*, 3:387.

65. *Shenbao*, September 10, 1924; Zhao, Xu, and Li, "Xuan Zhonghua," p. 98.

66. "Zhejiang dangbu baogao," p. 424; Zhao, Xu, and Li, "Xuan Zhonghua," p. 98.

67. "Zhejiang dangbu baogao," p. 427.

68. Ibid., p. 425.

69. Ibid.

70. Wilbur, *The Nationalist Revolution in China*, p. 20.

71. *MR*, December 7, 11, 12, 17, 20, 21, 1924.

72. Wilbur and How, *Missionaries of Revolution*, p. 120.

73. *MR*, December 17, 1924.

74. Zhao, Xu, and Li, "Xuan Zhonghua," p. 99.

75. *MR*, January 7, 1925.

76. *MR*, March 27, 1925.

77. *MR*, April 2, 27, 1925.

78. *MR*, May 12, 1925.

79. Wilbur and How, *Missionaries of Revolution*, pp. 148–49.

80. Mao Dun, "Mao Dunde huiyi," pp. 78–79.

81. Wang Ke-wen, "The Kuomintang in Transition," p. 62 and p. 355, n. 93.

82. "Shen Dingyi xiansheng beinan aiqi," pp. 162–63.

83. Mao Dun, "Mao Dunde huiyi," p. 79.

84. *Zhejiang dangbu baogao*, p. 425.

85. Wilbur and How, *Missionaries of Revolution*, p. 123.

86. Zhao, Xu, and Li, "Xuan Zhonghua," p. 99.

87. Wang Weilian, "Shen Xuanlu yu gongchandang," p. 160.

88. Zhao, Xu, and Li, "Xuan Zhonghua," p. 100.

89. Ibid.

90. *MR*, June 26, 1925.

91. *MR*, July 2, 1925.

92. *MR*, July 9, 1925. See also Li Yunhan, *Cong ronggong dao qingdang*, p. 411.

93. *SDX*, p. 10.

94. Zhong Baiyong, "Diyici guogong hezuo shiqi fasheng zai Xiaoshande yichu naoju," p. 213; and Zhao, Xu, and Li, "Xuan Zhonghua."

95. Michael Keith and Steve Pile, "Introduction, Part 2: The Place of Politics," p. 37.

96. Zhao, Xu, and Li, "Xuan Zhonghua," pp. 101–3.

97. Another report claims that Shen went so far in the debates as to forbid Ningbo representative Yu Bianqun from speaking. See Pan Nianzhi, "Da geming shiqi Zhejiangde fandui Guomindang youpai douzheng," p. 4.

98. Zhong Baiyong, "Diyici guogong hezuo shiqi fasheng zai Xiaoshande yichu naoju," pp. 212–13.

99. These policies were the bloc within, accepting direction from the Comintern, and supporting workers and farmers.

100. Zhong Baiyong, "Diyici guogong hezuo shiqi fasheng zai Xiaoshande yichu naoju," p. 213.

101. *XP*, May 1, 1920.

102. "Ta jiushi ni; ni jiushi wo" [He really is you; you really are I], *XP*, November 23, 1919.

103. *MR*, July 11, 1925.

104. Li Yunhan, *Cong ronggong dao qingdang*, p. 411. It should be stressed that Shen certainly had many supporters (some undoubtedly handpicked) at the meeting.

105. Zhao, Xu, and Li, "Xuan Zhonghua," pp. 104–105.

106. Quoted in Gao Yuetian, "Shen Dingyi xianshengde yisheng," part 1, p. 5.

107. Chen Tianxi, *Zengding Dai Jitao xiansheng biannian chuanji*, p. 67.

108. *Zhejiang bainian dashiji*, p. 199.

6. The Black Star

1. "Zhejiang sheng dangbu baogao," p. 428. See also Jiang Tianyi, "Diyici guogong hezuo shiqi Guomindang Zhejiang sheng dangbu huodong zhuiji," p. 198.

2. Wang Weilian, "Shen Xuanlu yu gongchandang," p. 160.

3. See, e.g., "Rensheng wenti" [Questions about life], *XP*, January 5, 1921.

4. Xu Xingzhi, "Dang chengliu shiqi Zhejiangde gongnong yundong," p. 43.

5. Zhao, Xu, and Li, "Xuan Zhonghua," p. 103.

6. "Zhejiang sheng dangbu baogao," p. 429.

7. Zhao, Xu, and Li, "Xuan Zhonghua," p. 103.

8. Wilbur and How, *Missionaries of Revolution*, p. 101.

9. Ibid., pp. 103–4.

10. Ibid., p. 171.

11. Ibid.

12. Jiang Tianyi, "Diyici guogong hezuo shiqi Guomindang Zhejiang sheng dangbu huodong zhuiji," p. 199.

13. *Qingdang shilu*, p. 212.

14. Zhao, Xu, and Li, "Xuan Zhonghua," p. 104.

15. Mao Zedong, from "Diguo zhuyi zuihoude gongju," in *Zhengzhi zhoubao*, 3, p. 11, as quoted in Zhou Zixin, "Xishan huiyipai zhaokaide liangci fandong huiyi," p. 98.

16. "Zhejiang sheng dangbu baogao," p. 429. Angus McDonald's suggestion seems on the mark: that the development of the Guomindang can be appropriately studied "as a function of factions and interests in conflict and alliance," *Urban Origins of Rural Revolution*, p. 139.

17. *Qingdang shilu*, pp. 151–53.

18. The meeting was held at the Azure Cloud Temple about fifteen kilometers from Beijing, in the mountains beyond the former Summer Palace. See the description in Vera Vladimirovna Vishnyakova-Akimova, *Two Years in Revolutionary China, 1925–1927*, pp. 50–53.

19. *Qingdang shilu*, pp. 50–67 and 142–210.

20. Ibid., pp. 51, 52, 61, and 64.

21. Wilbur and How, *Missionaries of Revolution*, p. 191.

22. For more on the Western Hills networks, see R. Keith Schoppa, "Shen Dingyi and the Western Hills Group: 'What's a Man Like You Doing in a Group Like This?'"

23. *Qingdang shilu*, p. 45.

24. *Zhejiang bainian dashiji*, p. 193.

25. *MR*, December 22, 1925.

26. Zhao, Xu, and Li, "Xuan Zhonghua," pp. 105–6.

27. *MR*, January 5, 1926.

28. *MR*, January 5, 7, 13, 1926.

29. *MR*, January 5, 1926.

30. Zhou Zixin, "Xishan huiyipai zhaokaide liangci fandong huiyi," p. 99.

31. Zhao, Xu, and Li, "Xuan Zhonghua," p. 106.

32. *Qingdang shilu*, pp. 324–25.

33. Ibid., p. 326.

34. Ibid., p. 129.

35. Ibid., p. 118.

36. Ibid., p. 272. Ruan Yicheng, "Shen Xuanlu," p. 6, says the new office was on Pishi Lane, but other sources corroborate the Little Cart Bridge address.

37. *Qingdang shilu*, p. 326, and *MR*, March 9, 1926.

38. *Qingdang shilu*, p. 322.

39. Zhao, Xu, and Li, "Xuan Zhonghua," p. 106.

40. *Qingdang shilu*, pp. 325–26.

41. Ibid., p. 325.

42. Jiang Tianyi, "Diyici guogong hezuo shiqi Guomindang Zhejiang sheng dangbu huodong zhuiji," p. 201.

43. Zhao, Xu, and Li, "Xuan Zhonghua," pp. 106–7.

44. Ibid., p. 106.

45. Jiang Tianyi, "Diyici guogong hezuo shiqi Guomindang Zhejiang sheng dangbu huodong zhuiji," pp. 200–201.

46. *Qingdang shilu*, p. 326.

47. *Zhejiang bainian dashiji*, pp. 194–96.

48. *SDX*, p. 11.

49. McDonald, *Urban Origins of Rural Revolution*, esp. chap. 5.

50. *Qingdang shilu*, p. 326.

51. Ibid.

52. Ibid., p. 322.
53. Ibid., pp. 322–23.
54. Ibid., pp. 326–27.
55. Ibid., pp. 209–10.
56. Ibid., p. 211.
57. *Zhejiang bainian dashiji*, p. 195.
58. See the account in *Zhejiang gongren yundong shi*, pp. 77–82.
59. *Qingdang shilu*, p. 211.
60. Ibid., p. 328.
61. *Zhejiang bainian dashiji*, p. 195.
62. *Qingdang shilu*, p. 328.
63. Ibid., pp. 325–26.
64. *Juewu*, March 8, 1923.
65. See the description in Jonathan Spence, *The Gate of Heavenly Peace*, pp. 193–94.
66. Jonathan Spence, *The Search for Modern China*, p. 344.
67. *Qingdang shilu*, p. 146.
68. Ibid., p. 156.
69. Ibid., p. 157.
70. Ibid., pp. 157–59.
71. Ibid., p. 173.
72. Ibid., p. 180.
73. Ibid., p. 181.
74. Ibid., p. 182.
75. Ibid., p. 170.
76. Ibid., p. 352.
77. Ibid., p. 359.
78. Ibid., p. 362.
79. *MR*, July 14, 1926.
80. *Zhejiang bainian dashiji*, pp. 197–98.
81. *Qingdang shilu*, p. 320.
82. Ibid., p. 315.
83. Ibid., p. 327.
84. Ibid., p. 284.
85. Jiang Tianyi, "Diyici guogong hezuo shiqi Guomindang Zhejiang sheng dangbu huodong zhuiji," pp. 201–2. See also *Zhejiang bainian dashiji*, p. 198. There is disagreement over the dates of the party closure. The latter source says it occurred on August 24, while *Qingdang shilu* puts it either on August 1 or August 20.
86. *Qingdang shilu*, p. 285. Jiang Tianyi claims that even though Shen's office was not closed, his group was nervous enough to take down the signboard; "Diyici guogong hezuo shiqi Guomindang Zhejiang sheng dangbu huodong zhuiji," p. 202.
87. Pan Nianzhi, "Da geming shiqi Zhejiangde fandui Guomindang youpai douzheng," p. 5. Pan and Wang were in charge because Xuan was in Shanghai much of this time; the other key leader, Ding Qimei, was at his home in Pinghu. The counties where organizing was proceeding included Cheng,

Shangyu, Yuyao, Jiande, Linhai, Pingyang, Fuyang, and Tonglu. Jiande was in the inner periphery.

88. Jiang Tianyi, "Diyici guogong hezuo shiqi Guomindang Zhejiang sheng dangbu huodong zhuiji," p. 202.

89. *SDX*, p. 12.

90. *Juewu*, March 2, 1922.

7. A Dangerous Time

1. *MR*, March 7, 1927.

2. *Shibao*, March 18–19, 1927.

3. *Shibao*, March 19, 1927.

4. Zhao, Xu, and Li, "Xuan Zhonghua," pp. 108–9.

5. Pan Nianzhi, "Da geming shiqi Zhejiangde fandui Guomindang youpai douzheng," p. 9.

6. Ibid., pp. 10–11.

7. Bergère, "The Shanghai Bankers' Association, 1915–1927," p. 26.

8. Zhao, Xu, and Li, "Xuan Zhonghua," p. 110.

9. Chesneaux, *Chinese Labor Movement*, p. 364.

10. Quoted in Zhao, Xu, and Li, "Xuan Zhonghua," p. 108.

11. *Shibao*, March 20, 1927.

12. Schoppa, *Chinese Elites and Political Change*, pp. 182–83.

13. *MR*, April 4, 1927.

14. *MR*, April 2, 1927.

15. Jiang Tianyi notes the two factions in the labor movement, indicating that the Communists had firm control of the GLU. See "Beifa qianhou Zhejiang Guomindang huodongde diandi huiyi," p. 74.

16. Zhao, Xu, and Li, "Xuan Zhonghua," p. 110.

17. Pan Nianzhi, "Da geming shiqi Zhejiangde fandui Guomindang youpai douzheng," p. 11.

18. *MR*, March 29, 1927.

19. *MR*, March 31, 1927.

20. Zhao, Xu, and Li, "Xuan Zhonghua," p. 110.

21. *Zhejiang gongren yundong shi* (p. 121) claims that Shen was actively involved in the party purge in Xiaoshan and Shaoxing in early April.

22. Zhao, Xu, and Li, "Xuan Zhonghua," p. 110. Jiang Tianyi, "Diyici guogong hezao shiqi Guomindang Zhejiang sheng dangbu huodong zhuiji," p. 207, contends that the Federation marchers were vagrants and bullies masquerading as various kinds of construction workers, but he claims that both sides attacked each other.

23. *Shibao*, April 3, 1927.

24. *MR*, April 2, 1927.

25. Zhao, Xu, and Li, "Xuan Zhonghua," p. 111.

26. Pan Nianzhi, "Da geming shiqi Zhejiangde fandui Guomindang youpai douzheng," p. 13. See Ma's description of his position in *Wo zai liushi sui yiqian*, p. 94.

27. Pan Nianzhi, "Da geming shiqi Zhejiangde fandui Guomindang youpai douzheng," p. 13.

28. Jiang Tianyi claims that the provincial Guomindang bureau was holding a commemorative gathering for Sun Yat-sen at the provincial Education Association on Pinghai Road when the purge began, but others do not corroborate this account. See "Beifa qianhou Zhejiang Guomindang huodongde diandi huiyi," p. 75.

29. Jiang Tianyi, " Diyici guogong hezuo shiqi Guomindang Zhejiang sheng dangbu huodong zhuiji," p. 208; Zhao, Xu, and Li, "Xuan Zhonghua," pp. 111–112.

30. Pan Nianzhi, "Da geming shiqi Zhejiangde fandui Guomindang youpai douzheng," p. 14.

31. Zhao, Xu, and Li, "Xuan Zhonghua," pp. 112–13; Jiang Tianyi, "Diyici guogong hezuo shiqi Guomindang Zhejiang sheng dangbu huodong zhuiji," p. 209. See also Xu Bainian, "Zhejiang zaoqi shuchude geming huodongjia—Xuan Zhonghua lieshi chuanlue," pp. 28–47.

32. Yang Zhihua, "Yang Zhihuade huiyi," p. 28.

33. Chen Gongmao, "Shen Dingyi qiren," p. 43.

34. Jiang Tianyi, "Diyici guogong hezuo shiqi Guomindang Zhejiang sheng dangbu huodong zhuiji," p. 208.

35. On the arrest and release of Cha Renwei, see Han Jingyi, "Cha Renwei beibu jingguo," pp. 83–84. On the release of Chu and Shen Junru, see Pan Nianzhi, "Da geming shiqi Zhejiangde fandui Guomindang youpai douzheng," p. 14. Pan claims that Ma Xulun had advocated the execution of Chu and Shen because of their closeness to the Communists, their reservoirs of power in the province, and his personal dislike of the two. Chiang Kai-shek, apprised of the situation, ordered Chu and Shen to Nanjing where he released them.

36. *Shibao*, April 17, 1927.

37. *Yaqian nongmin yundong*, 1987, pp. 113–14.

38. *MR*, May 20, 1927. See also the account in Jiang Tianyi, "Diyici guogong hezuo shiqi Guomindang Zhejiang sheng dangbu huodong zhuiji," p. 207.

39. *Shibao*, May 5, 1927.

40. *Shenbao*, June 22, 24, 1927.

41. *MR*, July 3, 1927.

42. *MR*, June 12, 1927.

43. *MR*, June 14, 1927.

44. *Shenbao*, June 25, 1927. His comment on the Communist position on colonization in the context of the purge is puzzling since this policy issue hardly seems one central to undertaking the purge. This remark seems more a personal reflection, for Shen felt strongly about the colonization question. But Shen's raising such an issue that was neither central to the reasons for the purge nor for the situation at hand raises questions about Shen's judgment; his personal views intruded into his public performance.

45. "Zhonghua minguo jichu zai nali?" [Where is the foundation of the Republic of China?] *XP*, October 26, 1919.

46. *MR*, June 26, 1927.

47. *Shenbao*, July 14, 1927.

48. "Xixing yu yurou" [Sacrifice and fish and pork], *XP*, September 7, 1919.

49. *MR*, July 19, 30, August 10, 1927; *Shenbao*, July 16, 1927.

50. *Shenbao*, July 16, 1927.

51. *MR*, August 10, 1927.

52. *Shenbao*, June 26, July 12, 1927.

53. Ruan Yicheng, "Shen Xuanlu," part 2, p. 18.

54. *Shenbao*, July 23, 1927.

55. *Shenbao*, September 3, 1927.

56. *MR*, September 19, 1927.

57. *MR*, July 29, 1927. This was an advance notice of his lecture.

58. *MR*, July 24, 1927.

59. *Shenbao*, July 6, 1927. This was the court case of Kong Jirong, where accountants figured in the case.

60. Chen Gongmao, "Shen Dingyi qiren," p. 43.

61. Ibid.

62. Gao Yuetian, "Shen Dingyi xianshengde yisheng," p. 10. This judgment on Xuan seems anachronistic; the Self-Examination Institute was not established until late in 1927. Xuan would most surely have been arrested in the immediate aftermath of April 11 well before Shen directed the purge, when there were executions in Zhejiang.

63. *Shenbao*, July 31, 1927.

64. *Shenbao*, September 9, 1927.

65. *Zhejiang bainian dashiji*, p. 203.

66. *Shenbao*, September 4, 1927.

67. *Juewu*, September 9, 1921.

68. Ruan Yicheng, "Xianjun Xunbo gong nianpu," p. 51.

69. *Shibao*, July 27, 1927.

70. Ibid.

71. Gao Yuetian, "Shen Dingyi xianshengde yisheng," p. 10.

72. *Shenbao*, July 27, 1927.

73. *Shenbao*, September 14, 1927.

74. Gao Yuetian, "Shen Dingyi xianshengde yisheng," p. 10.

75. Wilbur, *Nationalist Revolution in China*, p. 157.

76. Wang Ke-wen, *The Kuomintang in Transition*, p. 151.

77. *Shenbao*, October 12, 1927. Guangxi clique leader Li Zongren noted that in meetings to set up the Special Committee, "to my surprise, the majority of the Western hills leaders gave me the impression of being gentlemen of high principles." See Li Tsung-jen and Tong Te-kong, *The Memoirs of Li Tsung-jen*, p. 238.

78. *MR*, October 13, 1927. Men like Hong Ludong and Chen Xihao, former members of the reorganization committee, questioned its legality.

79. *SDX*, p. 13.

80. *Shenbao*, May 7, 1927.

81. *MR*, October 2, 15, 1927.

82. *MR*, November 6, 1927.

83. Ibid.
84. *MR*, October 22, 1927.
85. *Shenbao*, November 10, 1927.
86. *Shenbao*, November 7, 1927.
87. *MR*, December 8, 1927.
88. Wang Ke-wen, *The Kuomintang in Transition*, p. 160.
89. Ibid., p. 161.
90. *Shenbao*, November 9, 15, 1927.
91. *Shenbao*, January 12, 1928.
92. *MR*, December 20, 1927.
93. *Shenbao*, January 1, 1928.
94. *Shenbao*, January 11, 1928.
95. *Shenbao*, December 18, 1927.
96. Ruan Yicheng, "Shen Xuanlu," part 2, p. 17.
97. *MR*, October 13, 30, December 1, 1927; *Shenbao*, October 30, November 11, 28, 1927.

8. The Representative of the Masses

1. *Juewu*, June 23, 1921.
2. Kong Xuexiong, "Dongxiang zizhi shimo," p. 331.
3. *Shenbao*, October 13, 1927.
4. *MR*, October 23, 1927. An example of his involvement on the local level was his speaking on the Three Principles of the People as the standard for education at a November 13 meeting of party leaders from the two Xiaoshan branch bureaus. See *MR*, November 19, 1927.
5. Kong Xuexiong, "Dongxiang zizhi shimo," p. 398.
6. *MR*, February 26, 1928.
7. Kong Xuexiong, "Dongxiang zizhi shimo," p. 332.
8. *MR*, November 22, 1927.
9. Kong Xuexiong, "Dongxiang zizhi shimo," p. 396.
10. Ibid., p. 397.
11. Ibid., p. 395.
12. Ibid., pp. 333–35. For perhaps the most famous rural reconstruction project in the 1930s, see Charles Hayford, *To the People: James Yen and Village China*; for an overview of other rural reconstruction efforts in this period, see Guy Alitto, *The Last Confucian*, chap. 10.
13. *Shenbao*, January 14, 1928.
14. *Shenbao*, January 12, 1928.
15. *Shibao*, December 30, 1927.
16. Lin Weibao, "Yaqian yinxiang ji," p. 74.
17. Kong Xuexiong, "Dongxiang zizhi shimo," pp. 339–340.
18. Ibid., p. 398.
19. Ibid., pp. 334–35.
20. Ibid., p. 399.
21. Chen Gongmao, "Shen Dingyi qiren," p. 43.

22. Kong Xuexiong. "Dongxiang zizhi shimo," p. 334.

23. Ibid., p. 332.

24. These numbers are likely inflated, coming as they do from the account of Kong (pp. 332–33), one of Shen's strongest supporters.

25. Kong Xuexiong, "Dongxiang zizhi shimo," pp. 338, 347–48. Farmers associations had the largest membership and therefore the most money from membership dues.

26. Ibid., p. 347.

27. The following account comes from Kong, pp. 337–38.

28. SDX, p. 13.

29. Chen Gongmao, "Shen Dingyi qiren," pp. 43–44.

30. Sulamith Heins Potter and Jack M. Potter, *China's Peasants: The Anthropology of Revolution*, p. 195.

31. Kong Xuexiong, "Dongxiang zizhi shimo," pp. 387–88.

32. Ibid., pp. 389–90.

33. Ibid., pp. 392 and 394.

34. Ibid., p. 393.

35. Ibid., p. 390.

36. Ibid.

37. Ibid., pp. 373–74.

38. Chen Gongmao, "Shen Dingyi qiren," p. 46.

39. *Chinese Economic Bulletin*, February 5, 1927, p. 72.

40. *Chinese Economic Journal*, December 26, 1927, p. 571; *Chinese Economic Bulletin*, February 5, 1927, p. 72.

41. Kong Xuexiong, "Dongxiang zizhi shimo," p. 391.

42. Ibid., pp. 361–62.

43. Ibid., p. 392.

44. Ibid., p. 332.

45. Ibid., p. 338.

46. Ibid., p. 340.

47. Ibid.

48. *Shenbao*, September 15, 1927.

49. *Shenbao*, January 12, 1928.

50. *Shenbao*, February 1, 1928.

51. *Shenbao*, April 17, 19, 1928.

52. *Shenbao*, May 22, 1928.

53. *Shenbao*, July 3, 1928.

54. *Shenbao*, July 15, 1928; see also *Xiaoshan xianzhi, da shiji*, p. 29.

55. Kong Xuexiong, "Dongxiang zizhi shimo," p. 378.

56. Wang Zanyuan and Chen Dingshun, "Xianghu shifan jian wushinian huiyi," p. 64.

57. *Shenbao*, April 13, 1928.

58. *Shenbao*, August 13, 1928.

59. *Shenbao*, August 11, 1928.

60. Wilbur, *Nationalist Revolution in China*, pp. 185–86.

61. It is not only with individuals but also with larger communities that perceptions become reality. Emily Honig notes in regard to Subei residents in Shanghai that "ultimately it does not matter whether Subei people really were

collaborators [with the Japanese] or not; more significant is the popular perception that they were and the discrimination against them that ensued." See "Migrant Culture in Shanghai: In Search of a Subei Identity," p. 247.

62. Strauss, *Mirrors and Masks*, p. 25.

63. Murray Edelman, *Constructing the Political Spectacle*, p. 78.

64. See Potter and Potter, *China's Peasants*, pp. 281–95, for reflections on the party ethic. Though their comments apply specifically to the Communist Party, they also have relevance to some elements of the Guomindang.

65. Kong Xuexiong, "Dongxiang zizhi shimo," pp. 399–400.

66. *Shenbao*, July 2, 1928.

67. Chen Gongmao, "Shen Dingyi qiren," p. 44.

68. *MR*, August 19, 1928.

69. Kong Xuexiong, "Dongxiang zizhi shimo," p. 341.

70. See Fitzgerald, "Misconceived Revolution," pp. 337–39.

71. Kong Xuexiong, "Dongxiang zizhi shimo," p. 341.

72. See the provocative discussion of Edelmann in *Constructing the Political Spectacle*, chap. 4, "The Construction and Uses of Political Enemies."

9. Scenarios

1. This account is based on material in *SDX*, "Shen Dingyi xiansheng beici jingguo," and *MR* and *Shenbao*, August 30 to September 12, 1928.

2. Chen Gongmao, "Shen Dingyi qiren," p. 45.

3. *Shenbao*, September 3, 1928.

4. For discussion of this possibility, see *Shenbao*, September 3, 1928; Kong Xuexiong, "Dongxiang zizhi shimo," p. 387; and Chen Gongmao, "Shen Dingyi qiren," p. 46.

5. See *Shenbao*, September 3, 1928; Chen Gongmao, "Shen Dingyi qiren," p. 46.

6. "Silkworm Raising in Chekiang Province," *Chinese Economic Bulletin*, February 5, 1927, p. 72. See also "Agricultural Notes," *Chinese Economic Bulletin*, February 19, 1927, p. 103; and "Cocoon Crops of Chekiang," *Chinese Economic Bulletin*, May 24, 1930, pp. 261–63.

7. "Cocoon Trade in Chekiang," *Chinese Economic Journal*, December 1926, pp. 563–72.

8. Qian Fanglai, "Xinhai fengyunzhongde Cheng xianzhi shi," p. 199.

9. Chen Gongmao, "Shen Dingyi qiren," pp. 45–46.

10. Ibid., p. 46.

11. Schoppa, "Contours of Revolution in a Chinese County," p. 783.

12. Cao Juren, *Wo yu wode shijie*, p. 179, and Gao Yuetian, "Shen Dingyi xianshengde yisheng," p. 11.

13. Kong Xuexiong, "Dongxiang zizhi shimo," p. 340.

14. Chen Gongmao, "Shen Dingyi qiren," p. 45.

15. *Shenbao*, December 3, 1928.

16. *Shenbao*, February 20, 1929.

17. *Shenbao*, December 3, 1928.

18. Chen Gongmao, "Shen Dingyi qiren," p. 46.

19. Those who charge that the Communists were involved are all strong supporters of the Guomindang. See Gao Yuetian, "Shen Dingyi xianshengde yisheng", p. 11; and *MR*, August 30, 1928.

20. *MR*, August 30, 1928.

21. Schoppa, "Contours of Revolution in a Chinese County," p. 784.

22. Chen Gongmao, "Shen Dingyi qiren," p. 44, and Xu Xingzhi, "Dang chengliu shiqi Zhejiangde gongnong yundong," p. 43. See also, however, the implication of Guomindang involvement in Ruan Yicheng (Guomindang loyalist), "Shen Xuanlu," p. 18. He says, "After I came to Taiwan, Mr. Huang Jilu (who had been with Shen at the Western Hills meeting) whose personal exchanges were very sincere, asked me many times if I knew the facts of the case. I said that I really did not. Huang harbored doubts about whether people at the Zhejiang party bureau were involved. I said there was no proof and would not dare jump to a conclusion."

23. *Shenbao*, November 26, 1927, and January 28, 1928.

24. *Shenbao*, May 22, 1928.

25. Chen Gongmao, "Shen Dingyi qiren," p. 45.

26. *Shenbao*, January 7, 1928.

27. Kong Xuexiong, "Dongxiang zizhi shimo," p. 341; interview with Shen Jianyun, June 9, 1993.

28. *SDX*, p. 14.

29. *Shenbao*, September 2, 1928.

30. Wang Ke-wen, "The Kuomintang in Transition," pp. 148–61, 179, 200, and 211.

31. *Shenbao*, September 2, 1928.

32. Chen Gongmao, "Shen Dingyi qiren," pp. 44–45.

33. Xu Xingzhi, "Dang chengliu shiqi Zhejiangde gongnong yundong," p. 43.

34. Chen Gongmao, "Shen Dingyi qiren," p. 45.

35. *MR*, August 31, 1928.

36. *Shenbao*, September 2, 1928.

37. *MR*, August 31, 1928.

38. Chen Gongmao, "Shen Dingyi qiren," p. 45.

39. Ibid., p. 44.

40. *Shenbao*, September 2, 1928.

41. *MR*. September 3, 1928; Chen Gongmao, "Shen Dingyi qiren," p. 45.

42. Chen Gongmao, "Shen Dingyi qiren," p. 46.

43. Hong Ruijian, *Zhejiang zhi erwu jianzu*.

44. Personal letter to author, dated June 30, 1993.

45. Weigert, Teitge, and Teitge, *Society and Identity*, p. 31.

10. Shen and the Chinese Revolution of the 1920s

1. The revolution of 1911 had never gotten beyond this enemy-defining stage. The revolutionaries focused on overthrowing the Manchus; and within five months they were gone, the revolutionaries not having time to set forth

clearly and work through their ultimate goals. Although Sun's Revolutionary Alliance had indeed called for certain goals, the means by which they were to have been realized were not clear.

2. Michael J. Watts notes that identity in general is "labile and sliding." See "Space for Everything (A Commentary)," p. 124.

3. J. Clyde Mitchell, "The Concepts and Use of Social Networks," p. 24, argues that networks based on the traditional locality "were multiplex and the circuit of relations had a tendency to become closed." He quotes J. A. Barnes's description of such networks as having a "tight mesh."

4. See the arguments in George Revill, "Reading *Rosehill*: Community, Identity, and Inner-City Derby," pp. 119–20. Though Revill discusses community, his description is also appropriate for networks: they "have a part to play in the way people think about themselves, in the construction of subjectivity, and in the production of personal identity."

5. See Schoppa, *Chinese Elites and Political Change*, pp. 145–57.

6. The phrase is William Rowe's in *Hankow: Commerce and Society in a Chinese City, 1796–1889*, p. 213.

7. See Mary Rankin's comments on the locality and public identity in "Some Observations on a Chinese Public Sphere," p. 165.

8. See the statements on this idea in Michael Keith and Steve Pile, "Conclusion: Towards New Radical Geographies," p. 225.

9. See the comments by James Clifford in "On Ethnographic Allegory," as quoted in Akhil Gupta and James Ferguson, "Beyond 'Culture': Space, Identity, and the Politics of Difference," p. 9.

10. J. A. Barnes, *Social Networks*, p. 19.

11. Jonathan Friedman, "Myth, History, and Political Identity," p. 194.

12. Timothy Garton Ash, "Refolution in Hungary and Poland."

Bibliography

Works of Shen Dingyi

In the first section of this bibliography I have listed only those works that are cited in the text. In the second section I have selected others of Shen's writings that were particularly important in interpreting him and the 1920s revolution; they are selected from a large corpus of essays, poems, and recorded speeches, all of which informed my understanding of Shen. The majority of his writings are found in *Xingqi pinglun* (*Weekly Review*) in 1919–20, in *Minguo ribao* (*Republican Daily News*), and in its supplement *Juewu* (*Awakening*) from 1919 through 1924. Shen's poetry and essays from 1925 until his death have been lost.

WORKS CITED

"Bei chuang feng yu" [Wind and rain at the north window]. *Juewu*, June 26, 1921.
"Da Jiming" [Answering Jiming]. *Juewu*, February 12, 1920.
"Du Dabaide 'Duijing'" [On reading Liu Dabai's "Facing the Mirror"]. *Juewu*, September 20, 1920.
"Funu jiefang" [Women's liberation]. *Juewu*, September 15, 1920.
"Gege bu zhidao" [Older brother doesn't know]. *Xingqi pinglun*, February 15, 1920.
"Gongdu huzhu tuan" [Work-study mutual aid group]. *Xingqi pinglun*, February 8, 1920.
"Gongren yue" [The song of the worker]. *Xingqi pinglun*, January 11, 1920.

"Gu lao touzi di mishi" [Gu Lao Touzi's secret history]. *Juewu*, June 23, 1921.

"Gua yu Rihuo" [Watermelons and Japanese goods]. *Xingqi pinglun*, September 14, 1919.

"Haibian youyong" [Swimming at the beach]. *Xingqi pinglun*, October 10, 1919.

"Huibo" [Ripples]. *Xingqi pinglun*, June 6, 1920.

"Jieshao 'gongdu huzhu tuan'" [Introducing work-study mutual aid groups]. *Xingqi pinglun*, December 21, 1919.

"Jingzheng yu huzhu" [Competition and mutual aid]. *Xingqi pinglun*, July 13, 1919.

"Ju" [Chrysanthemums]. *Juewu*, November 3, 1920.

"Liubie liuE tongzhiminde yifeng xin" [A letter to comrades studying in Russia and elsewhere].*Juewu*, January 1, 1924.

"Mingyi zhong? Shishi zhong?" [Is the name or the deed more important?]. *Xingqi pinglun*, August 24, 1919.

"Ni xian wo chuo?" [Do you dislike the dirty?]. *Juewu*, March 25, 1920.

"Nongmin zijue" [Farmer self-determination]. In *Yaqian nongmin yundong*. Beijing, 1987.

"Pengyou? Jie?" [Friend? robbed?]. *Xingqi pinglun*, October 10, 1919.

"Qingkan minzhuguode xin falu" [Request to see a democracy's new laws]. *Xingqi pinglun*, July 27, 1919.

"Rensheng wenti" [Questions about life]. *Juewu*, January 5, 1921.

"Shanghai bagongde jianglai" [The future of the Shanghai strike]. *Xingqi pinglun*, June 15, 1919.

"Shei nide pengyou?" [Who is your friend?]. In *Yaqian nongmin yundong*. Beijing, 1987.

"Shei shi shuai? Shei shi di?" [Who is the leader? Who is the enemy?]. *Xingqi pinglun*, September 28, 1919.

"Sheng he si" [Life and death]. *Juewu*, October 14, 1920.

"Shui che" [Waterwheels]. *Juewu*, August 8, 1921.

"Si" [Death]. *Juewu*, January 1, 1922.

"Suibian tan" [Random talk]. *Xingqi pinglun*, June 8 and 15, 1919; July 13 and 20, 1919; August 10 and 17, 1919.

"Suiyang chuan Guangzhou boan" [Reaching the Guangzhou shore]. *Juewu*, February 2, 1921.

"Ta jiushi ni; ni jiushi wo" [He really is you; you really are I]. *Xingqi pinglun*, November 23, 1919.

"Tanjiang pianying" [Traces collapsing into the river]. *Juewu*, May 6, 1923.

"Toushi yihoude 'mao'" [The cat after stealing the food]. *Juewu*, November 8, 1921.

"Wei shenmo?" [Why?]. *Xingqi pinglun*, August 31, 1919.

"Wen xun" [To hear of the news]. *Juewu*, March 8, 1923.

"Wo zuo 'ren' de fuqin" [The meaning of fatherhood]. *Xingqi pinglun*, December 7, 1919.

"Xing yu hai" [Star and sea]. *Juewu*, March 2, 1922.

"Xixing yu yurou" [Sacrifice and fish and pork]. *Xingqi pinglun*, September 7, 1919.

"Xue" [Blood]. *Xingqi pinglun*, September 21, 1919.

"Xuexiao zizhide shenghuo" [The life of school self-government]. *Xingqi pinglun*, November 2, 1919.

"Yanzi fei" [Swallows fly]. *Juewu*, September 9, 1921.

"Yaqian nongmin xiehui jiesan hou" [After the dissolution of the Yaqian Farmers Association]. In *Yaqian nongmin yundong*. Xiaoshan, 1985.

"Ye you Shanghai you suojian" [What you see walking at night in Shanghai]. *Xingqi pinglun*, November 23, 1919.

"Yi nian" [A thought]. *Xingqi pinglun*, June 15, 1919.

"Yi ye" [One night]. *Juewu*, September 6, 1920.

"Yige qingniande meng" [A youthful dream]. *Juewu*, April 1, 1920.

"Yu" [Ignorance]. *Minguo ribao*, January 13, 1922.

"Zenmoyang hao?" [In what way good?]. *Xingqi pinglun*, February 22, 1920.

"Zhonghua minguo jichu zai nali?" [Where is the foundation of the Republic of China?] *Xingqi pinglun*, October 26, 1919.

"Zui" [Drunk]. *Juewu*, May 12, 1922.

SIGNIFICANT WORKS NOT CITED IN NOTES

"Ah Erde erzi" [The son of Ah Er]. *Juewu*, August 30, 1920.

"Ai Xiangjiang" [Grieving over the closure of the *Xiang River Review*]. *Xingqi pinglun*, August 3, 1919.

"Ai Zhixin" [Mourning Zhu Zhixin]. *Juewu*, October 15, 1920.

"Bi yu qiang" [Pens and guns]. *Xingqi pinglun*, August 24, 1919.

"Boli chuang" [Glass window]. *Xingqi pinglun*, January 1, 1920.

"Chongtian ren" [The farmer]. *Xingqi pinglun*, July 20, 1919.

"Chule" [Gone]. *Juewu*, February 28, 1922.

"Chuque qingnian wu xiwang" [Do away with youthful hopelessness]. *Xingqi pinglun*, June 29, 1919.

"Diguo zhuyide jihuo re jing le" [Imperialism's rare commodity incites the capital]. *Minguo ribao*, October 25, 1924.

"Duiyu jiaoshiyuan bagongde ganxiang" [My impressions about educators going on strike]. *Xingqi pinglun*, January 11, 1920.

"Fuweng ku" [Rich man's weeping]. *Xingqi pinglun*, January 11, 1920.

"Gao you jun" [Proclaiming a friendly army]. *Minguo ribao*, November 4, 1924.

"Geming yu rensheng" [Revolution and life]. *Juewu*, May 8, 1925.

"Guang" [Light]. *Xingqi pinglun*, September 7, 1919.

"Heping meng—xingle ba!" [Dreams of peace—Wake up!] *Minguo ribao*, October 16, 1924.

"Hu hua" [Protect the flowers]. *Juewu*, October 28, 1921.

"Hu-Hang yeche zhong" [On the overnight train from Shanghai to Hangzhou]. *Juewu*, October 10, 1921.

"Hunjia wenti" [The question of marriage]. *Xingqi pinglun*, December 7, 1919.

"Huo hua" [Sparks]. *Juewu*, January 1, 1922.

"Huo menshen" [Living door gods]. *Xingqi pinglun*, October 26, 1919.

"Jianglaide wenti" [Future problems]. *Xingqi pinglun*, October 10, 1919.

"Jiaoyu yu jingji" [Education and finance]. Presentation at Zhejiang First Normal School on October 9, 1921. Printed in *Xuanlu wencun*.

"Jiaoyudi shehuihua" [Socializing education]. *Juewu*, May 7, 1922.

"Kaoshi yu biye" [Examinations and graduation]. *Xingqi pinglun*, February 22, 1920.

"Liangge xiaoxuesheng tan hua" [Conversation of two elementary students]. *Juewu*, December 20, 1920.

"Meiguo gongshi Rui-en-shide hua yu Zhonghua minguode xianfa" [American Ambassador Reinsch's talk and the constitution of the Republic of China]. *Xingqi pinglun*, September 21, 1919.

"Nongjia" [Farmers]. *Xingqi pinglun*, January 18, 1920.

"Nongjia yefan qianhou" [At the time of the farmer's evening meal]. *Juewu*, July 3, 1921.

"Nuzi jiefang cong nali zuoqi?" [Where do we start with women's liberation?]. Printed in *Xuanlu wencun*.

"Pa si ma?" [Do you fear death?]. *Xingqi pinglun*, November 9, 1919.

"Pumie fan geming" [Get rid of the anti-revolutionaries]. *Minguo ribao*, October 20, 1924.

"Qian" [Money]. *Xingqi pinglun*, January 1, 1920.

"Qiantude deng" [The future light]. *Xingqi pinglun*, August 17, 1919.

"Qingniande shehui cong nali zuoqi?" [Where do we start to build a society of youth?]. *Xingqi pinglun*, April 4, 1920.

"'Ren' yu 'wu'" [People and animals]. *Xingqi pinglun*, August 24, 1919.

"Sha bian bing" [Killing changes a soldier]. *Juewu*, June 23, 1921.

"Shei neng ti junfa zuo zhanbao?" [Who can make the guarantee to take the place of the warlords?] *Minguo ribao*, October 27, 1924.

"Shengyihui yu shengyihuide bijiao" [A comparison of provincial assemblies]. *Xingqi pinglun*, December 21, 1919.

"Shenjizhongde miao yin" [Marvelous sounds amid intense silence]. *Juewu*, May 8, 1922.

"Shi yu laodong" [Poetry and labor]. *Xingqi pinglun*, May 1, 1920.

"Shizi" [Pebbles]. *Juewu*, August 21, 1921.

"Shuang shi jie" [Double Ten]. *Juewu*, October 10, 1921.

"Tan xuanju" [Speaking of elections]. *Juewu*, December 15, 1920.

"Ti Zhejiang chao zhaopian" [On a photograph of the Zhejiang Bore]. *Juewu*, November 4, 1920.

"Women zai bu yao lieqiangde zanzhu" [Again we do not want the approval of the Powers]. *Minguo ribao*, November 1, 1924.

"Xiang" [Thoughts]. *Xingqi pinglun*, August 24, 1919.

"Xie Chucang du Huang Hai'" [Accompanying Ye Chucang in crossing the Yellow Sea]. *Juewu*, January 15, 1921.

"Xin jiu wenxue yige dazhanchang" [The great battlefield in the struggle between old and new literature]. *Xingqi pinglun*, November 16, 1919.

"Xin xian duanhoude wei xiao" [The small laugh after the breaking of the heart strings]. *Juewu*, January 12, 1922.

"Xue ji" [Snow boundary]. *Juewu*, January 9, 1921.

"Xuesheng yu wenhua yundong" [Students and the new culture movement]. *Xingqi pinglun*, February 29, 1920.

"Yeqiao ren ying" [The image of a man on Ye bridge]. *Juewu*, October 16, 1921.

"Yige xiao haizi he Ah Ben" [A child and Ah Ben]. *Juewu*, January 10, 1921.

"Yu" [Rain]. *Xingqi pinglun*, February 1, 1920.

"Zai Hangzhou" [At Hangzhou]. *Juewu*, March 3, 1922.

"Zai shiju biandongde jihuishang guomin ying youde yaoqiu" [What the nation must seek at the opportunity of a changing situation]. *Minguo ribao*, October 26, 1924.

"Zhejiang Xiaoshan xian shuizai zhuangguang" [The flooding situation in Xiaoshan county]. *Minguo ribao*, October 6, 1922.

"Zhenli he jinqian" [Truth and money]. *Juewu*, October 1, 1920.

"Zhenya fan geming hou zhian wentide shangque" [The discussions about the question of establishing peace after the anti-revolutionaries are crushed]. *Minguo ribao*, October 24, 1924.

"Zhishi Zhejiang zizhi zhengfu yingzoude lu" [Pointing out the path of provincial self-government that Zhejiang should follow]. *Minguo ribao*, October 18, 1924.

"Zhongguode guoji diwei yu shiju" [China's international status and situation]. *Minguo ribao*, November 2, 1924.

Primary and Secondary Works

"Agricultural Notes." *Chinese Economic Bulletin*, February 19, 1927, 63.

Alitto, Guy. *The Last Confucian*. Berkeley and Los Angeles: University of California Press, 1979.

All about Shanghai and Environs. Shanghai: The University Press, 1934–35.

Ames, Roger T., ed., with Wimal Dissanayake and Thomas P. Kasulis. *Self as Person in Asian Theory and Practice*. Albany: State University of New York Press, 1994.

Ash, Timothy Garton. "Refolution in Hungary and Poland." *New York Review of Books* 36, no. 13 (August 17, 1989): 9.

Bailey, F. G. "Gifts of Poison." In F. G. Bailey, ed., *Gifts and Poison: The Politics of Reputation*. Oxford: Oxford University Press, 1971.

———. *Stratagems and Spoils: A Social Anthropology of Politics*. New York: Schocken Books, 1969.

Bao Huiceng. "Gongchandang diyici quanguo daibiao huiyi qianhoude huiyi" [Recollections of the time of the first National Congress]. In *"Yida" qianhou.* Vol. 2. Beijing, 1980.

Barnes, J. A. "Networks and Political Process." In Marc J. Swartz, ed., *Local-Level Politics.* Chicago: University of Chicago Press, 1968.

———. *Social Networks.* N.p.: Addison-Wesley Publishing Company, 1972.

Barnett, Eugene. "As I Look Back: Recollections of Growing Up in America's Southland and of Twenty-Six Years in Pre-communist China, 1888–1936." N.p., n.d.

Bergère, Marie-Claire. *The Golden Age of the Chinese Bourgeoisie, 1911–1937.* Translated by Janet Lloyd. Cambridge: Cambridge University Press, 1989.

———. "The Shanghai Bankers' Association, 1915–1927: Modernization and the Institutionalization of Local Solidarities." In Frederic Wakeman, Jr., and Wen-hsin Yeh, eds., *Shanghai Sojourners.* Berkeley: Institute of East Asian Studies, University of California, 1992.

Bernhardt, Kathryn. *Rents, Taxes, and Peasant Resistance: The Lower Yangzi Region, 1840–1950.* Stanford: Stanford University Press, 1992.

Boissevain, Jeremy. "An Exploration of Two First-Order Zones." In Jeremy Boissevain and J. Clyde Mitchell, eds., *Network Analysis: Studies in Human Interaction.* The Hague: Mouton, 1973.

Bondi, Liz. "Locating Identity Politics." In Michael Keith and Steve Pile, eds., *Place and the Politics of Identity.* London: Routledge, 1993.

Boorman, Howard L., ed. *Biographical Dictionary of Republican China.* 4 vols. New York: Columbia University Press, 1970.

Brown, S. C. *Objectivity and Cultural Divergence.* Cambridge: Cambridge University Press, 1984.

Cao Juren. "Dao Shen Xuanlu xiansheng" [Lamenting Mr. Shen Xuanlu]. *Juewu,* September 3, 1928.

———. *Wo yu wode shijie* [My world and I]. Hong Kong, 1971.

Carlstein, Tommy, Don Parkes, and Nigel Thrift, eds. *Human Activity and Time Geography.* New York: John Wiley, 1978.

———. *Making Sense of Time.* New York: John Wiley, 1978.

Chang Kuo-t'ao [Zhang Guotao]. *The Rise of the Chinese Communist Party, 1921–1927.* 2 vols. Lawrence: University of Kansas Press, 1971.

Chen Gongmao. "Shen Dingyi qiren" [A biographical sketch of Shen Dingyi]. In *Zhejiang wenshi ziliao xuanji* [A collection of historical materials on Zhejiang]. Vol. 21. Hangzhou, 1982.

Chen Gongpei. "Huiyi dangde faqi zu he fu faqin gongyingxue deng qingguang" [Remembering the circumstances of the party's formation and going to the Faqin Engineering School]. In *"Yida" qianhou.* Vol 2. Beijing, 1980.

Chen, Joseph T. *The May Fourth Movement in Shanghai.* Leiden: E. J. Brill, 1971.

Chen Juemu. "Liu Dabai xiansheng zhi shengping" [A brief biographical sketch of Liu Dabai]. In *Zhejiang wenshi ziliao xuanji* [A collection of historical materials on Zhejiang]. Vol. 43. Hangzhou, 1990.

Chen Shaokang, Luo Meiling, and Tian Ziyu. "Li Hanjun." In *Zhong-gongdangshi renwu chuan* [Biographies from Chinese Communist Party history]. Vol. 11. N.p., n.d.

Chen Tianxi. *Zengding Dai Jitao xiansheng biannian chuanji* [A supplement to Dai Jitao's chronological biography]. Taibei, 1967.

Chen Wangdao. "Huiyi dang chengli shiqide yixie qingguang" [Remembering a few things about the time of the establishment of the party]. In *"Yida" qianhou.* Vol. 2. Beijing, 1980.

Chen Xieshu. "Shaoxing guangfushi jianwen" [Experiences at the time of the revolution in Shaoxing]. In *Jindai shi ziliao.* No. 1. Beijing, 1954.

Cheng Hanchang. "Zhongguo xiandai nongmin yundong zuizao fasheng yu heshi hedi?" [Where and when was the earliest contemporary Chinese farmers' movement?]. *Jiaoxue yu yanjiu* [Educational study and research] 4 (1980): 55–57.

Chesneaux, Jean. *The Chinese Labor Movement, 1919–1927.* Stanford: Stanford University Press, 1968.

Chie Nakane. *Japanese Society.* New York: Penguin, 1970.

Chinese Economic Bulletin, 1927–30.

Chinese Economic Journal, 1926–28.

Chu Fucheng. "Zhejiang xinhai geming jishi" [An account of the 1911 revolution in Zhejiang]. In *Gesheng guangfu.* Vol. 2. Taibei, 1962.

Clayton, E. H. *Heaven Below.* New York: Prentice-Hall, 1944.

Clifford, James. "On Ethnographic Allegory." In James Clifford and George Marcus, eds., *Writing Culture: The Poetics and Politics of Ethnography.* Berkeley and Los Angeles: University of California Press, 1986.

Clifford, James and George Marcus, eds. *Writing Culture: The Poetics and Politics of Ethnography.* Berkeley and Los Angeles: University of California Press, 1986.

"Cocoon Crops of Chekiang." *Chinese Economic Bulletin,* May 24, 1930, 261–63.

"Cocoon Trade in Chekiang." *Chinese Economic Journal,* December 1926, 563–72.

Cohen, Abner. *The Politics of Elite Culture: Explorations in the Dramaturgy of Power in a Modern African Society.* Berkeley and Los Angeles: University of California Press, 1981.

Cohen, Myron. "Being Chinese: The Peripheralization of Traditional Identity." *Daedalus* 120, no. 2 (Spring 1991): 113–34.

Crossley, Pamela Kyle. *Orphan Warriors.* Princeton: Princeton University Press, 1990.

Crow, Carl. *The Travelers' Handbook for China.* San Francisco: San Francisco News Company, 1913.

Dai Jitao. *Dai Jitao xiansheng wencun* [Collected works of Mr. Dai Jitao]. Taibei, 1959.

Dangshi yanjiu ziliao [Research materials for party history]. 2 vols. Chengdu, 1981.

Darnton, Robert. *The Great Cat Massacre.* New York: Oxford University Press, 1985.

Darwent, C. E. *Shanghai: A Handbook for Travellers and Residents.* Shanghai: Kelly and Walsh, 1920.

Dirlik, Arif. *The Origins of Chinese Communism.* New York: Oxford University Press, 1989.

Duara, Prasenjit. *Culture, Power, and the State: Rural North China, 1900–1940.* Stanford: Stanford University Press, 1988.

Eastman, Lloyd E. "The May Fourth Movement as a Historical Turning Point: Ecological Exhaustion, Militarization, and Other Causes of China's Modern Crisis." In Kenneth Lieberthal, Joyce Kallgren, Roderick MacFarquhar, and Frederic Wakeman, Jr., eds. *Perspectives on Modern China: Four Anniversaries.* Armonk, N.Y.: M. E. Sharpe, 1991.

Edelman, Murray. *Constructing the Political Spectacle.* Chicago: University of Chicago Press, 1988.

———. *Political Language.* New York: Academic Press, 1977.

———. *Politics as Symbolic Action.* Chicago: Markham Publishing Company, 1971.

Eisenstadt, S. N., and L. Roniger. *Patrons, Clients, and Friends.* Cambridge: Cambridge University Press, 1984.

Elman, Benjamin A. "Political, Social, and Cultural Reproduction via Civil Service Examinations in Late Imperial China." *Journal of Asian Studies* 50, no. 1 (February 1991): 7–28.

Fei Xiaotong. *From the Soil: The Foundations of Chinese Society.* Translated by Gary G. Hamilton and Wang Zheng. Berkeley and Los Angeles: University of California Press, 1992.

Feigon, Lee. *Chen Duxiu: Founder of the Communist Party.* Princeton: Princeton University Press, 1983.

Fitzgerald, John. "The Misconceived Revolution: State and Society in China's Nationalist Revolution, 1923–26." *Journal of Asian Studies* 49, no. 2 (May 1990): 323–43.

Franck, Harry A. *Roving through South China.* New York: The Century Company, 1925.

Friedman, Jonathan. "Myth, History, and Political Identity." *Cultural Anthropology* 7, no. 2 (May 1992): 194–210.

Fu Binran. "Wusi qianhou" [At the time of May Fourth]. In *Wusi yundong huiyilu.* Vol. 2. Beijing, 1979.

Galbiati, Fernando. *P'eng P'ai and the Hai-Lu-feng Soviet.* Stanford: Stanford University Press, 1985.

Gao Yuetian. "Shen Dingyi xianshengde yisheng" [Mr. Shen Dingyi's life]. Parts 1 and 2. *Zhejiang yuekan* [Zhejiang monthly] 4, no. 3 (March 1972): 5–8; no. 4 (April 1972): 8–13.

Ge Jing'en. "Xinhai geming zai Zhejiang" [The 1911 revolution in Zhejiang]. In *Xinhai geming huiyilu.* Vol. 4. Beijing, 1961–63.

Geertz, Clifford. *The Interpretation of Cultures.* New York: Basic Books, 1973.

Gellner, Ernest. *Cause and Meaning in the Social Sciences.* London: Routledge and Kegan Paul, 1973.

———. *Patrons and Clients in Mediterranean Societies.* London: Duckworth, 1977.

Geming renwu zhi [Records of revolutionary personalities]. Edited by Dang-shi hui. Taibei, 1969—.

Gendai Shina jimmeikan [Biographical directory of contemporary Chinese]. Compiled by Gaimushō jōhōbu [Public Information Bureau, Ministry of Foreign Affairs]. Tokyo, 1928.

Gesheng guangfu [The revolution in the provinces]. In *Zhonghua minguo kaiguo wushinian wenxian* [Documents on the fiftieth anniversary of the founding of the Republic of China]. Edited by Zhonghua minguo kaiguo wushinian wenxian bianzuan weiyuanhui [Committee on the compilation of documents on the fiftieth anniversary of the founding of the Republic]. 3 vols. Taibei, 1962.

Gilmartin, Christina. "Mobilizing Women: The Early Experiences of the Chinese Communist Party, 1920–1927." Ph.D. dissertation. University of Pennsylvania, 1986.

Goodman, Bryna. "New Culture, Old Habits: Native Place Organization and the May Fourth Movement." In Frederic Wakeman, Jr., and Wen-hsin Yeh, eds., *Shanghai Sojourners*. Berkeley: Institute of East Asian Studies, University of California, 1992.

Gordon, Chad. "Self-Conceptions: Configurations of Content." In Chad Gordon and Kenneth J. Gergen, eds., *The Self in Social Interaction*. Vol. 1. New York: John Wiley, 1968.

Gregory, Derek. "Social Change and Spatial Structures." In Tommy Carlstein, Don Parkes, and Nigel Thrift, eds., *Making Sense of Time*. New York: John Wiley, 1978.

Gupta, Akhil, and James Ferguson. "Beyond 'Culture': Space, Identity, and the Politics of Difference." *Cultural Anthropology* 7, no. 1 (February 1992): 6–23.

Han Jingyi. "Cha Renwei beibu jingguo" [The arrest of Cha Renwei]. In *Zhejiang wenshi ziliao xuanji* [A collection of historical materials on Zhejiang]. Vol. 2. Hangzhou, 1962.

Hayford, Charles. *To the People: James Yen and Village China*. New York: Columbia University Press, 1990.

Hofheinz, Roy, Jr. *The Broken Wave: The Chinese Communist Peasant Movement, 1922–1928*. Cambridge: Harvard University Press, 1977.

Hong Ruijian. *Zhejiang zhi erwu jianzu* [Zhejiang's 25 percent rent reduction]. Nanjing, 1935.

Honig, Emily. "Migrant Culture in Shanghai: In Search of a Subei Identity." In Frederic Wakeman, Jr., and Wen-hsin Yeh, eds., *Shanghai Sojourners*. Berkeley: Institute of East Asian Studies, University of California, 1992.

Jiang Danshu. "'Fei Xiao' yu Zhejiang diyi shifande fan fengjian douzheng" ["Decry filial piety" and the struggle against feudalism at Zhejiang's First Normal School]. In *Wusi yundong huiyilu*. Vol. 2. Beijing, 1979.

Jiang Tianyi. "Beifa qianhou Zhejiang Guomindang huodongde diandi huiyi" [Memories of small points concerning the Guomindang movement in Zhejiang before and after the Northern Expedition]. In *Zhejiang wenshi ziliao xuanji* [A collection of historical materials on Zhejiang]. Vol. 2. Hangzhou, 1962.

————. "Diyici guogong hezuo shiqi Guomindang Zhejiang sheng dangbu huodong zhuiji" [A record of the Zhejiang provincial party bureau during the first period of cooperation between the Guomindang and the Communist party]. In *Sun Zhongshan yu Zhejiang*. Hangzhou, 1986.

Jindai shi ziliao [Materials on modern Chinese history]. Compiled by Zhongguo kexue yuan lishi yanjiusuo [The history research bureau of the Chinese Academy of Science]. 8 vols. Beijing, 1954–61.

Johnson, David. "Communication, Class, and Consciousness in Late Imperial China." In David Johnson, Andrew J. Nathan, and Evelyn Rawski, eds., *Popular Culture in Late Imperial China*. Berkeley and Los Angeles: University of California Press, 1985.

Juewu [Awakening]. Shanghai, 1919–24.

Keith, Michael, and Steve Pile. "Conclusion: Towards New Radical Geographies." In Michael Keith and Steve Pile, eds., *Place and the Politics of Identity*. London: Routledge, 1993.

————. "Introduction, Part 1: The Politics of Space." In Michael Keith and Steve Pile, eds., *Place and the Politics of Identity*. London: Routledge, 1993.

————. "Introduction, Part 2: The Place of Politics." In Michael Keith and Steve Pile, eds., *Place and the Politics of Identity*. London: Routledge, 1993.

————, eds. *Place and the Politics of Identity*. London: Routledge, 1993.

King, Ambrose Yeo-chi. "Kuan-hsi and Network Building: A Sociological Interpretation." *Daedalus* 120, no. 2 (Spring 1991): 63–84.

Kong Xuexiong. "Dongxiang zizhi shimo" [The complete story of the East Township self-government]. In *Zhongguo jinri nongcun yundong* [The rural movements in China today]. N.p., 1934.

Lai Weiliang. "Xinhai gongchengying Hangzhou qiyi ji" [A record of the engineers' battalion in the 1911 Hangzhou uprising]. In *Jindai shi ziliao*. No. 6. Beijing, 1957.

————. "Zhejun guangfu Hangzhou he chiyuan Nanjing qinli ji" [A personal account of the Zhejiang army at Hangzhou in the 1911 revolution and the rapid assistance at Nanjing]. In *Xinhai geming huiyilu*. Vol. 4. Beijing, 1961–63.

Lapidus, Ira. "Hierarchies and Networks: A Comparison of Chinese and Islamic Societies." In Frederic Wakeman, Jr., and Carolyn Grant, eds., *Conflict and Control in Late Imperial China*. Berkeley and Los Angeles: University of California Press, 1975.

Lary, Diana. *Region and Nation: The Kwangsi Clique in Chinese Politics, 1925–1937*. Cambridge: Cambridge University Press, 1974.

————. *Warlord Soldiers*. Cambridge: Cambridge University Press, 1985.

Lee, Leo Ou-fan. "In Search of Modernity: Some Reflections on a New Mode of Consciousness in Twentieth Century Chinese History and Literature." In Paul Cohen and Merle Goldman, eds., *Ideas across Culture*. Cambridge: Harvard University Press, 1990.

————. *Voices from the Iron House: A Study of Lu Xun*. Bloomington: Indiana University Press, 1987.

Lefebvre, Henri. *The Production of Space*. Oxford: Basil Blackwell, 1991.

"Legend of the White Snake." In *Collection of Myths about Madame White Snake*. Vol. 135 of *Minsu congshu* [A compendium of folklore]. Taibei, 1951.

Li Da. "Zhongguo gongchandang chengli shiqide sixiang douzheng qing-guang" [Ideological struggle at the time of the establishment of the Chinese Communist party]. In *"Yida" qianhou*. Vol. 2. Beijing, 1980.

————. "Zhongguo gongchandang faqi he diyici, dierci daibiao dahui jing-guode huiyi" [Recollections of the founding of the Chinese Communist party and the first and second party congresses]. In *"Yida" qianhou*. Vol. 2. Beijing, 1980.

Li Tsung-jen [Li Zongren] and Tong Te-kong. *The Memoirs of Li Tsung-jen*. Boulder: Westview Press, 1979.

Li Yunhan. *Cong ronggong dao qingdang* [From cooperation with the Communist party to the party purge]. Taibei, 1966.

Li Zhengtong. "Xinhai geming yihou shiliuniande Zhejiang zhengju" [The government situation in Zhejiang in the sixteen years after the 1911 revolution]. In *Zhejiang xinhai geming huiyilu*. Vol. 27 of *Zhejiang wenshi ziliao xuanji*. Hangzhou, 1984.

Lieberthal, Kenneth, Joyce Kallgren, Roderick MacFarquhar, and Frederic Wakeman, Jr., eds. *Perspectives on Modern China: Four Anniversaries*. Armonk, N.Y.: M. E. Sharpe, 1991.

Lin Weibao. "Yaqian yinxiang ji" [Impressions of Yaqian]. *Zhongguo nong-cun* [Rural China] 1, no. 7 (1935): 72–75.

Liu Dabai. "Zeng Shen Xuanlu qilu sishou" [A poem presented to Shen Xuanlu]. In Chen Juemu, "Liu Dabai xiansheng zhi shengping" [A brief biographical sketch of Liu Dabai]. In *Zhejiang wenshi ziliao xuanji* [A collection of historical materials on Zhejiang], vol. 43 (1990), 48–49.

Lu Gongwang. "Xinhai geming Zhejiang guangfu jishi" [An account of the 1911 revolution in Zhejiang]. In *Jindai shi ziliao*. No. 1. Beijing, 1954.

Lu Huangguang. "Xinhai Zhesheng guangfu qianhouzhi junzheng cangsang" [The vast changes in army administration before and after the 1911 revolution in Zhejiang]. *Zhejiang yuekan* [Zhejiang monthly] 1, no. 8 (1969): 8–9.

Lu Xun [Lu Hsun]. "The Misanthrope." In *Selected Stories of Lu Hsun*. Translated by Yang Hsien-yi and Gladys Yang. Beijing: Foreign Languages Press, 1972.

————. *Selected Works*. 4 vols. Beijing: Foreign Languages Press, 1956–60.

Lu Yichun and Ye Guangting. *Xihu manhua* [Random talks on West Lake]. Tianjin, 1982.

Ma Xulun. "Guanyu xinhai geming Zhejiang shengcheng guangfu jishide buchong ziliao" [Supplementary material on the 1911 revolution in Zhejiang's provincial capital]. In *Jindai shi ziliao*. No. 1. Beijing, 1957.

————. *Wo zai liushi sui yiqian* [Before I was sixty years old]. Shanghai, 1947.

————. "Wo zai xinhai zheyinian" [My activities in 1911]. In *Xinhai gem-ing huiyilu*. Vol. 1. Beijing, 1961–63.

Mao Dun [Shen Yanbing]. "Huiyi Shanghai gongchanzhuyi xiaozu" [Memories of the Shanghai Communist cell]. In *"Yida" qianhou*. Vol. 2. Beijing, 1980.

———. "Mao Dunde huiyi" [Mao Dun's recollections]. In *Yaqian nongmin yundong*. Beijing, 1987.

Marks, Robert. *Rural Revolution in South China: Peasants and the Making of History in Haifeng County, 1570–1930*. Madison: University of Wisconsin Press, 1984.

Mast, Herman, III. "An Intellectual Biography of Tai Chi-t'ao from 1891 to 1928." Ph.D. dissertation, University of Illinois, 1970.

Mast, Herman, III, and William G. Saywell. "Revolution Out of Tradition: The Political Ideology of Tai Chi-t'ao." *Journal of Asian Studies* 34, no. 1 (November 1974): 73–98.

McCord, Edward A. *The Power of the Gun: The Emergence of Modern Chinese Warlordism*. Berkeley and Los Angeles: University of California Press, 1993.

McDonald, Angus. *The Urban Origins of Rural Revolution*. Berkeley and Los Angeles: University of California Press, 1978.

Miner, Noel. "Chekiang: The Nationalists' Effort in Agrarian Reform and Construction, 1927–1937." Ph.D. dissertation, Stanford University, 1975.

Minguo ribao [Republican Daily News], 1915–29.

Minlibao [The People's Stand], 1911–13.

Mitchell, J. Clyde. "The Concept and Use of Social Networks." In J. Clyde Mitchell, ed., *Social Networks in Urban Situations*. Manchester: The University Press, 1969.

———, ed. *Social Networks in Urban Situations*. Manchester: The University Press, 1969.

Ni Weixiong. "Zhejiang xinchaode huiyi" [Recollections of the Zhejiang New Tide]. In *Wusi yundong huiyilu*. Vol 2. Beijing, 1979.

North China Herald and Supreme Court and Consular Gazette. Shanghai, 1917.

Pan Ling. *In Search of Old Shanghai*. Hong Kong: Joint Publishing Company, 1983.

Pan Nianzhi. "Da geming shiqi Zhejiangde fandui Guomindang youpai douzheng" [The struggle against the Guomindang right wing during the period of the 1920s revolution]. In *Zhejiang geming shiliao teji* [Special collection of historical materials on the revolution in Zhejiang]. Vol. 2. Hangzhou, 1980.

Peck, Graham. *Two Kinds of Time*. Boston: Houghton-Mifflin, Sentry Edition, 1967.

Perry, Elizabeth J. "Strikes among Shanghai Silk Weavers, 1927–1937: The Awakening of a Labor Aristocracy." In Frederic Wakeman, Jr., and Wenhsin Yeh, eds., *Shanghai Sojourners*. Berkeley: Institute of East Asian Studies, University of California, 1992.

Pomeranz, Kenneth. *The Making of a Hinterland: State, Society, and Economy in Inland North China, 1853–1937*. Berkeley and Los Angeles: University of California Press, 1993.

Potter, Sulamith Heins, and Jack M. Potter. *China's Peasants: The Anthropology of Revolution.* Cambridge: Cambridge University Press, 1990.

Qian Fanglai. "Xinhai fengyunzhongde Cheng xianzhi shi" [Famous persons in the 1911 revolution in the Cheng county gazetteer]. In *Cheng xian fengwu* [Customs of Cheng County]. Cheng county, Zhejiang, 1989.

Qian Gengshen. "Shen Dingyi xiansheng" [Mr. Shen Dingyi]. *Dongnan ribao* [Southeast Daily], January 4, 1945.

Qingdang shilu [A factual record of party purification]. Nanjing, 1928.

Qingdang yundong [The party purification movement]. Compiled by Qingdang yundong qijin hui [The radical purification society]. N.p., 1927–28.

Qingdang yundong [The party purification movement]. Compiled by Zhejiang sheng qingdang weiyuanhui [The Zhejiang provincial party purification committee]. N.p., n.d.

Qingdang yundong [The party purification movement]. Compiled by Zhongyang junshi zhengzhi xuexiao zhengzhibu [The political bureau of the Central military affairs and political school]. N.p., 1927.

Rankin, Mary Backus. *Early Chinese Revolutionaries: Radical Intellectuals in Shanghai and Chekiang, 1902–1911.* Cambridge: Harvard University Press, 1971.

———. *Elite Activism and Political Transformation in China: Zhejiang Province, 1865–1911.* Stanford: Stanford University Press, 1986.

———. "Some Observations on a Chinese Public Sphere." *Modern China* 19, no. 2 (April 1993): 158–82.

Rawski, Evelyn S. "Economic and Social Foundations of Late Imperial Culture." In David Johnson, Andrew J. Nathan, and Evelyn Rawski, eds., *Popular Culture in Late Imperial China.* Berkeley and Los Angeles: University of California Press, 1985.

Ren Wuxiong. "Guanyu Yu Xiusong lieshi" [Concerning martyr Yu Xiusong]. In *Dangshi yanjiu ziliao.* Vol. 2. Chengdu, 1981.

Returns of Trade and Trade Reports. Shanghai: Inspectorate General of the Maritime Customs, 1914.

Revill, George. "Reading *Rosehill*: Community, Identity, and Inner-City Derby." In Michael Keith and Steve Pile, eds., *Place and the Politics of Identity.* London: Routledge, 1993.

Rose, Arnold M. *Human Behavior and Social Processes.* Boston: Houghton-Mifflin, 1962.

Rowe, William T. *Hankow: Commerce and Society in a Chinese City, 1796–1889.* Stanford: Stanford University Press, 1984.

Ruan Xingcun, ed. *Ruan Xunbo xiansheng yiji* [The collected works of Mr. Ruan Xingcun]. 2 vols. Taibei, 1970.

Ruan Yicheng. *Sanju buli ben Hang* [Three periods of not leaving my home of Hangzhou]. Taibei, 1972.

———. "Shen Xuanlu." Parts 1 and 2. *Zhejiang yuekan* [Zhejiang monthly] 20, no. 228 (April 1988): 4–6; no. 229 (May 1988): 17–19.

———. "Xianjun Xunbo gong nianpu" [A biography by years of Mr. Xuan Xingcun]. In Ruan Xingcun, *Ruan Xunbo Xiansheng yiji* [The collected works of Mr. Ruan Xingcun]. Vol. 1. Taibei, 1970.

Sahlins, Marshall. *Culture and Practical Reason.* Chicago: University of Chicago Press, 1976.

Saich, Tony. *The Origins of the First United Front in China: The Role of Sneevliet (Alias Maring).* 2 vols. Leiden: E. J. Brill, 1991.

Schoppa, R. Keith. *Chinese Elites and Political Change: Zhejiang Province in the Early Twentieth Century.* Cambridge: Harvard University Press, 1982.

————. "Contours of Revolution in a Chinese County, 1900–1950," *Journal of Asian Studies* 51, no. 4 (November 1992): 770–96.

————. "Politics and Society in Chekiang, 1907–1927: Elite Power, Social Control, and the Making of a Province." Ph.D. dissertation, University of Michigan, 1975.

————. "Province and Nation: The Chekiang Provincial Autonomy Movement, 1917–1927." *Journal of Asian Studies* 36, no. 4 (August 1977): 661–74.

————. "Shen Dingyi and the Western Hills Group: 'What's a Man Like You Doing in a Group Like This?'" *Republican China* 16, no. 1 (November 1990): 35–50.

————. "Shen Dingyi in Opposition, 1921 and 1928." Unpublished paper presented at the Conference on Oppositional Politics in Twentieth Century China, Washington and Lee University, September, 1990.

Schwarcz, Vera. "No Solace from Lethe: History, Memory, and Cultural Identity in Twentieth Century China." *Daedalus* 120, no. 2 (Spring 1991): 159–79.

Schwartz, Benjamin I. "Notes on Conservatism in General and China in Particular." In Charlotte Furth, ed., *The Limits of Change.* Cambridge: Harvard University Press, 1976.

Shao Lizi. "Dang chengli qianhou yixie qingguang" [A few things about the situation during the period of the party's founding]. In *"Yida" qianhou.* Vol. 2. Beijing, 1980.

Shao Weizheng. "Yaqian nongmin xiehui shimo" [The complete story of the Yaqian farmers association]. In *Dangshi yanjiu ziliao* . Vol. 5. Chengdu, 1985.

Shaoxing xian xingzheng dier xingzheng huiyi tekan [Special publication of the second administrative conference of the Shaoxing county administration]. Shaoxing, 1946.

"Shen Dingyi xiansheng beici jingguo" [The assassination of Mr. Shen Dingyi]. N.p., n.d.

"Shen Dingyi xiansheng beinan aiqi" [Obituary notice following the killing of Mr. Shen Dingyi]. Edited by Shen Dingyi xiansheng xuehan zhisang weiyuanhui [The committee for covering the grief and managing the loss of Mr. Shen Dingyi]. In *Yaqian nongmin yundong.* Beijing, 1987.

Shen Dingyi xiansheng shilue [A brief biography of Mr. Shen Dingyi]. N.p., n.d.

Shenbao, 1923–30.

Shi Dazhong and Wang Siniu. "Shen Shuyan lai Dayi, Qianqing haozhao jianzu" [Uncle Word Shen comes to Dayi and Qianqing to call for rent reduction]. In *Yaqian nongmin yundong.* Beijing, 1987.

Shi Fuliang. "Wusi zai Hangzhou" [May Fourth in Hangzhou]. In *Wusi yundong huiyilu*. Vol. 2. Beijing, 1979.

———. "Zhongguo shehui zhuyi qingniantuan chengli qianhoude yixie qingguang" [A few things about the situation at the time of the founding of the Socialist Youth Corps]. In *"Yida" qianhou*. Vol. 2. Beijing, 1980.

Shibao [The Eastern Times], 1910–27.

Si Daoqing. "Xinhai geming Hangzhou guangfu bieji" [Another account of the 1911 revolution in Hangzhou]. In *Jindai shi ziliao*. No. 1. Beijing, 1954.

———. "Zhejun shibaniande huiyilu" [Recollections of eighteen years in the Zhejiang army]. In *Jindai shi ziliao*. No. 2. Beijing, 1957.

"Silkworm Raising in Chekiang Province." *Chinese Economic Bulletin*, February 5, 1927, 72.

Skinner, G. William. "Marketing and Social Structure in Rural China." *Journal of Asian Studies* 24, no. 1 (November 1964): 3–43; and 24, no. 2 (February 1965): 195–228.

———. "Regional Urbanization in Nineteenth Century China." In G. William Skinner, ed., *The City in Late Imperial China*. Stanford: Stanford University Press, 1977.

Soja, Edward. *Postmodern Geographies*. London: Verso, 1989.

Solomon, Robert C. "Recapturing Personal Identity." In Roger T. Ames, ed., *Self as Person in Asian Theory and Practice*. Albany: State University of New York Press, 1994.

Spence, Jonathan. *The Gate of Heavenly Peace*. New York: Viking, 1981.

———. *The Search for Modern China*. New York: W. W. Norton, 1990.

Stone, Gregory P. "Appearance and the Self." In Arnold M. Rose, ed., *Human Behavior and Social Processes*. Boston: Houghton-Mifflin, 1962.

Strand, David. *Rickshaw Beijing*. Berkeley and Los Angeles: University of California Press, 1989.

Strauss, Anselm L. *Mirrors and Masks: The Search for Identity*. Glencoe, Ill.: Free Press, 1959.

"Sun Zhongshan Hangzhouzhi xing" [Sun Yat-sen's Hangzhou travels]. In *Sun Zhongshan yu Zhejiang*. Hangzhou, 1986.

Sun Zhongshan yu Zhejiang [Sun Yat-sen and Zhejiang]. Vol. 4 of *Zhejiang xinhai geming huiyilu* [Recollections of the 1911 revolution in Zhejiang]. Hangzhou, 1986.

"Sun Zhongshan zai Hangzhoude yanshuo" [Sun Yat-sen's lectures in Hangzhou]. In *Sun Zhongshan yu Zhejiang*. Hangzhou, 1986.

Swartz, Marc J., Victor W. Turner, and Arthur Tuden, eds. *Political Anthropology*. Chicago: Aldine Publishing Company, 1966.

Tuan Yi-fu. "Space, Time, Place: A Humanistic Frame." In Tommy Carlstein, Don Parkes, and Nigel Thrift, eds., *Making Sense of Time*. New York: John Wiley, 1978.

Van de Ven, Hans J. *From Friend to Comrade: The Founding of the Chinese Communist Party, 1920–1927*. Berkeley and Los Angeles: University of California Press, 1991.

Vishnyakova-Akimova, Vera Vladimirovna. *Two Years in Revolutionary China, 1925–1927.* Translated by Steven I. Levine. Cambridge: Harvard University Press, 1971.

Wakeman, Frederic, Jr., and Wen-hsin Yeh, eds. *Shanghai Sojourners.* Berkeley: Institute of East Asian Studies, University of California, 1992.

Wang Guansan. "Jiating fangwen ji" [An account of home interviews]. In *Yaqian nongmin yundong.* Beijing, 1987.

Wang Huiyu. "Jian dang chuqide yixie qingguang" [A few things about the early days of building the party]. In *"Yida" qianhou.* Vol. 2. Beijing, 1980.

Wang Ke-wen. "The Kuomintang in Transition: Ideology and Factionalism in the 'National Revolution,' 1924–1932." Ph.D. dissertation. Stanford University, 1985.

Wang Weilian. "Shen Xuanlu yu gongchandang" [Shen Dingyi and the Communist Party]. In *Zhongguo gongchandang faqi ren fenlie shiliao* [Separate materials on founding members of the Chinese Communist Party]. Hong Kong, 1968.

Wang Xueqi. "Yijiuersinian wuyue Zhonggong zhongyang kuoda zhiweihui shuping" [An account of the May 1924 meeting of the enlarged central executive committee of the Chinese Communist Party]. *Hangzhou daxue xuebao* [Journal of Hangzhou University] 14, no. 2 (June 1984): 13–20, 81.

Wang Zanyuan and Chen Dingshun. "Xianghu shifan jian wushinian huiyi" [Memories at the fiftieth anniversary of the founding of Xiang Lake Normal School]. In *Zhejiang wenshi ziliao xuanji* [A collection of historical materials from Zhejiang]. Vol. 13. Hangzhou, 1981.

Wasserstrom, Jeffrey N. "The Evolution of the Shanghai Student Protest Repertoire; or, Where Do Correct Tactics Come From?" In Frederic Wakeman, Jr., and Wen-hsin Yeh, eds., *Shanghai Sojourners.* Berkeley: Institute of East Asian Studies, University of California, 1992.

———. *Student Protests in Twentieth-Century China: The View from Shanghai.* Stanford: Stanford University Press, 1991.

Watts, Michael J. "Space for Everything (A Commentary)." *Cultural Anthropology* 7, no. 1 (February 1992): 115–29.

Weigert, Andrew J., J. Smith Teitge, and Dennis W. Teitge. *Society and Identity: Toward a Sociological Psychology.* Cambridge: Cambridge University Press, 1986.

West Lake: A Collection of Folk Tales. Translated by Jan and Yvonne Walls. Hong Kong: Joint Publishing Company, 1983.

Wilbur, C. Martin. *The Nationalist Revolution in China, 1923–1928.* Cambridge: Cambridge University Press, 1983.

Wilbur, C. Martin, and Julie Lien-ying How. *Missionaries of Revolution: Soviet Advisers and Nationalist China, 1920–1927.* Cambridge: Harvard University Press, 1989.

Wolf, Margery. "Women and Suicide in China." In Margery Wolf and Roxanne Witke, eds., *Women and Chinese Society.* Stanford: Stanford University Press, 1975.

Wu, David Yen-ho. "The Construction of Chinese and Non-Chinese Identities." *Daedalus* 120, no. 2 (Spring 1991): 159–79.

Wusi shiqi qikan jieshao [An introduction to May Fourth periodicals].3 vols. Beijing, 1959.

Wusi yundong huiyilu [Memoirs of the May Fourth movement]. 2 vols. Beijing, 1979.

Wusi yundong zai Zhejiang [The May Fourth movement in Zhejiang]. Hangzhou, 1979.

Xia Yan. "Dang wusi liangchaozhong dao Zhejiangde shihou" [At the time of the May Fourth tide in Zhejiang]. In *Wusi yundong huiyilu*. Vol. 2. Beijing, 1979.

Xiang Shiyuan. *Zhejiang xinwen shi* [A history of journalism in Zhejiang]. N.p., 1930.

Xiaoshan xiangtu zhi [A gazetteer of the Xiaoshan locality]. N.p., 1931.

Xiaoshan xianzhi [A gazetteer of Xiaoshan County]. Xiaoshan, 1985.

Xie Chi. *Xie Chi wenji* [Collected works of Xie Chi]. Taibei, 1977.

Xinbian Zhejiang bainian dashiji, 1840–1949 [A new edition of the major events in Zhejiang in the last century]. Hangzhou, 1989.

Xinhai geming huiyilu [Recorded recollections of the revolution of 1911]. Edited by Zhongguo renmin zhengzhi xieshang huiyi quanguo weiyuanhui [Committee on written historical materials of the National Committee of the Chinese People's Consultative Conference]. 5 vols. Beijing, 1961–63.

Xinhai geming Zhejiang shiliao xuanji [A compilation of historical materials on the 1911 revolution in Zhejiang]. Edited by Zhejiang sheng xinhai geming yanjiuhui, Zhejiang sheng tushuguan [Research society of the Zhejiang provincial library on the 1911 revolution in Zhejiang]. Hangzhou, 1984.

Xingqi pinglun [Weekly Review], 1919–20.

Xu Bainian. "Zhejiang zaoqi shuchude geming huodongjia—Xuan Zhonghua lieshi chuanlue" [A biography of martyr Xuan Zhonghua—one of Zhejiang's outstanding revolutionaries of the early period]. In *Hangzhou yinglie* [Hangzhou heroes]. Vol. 1. Hangzhou, 1992.

Xu Bingkun. "Hangzhou guangfu zhi yede yici guanshen jinji huiyi" [An urgent meeting of officials and gentry on the eve of the Hangzhou revolution]. In *Xinhai geming huiyilu*. Vol. 4. Beijing, 1961–63.

Xu Xingzhi (Xu Meikun). "Dang chengliu shiqi Zhejiangde gongnong yundong." [The workers' and farmers' movement in Zhejiang at the time of the party's founding.] In *"Yida" qianhou*. Vol. 2. Beijing, 1980.

Xu Zhichen. "Guanyu Yuyangli liuhaode huodong qingguang" [Concerning the activity at Number 6, Yuyang Lane]. In *"Yida" qianhou*. Vol. 2. Beijing, 1980.

Xuanlu wencun [Collected works of Shen Xuanlu]. N.p., n.d.

Yang Fu. "Wusi shiqi Makesi Liening zhuyi zai Zhejiangde chuanbo" [The spread of Marxism-Leninism during the May Fourth period in Zhejiang]. *Hangzhou daxue xuebao* [Journal of Hangzhou University] 13, no. 1 (March 1983): 40–51.

Yang Fumao and Wang Zuoren. "Zhongguo xiandai nongmin yundongde xiansheng" [The first sound of China's contemporary farmers movement]. *Hangzhou daxue xuebao* [Journal of Hangzhou University] 4 (December 1980): 30–33, 53.

Yang Zhihua. "Yang Zhihuade huiyi" [Recollections of Yang Zhihua]. In *"Yida" qianhou*. Vol. 2. Beijing, 1980.

———. "Yang Zhihua tongzhi tan Xiaoshan nongyun" [Comrade Yang Zhihua talks of the Xiaoshan farmers movement]. In *Zhejiang wenshi ziliao xuanji* [A collection of historical materials from Zhejiang]. Vol. 13. Hangzhou, 1981.

Yao Zong. "Xinhai Zhejiang geming shi buyi" [Supplementary fragments to the history of Zhejiang's 1911 revolution]. *Zhejiang yuekan* [Zhejiang monthly] 1, no. 5 (1969): 8–9.

Yaqian nongmin yundong [The Yaqian farmers movement]. Xiaoshan, 1985.

Yaqian nongmin yundong [The Yaqian farmers movement]. Beijing, 1987.

Yeh Wen-hsin. *The Alienated Academy: Culture and Politics in Republican China, 1919–1937.* Cambridge: Harvard University Press, 1990.

———. "Middle County Radicalism: The May Fourth Movement in Hangzhou." Unpublished paper.

"Yida" qianhou: Zhongguo Gongchandang diyici daibiao dahui qianhou ziliao xuanbian [The period of the founding of the party: selected source materials for the period of the first national congress of the Chinese Communist party]. Edited by Zhongguo shehui kexueyuan xiandaishi yanjiushi/Zhongguo geming bowuguan dangshi yanjiushi [Contemporary history section of the Chinese Academy of Social Sciences/Party history section of the Museum of the Chinese Revolution]. 3 vols. Beijing, 1980.

You Hang jilue [A sketch for touring in Hangzhou]. Hangzhou, 1924.

Yu, George. *Party Politics in Republican China.* Berkeley and Los Angeles: University of California Press, 1966.

Yuezi ribao [Shaoxing Bell Daily], 1921–22.

Zhang Rentian. "Yi Guangfuhui Wang Wenjing" [Remembering the Restoration Society's Wang Wenjing]. In *Zhejiang xinhai geming huiyilu. Zhejiang wenshi ziliao xuanji*, Vol. 27. Hangzhou, 1984.

Zhang Ruisheng, Ping Liusan, Weng Ashun, et al. "Doumen, Gaoze dengcun jianzu qingguang diandi" [Bits about the rent reduction situation in Doumen, Gaoze, and other villages]. In *Yaqian nongmin yundong.* Beijing, 1987.

Zhang Xiaoxun. "Zhejiang xinhai geming guangfu jishi" [An account of the 1911 revolution in Zhejiang]. In *Jindai shi ziliao.* No. 1. Beijing, 1954.

Zhao Zijie, Xu Shaoquan, and Li Weijia. "Xuan Zhonghua." In *Buxiaode zhanshi* [Immortal Warriors]. Hangzhou, 1983.

Zhejiang bainian dashiji [The major events in Zhejiang in the last century]. Hangzhou, 1985.

Zhejiang gongren yundong shi [A history of the Zhejiang labor movement]. Edited by Zhejiang sheng conggonghui [Zhejiang province General Labor Union]. Hangzhou, 1988.

Zhejiang renwu jianzhi [Brief biographies of Zhejiangese]. 2 vols. Hangzhou, 1984.

"Zhejiang sheng dangbu baogao" [A report on the Zhejiang provincial party bureau]. In *Dangshi yanjiu ziliao*. Vol. 2. Chengdu, 1981.

Zhejiang wenshi ziliao xuanji [A collection of historical material on Zhejiang]. 46 vols. Hangzhou, 1962–92.

Zhejiang xinhai geming huiyilu [Recollection of the 1911 revolution in Zhejiang]. Vol. 27 of *Zhejiang wenshi ziliao xuanji*. Hangzhou, 1984.

Zhejiang yuekan [Zhejiang monthly], 1969–88.

"Zhejun Hangzhou guangfu ji" [An account of the Zhejiang army in the Hangzhou revolution]. Compiled by Zhejiang jun sishijiu lu siling bu [Headquarters of the Forty-Ninth Brigade of the Zhejiang army]. In *Gesheng guangfu*. Vol. 2. Taibei, 1962.

Zhong Baiyong. "Diyici guogong hezuo shiqi fasheng zai Xiaoshande yichu naoju" [The tragedy emerging from Xiaoshan in the first period of Guomindang-Communist cooperation]. In *Sun Zhongshan yu Zhejiang*. Hangzhou, 1986.

Zhong Liyu. "Guangfu Hangzhou huiyilu" [Recollection of the revolution in Hangzhou]. In *Jindai shi ziliao*. No. 1. Beijing, 1954.

Zhongguo gongchandang faqi ren fenlie shiliao [Separate materials on founding members of the Chinese Communist party]. Hong Kong, 1968.

Zhonghua xinbao [The China News], 1916–17.

Zhou Zixin. "Xishan huiyipai zhaokaide liangci fandong huiyi" [The two anti-movement conferences held by the Western Hills faction]. In *Dangshi yanjiu ziliao*. Vol. 6. Chengdu, 1985.

Zhu Shunzuo. *Shaoxing xianren zhi* [Biographies of worthy people of Shaoxing]. 2 vols. Shaoxing, 1984.

Zou Lu. *Hui gulu* [Memoirs]. Taibei, 1974.

Index

Yu Xiusong (*continued*)
    committee, 135, 164; in Shang-
    hai Communist cell, 82–83, 85–
    86
Yuan Shikai, 18–19, 32, 40, 59

Zhang Binglin, 44
Zhang Dongsun, 84, 86
Zhang Guotao, 142, 167
Zhang Ji, 12–13, 146, 246, 248
Zhang Jingjiang, 60, 189, 192–193, 249,
    272n.24; and Shen's death, 247, 248,
    249; warning to Shen, 245, 246
Zhang Lie, 191
Zhang Liusheng, 153
Zhang Qiuren, 139
Zhang Tinglin, 35
Zhang Xun, 49
Zhang Zuolin, 179
Zhejiang-Jiangsu war (1924), 143,
    146
Zhejiang Military Academy, 27, 40–41

Zhejiang Political Discussion Society,
    38–39, 43, 47, 268–269n.68,
    269n.69
Zhejiang Print Workers Club, 130, 139–
    140
Zhejiang province, 176, 256; political
    crisis in, 39–46; traditional geographi-
    cal units of, 267n.46
Zhejiang Provincial Assembly, 29–31, 34,
    102–103, 114–116
Zhejiang Provincial Education Associa-
    tion, 32, 34, 141, 172, 176
Zhejiang Special Arts School, 140
Zhong Baiyong, 155–157
Zhou Bonian, 12–13, 235, 246
Zhou Fengqi, 41
Zhou Renshou, 110–111, 261
Zhou Xinwei, 205, 221, 233
Zhu Jiabao, 105
Zhu Jiahua, 12–13, 219, 246, 247
Zhu Rui, 27, 40
Zou Lu, 165, 167, 182